Global Investment Competitiveness Report 2019/2020

Global Investment Competitiveness Report 2019/2020

Rebuilding Investor Confidence in Times of Uncertainty

WORLD BANK GROUP

1818 H Street NW, Washington, DC 20433
Telephone: 202-473-1000; Internet: www.worldbank.org

1 2 3 4 23 22 21 20

ISBN (paper): 978-1-4648-1536-2
ISBN (electronic): 978-1-4648-1543-0
DOI: 10.1596/978-1-4648-1536-2

Cover design: Bill Pragluski, Critical Stages, LLC.

Library of Congress Cataloguing-in-Publication data has been requested.

Contents

Boxes

Figures

Tables

Foreword

The *Global Investment Competitiveness Report 2019/2020* comes at a critical time—a period of economic uncertainty marked by the coronavirus (COVID-19) outbreak, a challenging global policy environment for investment and trade, rising protectionism, and shifting trade and investment preferences. These forces are changing the patterns of international production and corporate decision-making, creating both opportunities and risks for foreign investment.

The report was developed in the months that preceded the outbreak of COVID-19 and focuses on trade and investment policy uncertainty due to policy shifts, globally and nationally. It finds that rising policy uncertainty is darkening the outlook for foreign direct investment. Unfortunately, these negative effects will only be exacerbated by the economic challenges and policy uncertainty brought by the spread of the virus. Considering the difficult global environment, this report focuses on what the governments of developing countries can do to enhance investor confidence, maximize investments' contributions to inclusive growth, and foster the investment competitiveness of their economies. It delivers novel analytical insights, fresh empirical evidence, and actionable recommendations for governments eager to raise investor confidence in times of uncertainty.

Although responsible fiscal and monetary policies underpin macroeconomic stability, governments can further reduce risk and build confidence by implementing transparent and predictable regulatory regimes. Reaffirming commitments to market access and rules-based international systems would decrease uncertainty related to protectionism and economic nationalism. Better regulation and implementation would reduce obstacles to investment. Finally, governments do not need to forgo growth to improve inclusion. Measures to improve labor market skills and local supplier linkages to multinational companies can promote more equitable, broad-based economic growth.

These recommendations reflect the results of the 2019 Global Investment Competitiveness Survey of more than 2,400 business executives representing foreign direct investment (FDI) in 10 large developing countries: Brazil, China, India, Indonesia, Malaysia, Mexico, Nigeria, Thailand, Turkey, and Vietnam. Two-thirds of investors said that policy uncertainty due to protectionism and economic nationalism in trade and investment is "important" or "critically important" in their investment decisions. Over half of those who said policy uncertainty is a "critically important" investment factor reported a decrease in employment, firm productivity, or investments over the past year. A majority of investors surveyed overall did not expect to expand investments over the next three years. Interviews were conducted from June to November 2019.

Foreign investors said that supportive political environments, stable macroeconomic conditions, and conducive regulatory regimes are their top three investment decision factors—even more important than low taxes, low labor and input costs, or access to natural resources. Moreover, the report's new global database of regulatory risk shows that predictability and transparency increase investor confidence and FDI flows.

The report assesses the impact of FDI on poverty, inequality, employment, and firm performance using empirical evidence from various countries. It shows that FDI in developing countries yields benefits to firms and citizens—including more and better-paid jobs, technology transfers, and stronger linkages to global value chains. Still, governments need to remain vigilant about the potential for worsening income inequality. A final chapter articulates priorities for investment promotion agencies and other stakeholders seeking to enhance their countries' investment competitiveness.

The *Global Investment Competitiveness Report 2019/2020* draws insights from a variety of sources, including the survey of business executives, extensive analysis of data and evidence, and a thorough review of international best practices in investment policy design and implementation. Together, these sources underscore the significant threat to global economic growth from high levels of international and domestic policy uncertainty in trade and investment. They also indicate that with timely action, policy makers can bolster foreign direct investment and reap its benefits for short-term growth and long-term economic transformation—both critical for poverty reduction.

Ceyla Pazarbasioglu
Vice President
Equitable Growth, Finance and Institutions
World Bank Group

Hans Peter Lankes
Vice President
Economics and Private Sector Development
International Finance Corporation

Acknowledgments

This report was developed by the World Bank Group's Global Investment Climate team. It was managed by Peter Kusek, under the guidance of Christine Zhenwei Qiang (Practice Manager of the Investment Climate Unit), Caroline Freund (Global Director for Trade, Investment, and Competitiveness), and William Maloney (Chief Economist of the Equitable Growth, Finance, and Institutions Vice Presidency).

The team would like to thank the following donor partners of the World Bank Group for making this report possible through their generous financial contributions: the Prosperity Fund of the United Kingdom's Foreign and Commonwealth Office and the Government of Austria's Federal Ministry of Finance.

The team is grateful to the many internal and external technical reviewers and contributors who provided insight and guidance at various stages of the report preparation, including Laura Alfaro, Robert Beschel, Richard Bolwijn, Paul Brenton, Jansen Calamita, Deepa Chakrapani, Ritam Chaurey, Jieun Choi, Andrea Ciani, Riccardo Crescenzi, Stephan Dreyhaupt, Marcello Estevao, Neil Gregory, Mona Haddad, Mary Hallward-Driemeier, Nathen Jensen, Mark Kantor, Ayhan Kose, Aart Kraay, Anuj Mathew, Sebastien Miroudot, Gaurav Nayyar, Richard Newfarmer, Habib Rab, Rita Ramalho, Carlos Rodriguez Castelan, Jorge Luis Rodriguez Meza, Miguel Eduardo Sanchez Martin, Karl Sauvant, Pierre Sauve, Bostjan Skalar, and Joshua Wimpey.

The report's authors are grateful for the excellent research assistance and overall support of Sarur Chaudhary, Philippe Armand De Bonneval, Maximilian Philip Eltgen, Jingyu Gao, Nisan Gorgulu, Carlos Griffin, Nadia Hasham, Sarah Hebous, Benjamin Kett, Yan Liu, Alex Sanchiz Vicente, and Ramprakash Sethuramasubbu.

The team would also like to recognize numerous World Bank Group and other colleagues for their helpful guidance and assistance, without whom this report would not have been complete. These include Gokhan Akinci, Ivor Beazley, Tania Begazo Gomez, David Bridgman, Pascaline della Faille, Wim Douw, Thomas Farole, Tania Ghossein, Daniela Gomez-Altamirano, Justin-Damien Guénette, Georges Vivien Houngbonon, Lee Ann Jackson, Sergiy Kasyanenko, Anju Lamichhane, Jan Loeprick, Syed Akhtar Mahmood, Graciela Miralles Murciego, Ngan Thuy Nguyen, Ivan Nimac, Celia Ortega Sotes, Rodrigo Ortiz, Cecilia Sager, Damien Shiels, Matthew Stephenson, Temel Taskin, Robert Whyte, and Sandy Ye.

Nancy Morrison and Mary Anderson were the editors of the report. Mary Fisk and Jewel McFadden provided editorial production and logistics support. Aarushi Sinha provided additional editorial and production assistance. The communications efforts were led by Elizabeth Price and Melissa Knutson.

The 2019 Global Investment Competitiveness Survey analyzed in chapter 1 was undertaken on behalf of the World Bank Group by Kantar Public, a global survey firm. We are particularly grateful for the contributions of the following Kantar colleagues: Jamie Burnett, Stephan Paetz, and Marco Pelucchi.

The team acknowledges the many formal and informal contributions of individuals, groups, and organizations that provided meaningful comments and inputs to enable the successful publication of this report. Keeping in mind these contributions, the team apologizes if it has inadvertently omitted formally acknowledging any such valuable contributions.

About the Authors

Sarah Hebous is a consultant at the World Bank Group. She has extensive experience in data analysis and empirical economics including conducting household surveys and analyzing job creation and sources of agrarian distress. She holds a master's degree in mathematics from the University of Münster, Germany.

Armando Heilbron leads the World Bank Group's investment promotion workstream. His global experience spans international business, investment promotion, private sector development, and special economic zones. He is a Fulbright scholar with a master's degree in international business from the University of California, Berkeley.

Priyanka Kher is a private sector specialist in the Investment Climate Unit of the World Bank Group. She leads research and policy advisory on investment climate reforms, investment retention and expansion, and international trade and investment law. She holds a master's degree in law from Harvard Law School.

Hania Kronfol is a private sector specialist in the Investment Climate Unit of the World Bank Group, where she leads analytical and advisory projects on investment policy and promotion. Her areas of expertise include foreign direct investment–led development, investment attraction, institutional strengthening, and trade and investment policy reform. She holds a master's degree in public policy from Harvard University.

Ryan Kuo is a consultant in the Investment Climate Unit of the World Bank Group, where he conducts research and advises governments on foreign direct investment and competition policy. His experience also includes work in the public and private sectors across East Africa and Southeast Asia. He holds a master's degree in public affairs from Princeton University.

Peter Kusek is a senior economist at the World Bank Group. He leads the Applied Research Program on Investment Climate and is the managing editor of the *Global Investment Competitiveness Report* series. His research and advisory work focus on international investment, competitiveness, and private sector development. He holds a master's degree in economic policy and international development from Princeton University.

Christine Zhenwei Qiang is the practice manager of the Investment Climate Unit of the World Bank Group. Her team advises governments in more than 90 countries on catalyzing investment and business competitiveness through legal, policy, regulatory, and institutional reforms in the areas of business regulation, competition policy, and investment policy and promotion. She holds a doctorate in economics from Johns Hopkins University.

Alexandros Ragoussis is an economist at the International Finance Corporation of the World Bank Group and an associate fellow at the German Development Institute. He holds a doctorate in economics from the University of Sydney and has been working on firm dynamics, investment, and their links with international development.

Abhishek Saurav is an economist in the Investment Climate Unit of the World Bank Group. He leads policy research on private investment, job creation, women's economic empowerment, and productivity. He also provides evidence-based policy advice to governments. He holds a doctorate in public policy and administration from George Washington University.

Victor Steenbergen is an economist in the Investment Climate Unit of the World Bank Group. He has quantitative research expertise in investment, tax, trade, and public finance policy. He has also provided longer-term technical assistance to the governments of Malawi, Mexico, Nigeria, and Rwanda. He holds a master's degree in public administration and development economics from the London School of Economics.

Trang Thu Tran is a senior economist in the Firms, Entrepreneurship, and Innovation Unit of the World Bank Group. Her analytical and advisory work have focused on entrepreneurship and innovation policy, international investment, and business regulatory issues. She is an applied microeconomist with a doctorate from the University of Maryland, College Park.

Abbreviations

ABA	Austrian Business Agency
B2G	business-to-government
BIT	bilateral investment treaty
BPP	Benchmarking Public Procurement (World Bank)
CATI	computer-assisted telephone interview
CEO	chief executive officer
CINDE	Costa Rican Investment Promotion Agency
CISF	comprehensive investor services framework
CRM	customer relationship management
DDI	domestic direct investment
EIU	Economist Intelligence Unit
EPU	Global Economic Policy Uncertainty Index
EU	European Union
FDI	foreign direct investment
FET	fair and equitable treatment
FIAS	Foreign Investment Advisory Service (World Bank)
FTA	free trade agreement
GDP	gross domestic product
GIC	Global Investment Competitiveness (survey)
GIPB	Global Investment Promotion Best Practice
GIRG	Global Indicators of Regulatory Governance (World Bank)
GST	goods and services tax
GVC	global value chain
HICs	high-income countries
ICRG	International Country Risk Guide

ICT	information and communication technology
IFC	International Finance Corporation
IIA	international investment agreement
IPA	investment promotion agency
IPI	investment promotion intermediaries
ISDS	investor-state dispute settlement
ISIC	International Standard Industrial Classification of All Economic Activities
ISIC2	ISIC two-digit classification
IT	information technology
IV	instrumental variables
JV	joint venture
KPIs	key performance indicators
LICs	low-income countries
M&A	mergers and acquisitions
MFN	most-favored nation
MICs	middle-income countries
MNE	multinational enterprise
MREL	monitoring, reporting, evaluation, and learning
OECD	Organisation for Economic Co-operation and Development
OFDI	outward foreign direct investment
OSS	one-stop-shop
PCA	principal component analysis
PPP	public-private partnership
R&D	research and development
SBU	Survey of Business Uncertainty
SDG	Sustainable Development Goal
SDI	Scottish Development International
SEZ	special economic zone
SMEs	small and medium enterprises
UNCTAD	United Nations Conference on Trade and Development
WAIPA	World Association of Investment Promotion Agencies
WTO	World Trade Organization

Main Messages

Overall

1. Even before the COVID-19 outbreak, global foreign direct investment (FDI) was in decline due to trade policy uncertainty, rising protectionism, falling rates of return on FDI, and changing forms of international production.
2. The COVID-19 crisis is presenting a new, unprecedented source of investor risk that is depressing business confidence to historic lows, resulting in a projected fall in global FDI by more than 40 percent in 2020.
3. More than two-thirds of multinational investors in developing countries are reporting disruptions in supply chains, declines in revenues, and falls in production as a result of COVID-19—and the impacts are projected to worsen in the coming months—based on a new World Bank survey on the impact of the pandemic.
4. FDI can alleviate the impact of the COVID-19 crisis and boost countries' economic resilience by providing a critical source of external capital for financing public debt and continuing to create more and better-paid jobs, lift people out of poverty, and boost productivity.
5. Foreign acquisitions of local firms in developing countries have doubled as a share of FDI over the past decade, and they have made the acquired companies more export oriented, productive, and diversified in their product offering.
6. At the same time, the possible adverse effects of FDI on income inequality and on lower-skilled workers emphasize the critical mitigating role of labor market and education policies.
7. An extensive survey of more than 2,400 global business executives in 10 large middle-income countries conducted between June and November 2019 shows that government policies can influence FDI location decisions.
8. Government actions—such as reducing investor risk and increasing policy predictability—can rebuild investor confidence, based on the report's new global database of regulatory risk.
9. Investment promotion agencies can boost their countries' investment competitiveness by better aligning their FDI attraction and retention efforts with market signals and changing investor preferences.
10. Governments can leverage FDI for robust economic recovery from COVID-19 by avoiding protectionist policies, seizing new opportunities from changing FDI and supply chain trends, and fostering global cooperation.

Overview

Christine Zhenwei Qiang and Peter Kusek

Global FDI Flows Face an Unprecedented Decline

The COVID-19 pandemic is severely impacting multinational enterprises (MNEs) globally. The economic shock of the crisis to the private sector is being transmitted through multiple channels, including falling demand, reduced and disrupted input supply, tightening of credit conditions, a liquidity crunch, and rising uncertainty. The pre-COVID-19 global environment for foreign direct investment (FDI) was already characterized by rapidly eroding investor confidence because of trade and investment policy uncertainty, lagging global growth, falling commodity prices, and rising protectionism. The COVID-19 crisis presents a new, unprecedented source of investor risk that is depressing investor confidence to new lows.

Even before the COVID-19 pandemic upended the global economy, global FDI was sliding to levels even below those last seen in the aftermath of the global financial crisis a decade ago (figure O.1, panel a).[1] The decline was more concentrated in high-income countries, where inflows of FDI fell by nearly 60 percent in recent years. Although FDI to developing countries did not decline as steeply, it nonetheless fell to its lowest levels in decades relative to gross domestic product (GDP).[2] Compared with the mid-2000s, when FDI reached nearly 4 percent of GDP in developing countries, that share fell to under 2 percent in 2017 and 2018 (figure O.1, panel b).

This worrisome global trend in recent years has reflected a mix of (a) *economic factors,* including declining rates of return on FDI; (b) *business factors,* including adoption of digital technologies and increasingly asset-light forms of international production; and (c) *policy factors,* including the erosion of investor confidence due to policy uncertainty and changes in US tax policy that drove repatriation of capital back to the United States.[3] More specifically, worsening business fundamentals have driven much of the decline in FDI since 2015, when FDI flows reached their postcrisis peak. The global average rate of return on FDI decreased from 8.0 percent in 2010 to 6.8 percent in 2018 (UNCTAD 2019). While the rates of return have dropped in both developing and developed countries, the declines have been especially large in developing countries.

Furthermore, changing business models resulting from technological advances have driven declines in FDI levels and returns. In particular, increases in labor costs and the rise of advanced manufacturing technologies have

FIGURE O.1 FDI Inflows to Developing Countries over the Past Decade Have Been Mostly Flat and Have Declined as a Share of GDP

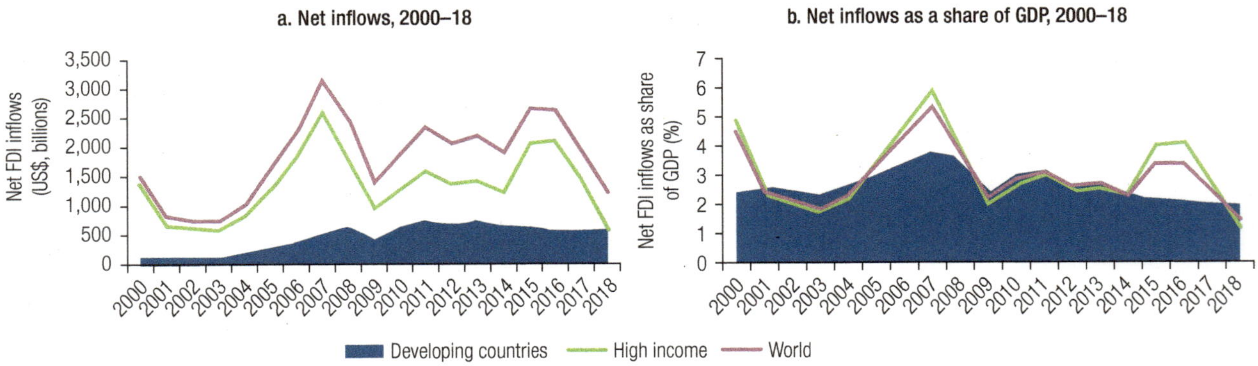

Source: World Development Indicators database.
Note: All country income categories use World Bank-defined classifications; "developing" countries refers collectively to all low and middle-income countries. FDI = foreign direct investment; GDP = gross domestic product.

eroded or decreased the significance of many developing countries' labor cost advantages. At the same time, the increasing importance of the digital economy and services is shifting businesses toward more asset-light models of investment (UNCTAD 2019). In addition, commodity price slumps have adversely affected returns on FDI in more commodity-dependent markets (such as many economies in Latin America and the Caribbean, the Middle East and North Africa, and Sub-Saharan Africa).

Uncertainty Has Been Rising and FDI Rules Tightening

Even before the COVID-19 crisis, the number and magnitude of various global economic, geopolitical, technological, and social shifts have increased uncertainty for citizens, businesses, and policy makers. These changes are reflected in the high values registered in 2019 by various indicators such as the World Uncertainty Index, the Global Economic Policy Uncertainty Index, and the Trade Policy Uncertainty Index (Baker, Bloom, and Davis 2019; Caldara et al. 2019). In 2020, these indexes have reached unprecedented levels.

Citizens are increasingly attributing growing economic disparity and losses in local economic opportunities to globalization. Less than half the citizens in some of the world's largest 27 countries believe that trade and globalization help create jobs, and less than one-third find that they are good for wages, recent data from the Pew Research Center indicate (Gramlich 2019).[4] The antiglobalization sentiment is also heightened by the ongoing shifts in economic and geopolitical power as well as concerns about national security. Such anxiety and discontent are fueling a rise in economic nationalism and protectionism.

Recent events such as withdrawals from global trade agreements, tariff escalations, and other trade tensions have contributed to a new rise in trade and investment policy uncertainty (Baker, Bloom, and Davis 2019). Free trade, unhindered investment, and open markets are under threat. Although these fears are particularly pronounced in the industrialized world, a growing number of developing country governments are also building their policy agendas along similar themes.

The growing protectionist views have gradually translated into more restrictive rules on the entry of FDI. The United States and the European Union have enacted strict screenings of foreign acquisitions in response to perceived risks to national or economic security. Cases of investment withdrawals—investments that are either rejected or withdrawn over security concerns—tripled in

2018 alone, often receiving high publicity (UNCTAD 2019).

Governments have also become increasingly anxious about the potentially noncommercial objectives of foreign investment by state-owned enterprises or sovereign wealth funds. Of particular concern has been foreign ownership of core technologies, manufacturing of health care products, sensitive business assets, and critical infrastructure. Various governments blocked mergers and acquisitions (M&A) deals worth more than US$150 billion in 2018 (more than 10 percent of total global FDI) on the basis of national security concerns (UNCTAD 2019). Member countries of the Organisation for Economic Co-operation and Development (OECD) on both sides of the Atlantic are tightening—or proposing to tighten—their rules governing the entry of FDI.

In fact, a global cross-country analysis of policy trends shows that the share of restrictive and regulatory measures against FDI is the highest it has been in more than 20 years—and the trend may be worsening. The United Nations Conference on Trade and Development's data on FDI policy trends around the world show that 55 countries undertook at least 112 policy measures related to FDI in 2018 (UNCTAD 2019). Of these, more than one-third restricted or regulated FDI more tightly, whereas the share of measures that liberalized and promoted FDI fell to less than two-thirds (figure O.2). In contrast, it was only the previous year (2017) when around 80 percent of the measures promoted FDI. High-income countries have been the primary drivers of the trend toward more restrictive rules on FDI. In 2018, more than 70 percent of new FDI policy measures in developed countries were aimed at restricting or regulating FDI (UNCTAD 2019).

Although most developing countries have so far largely resisted increasing the restrictiveness of their FDI regimes, there is a growing concern that the actions of the governments of developed countries will either set a precedent for the developing countries to follow, or that developing countries will do so as a retaliatory measure. For example, China and South Africa have recently introduced new regulatory frameworks for FDI screening for national security concerns (UNCTAD 2019).

FIGURE O.2 Investment Policies Regarding FDI Are Becoming More Restrictive

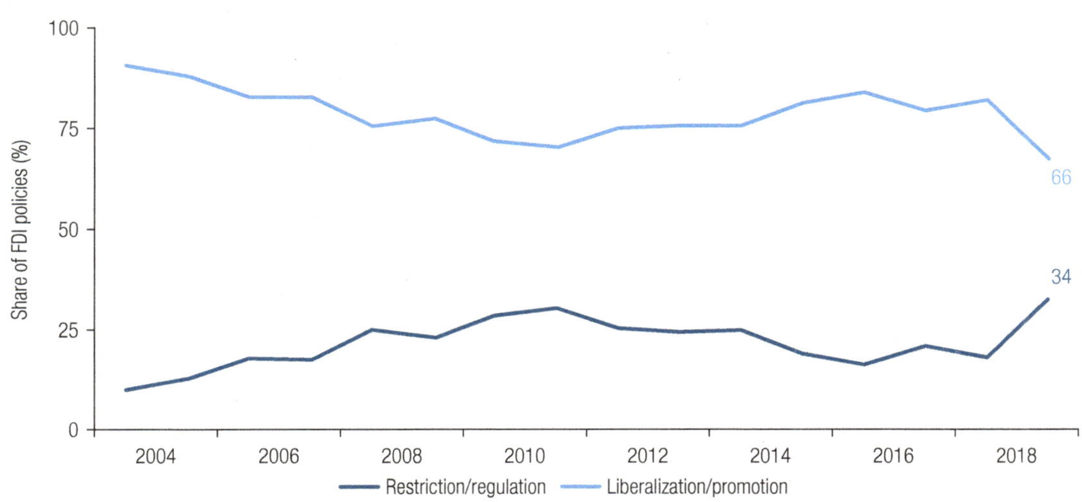

Source: UNCTAD 2019.
Note: Sample in 2018 comprised 55 countries that undertook at least 112 FDI-related policy measures. FDI = foreign direct investment.

Policy and COVID-19 Uncertainties Adversely Affect Jobs, Investment, and Productivity

Between June and November 2019, a Global Investment Competitiveness (GIC) Survey of more than 2,400 global business executives in 10 large middle-income countries was conducted for this report (see chapter 1). Without taking into account the additional effects of the COVID-19 pandemic, two-thirds of investors—particularly firms that import a greater share of their inputs and larger firms (employing more than 250 people)—reported that policy uncertainty due to protectionism and economic nationalism in trade and investment was "important" or "critically important" in their investment decisions in the past year (figure O.3, panel a). Furthermore, among those investors who considered such policy uncertainty in trade and investment to be a "critically important" investment factor, more than half have already experienced a decrease in employment, firm productivity, or investments as a result (figure O.3, panel b).

These negative effects have been further exacerbated by the economic challenges and

FIGURE O.3 Even before the COVID-19 Crisis, Investors Were Sensitive to Policy Uncertainty in Trade and Investment and Have Been Adversely Affected in the Past Year

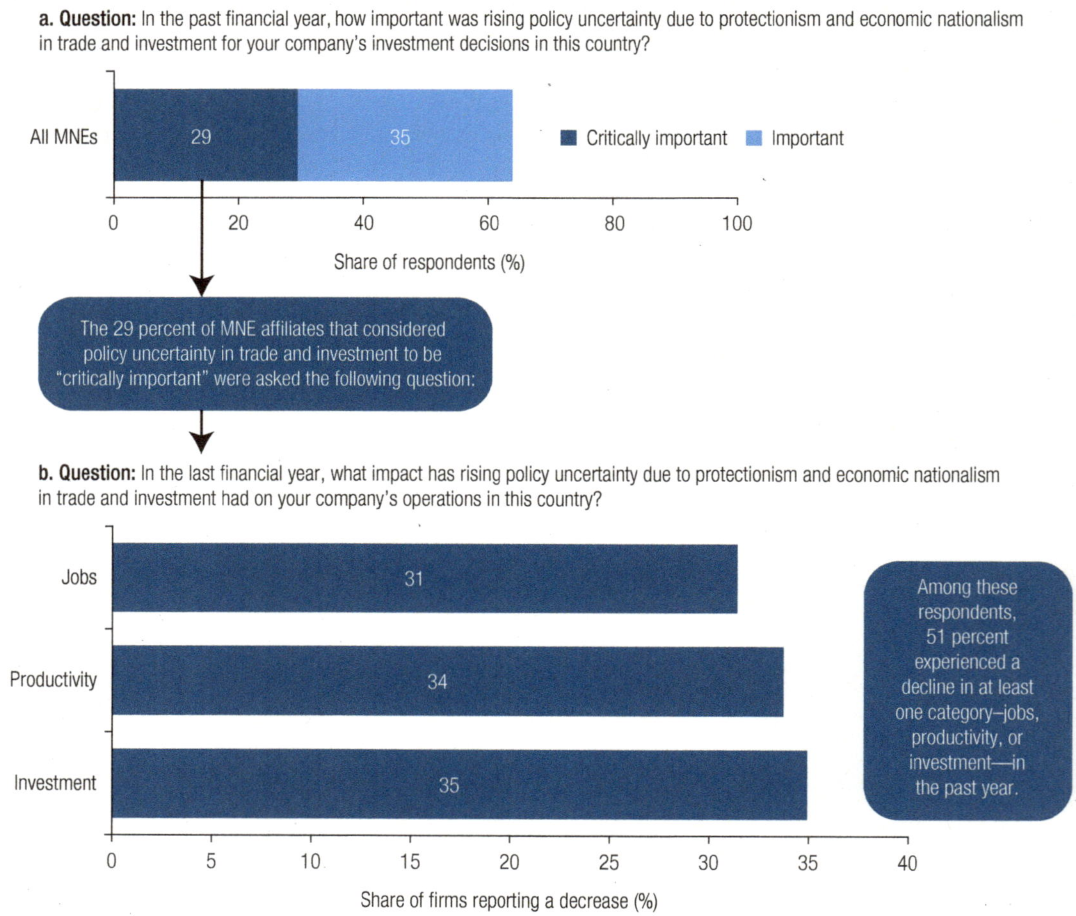

Source: Computation based on the 2019 GIC Survey.
Note: Affiliates of multinational enterprises were surveyed in 10 middle-income countries: Brazil, China, India, Indonesia, Malaysia, Mexico, Nigeria, Thailand, Turkey, and Vietnam. MNEs = multinational enterprises. The "past financial year" was a 12-month period between January 1, 2018, and September 30, 2019, depending on the country.

policy uncertainty brought by the spread of COVID-19. The closing of factories, disruptions in transport, and unavailability of production inputs are directly affecting how companies operate across the globe. The shocks, having already spread from directly hit sectors to others, are also spreading across regions through supply linkages. At the epicenter of this turmoil are multinational corporations that have shaped the geography of global value chains (GVCs) over the past three decades.

To assess the impact of the pandemic on MNE affiliates in developing countries, the World Bank conducted a foreign investor "pulse" survey in March–April 2020.[5] The results show that the COVID-19 pandemic has already adversely affected more than three-fourths of investors through both demand- and supply-side channels. Nearly four in five MNEs report reductions in revenues and profits over the past three months, on average by 40 percent (figure O.4, panel a). Demand has fallen sharply because of high uncertainty and precautionary behavior of consumers, resulting in reduced consumer spending and corporate orders.

On the supply side, three in four MNEs report declines in supply chain reliability, on average by 30 percent. Along with the liquidity crunch (experienced by more than 60 percent of respondents) and a decline in worker productivity (reported by three-fourths of businesses), the aggregate effects of these shocks include reductions of roughly one-third in output and investment, reported by most businesses. The shock waves are also reaching companies' employees: two in five businesses report declines in jobs, on average by 16 percent.

Even more worrisome than these shocks over the first quarter of 2020 are companies' dire predictions that the impacts will likely intensify over the second quarter, with performance deteriorating along every measured dimension (figure O.4, panel b). More than 85 percent of surveyed businesses expect that their revenues and profits will decline in April through June 2020, on average by more than 40 percent. Four in five businesses also expect

FIGURE O.4 The COVID-19 Pandemic Had Adversely Affected a Vast Share of MNEs by April 2020

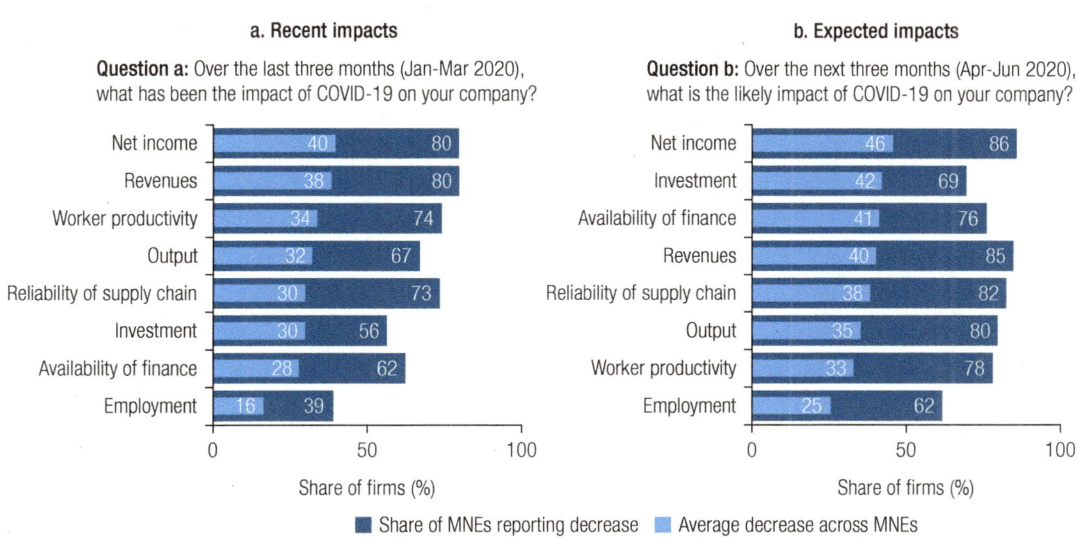

Source: World Bank, forthcoming.
Note: Computation based on the World Bank's Investor Confidence Global Pulse Survey, conducted March–April 2020. Sample represents 105 multinational enterprise (MNE) affiliates operating in 26 developing countries. The reference period of "last three months" ranges approximately from January to March 2020.

an average 35 percent reduction in output in the second quarter. The employment impacts are particularly likely to worsen: three in five businesses expect to have to reduce employment in the second quarter, on average by 25 percent. In addition to the likely downsizing of the workforce, the most precipitous declines are anticipated in the availability of finance (by 41 percent) and in investments (by 42 percent).

The gloomy outlook reported by the survey respondents is consistent with emerging evidence on declining investment activity. UNCTAD (2020) estimates that global FDI could decline by up to 40 percent in 2020–21. The world's largest 5,000 MNEs, which account for a significant share of global FDI, have revised their earnings estimates downward by an average of 30 percent. Because a major share of FDI materializes through reinvested earnings, FDI activity among existing investors is set to decline. Furthermore, in the first quarter of 2020, M&A activity is expected to drop by up to 70 percent. In February 2020, new cross-border acquisitions fell below US$10 billion, compared with the normal monthly average of US$40 billion—US$50 billion before the crisis.[6]

FDI Can Help Countries Alleviate the Impact of the Crisis, But Governments Must Rebuild Investor Confidence

With the expected massive global decline in FDI, competition among developing countries to attract foreign investment has only intensified. What can developing countries do to counter prevailing global headwinds and uncertainty and to rebuild investor confidence? How will the factors that affect countries' investment competitiveness change as a result of COVID-19? The report's findings pertaining to these questions are organized around two core pillars focused on (1) FDI contributions to development and economic resilience, and (2) policy actions to rebuild investor confidence and boost investment.

The individual chapters of this report analyze various facets of countries' foundations for investment competitiveness. The GIC Survey analyzes the drivers of FDI and identifies priorities for countries to increase their FDI attractiveness. Several chapters provide new evidence on FDI's contributions to job creation, poverty alleviation, and firm productivity. The report also explores how to boost investor confidence through specific policy and regulatory actions that reduce regulatory risks. The report concludes with an assessment of what governments—and especially their investment promotion agencies (IPAs)—can do to help attract high-quality FDI and transform their economies. If they succeed, FDI can continue to play a critical role in a robust economic recovery from the COVID-19 pandemic.

Pillar 1: FDI Boosts Economic Resilience—Easing the Impact of Economic Crises by Creating Jobs, Alleviating Poverty, and Boosting Productivity

FDI has always been a key building block for the economic growth of developing countries, often providing the largest source of external finance—surpassing remittances, official development assistance, and portfolio investment flows. In the post-COVID recovery phase, FDI's role is likely to further increase. Countries' crisis-response policies, such as financial and fiscal stimulus measures, are generating debt. Domestic revenue sources will be insufficient to service that debt. FDI is therefore likely to remain an essential source of capital.

Beyond capital, foreign investment also helps create jobs and reduce poverty. FDI can affect welfare through three main channels (figure O.5):

- *Employment income:* As FDI brings capital and new technologies to a sector, it often raises overall labor demand and productivity in the sector. This can raise total employment and average wages, leading to higher household incomes.

FIGURE O.5 FDI Affects Household Incomes through Several Broad Channels

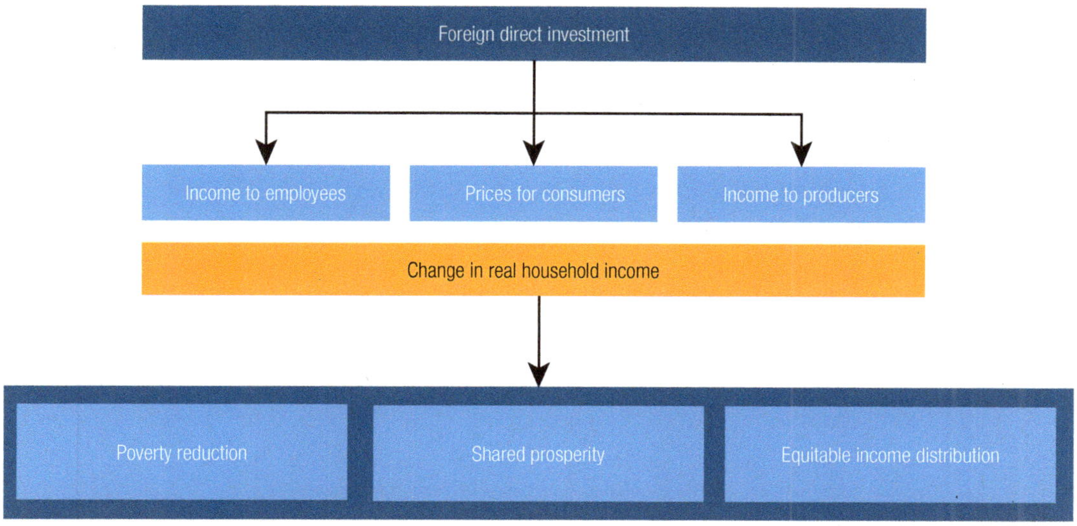

Source: World Bank and OECD 2017.
Note: FDI = foreign direct investment.

- *Consumer prices:* The entry of new foreign firms increases competition in markets. This may lower the prices of goods and services, thus raising household purchasing power and consumption possibilities.
- *Producer income:* As foreign firms compete with, buy from, or sell to domestic firms, they may influence the productivity and profitability of these enterprises, increasing or cutting into incomes of domestic producers.

These FDI effects are seemingly more obvious when it comes to greenfield FDI. Greenfield investment adds new elements to the economy: new facilities, new jobs, new production capacity. In contrast, brownfield FDI—acquisitions of domestic firms by foreign investors—transforms existing production. Any positive effect of brownfield investment would therefore tend to materialize over longer time frames and with varying intensity.

Most of the previous evidence on brownfield FDI has come from high-income countries and has focused on macroeconomic growth, overlooking development outcomes at the level of firms, the jobs they create, or the wages they offer.[7] To help fill this gap, this report focuses on acquired firms in developing countries—what they look like, how they evolve, and whether conventional narratives do justice to their contributions to development goals. This is particularly pertinent as brownfield investment has doubled as a share of FDI in developing countries over the past 10 years (figure O.6, as further discussed in chapter 2).

This report analyzes a unique set of industrial censuses from six developing countries—China, Côte d'Ivoire, Indonesia, Moldova, Serbia, and Vietnam—to show that brownfield FDI firms perform better than local firms on some of the key dimensions that matter for development, such as export orientation, product diversification, asset accumulation, labor productivity, and employment (figure O.7).

Results show that firms acquired by MNEs not only perform better than the average domestic firm at the time of the acquisition, but also improve their performance after acquisition faster than local firms along some of the key dimensions that matter for development. For example, over the first five years of a firm's operation, a brownfield affiliate is

FIGURE O.6 Brownfield Investment Rose as a Share of Total FDI in Developing Countries, 2010–17

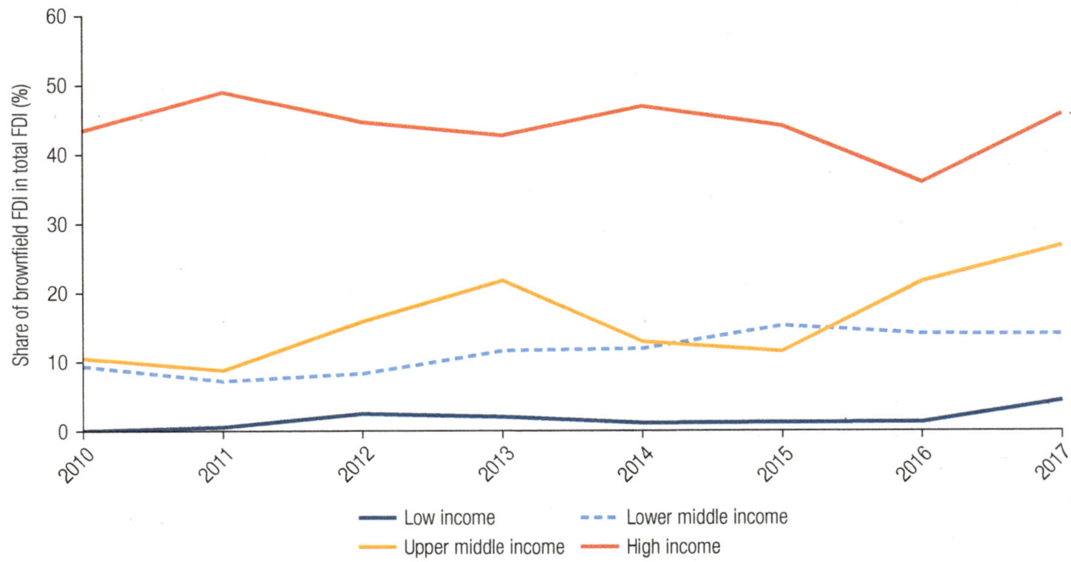

Source: World Bank, based on the 2019 United Nations Conference on Trade and Development (UNCTAD) Mergers and Acquisitions (M&A) database, http://www.unctad.org/fdistatistics.
Note: The trend is illustrated using a two-year moving average. All country income categories use 2017 World Bank-defined classifications; "developing countries" refers collectively to low- and middle-income countries. FDI = foreign direct investment.

70–100 percent more likely to export than a domestic firm (figure O.7, panel e). Wages in foreign takeovers at the end of the first five years of operations are 40–50 percent higher than in domestic firms (figure O.7, panel a).

Furthermore, contrary to conventional belief about the potential job-destroying effects of foreign M&A, employment in newly acquired firms tends to grow faster in most countries than employment in domestic firms with similar characteristics. Specifically, two years after acquisition, the average employment in brownfield affiliates expands by approximately 4 percent, compared with 1.5 percent in domestic firms with similar characteristics (figure O.8, panel a). The firms' asset value after the acquisition follows a similar path. The experience of the six countries analyzed in this study suggests that foreign acquisitions can be a helpful complement to greenfield FDI in all developing countries seeking to leverage foreign investment for advancing their development goals.

Looking beyond formal enterprises, the report further finds that FDI has a significant effect on household employment and wages in three developing countries: Ethiopia, Vietnam, and Turkey (see chapter 3). Workers in sectors and regions with a higher presence of foreign firms are generally more likely to be formally employed and receive higher wages.

In Vietnam, FDI allowed more than 350,000 individuals to enter formal manufacturing employment between 2007 and 2016. In Turkey, FDI brought in at least 40,000 additional formal manufacturing jobs between 2009 and 2016. FDI also raised average manufacturing wages, which increased by 32 percent in Ethiopia, 12 percent in Vietnam, and 8 percent in Turkey. Consequently, these wage increases brought about by FDI helped reduce poverty in all three countries. Conservative estimates suggest that FDI contributed to lifting at least 35,000 individuals out of poverty in Ethiopia (2009–14), 24,000 in Vietnam (2007–16), and 15,000 in Turkey (2009–16).

Growth in formal jobs and wages due to FDI has also translated into increased shared prosperity: the FDI-induced wage increases helped improve the income of

FIGURE O.7 Greenfield and Brownfield FDI Firms Perform Better than Domestic Firms over the First Five Years of Operation

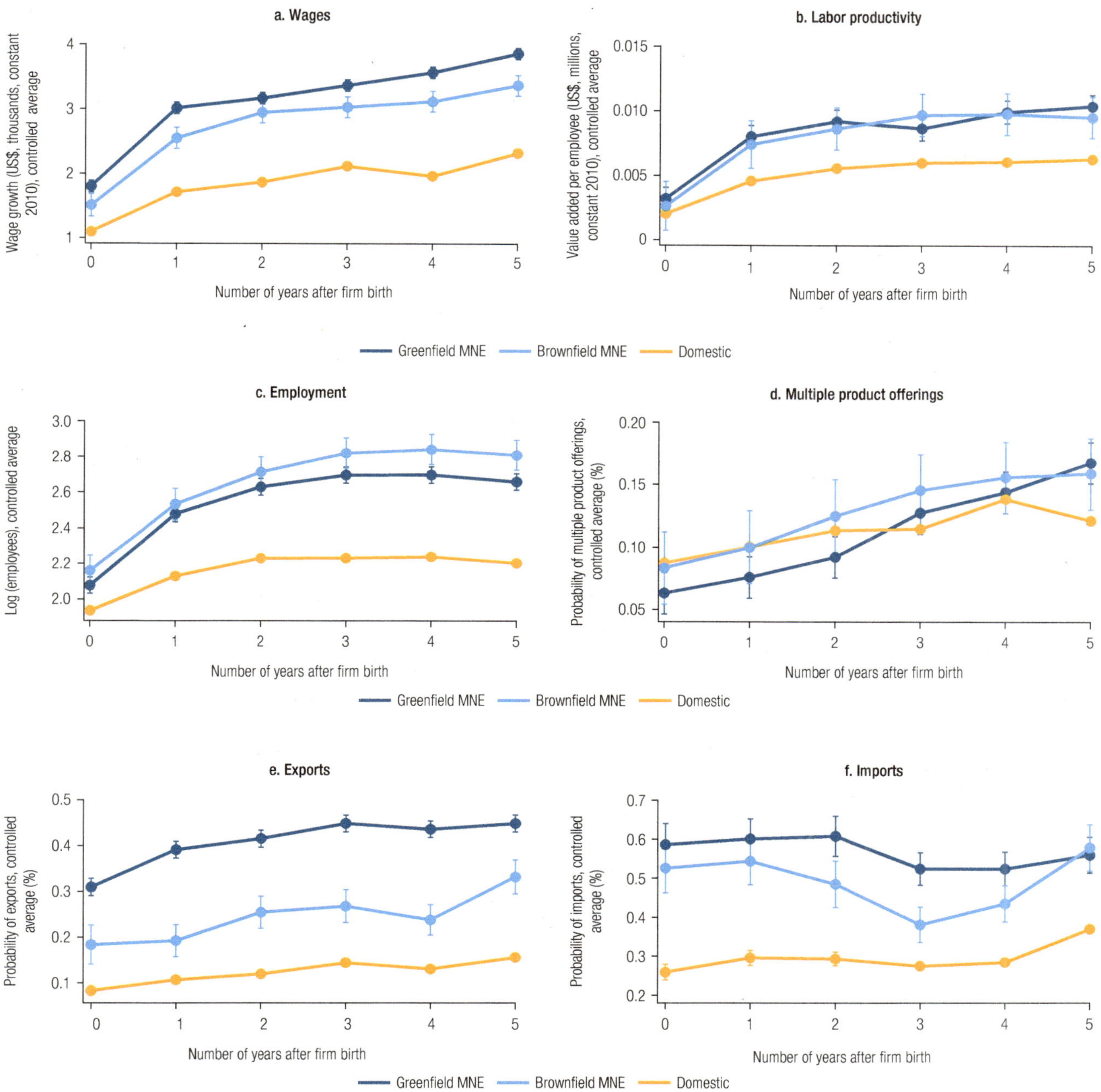

Source: World Bank calculations, based on industrial censuses from six countries.

Note: For this figure, industrial census data were analyzed from China, Côte d'Ivoire, Indonesia, Moldova, Serbia, and Vietnam (as further described in chapter 2, annex 2A). Vertical bars indicate the margin of error. "Domestic" refers to the firms that originated as domestic enterprises. Growth paths of firm outcomes can be captured in a simple framework using an interaction between indicators of firm group (greenfield, brownfield, and domestic) and years after entry in the following specification: $y_{ics} = group_i \beta \cdot d_t + \alpha_{cs} + \delta d_{it_c} + \varepsilon_{ics}$. The sample is restricted to cohorts whose entry is observed. To account for differences that might be driven by country characteristics, sector composition, and macroeconomic trends, the regressions also control for country-sector fixed effects and cohort fixed effects. FDI = foreign direct investment; MNE = multinational enterprise.

FIGURE O.8 Employment and Wages in Brownfield Firms Grow Faster than in Domestic Firms with Similar Characteristics

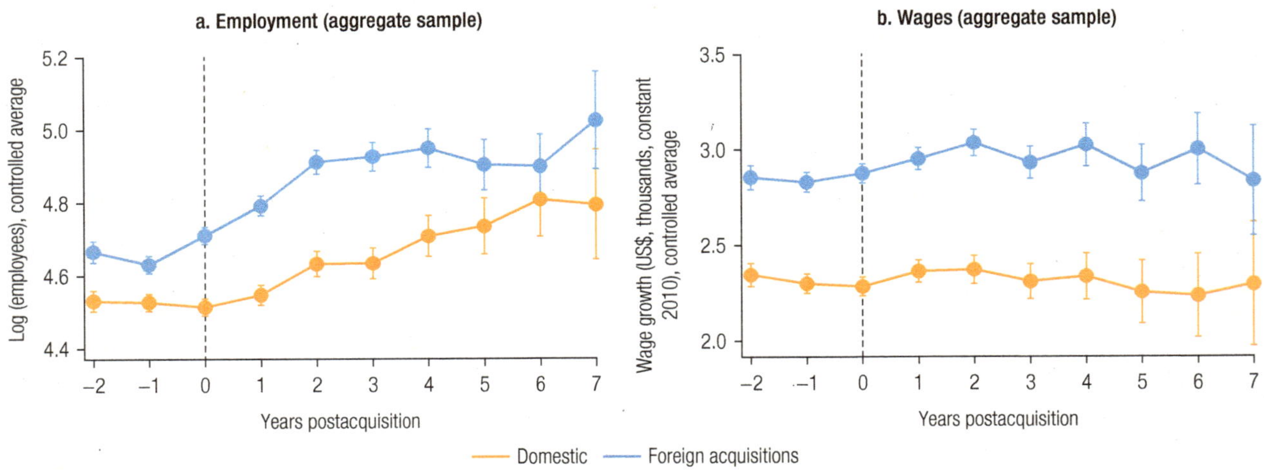

Source: World Bank calculations, based on industrial censuses from six countries.
Note: For this figure, industrial census data were analyzed from China, Côte d'Ivoire, Indonesia, Moldova, Serbia, and Vietnam (as further described in chapter 2, annex 2A). Vertical bars indicate the margin of error. "Domestic" refers to the firms that originated as domestic enterprises. Growth paths of firm outcomes can be captured in a simple framework using an interaction between indicators of firm group (greenfield, brownfield, and domestic) and years after entry in the following specification: $y_{ics} = group_i \beta \cdot d_t + \alpha_{cs} + \delta d_{it_0} + \varepsilon_{ics}$. The sample is restricted to cohorts whose entry is observed. To account for differences that might be driven by country characteristics, sector composition, and macroeconomic trends, the regressions also control for country-sector fixed effects and cohort fixed effects. Wage growth paths are calculated using constant deflated values in US dollars. FDI = foreign direct investment.

the bottom 40 percent of the population in all studied countries. However, the distributional effects differ significantly across the three countries (figure O.9). In Ethiopia, the benefits of FDI are more concentrated in the bottom 40 percent, while in Vietnam, the welfare gains are evenly distributed across the income distribution. Turkey had the greatest average wage benefits from FDI but also experienced increases in income inequality in services.[8]

These differences in the distributional effects of FDI across the three countries are likely driven by differences across sectors and workers' education levels (table O.1). In general, the average effects of FDI on formal employment and wages are positive for manufacturing and high-skilled services but neutral for extractive sectors and low-skilled services.

The analysis also finds significant evidence of a skill premium for high-skilled versus low-skilled workers in FDI affiliates. In regions and sectors with higher MNE activity (relative to those not receiving FDI), higher-skilled workers experience large benefits while low-skilled workers may see no changes or even see relative declines in formal employment and wages. Overall, this skill premium is more pronounced for FDI in services than in manufacturing.

Given that FDI disproportionately benefits better-educated and higher-skilled workers, those labor force participants who lack these characteristics tend to be left behind. Such workers tend to be more concentrated in the less economically advanced parts of their countries; as a result, FDI can exacerbate geographic disparities within economies. In particular, the analysis of Turkey presents a case of FDI-led skill premiums leading to wage dispersion, explaining why FDI in Turkey is associated with an increase in income inequality. This dynamic emphasizes the importance of a country's labor market and education policies.

The effects of multinational firms' production patterns on income and wage disparities are also explored in the recent *World Development Report* on global value chains (World Bank 2020). The report finds that GVCs increase wage inequality in countries at all income levels for at least three reasons: First, FDI and offshoring increase the

FIGURE O.9 FDI Has Had Varied Effects on National Income Distributions in Ethiopia, Vietnam, and Turkey

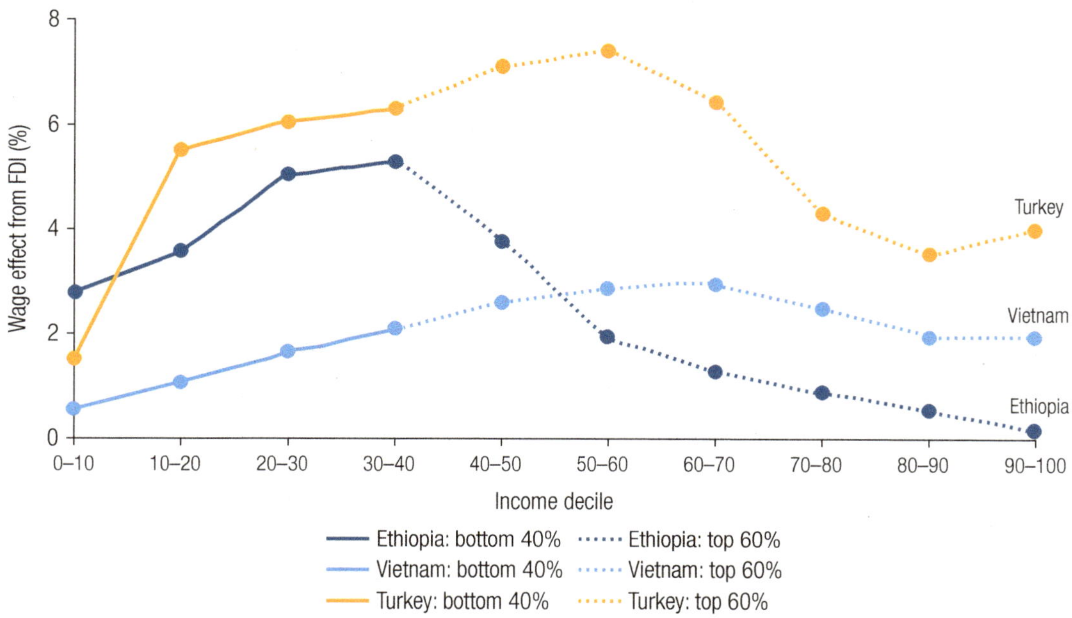

Source: World Bank calculations; individual labor market data from World Bank's International Income Distribution Database (I2D2), supplemented with Labor Force Surveys; firm-level data from sources including Ethiopia's Large and Medium Manufacturing Survey, Vietnam's Enterprise Census, and Turkey's Enterprise Information System data.
Note: FDI = foreign direct investment.

TABLE O.1 The Effects of FDI on Labor Markets Vary by Sector and Workers' Skill Levels

Broad sector	*Average effect*	*Low-skilled workers*	*High-skilled workers*
Extractives	No effect	No effect	No effect
Low-skilled manufacturing	Positive	Positive	Positive
High-skilled manufacturing	Positive	Neutral	Positive
Low-skilled services	Neutral	Negative	Positive
High-skilled services	Positive	Negative	Positive

Source: World Bank calculations; individual labor market data from World Bank's International Income Distribution Database (I2D2), supplemented with Labor Force Surveys; firm-level data from sources including Ethiopia's Large and Medium Manufacturing Survey, Vietnam's Enterprise Census, and Turkey's Enterprise Information System data.
Note: In the table title, "effects of FDI on labor markets" refers to the effects on both wages and the probability of formal employment. The table summarizes an analysis of data from three countries: Ethiopia, Turkey, and Vietnam. (For complete results, see chapter 3, annex 3C.) "Low-skilled" workers are those with primary education or less, while "high-skilled" workers have completed at least secondary education. All results are *relative* to workers in sectors with less or no investment by multinational enterprises (MNEs). FDI = foreign direct investment.

demand for skilled workers in low- and middle-income economies and put upward pressure on wage inequality. Second, GVCs are often more skill-sensitive because they tend to produce goods destined for quality-sensitive consumers in high-income countries. This can in turn create "a war for talent" in the developing countries and bid up the wages of skilled workers. Third, firms in GVCs tend to adopt more capital-intensive techniques than comparable domestic firms. The deepening and upgrading of physical capital contribute to the increase in the relative demand for skilled workers.

Pillar 2: Government Actions Can Rebuild Investor Confidence—Reducing Investor Risk, Fostering Investment Expansion, and Attracting New FDI through Policy Predictability, Regulatory Certainty, and Targeted Investment Promotion

The COVID-19 pandemic has rapidly escalated business uncertainty, in turn magnifying investment risks and depressing foreign investor confidence. Multinational firms are realizing that their historical push toward low-cost, low-inventory supply chains has opened them up to significant risk. In response, some of them are changing their corporate strategies, reassessing their approaches to sourcing production inputs, diversifying their suppliers, and making greater use of digital technologies (Baldwin and Evenett 2020).

They are also responding to changes in the policy environments, which in some markets have seen introductions of more-restrictive regulations, including during the outbreak. For example, to protect sensitive assets from foreign takeovers—notably in sectors such as health, medical research, biotechnology, and infrastructure—some countries are adopting new foreign investment screening mechanisms.

Traditionally, investors rely on a country's legal and regulatory framework to recognize their property rights and enforce those rights in a predictable and efficient manner. Economic theory suggests that when investors incur fixed and irreversible setup costs, uncertainty about the local conditions—especially policy uncertainty—will have a dampening effect that reduces investors' response to new investment opportunities (Bernanke 1983; Bloom 2009; Dixit 1989). Amid the COVID-19 outbreak, nationalization of essential supply chains, cancellation of government procurement contracts, and exchange control restrictions have come as sudden regulatory changes. Investors identify these political risks among their top concerns in the current crisis. It is therefore vital for governments to endeavor to reduce investor risk and help restore their confidence.

This report presents a new global database and a novel quantitative measure of regulatory risk (see chapter 4). This measure draws on, among others, data on the content of domestic laws and international treaties to assess countries' regulatory frameworks for investment in three dimensions (figure O.10): transparency, protection, and recourse. More specifically, it evaluates (a) transparency and predictability in both the content and process of making laws and regulations that apply to investors; (b) legal protection of investors against arbitrary and nontransparent government interference; and (c) investor access to

FIGURE O.10 Three Pillars of Addressing Regulatory Risk

Pillar 1. Transparency	Pillar 2. Protection	Pillar 3. Recourse
Is there *transparency* regarding the content as well as the process of making laws and regulations that apply to investors?	What is the extent of legal *protection* provided to investors against arbitrary, unpredictable, or nontransparent government actions?	Do investors have access to effective mechanisms for *recourse* in case of grievances or disputes?
• Systematic publication of and consultation on laws and regulations • Registries or ICT platforms and similar mechanisms to allow investors to find information about relevant laws and regulations • Specificity and clarity of legal provisions (to reduce space for discretion)	• Absolute treatment standards • Protection guarantees against direct and indirect expropriation, transfers of funds, fair and equitable treatment (FET)	• Investor-state dispute settlement and prevention • Land dispute resolution • Quality of judicial processes

Source: World Bank GIC Report team.
Note: ICT = information and communication technology.

effective mechanisms for recourse, including grievance management and dispute settlement.

Evidence at both the country and investor levels suggests that regulatory risk—as measured in this framework—matters for investment decisions. First, at the country level, higher regulatory risk is correlated with higher risk premia measured by other indexes. Second, higher regulatory risk is associated with lower FDI inflows (figure O.11).

Consistent with this result, investor data lend support at the microeconomic level to the negative relationship found between regulatory risk and FDI. To test the relationship between a host country's regulatory risk and foreign companies' investment entry and expansion decisions, the report uses a dataset of over 14,000 parent companies investing in nearly 28,000 FDI greenfield and expansion projects across 168 host countries between 2014 and 2016.[9] Estimations from this investor location decision model suggest that regulatory risk can deter MNEs from entering or expanding operations in a country.

The effect of regulatory risk on FDI is sizable and comparable in magnitude to the investment-enhancing effects of trade openness in the same regression models. In fact, in some of the models, the effect of regulatory risk on FDI exceeds that of trade openness, showing that a 1 percentage point reduction in regulatory risk increases the likelihood of an investor entering or expanding in a host country by 0.5–2 percentage points. In contrast, a 1 percentage point increase in the host country's trade-GDP ratio is associated with a 0.3–0.6 percentage point increase in an investor's likelihood to enter or expand.

The critical importance of the regulatory environment is further confirmed by results from the 2019 GIC Survey, in which investors rank countries' legal and regulatory environments as one of the top three factors for investment. In line with findings from the 2017 GIC Survey (World Bank 2018), 84 percent of respondents list regulatory environment as an "important" or "critically important" factor in their investment decisions (figure O.12).

FIGURE O.11 FDI Inflows Are Higher in Countries with Lower Regulatory Risk

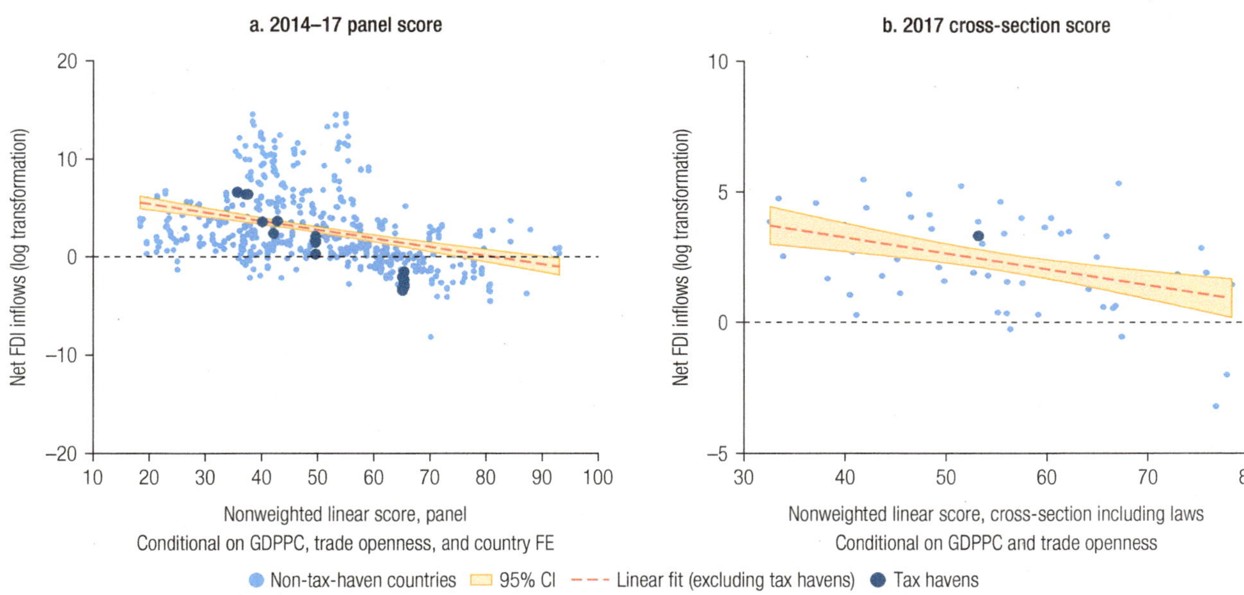

Source: World Bank calculations, from the World Development Indicators database.
Note: The scatterplots show the correlation between net foreign direct investment (FDI) inflows and regulatory risk index. Panel a uses a 2014–17 panel score; panel b uses a 2017 cross-section score. CI = confidence interval; FE = fixed effects; GDPPC = GDP per capita.

FIGURE O.12 The Legal and Regulatory Environment Was among the Top Three Factors for FDI in 2019

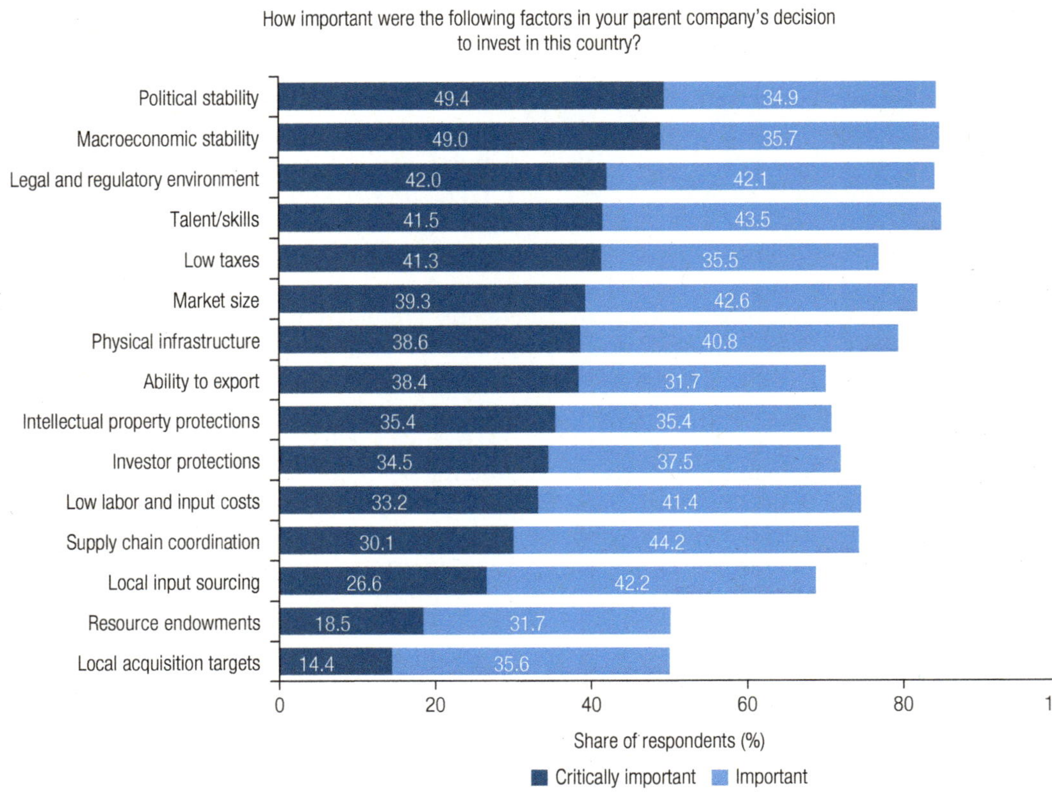

Source: Computation based on 2019 GIC Survey.
Note: Affiliates of multinational enterprises (MNEs) were surveyed in 10 middle-income countries: Brazil, China, India, Indonesia, Malaysia, Mexico, Nigeria, Thailand, Turkey, and Vietnam. FDI = foreign direct investment.

When it comes to investors who consider these factors "critically important," the legal and regulatory conditions of the host countries rank behind only political and macroeconomic stability, and ahead of considerations such as low taxes and low input costs. The legal and regulatory environment is especially important for larger firms. On average, large firms rank it as their top investment consideration.[10]

Overall, to reduce risks, governments need to remain committed to creating open and predictable environments for FDI. Given that the sources of policy uncertainty that erode investor confidence are both international and domestic, solutions at both levels are needed.

Internationally, reaffirming commitments to market access and rules-based international systems would decrease policy uncertainty related to protectionism and economic nationalism. To further advance this objective, a growing group of countries is calling for a new multilateral framework on investment facilitation. Although the framework's future is not yet clear, its emerging contours suggest it could encompass a set of practical measures concerned with improving the transparency and predictability of investment frameworks; streamlining procedures related to foreign investors; and enhancing coordination and cooperation between stakeholders such as host and home country governments, foreign investors, and domestic corporations as well as societal actors (Berger, Gsell, and Olekseyuk 2019; WTO 2017).

In addition to pursuing global, multilateral, or bilateral efforts toward providing clearer policy directions and investment frameworks, the 2019 GIC Survey results presented in this report point to the central role of domestic policy stability, with a particular emphasis on political and macroeconomic conditions. Indeed, evidence shows that the key elements of stable political environments include strong institutions, a level playing field, and predictable policy making. Macroeconomic stability is also vital, centered on implementing macroprudential policies, ensuring central bank independence, and optimizing fiscal policy.

Governments can further help reduce risks for investors by improving the legal, regulatory, and institutional frameworks for FDI. Business operations can be made more predictable by improving transparency and reducing room for bureaucratic discretion. Transparency can be strengthened by systematically consulting with the private sector and other stakeholders, developing information portals to make laws and regulations publicly available, and articulating clear and specific FDI-related legal provisions and administrative procedures.

Investment promotion agencies can play a critical role in these efforts given their role as governments' key interlocutors with foreign businesses. Empirical evidence shows that IPAs can help increase FDI inflows, attract higher-quality FDI, and even transform their economies (Charlton and Davis 2007; Freund and Moran 2017; Harding and Javorcik 2012; Moran et al. 2018; Morisset and Andrews-Johnson 2004; Wells and Wint 2000). They can play a significant role in strengthening their countries' investment competitiveness (see chapter 5).

Yet although IPAs have proliferated over the past two decades, success stories are still scarce, especially in the developing world. Many IPAs are unfocused—with too many mandates and target sectors—and are not providing the key services investors expect. At the same time, many IPAs are not evolving dynamically enough to align with both challenges and opportunities in the changing FDI landscape. The current literature, combined with surveys of IPAs and operational experience by the World Bank Group, suggests that IPAs can have greater positive impact if they sharpen their strategic alignment and focus, adopt a coherent institutional framework, and strengthen their delivery of investor services (figure O.13). In contrast, IPAs should not overestimate the role of investment

FIGURE O.13 **Core Elements for Increasing the Development Impact of Investment Promotion Agencies**

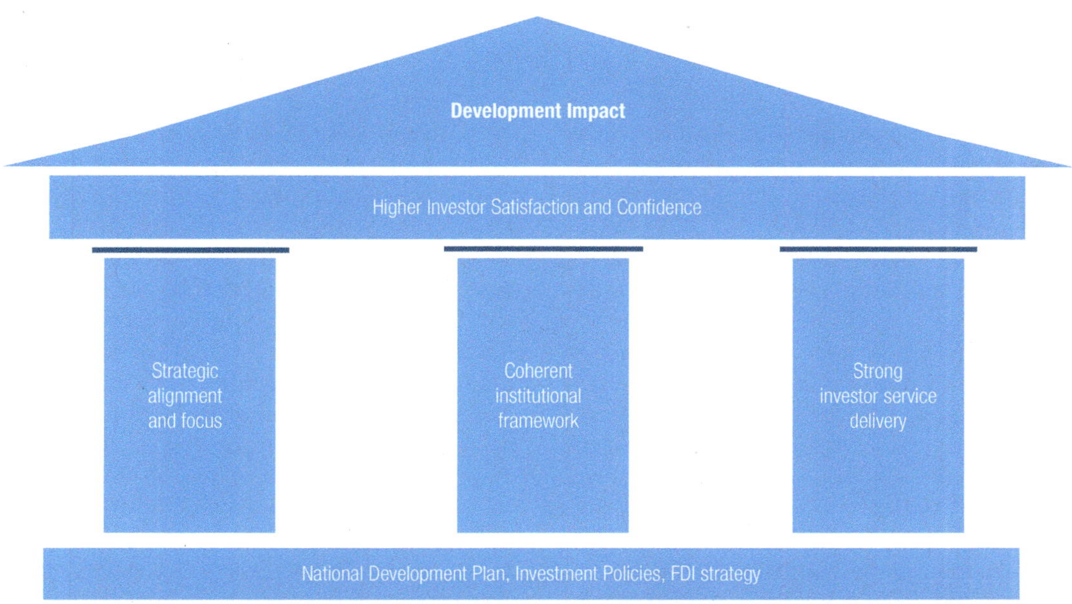

Source: World Bank, based on Heilbron and Aranda-Larrey 2020.
Note: FDI = foreign direct investment.

BOX 0.1

Key Success Factors in High-Performing IPAs in Developing Countries

World Bank research and operational experience have identified the following key success factors common to high-performing investment promotion agencies (IPAs) in developing countries:

- *High-level government support* (from the president or prime minister), granting a high priority to investment (or foreign direct investment [FDI]) and directly or indirectly championing the needed legal, regulatory, and institutional reforms for investment.
- *Strong strategic alignment* stemming from consultations with public and private sectors and cascading from a national development plan or FDI strategy to IPA corporate plans and industry-specific strategies.
- *A clear, uncontested mandate*, ideally focused on investment promotion, especially when starting or restructuring the IPA. Developing-country IPAs with multiple mandates take much longer to, or never do, deliver substantial FDI impact. Regulatory functions (including one-stop shops) are best performed by a separate public institution that ensures proper delivery of this essential function without compromising the equally essential investment promotion mandate of an IPA.
- *A high degree of institutional and financial autonomy* (or semiautonomy), emulating private sector flexibility to act according to agreed-upon strategic plans and to hire staff using specified and transparent job qualifications; avoiding political interference; and providing sustainability through political cycles.
- *An independent and well-functioning board of directors* or advisory board with strong and active private sector representation to better understand investors and provide direction in catering to their needs.
- *A strong investor-centric service orientation* to design and provide relevant and high-quality services to investors throughout their investment cycle.
- *Management and key promotion staff with strong private sector experience*, as well as international exposure and language skills, within the IPA's mix of employees with public and private sector experience.
- *Sufficient and sustained financial resources* over three- to five-year periods to provide continuity of strategic efforts over the long-cycle nature of investment promotion and to avoid struggling over funds every year or having to charge fees.

Source: Adapted from Heilbron and Whyte 2019.

incentives in increasing a location's overall investment competitiveness, although these may be needed to help companies during the pandemic crisis.[11]

When creating or strengthening their IPAs, policy makers should consider critical success factors (box O.1). The right strategic and institutional frameworks vary, depending on the country's political economy, the government's existing institutional setup, available legal formats, the civil service culture, and the institutional collaboration culture (Heilbron and Whyte 2019).

In the current COVID-19 crisis situation, IPAs are in large part shifting their principal focus from FDI attraction to retention of existing foreign investors as well as preservation of supply chains connecting foreign firms and their domestic suppliers. Through IPAs' responses to market signals and MNEs' needs, governments have an opportunity to minimize the risk exposure of MNEs and their associated supply chain linkages. Specific investment services to be prioritized by IPAs include (a) identifying and directly contacting at-risk or systemically strategic firms according to number of employees, region, or sector; (b) expediting foreign exchange approvals; and (c) advocating for urgent government actions to solve the firms' grievance issues more systematically.

Governments Can Leverage FDI for Robust Recovery from COVID-19

What can governments do, on the one hand, to leverage FDI to strengthen the resilience of their economies and help absorb future shocks, and on the other hand, to turn the current COVID-19 crisis into new opportunities to increase their competitiveness for FDI?

Avoid Protectionist Policies

Governments should avoid protectionist policies, which would further exacerbate disruptions to GVCs and amplify the already elevated uncertainty. Instead, to attract additional investment, countries should counter the global protectionist trend by further easing FDI entry and operational restrictions. Being more open to FDI relative to peers helps attract new investment. In fact, some countries are already using this crisis as an opportunity to open new sectors of their economies to foreign investment.

Enhanced regional cooperation can also be a critical element in the removal of barriers to intraregional trade and investment. Regional integration helps countries overcome divisions that impede the flow of goods, services, capital, people, and information. These divisions are a constraint to economic growth, especially in developing countries. While Europe, North America, and East Asia have historically led the way in regional integration, the momentum has lately also increased in some of the less integrated regions—as evidenced, for example, by the recently concluded negotiations on the African Continental Free Trade Area (AfCFTA). Experience has shown that deepened regional integration allows countries to improve market efficiency, accelerate reform processes in a coordinated and predictable manner, and foster multiregional cooperation.[12] Bilateral and regional trade and investment agreements also help enhance policy certainty by committing national governments to specific policy priorities and by fostering open and conducive trade and investment environments.

Seize New Opportunities from Changing FDI and GVC Patterns

Countries can seize new opportunities to increase their competitiveness for FDI as a result of shifting trade and investment patterns and policies. In the face of higher tariffs resulting from the 2019 trade war between China and the United States, importers have already sought new sourcing locations in the global marketplace (Constantinescu et al. 2019). Trade diversion may in turn cause a shift in FDI as firms adjust global supply chains and centers of production (Blanchard 2019). Developing economies with large export bases could emerge as suitable FDI hosts. Specifically, countries that already export similar products are likely to attract greater investment (Cali 2018).

With the COVID-19 crisis, the push to diversify supply chains will likely be intensified. Yet no consensus has emerged on how the global FDI and GVC landscape will look after COVID-19. Some economists hold the view that no major changes will take place and that adjustments will concentrate in health-related industries, as the economic rationale for GVCs holds the same (Baldwin and Evenett 2020; Freund 2020; Miroudot 2020). Others believe that COVID-19 has become a wake-up call for a new balance between risk and reward for GVCs, as pandemics, climate change, natural disasters, and other man-made crises may expose the world to increased risks (Goldberg 2020; Javorcik 2020). Regardless of which outcome prevails, as the main architects of GVCs, multinational firms will adjust production networks to improve their resilience and robustness in response to COVID-19.

Policy makers should reflect on these possible shifts in investment preferences and let business realities guide their policy response. Countries should assess which sectors and value chains have proven resilient during the

COVID-19 crisis. This will involve evaluating the risk exposure, value proposition, and competitiveness factors of individual sectors and value chains. In addition, governments should identify emerging competitive sectors in their countries that may arise from the possible reorganization of GVC and FDI landscapes.

Should new investment patterns emerge, they will require new priorities in investment policy and promotion reforms. These will entail realigning the investment incentive regimes to the new national development priorities likely to emerge after COVID-19, such as job creation. Reforms may also be needed to limit or phase out crisis-related investment screening and approval mechanisms. In addition, measures to address investor protections and grievance issues might be appropriate in some countries to enable governments to resolve grievances before they become legal disputes. Finally, measures to increase local firms' resilience and to strengthen supplier development programs will be needed to enhance FDI linkages to the local economies.

Strengthen Global Cooperation

Tackling the complex challenges presented by the current global environment will require global cooperation. The pandemic has illustrated the shared public health and economic vulnerabilities that countries face. It has also highlighted the critical importance of exchanging data, sharing information on good practices, and strengthening collaboration.

The magnitude and scale of the crisis require policy makers to employ their full arsenal of policy tools to improve business confidence and boost countries' investment competitiveness. During the global financial crisis, an unprecedented synchronized, coordinated policy response was critical to containing it. Once again, the times are testing policy makers. They must rise to the occasion by acting quickly, decisively, and collaboratively.

Notes

1. FDI data (here taken from the World Bank's World Development Indicators database) should be interpreted with caution. Research shows that multinational corporations' tax engineering and the role of investment hubs distort traditional FDI statistics. A growing body of evidence demonstrates that multinational corporations are reallocating royalties and other intangible assets to low-tax locations to reduce their aggregate corporate tax liability. Such "phantom investment" into corporate shells may account for almost 40 percent of global FDI (Damgaard, Elkjaer, and Johannesen 2019). At the same time, the main results reported in figure O.1 still hold, even if the analysis excludes tax havens as FDI destinations.
2. "Developing" countries in this report refers to low- and middle-income countries as defined by the World Bank. "Developed" countries are high-income countries. For the definitions of all income classifications and the countries therein, see "World Bank Country and Lending Groups," World Bank Knowledge Base: https://datahelpdesk.worldbank.org/knowledgebase/articles/906519-world-bank-country-and-lending-groups.
3. The 2017 Tax Cuts and Jobs Act (TCJA) essentially exempts US companies' foreign earnings from taxation, albeit with a one-off tax on past profits to ease the transition to the new system (Toder 2018). The implementation of the TCJA led to a massive increase in the repatriation of foreign-earned profits by the US multinationals back to the United States, resulting in negative FDI inflows from the United States for the affected host countries (OECD 2019). Although reinvested FDI earnings returned to positive levels in the first half of 2019—suggesting that many of the negative FDI flows were from one-time repatriations of past profits—rates of reinvestment remain below averages observed in the five years leading up to the implementation of the TCJA (OECD 2019). This pattern may signal a "new normal" for reinvestment levels as US companies now have fewer incentives to reinvest their foreign earnings to avoid taxation (OECD 2019).
4. The Pew Research Center's Spring 2018 Global Attitudes Survey included respondents from 27 countries: Argentina, Australia,

Brazil, Canada, France, Germany, Greece, Hungary, India, Indonesia, Israel, Italy, Japan, Kenya, the Republic of Korea, Mexico, the Netherlands, Nigeria, the Philippines, Poland, the Russian Federation, South Africa, Spain, Sweden, Tunisia, the United Kingdom, and the United States.

5. This short, English language, web-based survey was sent to known email addresses of MNEs, leveraging existing sampling frames for developing countries (World Bank, forthcoming). To extend reach, the survey was also circulated to known foreign investors through the countries' investment promotion agencies (IPAs). The period of data collection was March 24 to April 24, 2020. Data underlying the analysis comprise responses from 105 MNE affiliates operating in 26 developing countries. The results of the pulse survey are not generalizable to all developing countries but are an indicative estimate of impact of MNEs operating in developing countries.
6. Cross-border acquisition data are from the Thomson Reuters Refinitiv Mergers and Acquisitions Database (https://www.refinitiv.com/en/financial-data/company-data).
7. At the same time, several notable exceptions exist. These studies tend to focus on the employment and productivity of acquired firms in the context of a single developing country: Arnold and Javorcik (2009); Bircan (2019); Gong, Görg, and Maioli (2007); and Lipsey, Sjöholm, and Sun (2013).
8. Data analysis conducted for this chapter finds that Turkey's Gini coefficient currently stands at 0.35, but it would have been 0.33 (indicating lower inequality) without FDI.
9. These data are from fDi Markets, a *Financial Times* dataset (https://www.fdimarkets.com).
10. These differences may be driven by the presence of restrictions that are applicable only to larger firms and the greater regulatory scrutiny that large companies tend to experience.
11. This guidance suggests that developing countries should be careful and conservative in their use of tax incentives to stimulate their investment competitiveness. Other factors such as good investment climates, political stability, regulatory quality, and market opportunities are more critical to investors' initial location considerations than are tax rates and incentives (Andersen, Kett, and von Uexkull 2018; UNIDO 2011; World Bank 2018). Effective use of incentives requires greater regional and international coordination, political commitment, and common reporting standards to enhance transparency (IMF et al. 2015).
12. See "Overview," Regional Integration topic page, World Bank website: https://www.worldbank.org/en/topic/regional-integration/overview.

References

Akame, Afuge Junior, Metougue Eric Ekwelle, and George Ndonghandou Njei. 2016. "The Impact of Business Climate on Foreign Direct Investment in the CEMAC Region." *Journal of Economics and Sustainable Development* 7 (22): 66–74.

Alfaro, Laura, Sebnem Kalemli-Ozcan, and Vadym Volosovych. 2008. "Why Doesn't Capital Flow from Rich to Poor Countries? An Empirical Investigation." *Review of Economics and Statistics* 90 (2): 347–68.

Andersen, Maria R., Benjamin R. Kett, and Erik von Uexkull. 2018. "Corporate Tax Incentives and FDI in Developing Countries." In *2017/2018 Global Investment Competitiveness Report: Foreign Investor Perspectives and Policy Implications*, 73–100. Washington, DC: World Bank.

Arnold, Jens Matthias, and Beata S. Javorcik. 2009. "Gifted Kids or Pushy Parents? Foreign Direct Investment and Plant Productivity in Indonesia." *Journal of International Economics* 79 (1): 42–53.

Baker, Scott R., Nicholas Bloom, and Steven J. Davis. 2016. "Measuring Economic Policy Uncertainty." *Quarterly Journal of Economics* 131 (4): 1593–636.

Baker, Scott R., Nicholas Bloom, and Steven J. Davis. 2019. "The Extraordinary Rise in Trade Policy Uncertainty." *VoxEU*, September 17 (accessed November 7, 2019), https://voxeu.org/article/extraordinary-rise-trade-policy-uncertainty.

Baldwin, Richard E., and Simon J. Evenett, eds. 2020. *COVID-19 and Trade Policy: Why Turning Inward Won't Work*. London: CEPR Press.

Berger, Axel, Sebastian Gsell, and Zoryana Olekseyuk. 2019. "Investment Facilitation for Development: A New Route to Global Investment Governance." Briefing Paper

No. 5/2019, German Development Institute (DIE), Bonn.

Bernanke, Benjamin S. 1983. "Irreversibility, Uncertainty, and Cyclical Investment." *Quarterly Journal of Economics* 98 (1): 85–106.

Bircan, Çağatay. 2019. "Ownership Structure and Productivity of Multinationals." *Journal of International Economics* 116: 125–43.

Blanchard, Emily J. 2019. "Trade Wars in the Global Value Chain Era." In *Trade War: The Clash of Economic Systems Endangering Global Prosperity*, edited by Meredith A. Crowley, 57–63. London: CEPR Press.

Bloom, Nicholas. 2009. "The Impact of Uncertainty Shocks." *Econometrica* 77 (3): 623–85.

Bloom, Nicholas. 2014. "Fluctuations in Uncertainty." *Journal of Economic Perspectives* 28 (2): 153–76.

Caldara, Dario, Matteo Iacoviello, Patrick Molligo, Andrea Prestipino, and Andrea Raffo. 2019. "The Economic Effects of Trade Policy Uncertainty." International Finance Discussion Paper 1256, Board of Governors of the Federal Reserve System, Washington, DC. doi:10.17016/IFDP.2019.1256.

Cali, Massimiliano. 2018. "The Impact of the US-China Trade War on East Asia." *VoxEU*, October 16. https://voxeu.org/article/impact-us-china-trade-war-east-asia.

Charlton, Andrew, and Nicholas Davis. 2007. "Does Investment Promotion Work?" *The B.E. Journal of Economic Analysis & Policy* 7 (1): 1–21.

Constantinescu, Cristina, Aaditya Mattoo, Michele Ruta, Maryla Maliszewska, and Israel Osorio-Rodarte. 2019. "Global Trade Watch 2018: Trade Amid Tensions." Report No. 137201, World Bank, Washington, DC.

Damgaard, Jannick, Thomas Elkjaer, and Niels Johannesen. 2019. "What Is Real and What Is Not in the Global FDI Network?" Working Paper No. 19/274, International Monetary Fund, Washington, DC.

Dixit, Avinash. 1989. "Entry and Exit Decisions under Uncertainty." *Journal of Political Economy* 97 (3): 620–38.

Freund, Caroline. 2020. "Governments Could Bring Supply Chains Home. It Would Defy Economic Rationality." *Barron's*, May 1.

Freund, Caroline, Michael Ferrantino, Maryla Maliszewska, and Michele Ruta. 2018. "Impacts on Global Trade and Income of Current Trade Disputes." Macroeconomics, Trade & Investment (MTI) Practice Notes, No. 2, World Bank, Washington, DC.

Freund, Caroline, and Theodore H. Moran. 2017. "Multinational Investors as Export Superstars: How Emerging Market Governments Can Reshape Comparative Advantage." Working Paper No. 17-1, Peterson Institute for International Economics, Washington, DC.

Goldberg, Pinelopi Koujianou. 2020. "A Silent Hero of the Coronavirus Crisis." *Project Syndicate*, March 17.

Gong, Yundan, Holger Görg, and Sara Maioli. 2007. "Employment Effects of Privatisation and Foreign Acquisition of Chinese State-Owned Enterprises." *International Journal of the Economics of Business* 14 (2): 197–214.

Gramlich, John. 2019. "5 Trends in International Public Opinion from Our Searchable Global Indicators Database." *Fact Tank* (online platform) report, April 25, Pew Research Center, Washington, DC.

Harding, Torfinn, and Beata S. Javorcik. 2012. "Investment Promotion and FDI Inflows: Quality Matters." Economics Series Working Papers 612, University of Oxford.

Heilbron, Armando, and Yago Aranda-Larrey. 2020. "Strengthening Service Delivery of Investment Promotion Agencies: The Comprehensive Investor Services Framework." Finance, Competitiveness and Innovation in Focus. World Bank, Washington, DC.

Heilbron, Armando, and Robert Whyte. 2019. "Institutions for Investment: Establishing a High-Performing Institutional Framework for Foreign Direct Investment (FDI)." Investment Climate *In Focus* Note, World Bank, Washington, DC.

IMF, OECD, UN, and World Bank (International Monetary Fund, Organisation for Economic Co-operation and Development, United Nations, and World Bank). 2015. "Options for Low Income Countries' Effective and Efficient Use of Tax Incentives for Investment." Report to the G-20 Development Working Group, issued as an IMF Policy Paper, Washington, DC.

Javorcik, Beata. 2020. "Global Supply Chains Will Not Be the Same in the Post-COVID-19 World." In *COVID-19 and Trade Policy: Why Turning Inward Won't Work*, edited by Richard E. Baldwin and Simon J. Evenett, 111–16. London: CEPR Press.

Knight, Frank H. 1921. *Risk, Uncertainty, and Profit*. Boston: Hart, Schaffner, and Marx; Houghton Mifflin.

Lipsey, Robert E., Fredrik Sjöholm, and Jing Sun. 2013. "Foreign Ownership and Employment

Growth in a Developing Country." *Journal of Development Studies* 49 (8): 1133–47.

Miroudot, Sébastien. 2020. "Resilience versus Robustness in Global Value Chains: Some Policy Implications." In *COVID-19 and Trade Policy: Why Turning Inward Won't Work*, edited by Richard E. Baldwin and Simon J. Evenett, 117–30. London: CEPR Press.

Moran, Theodore H., Holder Görg, Adnan Serič, and Christiane Krieger-Boden. 2018. "Attracting FDI in Middle-Skilled Supply Chains." Discussion Paper No. 2018-2, Kiel Institute for the World Economy, Kiel, Germany.

Morisset, Jacques, and Kelly Andrews-Johnson. 2004. *The Effectiveness of Promotion Agencies at Attracting Foreign Direct Investment.* Occasional Paper No. 16, Foreign Investment Advisory Service, World Bank, Washington, DC.

OECD (Organisation for Economic Co-operation and Development). 2019. "FDI in Figures, October 2019." Semiannual data report, OECD, Paris.

Rodrik, Dani. 1991. "Policy Uncertainty and Private Investment in Developing Countries." *Journal of Development Economics* 36 (2): 229–42.

Toder, Eric. 2018. "Explaining the TCJA's International Reforms." *TaxVox* (blog), February 2. http://www.taxpolicycenter.org/taxvox/explaining-tcjas-international-reforms.

UNCTAD (United Nations Conference on Trade and Development). 2019. *World Investment Report 2019: Special Economic Zones.* New York: UNCTAD.

UNCTAD. 2020. *Investment Trends Monitor (Special Issue): Impact of the Coronavirus Outbreak on Global FDI.* Geneva: UNCTAD.

UNIDO (United Nations Industrial Development Organization). 2011. *Africa Investor Report 2011: Towards Evidence-based Investment Promotion Strategies.* Vienna: UNIDO.

Wells, Louis T. Jr., and Alvin G. Wint. 2000. "Marketing a Country: Promotion as a Tool for Attracting Foreign Investment." Revised ed. Occasional Paper No. 13, Foreign Investment Advisory Service, World Bank, Washington, DC.

Wernick, David A., Jerry Haar, and Shane Singh. 2009. "Do Governing Institutions Affect Foreign Direct Investment Inflows? New Evidence from Emerging Economies." *International Journal of Economics and Business Research* 1 (3): 317–22.

World Bank. 2018. *Global Investment Competitiveness Report 2017/2018: Foreign Investor Perspectives and Policy Implications.* Washington, DC: World Bank. doi:10.1596/978-1-4648-1175-3.

World Bank. 2019. *Global Economic Prospects, June 2019: Heightened Tensions, Subdued Investment.* Washington, DC: World Bank.

World Bank. 2020. *World Development Report 2020: Trading for Development in the Age of Global Value Chains.* Washington, DC: World Bank.

World Bank and OECD (Organisation for Economic Co-operation and Development). 2017. *A Step Ahead: Competition Policy for Shared Prosperity and Inclusive Growth.* Washington, DC: World Bank and OECD.

WTO (World Trade Organization). 2017. "Joint Ministerial Statement on Investment Facilitation for Development." Adopted at the 11th Ministerial Conference, December 13, WTO, Geneva.

1 Outlook and Priorities for Foreign Investors in Developing Countries: Findings from the 2019 Global Investment Competitiveness Survey in 10 Middle-Income Countries

Peter Kusek, Abhishek Saurav, and Ryan Kuo

Note: Since the Global Investment Competitiveness survey was conducted between June and November 2019, the results do not capture the effects of the COVID-19 pandemic on foreign investors.

Key Findings

- **An extensive survey of more than 2,400 foreign investors in 10 large middle-income countries, conducted between June and November 2019, shows that foreign-owned firms face significant trade and investment policy uncertainty that can negatively affect future investment decisions.** Since the survey was conducted before the COVID-19 outbreak, the results do not capture the effects of the pandemic on foreign-owned firms. The 10 countries covered by the survey are Brazil, China, India, Indonesia, Malaysia, Mexico, Nigeria, Thailand, Turkey, and Vietnam. The surveyed companies cumulatively represent around US$400 billion in total investment (about 10 percent of FDI stock in the surveyed countries) and employ nearly 1 million workers, based on conservative estimates.
- **Two-thirds of investors report that policy uncertainty due to protectionism and economic nationalism in trade and investment is either "important" or "critically important" in their investment decisions—and among the latter group, more than half have already experienced a decrease in employment, firm productivity, or investments in the last year.** Investor confidence decreases when the direction of policy making is unclear or unpredictable. Large firms and importers have been particularly sensitive to the effects of policy uncertainty in trade and investment.
- **Even before the COVID-19 outbreak, many investors were holding off expansion plans—based on the survey, less than half of foreign businesses planned to expand investment over the next three years.** However, results vary by country. Foreign businesses in China (17 percent of investors planning to expand investments) and Turkey (35 percent) report being much less likely to expand in the future than those in other surveyed countries. In contrast, about four-fifths of foreign affiliates in Nigeria and two-thirds in India plan to expand their investment stocks over the next three years. The effect of policy uncertainty in trade and investment—combined with domestic factors, such as macroeconomic fundamentals, political developments, and the legal and regulatory environment—are likely to shape foreign investors' investment plans in the surveyed countries.
- **The top three factors influencing investment decisions are political stability, macroeconomic stability, and a country's legal and regulatory environment; nearly 9 in 10 businesses consider them to be "important" or "critically important."** These factors rank ahead of considerations such as low tax rates, low labor and input costs, and access to resource endowments. Furthermore, large firms (those with more than 250 employees) rank an enabling regulatory environment as their top investment consideration. Investors that encounter major legal and regulatory obstacles are more likely to reduce or withdraw investment.
- **The COVID-19 pandemic represents an unprecedented shock to the global economy and MNEs, underscoring the need for policies to bolster investor confidence.** Against the backdrop of heightened policy uncertainty in trade and investment, the pandemic is set to further escalate uncertainty, magnify investment risks, and depress foreign investor confidence. These extraordinary challenges warrant a crisis management approach to governments' responses. In addition to short-term crisis response, governments should address international and domestic sources of policy uncertainty by reaffirming commitments to global and regional trade and investment systems, promoting political stability, enhancing macroeconomic stability, and improving legal and regulatory frameworks for FDI. Creating a predictable, business-friendly regulatory environment goes beyond the rules on the books and includes their full and consistent implementation in practice.

Introduction

This chapter presents the results of the 2019 Global Investment Competitiveness Survey (GIC Survey), a survey of executives of the affiliates of multinational enterprises (MNEs) in 10 developing countries.[1] The phone-based survey data cover more than 2,400 foreign investors with operations in 10 middle-income countries (MICs): Brazil, China, India, Indonesia, Malaysia, Mexico, Nigeria, Thailand, Turkey, and Vietnam. Using self-reported data from surveyed executives, the chapter serves two analytical objectives: First, it assesses the effect of rising trade and investment policy uncertainty on investors' confidence and future investment prospects. Second, it examines the role of a country's legal and regulatory environment in shaping investment decisions and identifies specific market entry and operational constraints faced by foreign investors.

The countries covered by the survey account for more than half of the global population, one-quarter of global gross domestic product (GDP), and one-fifth of global trade. From a foreign direct investment (FDI) perspective, they accounted for 37 percent of global inflows and 75 percent of inflows to developing countries in 2018. As with developing countries in general, FDI as a share of GDP has declined in the selected countries since the global financial crisis in 2008–09 (figure 1.1). From a precrisis average of 3 percent of GDP per year, FDI inflows have contracted to less than 2 percent in recent years.[2]

Most of the surveyed countries have high statutory restrictions on FDI relative to the global average (figure 1.2). Furthermore, countries more exposed to global megatrends such as rising protectionism, economic nationalism, and trade policy tensions are in turn more vulnerable to investment risks and declines in investor confidence.

In most of the selected countries, FDI growth rates have stalled or declined from

FIGURE 1.1 FDI Inflows to Middle-Income Countries Have Been Declining since the 2008–09 Global Financial Crisis

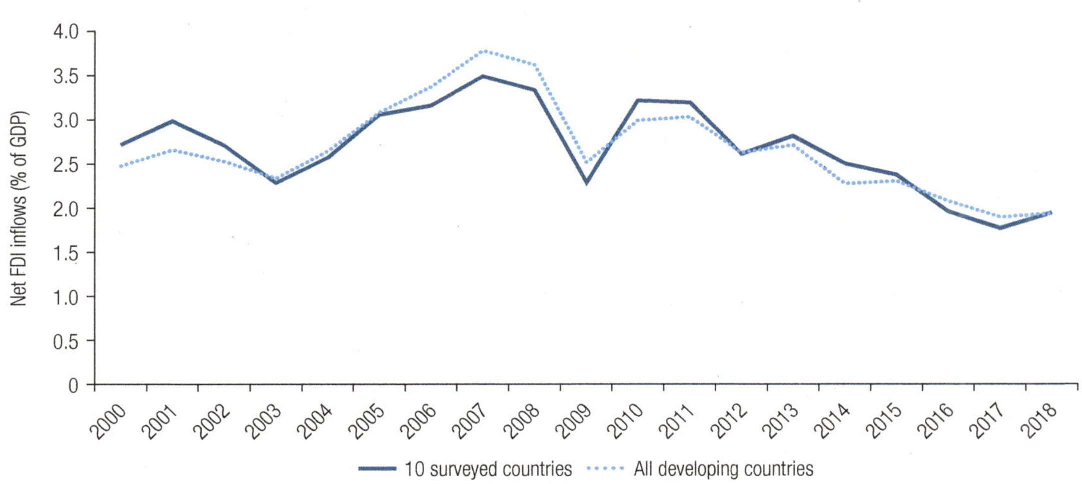

Source: World Development Indicators database.
Note: FDI = foreign direct investment. Surveyed countries are Brazil, China, India, Indonesia, Malaysia, Mexico, Nigeria, Thailand, Turkey, and Vietnam. "Developing" countries refers to low- and middle-income countries as defined by the World Bank.

FIGURE 1.2 Surveyed Countries Have High FDI Restrictiveness

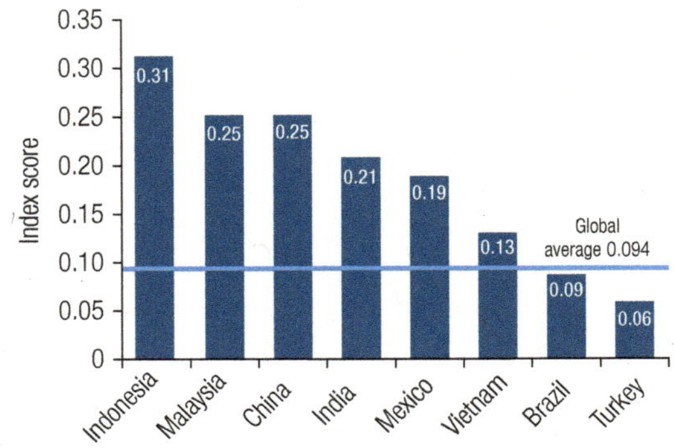

Source: Organisation for Economic Co-operation and Development (OECD) 2018 FDI Regulatory Restrictiveness Index, https://www.oecd.org/investment/fdiindex.htm.
Note: FDI = foreign direct investment. FDI Regulatory Restrictiveness Index scores range from 0 (open) to 1 (closed). The index scores are not available for Nigeria and Thailand.

their levels a decade ago, and growth has even been negative in some countries (such as Brazil and Nigeria) in recent years. An acute slowdown in FDI can sap growth momentum, lower participation in global value chains, and limit positive spillovers to domestic firms. Sluggish growth exacerbates the countries' risk of being trapped in middle-income status, limiting their ability to undertake "second generation" structural reforms.

FDI has been the largest source of external finance for many developing countries—greater than remittances, private debt and portfolio equity, or official development assistance.[3] Higher FDI inflows can ease capital constraints, contribute to output and employment growth, and increase aggregate productivity through positive productivity spillovers and technology transfers.

This chapter offers practical evidence to strengthen investment competitiveness by identifying policy levers that can relax FDI barriers, de-risk countries' investment climates, and facilitate additional FDI inflows. Through its systematic, data-driven identification of investment climate policy barriers, the chapter reflects the collective voice of foreign investors on the design and prioritization of investment policy reforms.

Survey Methodology and Respondent Profile

The data used in this study are from the 2019 GIC Survey, conducted June–November 2019 through 30-minute phone interviews in the primary business language(s) of the host economies. The survey was administered to senior executives of foreign-owned firms. Information was collected on the companies' general characteristics, the importance and effect of global megatrends on business operations, contribution to the host economy, and the importance of investment policy factors and operational obstacles they face.

The 2019 GIC Survey was designed to generate results that are representative at the country level and comparable across countries. It targeted a statistically representative sample of foreign-owned firms across the 10 surveyed MICs.[4] The target was to reach 125 interviews per sector (manufacturing and services). Each country sample comprises roughly 250 MNE affiliates with at least five employees. The only exception is Nigeria, where because of sampling frame limitations, the sample comprises 164 respondents (55 manufacturing and 109 services). Thus, across the 10 target countries, more than 2,400 responses were collected.

To assess changes in investor experience and perceptions, a second round of the survey is planned in 2020–21. To the extent possible, the second round will target respondents from the first round. For more details on the survey methodology, including sample representation and survey administration, see annex 1A.

The remainder of this section outlines the survey respondent profiles and additional methodological features, as follows:

- *Sector and subsector:* Survey respondents represent a range of sectors and source countries. By design, about half of the MNE affiliates were in the manufacturing sector, and about half were in services. Within each sector, the sample covers many subsectors (figure 1.3 and annex 1A, table 1A.2).
- *Size:* About one-quarter of surveyed MNE affiliates are large, with more than 250 employees. The remainder are small and medium enterprises (SMEs) with 250 or fewer employees, roughly half of which have 100 or fewer employees (figure 1.4, panel a).
- *Investment stock:* Roughly one-quarter of the MNE affiliates have invested more than US$10 million in host countries. More than one-tenth have invested more than US$50 million (figure 1.4, panel b).
- *Age:* On average, the surveyed MNE affiliates are fairly established in their respective markets. Nearly two-thirds of them have been in the host country for more than a decade, and one-third for more than 20 years (figure 1.4, panel c).
- *Ownership:* Roughly two-thirds of respondents are fully owned by foreign investors (that is, foreign MNEs hold a

FIGURE 1.3 Respondents Are Evenly Split between Manufacturing and Services Firms and Represent Firms across Various Specific Sectors

Share of 2019 GIC Survey respondents, by subsector (percent)

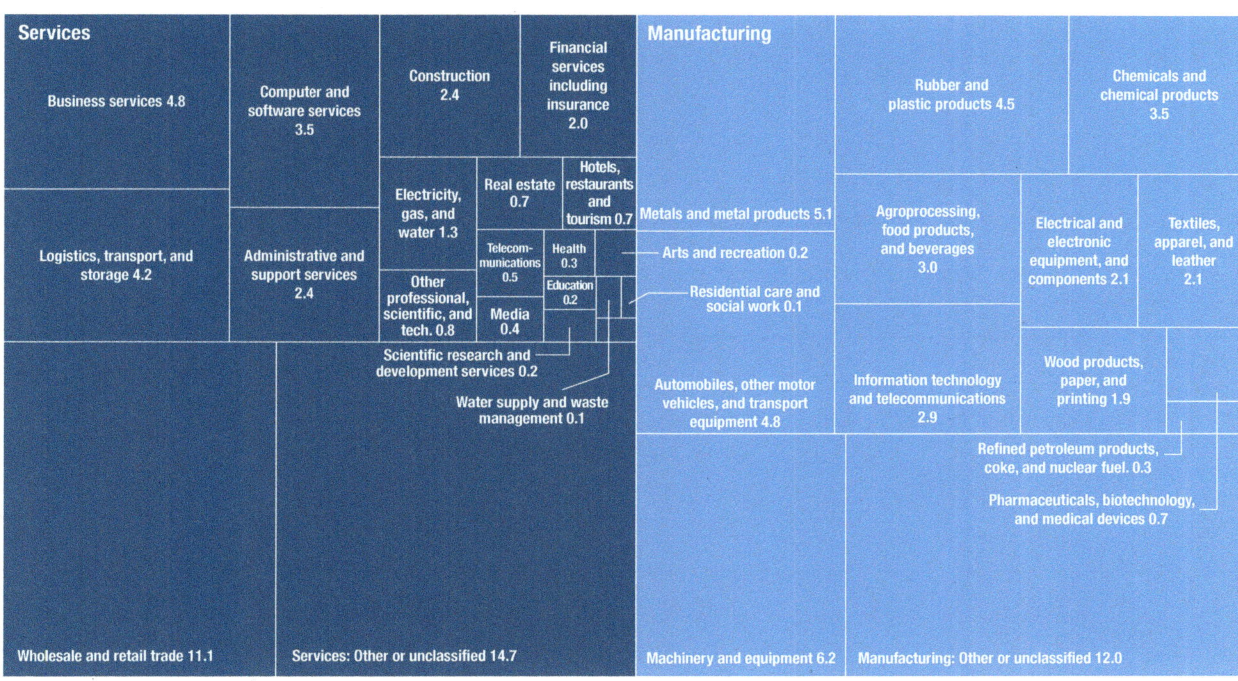

Source: Computation based on the 2019 GIC Survey.
Note: The relative size of the rectangles represents the relative share of respondents in each overall sector ("services" or "manufacturing"). Services subsectors comprising less than 1 percent include scientific research and development (R&D), arts and recreation, and others. For the number and shares of respondents by subsector, see annex 1A, table 1A.2.

FIGURE 1.4 The Median MNE Affiliate Is Relatively Small, Well-Established, and Majority Foreign Owned

Share of 2019 GIC Survey respondents (percent)

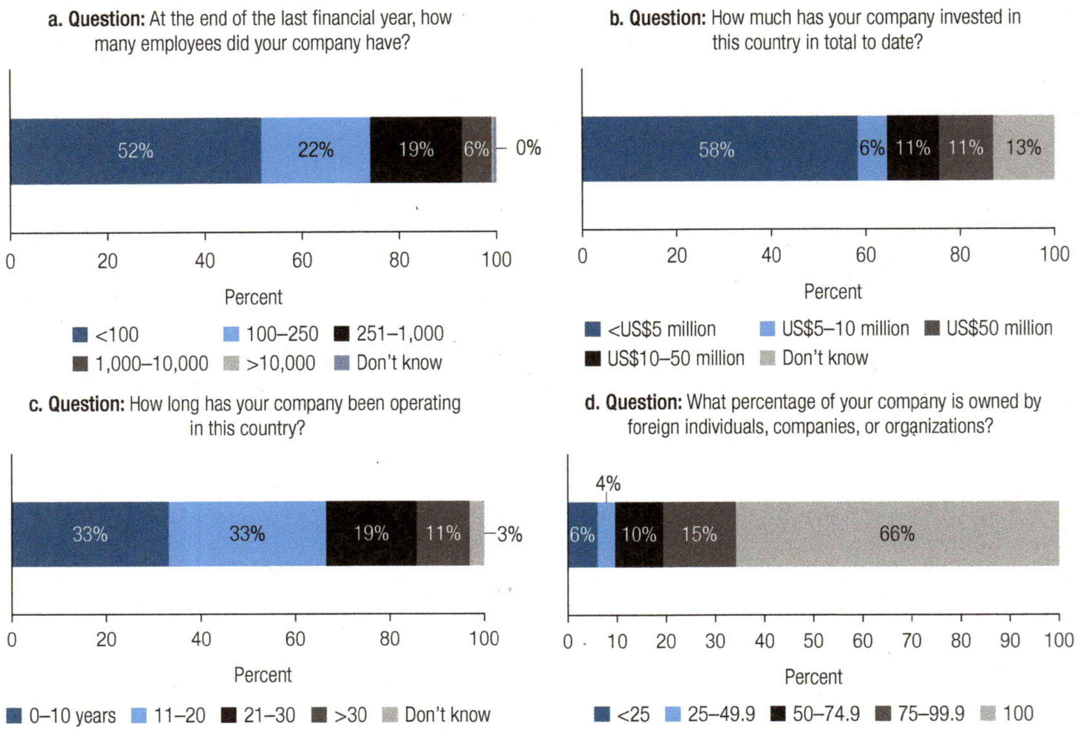

Source: Computation based on the 2019 GIC Survey.
Note: MNE = multinational enterprise. Percentages may not total 100 because of rounding.

TABLE 1.1 Most Investors Come from High-Income Countries in Asia or Europe

Share of 2019 GIC Survey respondents (percent)

Question: In which country is your parent company or your company's largest foreign owner located?

Region	*Developed*	*Developing*	*Total*
East Asia and Pacific	37	7	44
Europe and Central Asia	33	1	34
North America	13	0	13
Sub-Saharan Africa	0	3	3
Middle East and North Africa	1	1	2
Latin America and the Caribbean	1	1	2
South Asia	0	2	2
Total	**85**	**15**	**100**

Source: Computation based on the 2019 GIC Survey.
Note: "Developing" countries are low- and middle-income countries, and "developed" countries are high-income countries, as defined by the World Bank. "North America" is defined here as Canada and the United States.

100 percent stake), and about 10 percent are minority owned by foreign investors (that is, MNEs hold less than a 50 percent stake) (figure 1.4, panel d).

- *Origin:* Eighty-five percent of the foreign investors come from high-income countries, while the vast majority of the remainder come from middle-income countries (table 1.1). Low-income countries account for less than 1 percent of the foreign investors surveyed.

The Development Contributions of FDI in Host Economies

A large body of literature explores FDI's contribution to host economies through capital infusion and productivity spillovers. Researchers theorize that MNE affiliates may benefit local economies by introducing more advanced technology and management practices (especially to their suppliers), increasing demand for local products, providing improved inputs, driving exports, and introducing competition (Arnold and Javorcik 2009; Djankov and Hoekman 2000; Javorcik 2004; Lin and Saggi 2005; UNCTAD 2013; World Bank 2020).

At the same time, FDI may be harmful if local firms lose market share to foreign-backed competitors (Aitken and Harrison 1999). From an empirical standpoint, the literature has generally found positive upstream spillovers (that is, benefits of FDI for firms that are suppliers to MNE affiliates) and insignificant and sometimes negative spillovers for competitors of MNEs (Havránek and Iršová 2011; Iršová and Havránek 2013).

To assess the development contributions of MNE affiliates in host economies, the 2019 GIC Survey asked respondents about their investments and reinvestment behavior, input sourcing, export and import activity, and competition dynamics in host countries.

The survey data suggest that MNE affiliates make strong contributions to local economies through capital infusions. Roughly one-third of respondents have invested more than US$5 million in host economies, and more than 10 percent have invested more than US$50 million (figure 1.4, panel b). Not all of this capital comes from abroad: MNE affiliates reinvest about 60 percent of their profits back into host economies. This result is in line with earlier survey evidence and literature showing that reinvested earnings are an important source of FDI (Kusek and Silva 2018; UNCTAD 2016).

Parent-affiliate relationships observed in survey data reveal both North-South and South-South FDI flows. As noted earlier, 85 percent of parent MNEs are headquartered in high-income countries, the remainder coming mostly from middle-income countries.

A breakdown of country-level investments, by source region, shows that the respondents in surveyed countries in two regions—East Asia and Pacific, and Europe and Central Asia—exhibit strong intraregional links (table 1.2). Roughly three-quarters of respondents from these regions have parent MNEs based within the same region, confirming high regional economic integration. In contrast, MNE affiliates in countries such as Brazil, India, Mexico, and Nigeria are more likely to have parent companies from other regions.

Many surveyed MNE affiliates are active in sourcing from local suppliers. On average, the GIC Survey respondents source 55 percent of their inputs locally However, there is significant cross-country variation, likely driven by the availability and quality of local suppliers. In China and India, which have well-developed domestic product markets, MNE affiliates source a higher share of their inputs locally (67 percent and 60 percent, respectively), while respondents in Turkey and Vietnam source less than half of their inputs locally. In addition, services sector MNE affiliates, minority foreign-owned affiliates, large employers (more than 250 employees), and domestic market-oriented affiliates (those with less than half of revenues from exports) source a greater share of their inputs locally.

TABLE 1.2 Intraregional Investment Links Are Strong in East Asia and Pacific, and in Europe and Central Asia, While Interregional Investment Is Greater in Other Regions

Share of respondents (percent)

	Source region						
Host country	*East Asia and Pacific*	*Europe and Central Asia*	*Latin America and the Caribbean*	*South Asia*	*Sub-Saharan Africa*	*North America*	*Middle East and North Africa*
China	**58**	25	1	1	0	15	0
Indonesia	**77**	17	0	1	0	4	1
Malaysia	**64**	22	1	2	0	11	1
Vietnam	**86**	13	0	0	0	1	0
Thailand	**80**	11	0	1	1	7	1
Turkey	10	**77**	1	0	1	8	4
Brazil	15	60	**6**	1	0	17	1
Mexico	15	38	**9**	1	0	37	0
India	21	51	1	**1**	2	23	2
Nigeria	9	33	0	8	**26**	12	11

Source: Computation based on the 2019 GIC Survey.

Note: The figure excludes respondents who reported they did not know where their foreign parent multinational enterprises (MNEs) were based (less than 1 percent of the sample). Shaded cells denote investments originating from the same region as the host country (i.e., intraregional investment).

From a trade perspective, many surveyed MNE affiliates are active in driving exports. Survey respondents derive about one-third of their revenues from exports on average, and nearly one-quarter are majority exporters (at least 50 percent of revenues derived from exports). In general, MNE affiliates in the services sector derive a smaller share of their revenues from exports than do affiliates in the manufacturing sector (figure 1.5, panel a). Lower tradability of certain services and higher barriers to trade in services potentially explain these results. This pattern holds across most surveyed countries: in Vietnam, MNE affiliates in the manufacturing sector derive 74 percent of their revenues from exports on average, compared with a modest 29 percent for services affiliates. Similar trends are observed in China, Indonesia, Malaysia, and Mexico.

Finally, survey data show that MNE affiliates promote competition in host countries. Owing to technological, financial, and management advantages, foreign affiliates perform well on average in the surveyed countries: about half report having gained market share in the past three years, compared with just 16 percent that lost market share (figure 1.6, panel a). In addition, roughly two-thirds report primarily competing with firms operating in the host economy: 29 percent compete primarily with other MNE affiliates, and 35 percent compete with local firms (figure 1.6, panel b). These results suggest that MNEs apply competitive pressure on domestic competitors, although the net effect on domestic competitors' productivity is unclear.

Policy Uncertainty and Foreign Investors' Outlook

The slowdown in FDI flows has come amid rising policy uncertainty in trade and investment. Policy uncertainty increases when the direction of policy decision making is unclear or erratic, limiting businesses' ability to forecast the likelihood of future events and outcomes (Bloom 2014; Knight 1921). The increase in policy uncertainty is reflected in the high values registered in 2019 by various indicators such as the Global Economic Policy Uncertainty (EPU)

FIGURE 1.5 MNE Affiliates' Trading Behavior Differs Widely across Host Countries

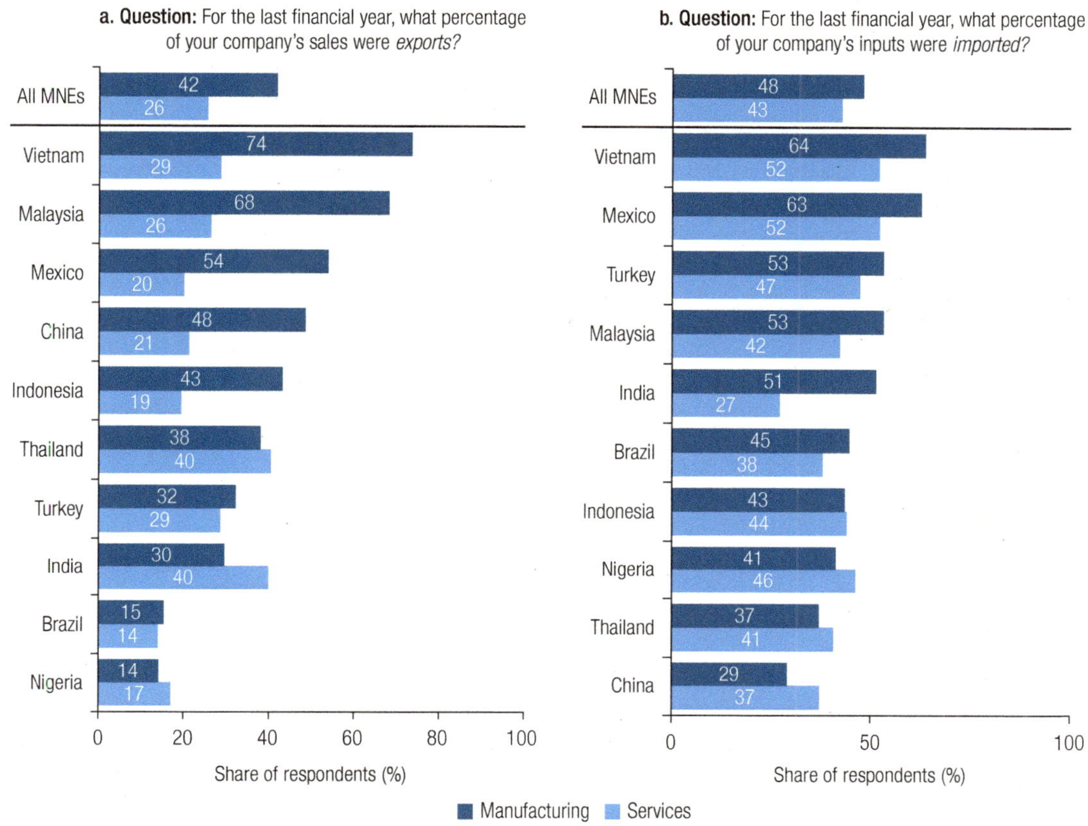

Source: Computation based on the 2019 GIC Survey.

Index, World Uncertainty Index, World Trade Uncertainty Index, and Trade Policy Uncertainty Index (Baker, Bloom, and Davis 2019; Caldara et al. 2019).[5]

For MNE affiliates, both international and domestic sources of policy uncertainty could escalate risk sentiment.[6] Recent and ongoing global events such as withdrawals from global trade agreements; new trade barriers (such as bilateral tariff escalations); geopolitical developments (such as Brexit); and other trade tensions have contributed to an unprecedented rise in trade and investment policy uncertainty (Baker, Bloom, and Davis 2019). In host economies, MNE affiliates can further be subject to uncertainties related to domestic political and electoral outcomes; unpredictable FDI rules (such as restrictive screenings and approval requirements); and economic nationalism. The pattern of economic nationalism extends to investment policy as well as trade: more than a third of national investment policies introduced in 2018 were measures related to new FDI restrictions or regulations (UNCTAD 2019).

Business survey data enhance our understanding of investor behavior amid trade and investment policy uncertainty. A growing body of literature has investigated the behavior of foreign investors in times of policy uncertainty more generally (Bonaime, Gulen, and Ion 2018; Cao, Li, and Liu 2017; Chen and Funke 2003; Chen, Nie, and Ge 2019; Julio and Yook 2016;

FIGURE 1.6 The Competitive Dynamics of FDI Firms in Host Markets Are Complex

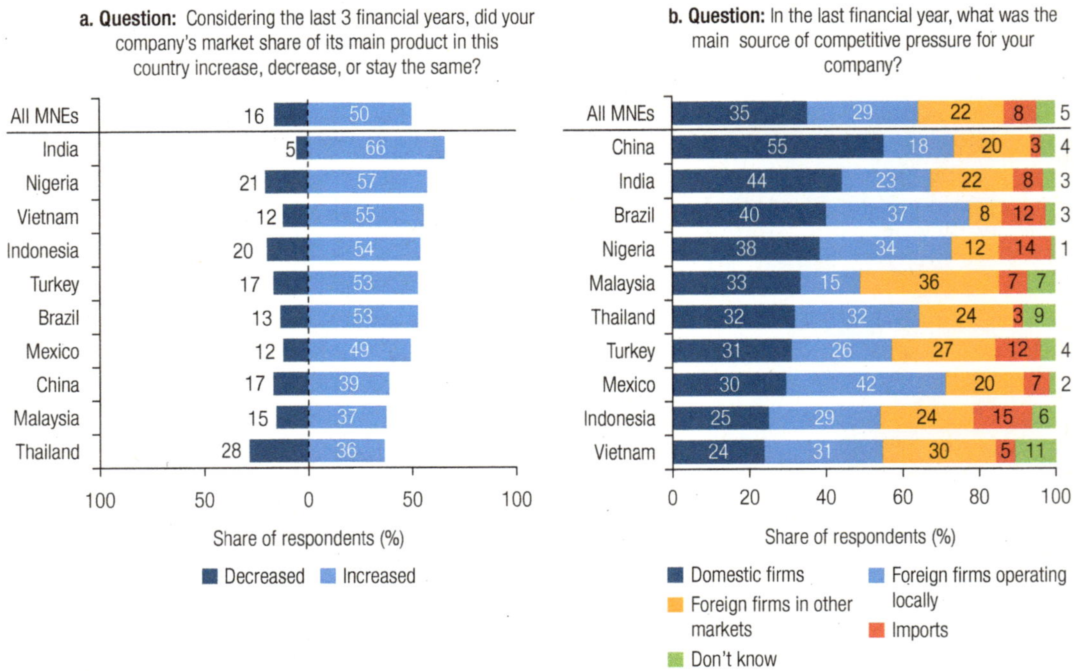

Source: Computation based on the 2019 GIC Survey.
Note: In panel b, percentages may not total 100 because of rounding. FDI = foreign direct investment; MNEs = multinational enterprises.

Rodrik 1991), but little research directly examines the business effects of trade and investment policy uncertainty on foreign-owned firms.[7]

The 2019 GIC Survey data provide direct evidence of the effects of trade and investment policy uncertainty on business operations of foreign-owned firms in the 10 MICs. By capturing current perceptions and expectations of foreign investors with investments in the surveyed MICs, the survey addresses the following questions related to policy uncertainty and investments:

- How important is the increasing policy uncertainty due to protectionism and economic nationalism in trade and investment in shaping foreign companies' investment decisions?
- How has policy uncertainty affected foreign-owned businesses in terms of jobs, productivity, investments, and changes in production locations?
- What are foreign investors' predominant investment plans in relation to expanding, maintaining, and reducing investments in host countries over the next three years?

Effects of Policy Uncertainty on Foreign-Owned Businesses

Survey results show that foreign-owned firms are sensitive to recent increases in policy uncertainty due to protectionism and economic nationalism in trade and investment. Nearly two-thirds of respondents report that such policy uncertainty was "important" or "critically important" to their investment decisions in the last year (figure 1.7, panel a).[8] The survey data indicate that, on average, MNE affiliates that import a greater share of their inputs and those that employ more than 250 workers (large firms) are more sensitive to policy

FIGURE 1.7 Investors Are Sensitive to Policy Uncertainty in Trade and Investment and Have Been Adversely Affected in the Last Year

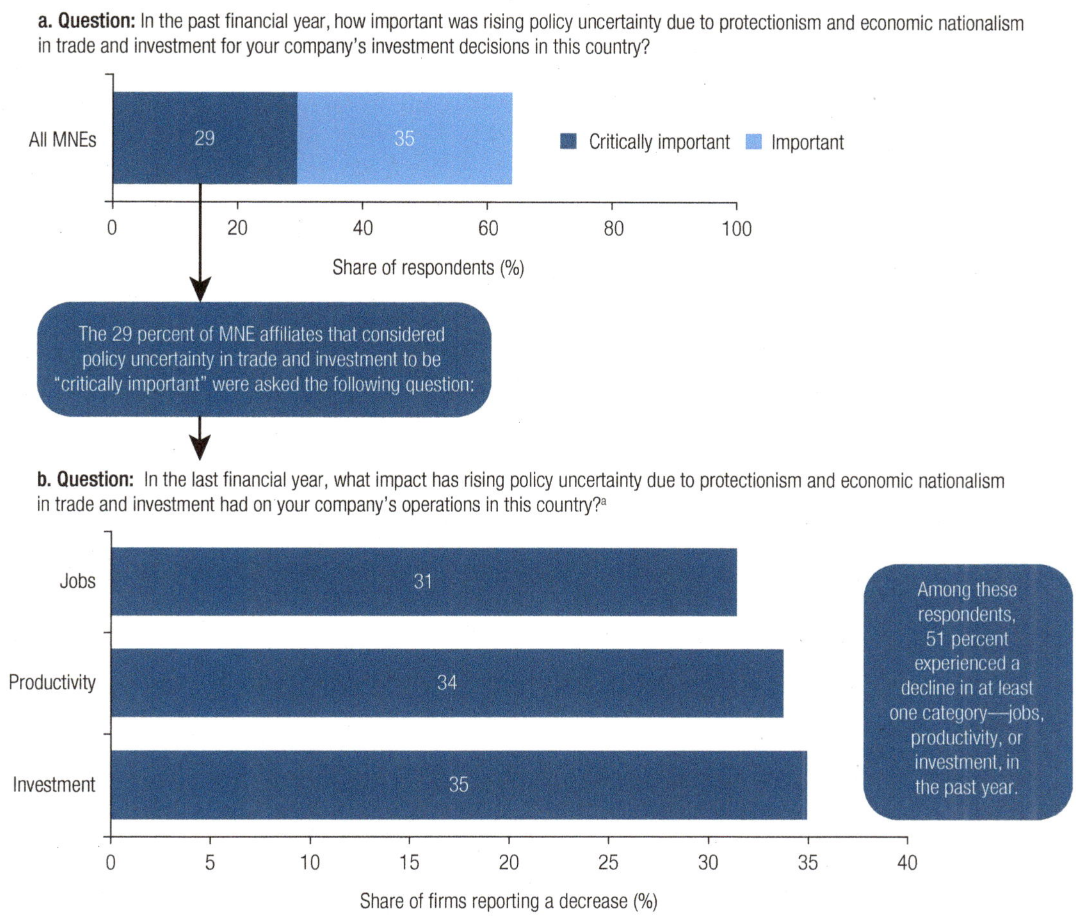

Source: Computation based on the 2019 GIC Survey.
Note: Affiliates of multinational enterprises were surveyed in 10 middle-income countries: Brazil, China, India, Indonesia, Malaysia, Mexico, Nigeria, Thailand, Turkey, and Vietnam. MNEs = multinational enterprises.
a. Questions about the impact of rising policy uncertainty on business operations were only asked of respondents who reported rising policy uncertainty as "critically important" in the past financial year (a 12-month period between January 1, 2018, and September 30, 2019, depending on the country).

uncertainty (both differences being significant at $p < 0.01$).[9]

To assess the direct impact of policy uncertainty on foreign-owned firms, MNE affiliates that consider policy uncertainty to be "critically important" were also asked whether policy uncertainty has caused increases, decreases, or no impact in terms of the number of jobs, productivity, investments, and changes in production locations (such as global supply chain adjustments). A substantial share of these MNE affiliates reported being adversely affected by policy uncertainty (figure 1.7, panel b). About a third of respondents to this question reported declines in the number of jobs (31 percent), productivity (34 percent), and investment (35 percent) in the last year. Taken together, over half (51 percent) the respondents have experienced a decline in jobs, productivity, or investments owing to rising policy uncertainty in the past financial year. About a third (32 percent) reported positive impacts along at least one outcome (and no negative impact on any outcome). The remaining 17 percent reported no effect or did not know.

The increase in trade and investment policy uncertainty could disrupt existing global value chains, reflecting MNEs' gradual shift toward reshoring or other changes to the locations of production (World Bank 2020). Thus, the survey asked the MNE affiliates that considered policy uncertainty to be "critically important" whether their decision making about production locations had changed as a result of policy uncertainty in the last financial year. Over 40 percent of respondents in China, Indonesia, Mexico, Nigeria, and Thailand have adjusted how they organize their supply chains as a result of policy uncertainty. In other countries, the results are less pronounced: less than one-third of respondents in Brazil, India, and Malaysia reported adjusting their supply chains because of policy uncertainty.

Policy uncertainty is most likely to have affected the configuration of supply chains and adjustments of production locations among the smaller MNE affiliates. Among those that are SMEs (with fewer than 250 employees), 40 percent report having adjusted how they organize their production locations, compared with 30 percent of large firms.[10] This pattern may reflect the larger firms' greater capacity to weather policy-related challenges as well as the smaller affiliates' greater organizational agility in adjusting production locations.

Predominant Investment Plans

The nature of FDI (being partially sunk after the investment is made) renders it particularly vulnerable to trade and investment policy uncertainty. Adopting a "wait and see" approach, cautious firms delay or cancel planned investments and technological upgrades.

Theoretical explanations posit that an increase in uncertainty increases the option value of delaying investments when faced with adjustment costs, resulting in declines in both investments and new hiring (Abel, Dixit, and Eberly 1996; Abel and Eberly 1996; Bernanke 1983). These theoretical predictions consistently find support in the empirical literature (Anand and Tulin 2014; Baker, Bloom, and Davis 2013; Bloom et al. 2012; Cebreros, Heffner, and Salcedo 2019; Gulen and Ion 2016). In turn, stalled investment activity impedes productivity growth because of limited reallocation across companies (Bloom 2009). In the face of trade and investment policy uncertainty, MNEs have incentives to revisit global production and sourcing decisions to avert vulnerabilities from possible supply chain dislocations (Blanchard 2019; IMF 2019). Firms' cautious investment behavior can thus curtail global economic activity and slow growth (Caldara et al. 2019).

To assess the investment outlook of MNEs operating in the surveyed economies, their affiliates were asked about their predominant investment plans in relation to expanding, maintaining, and reducing investments in host countries over the next three years.[11] Figure 1.8 presents aggregate results for the 10-country pooled sample. Fewer than half (48 percent) are planning to expand their investments over the next three years. A similar share of respondents (44 percent) across both manufacturing and services sectors are planning not to invest further, keeping their investment stock at current levels in respective host economies. A small share of existing respondents (4 percent) are planning to withdraw or reduce their investments.

MNE affiliates that are more exposed to policy uncertainty exhibit more cautious investment outlooks. In line with the literature, survey data suggest that policy uncertainty in trade and investment is poised to shift investment patterns. Firms that cite policy uncertainty in trade and investment as a "critically important" investment

FIGURE 1.8 Larger Firms and Those from Developing Countries Are More Likely to Expand Investment, on Average

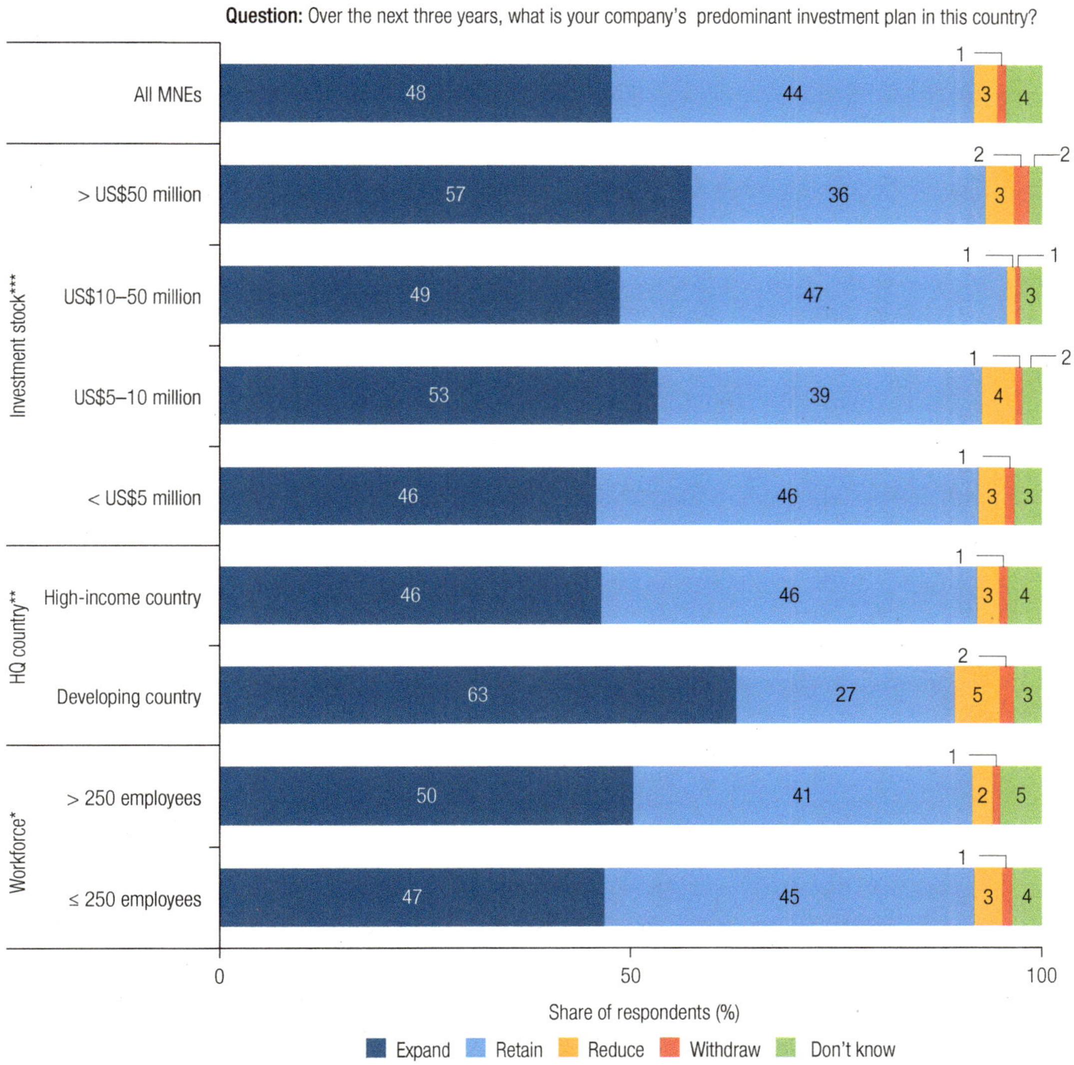

Source: Computation based on the 2019 GIC Survey.
Note: Affiliates of multinational enterprises (MNEs) were surveyed in 10 middle-income countries: Brazil, China, India, Indonesia, Malaysia, Mexico, Nigeria, Thailand, Turkey, and Vietnam. "Developing countries" refers to low- and middle-income countries as defined by the World Bank. Differences for investment stock were tested by comparing the " > US$10 million" group with the rest of the sample. Percentages may not total 100 because of rounding. The interviews were conducted June–November 2019, so the implied three-year time horizon for this question is 2019–22. HQ = headquarters.
*$p < .10$ **$p < .05$ ***$p < .01$

consideration are more than twice as likely as other affiliates (7 percent versus 3 percent) to reduce or withdraw their investments. Even after controlling for host country and various firm characteristics, MNE affiliates that cite policy uncertainty as a "critically important" investment consideration expect to be less expansionary on average.[12] Relatedly, those respondents that experienced reductions in either workforce, productivity, or investments as a result of policy uncertainty are nearly four times more likely to expect to reduce or withdraw investments in the next three years (9.2 percent versus 2.4 percent).[13]

Larger MNE affiliates (by size of workforce or investment) are more positive in their investment outlook. Foreign-owned firms with more than US$10 million in investment stock are nearly 10 percentage points more likely to expand investments in the next three years.[14] Similarly, foreign-owned firms with more than 250 employees are also more likely to expand and less likely to reduce investment over the next three years.[15] Results are consistent with literature that suggests that firms with greater financial resources are better equipped to weather uncertainty if they continue to believe that the long-term fundamentals of their investments are attractive (Ghosal and Loungani 2000).

MNE affiliates with parents from other developing countries are also significantly more likely to plan on expanding their investments. Nearly two-thirds of affiliates with global headquarters in other developing countries plan to expand their investments over the next three years. The factors driving this result could include a higher appetite for risk and policy uncertainty among investors from developing countries as well as current trade tensions being concentrated between developed and developing countries (Beamish and Banks 1987; Gonzalez, Qiang, and Kusek 2018; Wei, Liu, and Wang 2008).

MNE affiliates report heterogeneous future investment plans across the surveyed countries. Figure 1.9 presents disaggregated results by country for the question on predominant investment plans in relation to expanding, maintaining, and reducing investments in host countries over the next three years. In terms of expansion, foreign affiliates in China

FIGURE 1.9 Investors in China and Turkey Have Less Ambitious Investment Plans than Those in Other Countries

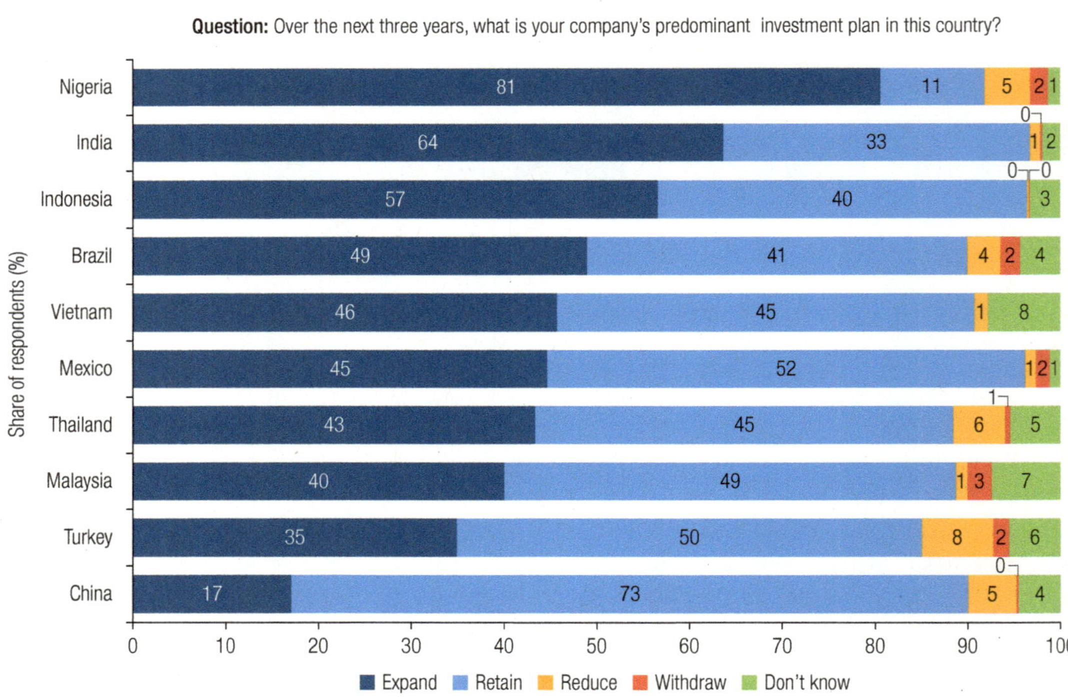

Source: Computation based on the 2019 GIC Survey.
Note: For sample composition, see annex 1A. Percentages may not total 100 because of rounding. The interviews were conducted June–November 2019, so the implied three-year time horizon for this question is 2019–22.

(17 percent) and Turkey (35 percent) are much less likely to expand than those in other surveyed countries. In stark contrast, about four-fifths of foreign affiliates in Nigeria and two-thirds in India plan to expand their investment stocks over the next three years. The effect of policy uncertainty in trade and investment—combined with domestic factors such as macroeconomic fundamentals, political developments, and the legal and regulatory environment, among others—is likely to shape foreign companies' investment plans in the surveyed countries.

In China, both efficiency-seeking and market-seeking investors report similar and relatively pessimistic investment outlooks for the next three years. However, the future investment plans for these two subgroups are likely shaped by different factors.

Efficiency-seeking investors (majority exporters) that primarily export to the United States are about 15 percentage points more likely than those with other primary export destinations to consider policy uncertainty to be "important" or "critically important" in their investment decisions.[16] Plausibly, the investment sentiment of efficiency-seeking investors reflects the detrimental effect of ongoing trade tensions with the United States. Although investment flows to China have not slowed to date (UNCTAD 2019), the relative pessimism of affiliates in China suggests that changes in trade patterns may lead to investment diversion in the near future.

In contrast, the subdued future investment plans for domestic market-seeking investors are plausibly driven by domestic factors, including high levels of corporate indebtedness (a future growth risk) and an overall slowdown in China's economic growth (World Bank 2019b).

In Turkey, MNE affiliates with different characteristics exhibit similar future investment plans: on average, only 35 percent plan to expand. There are no significant differences across major dimensions of interest (manufacturing and services, efficiency seeking and market seeking, large and small affiliates, older and newer affiliates) in terms of either sensitivity to policy uncertainty in trade and investment or average investment outlook.

This relative homogeneity suggests that foreign-owned firms' relative pessimism in Turkey is driven by domestic macroeconomic uncertainty. The Turkish economy has recently suffered from sharp financial outflows driven by concerns related to high current account deficits, high corporate indebtedness, and the direction of domestic economic policy (World Bank 2019b). Such issues are likely to affect all MNE affiliates in the country.

In contrast to China and Turkey, more than 80 percent of the surveyed MNE affiliates in Nigeria plan to expand their investment stocks in the next three years. This expansionary outlook holds regardless of the affiliates' sector, export intensity, and primary export destination, suggesting that economy-wide factors are driving investors' relative optimism.

Survey results suggest that Nigeria may experience a strengthening in investor confidence following a period of declining FDI inflows. The positive investment outlook observed in the survey is also supported by investment forecasts for the next three years. The projected investment growth rate is higher in Nigeria than in all other surveyed countries (see annex 1B). In recent years, FDI inflows to Nigeria have declined because of factors such as falling commodity prices, uncertainty regarding elections, new regulations establishing local content requirements, restrictions on visas for expatriate workers, and disputes between the government and foreign investors related to repatriation of profits and taxation (UNCTAD 2019; World Bank 2019b). Foreign affiliates' positive outlook for investment over the next three years reflects developments including political stability after completion of the 2019 election cycle, a marked improvement in the ease of doing business as a result of business environment reforms, and a new policy to reduce public ownership in joint-venture oil assets (UNCTAD 2019; World Bank 2019a). However, the longer-term outlook may depend on further strengthening of the country's economic governance framework (World Bank 2019b).

In India, most of the MNE affiliates—about two-thirds—also plan to expand their investment stocks in the next three years. They display no significant differences in either sensitivity to policy uncertainty in trade and investment or future investment plans across most major respondent characteristics.

The overarching trend observed across major respondent categories (manufacturing and services, efficiency seeking and market seeking, large and small affiliates, older and newer affiliates) suggests that foreign investors are likely responding to a base set of supportive economic fundamentals in India. A variety of positive factors can plausibly explain their robust investment outlook, including an accommodating monetary policy that has supported credit growth and policy stability as a result of political continuity. Investor confidence further stands to gain from the country's strong performance on business regulatory reforms and a streamlined nationwide goods and services tax (GST) regime, among other factors (IMF 2019; Kazmin 2019; World Bank 2019a, 2019b).

Importance of Predictability for Foreign Investment

Evidence presented in the preceding section suggests that policy uncertainty has adversely affected many investors. These impacts, combined with the looming threat of a synchronized global economic slowdown, mean that competition between countries for FDI is likely to further intensify.

This raises important questions for host-country policy makers. Crucially, what can developing countries do to inspire investor confidence, counter prevailing global headwinds and policy uncertainty, and leverage FDI for their development objectives? With nearly two-thirds of the 2019 GIC Survey respondents considering policy uncertainty to be "important" or "critically important" for investments, a credible policy response should enhance predictability and investor confidence.

Key Role of Political, Macroeconomic, and Regulatory Environments

The survey results show that nearly 9 in 10 respondents consider political stability, macroeconomic stability, and a country's legal and regulatory environment to be "important" or "critically important" for investment decisions (figure 1.10). These factors rank ahead of considerations such as low tax rates, low labor and input costs, and access to resource endowments.

The findings are consistent with the 2017/2018 GIC Survey and extant empirical literature showing that higher instability related to the political and macroeconomic environment[17] imposes additional transaction costs and risks for businesses. It thus plays a critical role in shaping long-term investment decisions. Empirical research shows that there is significant negative effect of the resulting risk and uncertainty on FDI inflows (Asiedu 2006; Busse and Hefeker 2007; Jun and Singh 1996; Krifa-Schneider and Matei 2010; Schneider and Frey 1985; Sekkat and Veganzones-Varoudakis 2007; Walch and Wörz 2012).

Relatedly, a transparent and predictable regulatory environment is crucial for attracting new investment as well as for retaining existing foreign investors. A large body of research suggests that the quality of a country's legal and regulatory environment is positively associated with FDI (Akame, Ekwelle, and Njei 2016; Buchanan, Le, and Rishi 2012; Daude and Stein 2007; Gani 2007; Globerman and Shapiro 2002; Vogiatzoglou 2016; Wei 2000; Wernick, Haar, and Singh 2009). Furthermore, evidence from previous investor surveys reinforces the claim that a supportive business climate is among the top priorities for foreign investors (A.T. Kearney 2019; Kusek and Silva 2018).

Countries' legal and regulatory environments are especially important for larger

FIGURE 1.10 Legal and Regulatory Environment Is among the Top Three Investment Decision Factors

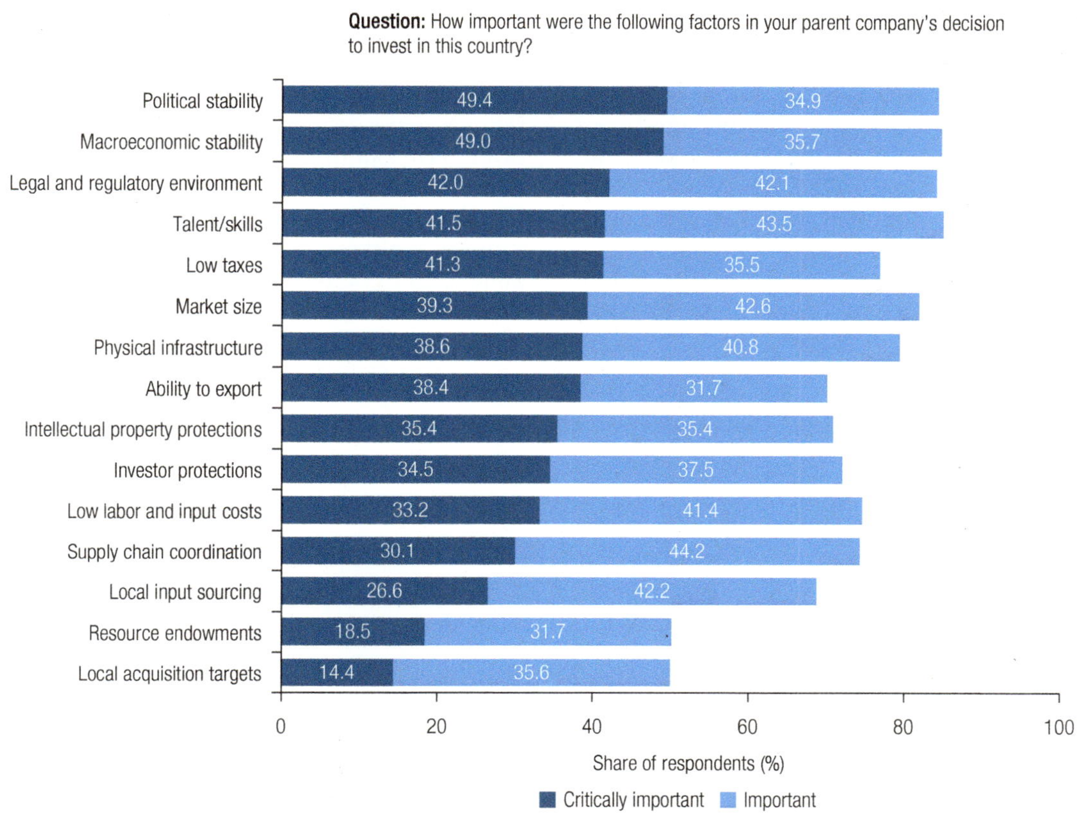

Source: Computation based on the 2019 GIC Survey.
Note: Affiliates of multinational enterprises (MNEs) were surveyed in 10 middle-income countries: Brazil, China, India, Indonesia, Malaysia, Mexico, Nigeria, Thailand, Turkey, and Vietnam.

firms. On average, large firms (those with more than 250 employees) rank the legal and regulatory environment as their top investment consideration, while smaller affiliates consider it to be only the fourth most important consideration.[18] These differences may be driven by investment restrictions that are applicable only to larger firms and by the greater regulatory scrutiny that large firms tend to experience.

Investment Policy and Regulatory Regimes that Enable FDI

The 2019 GIC Survey assessed which specific investment policy and regulatory obstacles hinder an enabling regime for FDI. Cumbersome investment approval processes and operational restrictions are the most-cited regulatory barriers for FDI in the surveyed MICs.

Respondents most commonly identify investment approval processes as a key issue, with 56 percent listing them as "moderate" or "major" obstacles to operations. On average, MNE affiliates need more than two months (64 days) to obtain such approvals, but times vary widely across countries and types of investment—and 10 percent of affiliates report wait times of five months or more. Restrictions on prices, technology, or products are another key barrier, with 44 percent of respondents citing them as "moderate" or "major" obstacles. The salience of these top two concerns holds across most countries and sectors. In addition, these findings are consistent with prior work that also finds that investment approval processes and restrictions on prices, technology, or products can be significant obstacles for foreign affiliates (Mistura and Roulet 2019; UNCTAD 2019).

The survey data also show that firms planning to *reduce or withdraw* investments in the next three years are more likely than those planning to *retain or expand* investments to have experienced higher legal and regulatory obstacles in investment approvals, local sourcing requirements, research and development (R&D) investment requirements, minimum investment requirements, and expatriate staff restrictions. For example, 35 percent of respondents planning to reduce or withdraw investments cite investment approvals as a "major" obstacle, compared with just 26 percent of other respondents (figure 1.11). These stark differences suggest that legal and

FIGURE 1.11 MNE Affiliates That Experience Legal and Regulatory Obstacles Are More Likely to Reduce or Withdraw Investments in the Future

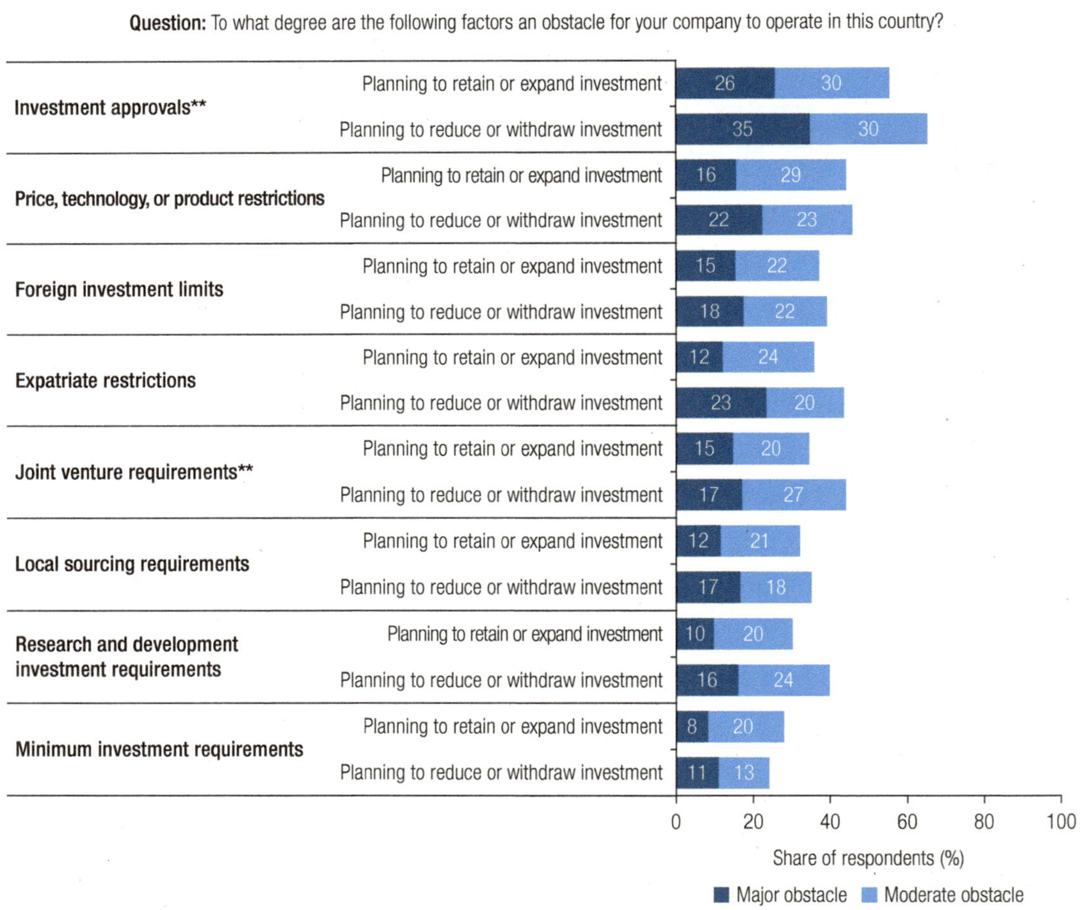

Source: Computation based on the 2019 GIC Survey.
Note: Affiliates of multinational enterprises (MNEs) were surveyed in 10 middle-income countries: Brazil, China, India, Indonesia, Malaysia, Mexico, Nigeria, Thailand, Turkey, and Vietnam. The interviews were conducted June–November 2019, and the implied future time horizon for this question is a three-year period: 2019–22.
$^{**}p < .05$

regulatory barriers play a key role in MNE affiliates' investment decisions.

Notably, some factors that are only rarely considered major obstacles by most MNE affiliates (such as restrictions on expatriate staff) rank among the top obstacles for affiliates looking to reduce or withdraw their investments. Some of these issues may matter a great deal to a subset of affiliates, while others may be relatively rare but important when they do arise.

Table 1.3 disaggregates the top three legal and regulatory obstacles, by country. Cumbersome investment approvals to start and operate a business are the top-cited obstacle in most countries and rank in the top two in all surveyed MICs. Restrictions on setting prices, production technology, or the format of products also rank in the top three in all surveyed MICs except Vietnam.

Other top-three obstacles vary by country: for example, affiliates in Brazil and Mexico cite those countries' relatively stringent joint venture requirements as hindering MNE affiliates' operations. In contrast, limits on the amount of foreign investment are relatively bigger concerns for affiliates in China, India, Indonesia, Thailand, and Turkey. In Vietnam, local sourcing requirements and restrictions on hiring expatriate staff routinely hold back affiliates' operations.

Recent literature has shed light on how businesses navigate the regulatory environment in developing countries and the divergence between regulatory provisions and their implementation (Freund, Hallward-Driemeier, and Rijkers 2014; Hallward-Driemeier and Pritchett 2015). To assess factors that contribute to obstacles for foreign-owned firms in the surveyed countries, the survey asked respondents about specific aspects of government conduct related to the quality and implementation of investment rules. MNE affiliates cite both the quality of laws (rules and regulations) and challenges in their implementation as contributing to their obstacles in the surveyed countries (figure 1.12).

TABLE 1.3 Investment Approval Processes Are the Top Most-Cited Obstacle across Surveyed Countries, Followed by Price, Technology, or Product Restrictions

Country	*Most-cited obstacle*	*Second most-cited obstacle*	*Third most-cited obstacle*
Brazil	Investment approvals	Price, technology, or product restrictions	JV requirements
China	Investment approvals	Price, technology, or product restrictions	Foreign investment limits
India	Investment approvals	Foreign investment limits	Price, technology, or product restrictions
Indonesia	Investment approvals	Price, technology, or product restrictions	Foreign investment limits
Malaysia	Expatriate restrictions	Investment approvals	Price, technology, or product restrictions
Mexico	Investment approvals	Price, technology, or product restrictions	JV requirements
Nigeria	Investment approvals	Expatriate restrictions	Price, technology, or product restrictions
Thailand	Investment approvals	Price, technology, or product restrictions	Foreign investment limits
Turkey	Investment approvals	Price, technology, or product restrictions	Foreign investment limits
Vietnam	Investment approvals	Local sourcing requirements	Expatriate restrictions

Source: Computation based on the 2019 GIC Survey.
Note: Rankings are based on frequency counts. JV = joint venture.

FIGURE 1.12 Foreign-Owned Firms Perceive the Quality of Rules and Their Implementation as Obstacles in Government Conduct

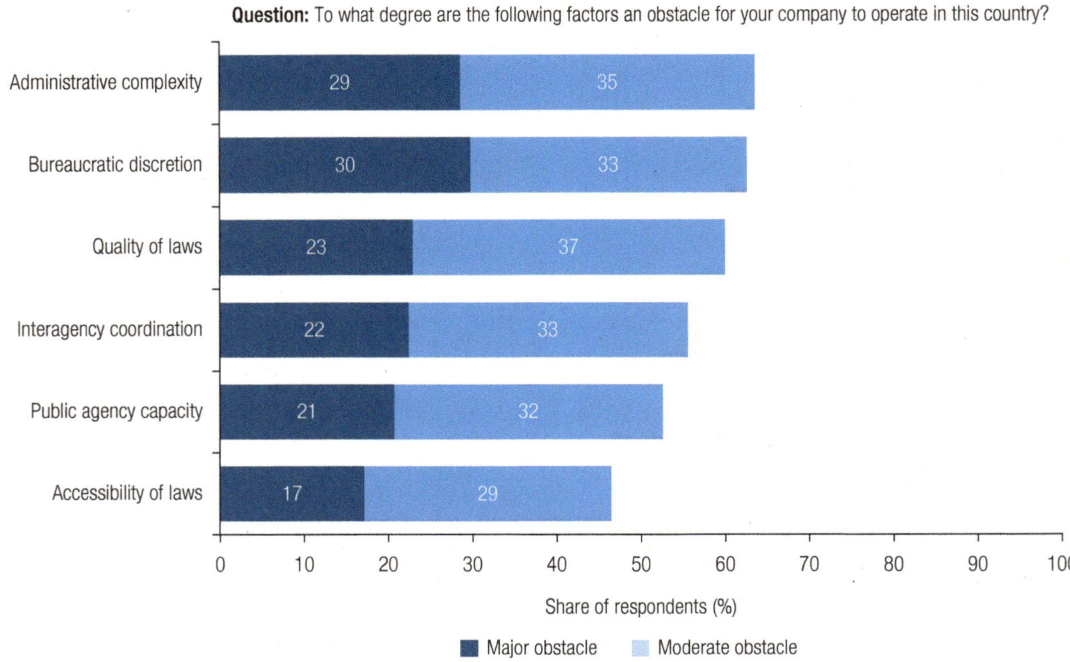

Source: Computation based on the 2019 GIC Survey.
Note: Affiliates of multinational enterprises were surveyed in 10 middle-income countries: Brazil, China, India, Indonesia, Malaysia, Mexico, Nigeria, Thailand, Turkey, and Vietnam.

Major drivers of legal and regulatory challenges include the complexity of administrative procedures, discretion exercised by the bureaucracy, and the quality of laws and regulations. In other words, both the substantive content of laws and the way in which they are implemented contribute to legal and regulatory obstacles in the surveyed countries.

Outside of the main findings of this report, the 2019 GIC survey also revealed important differences between various categories of MNE affiliates (box 1.1).

Conclusions and Policy Implications

High levels of international and domestic policy uncertainty in trade and investment have emerged as an investment risk. If not curtailed, such uncertainty can present a significant threat for the global economy. Survey data suggest that policy uncertainty has already adversely affected many investors and could drive future investment slowdowns. Over the next three years, most investors in the surveyed MICs are not planning to expand their investment stock. Given the demonstrated contributions of FDI to host economies in terms of capital infusion, technology transfer, and linkages to global and local value chains, policy uncertainty poses a serious threat to both short-term growth and long-term structural transformation.

In this environment of uncertainty, governments of developing countries can nevertheless take steps to bolster FDI by strengthening their investment competitiveness. Current insights from the 2019 GIC Survey highlight several policy priorities:

BOX 1.1

Key Findings of the 2019 GIC Survey Results, by Foreign Investor Type

The 2019 GIC survey revealed some important differences between various categories of multinational enterprise (MNE) affiliates.[a] Some of the results listed below concern topics addressed in the survey but not covered in detail in this chapter (such as incentives and investment promotion agencies). These topics are addressed in detail in subsequent chapters of this report.

Differences by Sector (Manufacturing versus Services)

- Manufacturers are more sensitive than services affiliates to the availability and costs of local inputs.
- Services affiliates consider joint venture requirements and limits on foreign investment to be larger obstacles, on average, than do manufacturers.
- Manufacturers tend to use and value investment incentives more than services affiliates do.

Differences by Degree of Export Activity

Several findings showed differences between "majority exporters" (MNE affiliates whose revenues come mostly from exports) and affiliates with less than half of revenues from exports:

- Majority exporters are less sensitive to local market size and stability but are more sensitive to input cost, availability, and quality.
- Majority exporters consider local sourcing requirements and restrictions on hiring expatriate staff to be bigger obstacles, on average.
- Majority exporters use and value investment incentives more, on average.

Differences by Origin Country (Developed versus Developing)

- Investors from developing countries are more likely to plan on expanding investments over the next three years.
- Investors from developing countries value investment incentives and investment promotion agency (IPA) services more than investors from developed countries do, on average.

Differences by Size (Firm Employment Level)

- Large employers (those with more than 250 employees), on average, place greater importance on the legal and regulatory environments of their host countries.
- Smaller employers, on average, encounter more legal and regulatory obstacles, particularly concerning investment approvals, joint venture requirements, research and development (R&D) investment requirements, and minimum investment requirements.
- Large employers receive more fiscal or financial incentives, on average, but do not necessarily value them more than smaller firms do.

a. Unlike other analyses in this chapter, differences presented in this box are from logistic and ordered logistic regressions without controls, because they are meant primarily for descriptive purposes. They should not be interpreted as indicative of causal impacts.

1. *Counter international policy uncertainty by reaffirming commitments to global and regional trade systems.* Survey data consistently demonstrate how rising policy uncertainty due to protectionism and economic nationalism in trade and investment weighs on investor sentiment. To counter such uncertainty, policy makers should signal and follow through on their commitments to multilateral and regional trade and investment arrangements in several ways:
   a. *Uphold the multilateral trading system.* Honoring existing global and regional trade and investment agreements would improve the government's credibility and commitment regarding the course of future policy. In the absence of such commitments, foreign-owned firms may be hesitant to invest if they think existing rules may not be honored in the future.
   b. *Continue trade and economic liberalization.* The continuation of

ongoing trade and investment liberalization efforts through multilateral and regional mechanisms would increase investor confidence by setting expectations of further reductions in trade and investment restrictions in the future. In parallel, governments should continue to reduce economic distortions (for example, from subsidies) through domestic reforms, which would both facilitate domestic growth and contribute to the resolution of ongoing trade disputes.

   c. *Clearly communicate policy directions.* Clearly communicating changes in trade and investment policy in advance would reduce investors' uncertainty on the direction of future policy.

2. *Promote political stability, strong institutions, and good governance.* On average, MNE affiliates cited political stability as their top investment decision-making factor. Indeed, research highlights how potential reescalation of conflicts, electoral violence, and political turbulence pose risks to many countries' economic outlooks. Hence, policy makers should focus on these overarching goals:
   a. *Strengthen institutions.* Political and economic institutions establish "rules of the game" by promoting, among other things, openness, transparency, and stability. Strengthening institutions to ensure peaceful transitions of power and some degree of continuity in structures of governance and policy making thus contributes to greater predictability and investor confidence.
   b. *Ensure fair governance.* Establishing rules and building institutional capacity to ensure a level playing field for investors and to eliminate political favoritism toward specific businesses is also crucial for attracting investments. A level playing field ensures that the most efficient MNEs have adequate incentives to invest, helping to maximize benefits from FDI.
3. *Optimize macroeconomic policy.* Macroeconomic stability is the second most-cited investment decision-making factor among MNE affiliates. Underlying inflationary pressures are still present in many low- and middle-income countries, as are risks of short-term capital outflows. To counter those pressures, governments should pursue the following measures:
   a. *Implement macroprudential policies.* Policies such as countercyclical capital buffers and limits on foreign currency borrowing can help limit exposure to future currency, interest rate, or debt rollover shocks.
   b. *Ensure central bank independence.* Insulating central banks from political interference would help establish currency and interest rate credibility.
   c. *Optimize fiscal policy.* From a fiscal perspective, individual country situations vary widely. In general, however, countries would do well to preserve growth-enhancing spending and tax reforms while ensuring fiscal space through fiscal consolidation, broadening of the tax base, and strengthening of tax administration. Such measures would help keep debt-to-GDP ratios manageable while limiting adverse effects on economic growth.
4. *Improve the legal and regulatory framework for FDI.* Foreign investors consistently identify the legal and regulatory environments for FDI in host countries as being critical considerations for their investment decisions. Indeed, these issues are even more important to the large firms that disproportionately contribute to employment growth in host countries. Policy makers should thus remain committed to fair market access for foreign firms while removing critical administrative barriers to investment, as follows:
   a. *Remain committed to fair access.* Policy makers should resist the temptation to engage in protectionism and economic nationalism in their own markets. This entails minimizing foreign investment limits, excessive and discretionary foreign investment screening, and discrimination against foreign firms.

b. *Remove critical administrative barriers.* Across all countries, survey respondents consistently cite cumbersome investment approval processes as well as restrictions on pricing, technology, or products as key obstacles to their operations. Governments of developing countries should thus invest in making approval processes more efficient and optimize operational regulations to minimize adverse impacts on business operations without sacrificing the regulations' original policy objectives.
c. *Focus on improving both the implementation and quality of laws.* Survey data suggest that both suboptimal design of regulations and the ways in which they are enforced contribute to operational obstacles. Thus, although improving the regulations should remain a priority, governments should also work to streamline procedures and clarify roles to limit administrative complexity and bureaucratic discretion.

The COVID-19 pandemic reinforces the importance of these policy priorities, especially measures to build investor confidence. Against the backdrop of heightened policy uncertainty in trade and investment, the pandemic will further escalate uncertainty, magnify investment risks, and depress foreign investor confidence. With higher dependence on imports of intermediate goods and broader exposure to export markets, MNEs are particularly vulnerable to supply and demand shocks induced by the pandemic. Although large-scale impacts are already observable, the full extent and duration of the effects of the pandemic remain uncertain.

Beyond such medium- to long-term measures, the extraordinary challenges associated with the pandemic also warrant crisis management measures by governments. The pandemic represents an unprecedented shock to the global economy, and the economic fallout for MNEs is expected to be very high (IMF 2020; UNCTAD 2020). Support to MNEs should be deployed rapidly, benefit a broad cross-section, and respond to pressing vulnerabilities. The prospects for recovery rest on the breadth and depth of policy support extended to MNEs in the face of the extraordinary global shock.

Finally, the severity of the pandemic underscores the need for timely policy insights. A responsive policy research agenda should seek to fill knowledge gaps (for example, estimate the effects on markets, businesses, and workers) and enable the design of policy measures that increase the resilience of MNEs to shocks and preserve their viability.

Annex 1A. Survey and Data Analysis Methodology

The data used in this study are from the 2019 Global Investment Competitiveness (GIC) Survey, which captures the experiences and perceptions of multinational enterprise (MNE) affiliates on global megatrends and investment climate factors in 10 middle-income countries (MICs). The survey involved interviewing senior executives of foreign-owned firms who possess a broad understanding of their companies' business strategies, policy barriers, operational obstacles, and investments in the host economy.

The survey complements other investor surveys by focusing on investment climate variables, such as administrative and legal barriers, rather than on broader economywide factors. These specific investment climate variables are actionable areas for policy makers.

The survey comprised four sections:

1. *General information on the company*, including sector, number of employees, the total investment stock to date, and predominant investment plan over the next three years in the host country.
2. *Importance and effect of global megatrends on the company's business operations*—including on jobs, productivity, investments, and changes in location of production—in the last year.
3. *Foreign-owned firms' contribution to the host economy* through reinvestments, local sourcing, and pro-competition effects, as well as *foreign-owned firms' integration in*

global value chains through estimates of imports and exports.

4. *Importance of investment policy factors and operational obstacles faced by the foreign-owned firms' affiliates*, including investment restrictions, services offered by investment promotion agencies (IPAs), tax and financial incentives, and investment protection guarantees.

The survey was designed to generate results that are representative at the country level and comparable across countries. An assessment of changes in affiliate experience and perceptions over time will be possible with a second wave of data collection in 2020–21. To the extent possible, the second round will target foreign-owned businesses from the first round.

Sample Representation

The survey represents experiences and perceptions of a representative sample of foreign-owned firms in each of 10 MICs: Brazil, China, India, Indonesia, Malaysia, Mexico, Nigeria, Thailand, Turkey, and Vietnam. Each country sample comprises roughly 250 foreign-owned firms with at least five employees.[19] In each country, roughly 125 respondent firms operate in the manufacturing sector, and roughly 125 respondent firms operate in the services sector (tables 1A.1 and 1A.2).[20] The only exception is Nigeria, where because of sampling frame limitations, the sample comprises 164 respondents (55 manufacturing and 109 services). Thus, across the 10 target countries, more than 2,400 responses were collected.

Sampling frames comprising partially or fully foreign-owned businesses in the 10 MICs were constructed using commercially available and proprietary sources (Dunn & Bradstreet, Orbis/Bureau van Dijk, Sample Solutions, and others). The sampling frame sizes by country are presented in table 1A.3. The frames were de-duplicated and cleaned, and data quality was enhanced using standard sample framing and data manipulation techniques. In some sampling frames, all affiliates were contacted to reach the target sample size. In others, only select affiliates were contacted before the target was reached.

TABLE 1A.1 2019 GIC Survey Sample, by Country and Sector

Country	Manufacturing MNE affiliates	Services MNE affiliates	Total
Brazil	125	125	250
China	125	125	250
India	125	125	250
Indonesia	133	125	258
Malaysia	125	125	250
Mexico	124	125	249
Nigeria	55	109	164
Thailand	125	125	250
Turkey	125	125	250
Vietnam	128	125	253
Total	**1,190**	**1,234**	**2,424**

Source: Computation based on the 2019 GIC Survey.
Note: MNE = multinational enterprise.

Nonresponse bias can occur when those who respond to the survey are systematically different from nonrespondents in terms of basic characteristics. The likelihood of nonresponse bias in this survey is minimal because no systematic differences were found when respondents and nonrespondents were compared based on observed characteristics (such as sectoral affiliation and country of origin). To address any possibility of nonresponse bias due to target respondents' varying willingness or ability to respond to the survey, data were weighted for nonresponse. This did not change the results and findings derived from the survey and presented in the chapter.

To ensure representativeness, analyses contained in the chapter incorporate weights to account for different sample sizes across countries, different probabilities of sampling, and bias due to nonresponse. Design weights have been included to ensure that the different strata (country-sector intersections) are given equal weight. Sampling weights were included to account for different probabilities of being sampled, weighting each observation by the inverse probability of selection. Finally, nonresponse weights are applied to maintain consistency between the distribution of MNE affiliates in the sampling frame and results from the sample along observable characteristics To check the robustness of results in this

TABLE 1A.2 Share of 2019 GIC Survey Respondents, by Subsector

Sector and subsector	*N*	*Share of total sample (%)*
Manufacturing	**1,190**	**49.1**
Machinery and equipment	151	6.2
Metals and metal products	124	5.1
Automobiles, other motor vehicles, and transport equipment	116	4.8
Rubber and plastic products	108	4.5
Chemicals and chemical products	84	3.5
Agroprocessing, food products, and beverages	72	3.0
Information technology and telecommunications	71	2.9
Electrical and electronic equipment and components	52	2.1
Textiles, apparel, and leather	51	2.1
Wood products, paper, and printing	45	1.9
Pharmaceuticals, biotechnology, and medical devices	18	0.7
Refined petroleum products, coke, and nuclear fuel	8	0.3
Manufacturing: Other or unclassified	290	12.0
Services	**1,234**	**50.9**
Wholesale and retail trade	270	11.1
Business services	116	4.8
Logistics, transport, and storage	101	4.2
Computer and software services	85	3.5
Administrative and support services	59	2.4
Construction	58	2.4
Financial services, including insurance	49	2.0
Electricity, gas, and water	32	1.3
Other professional, scientific, and technical services	20	0.8
Real estate	18	0.7
Hotels, restaurants, and tourism	16	0.7
Telecommunications	13	0.5
Media	9	0.4
Health	7	0.3
Arts and recreation	6	0.2
Education	5	0.2
Scientific research and development services	5	0.2
Water supply and waste management	3	0.1
Residential care and social work	2	0.1
Public administration and defense services	1	0.0
Services: Other or unclassified	359	14.8

Source: Computation based on the 2019 GIC Survey.

TABLE 1A.3 Sampling Frame Sizes, by Country

Country	*Total number of affiliates*
Brazil	5,007
China	15,668
India	9,120
Indonesia	4,153
Malaysia	5,673
Mexico	7,992
Nigeria	7,089
Thailand	9,789
Turkey	4,248
Vietnam	2,739

Source: Computation based on the 2019 GIC Survey.

chapter to different weighting approaches, all analyses in this report were also run without weights and with sampling weights only. The results in this chapter were found to be robust to these changes in weighting approach.

Survey Administration

The World Bank Group commissioned an international survey firm, Kantar Public, to conduct 30-minute phone interviews with target respondents. The interviews were conducted by enumerators, and response data were entered in a computer system, a setup commonly referred to as computer-assisted telephone interviews (CATIs). The interviews were conducted in nine languages: Bahasa Indonesia, Mandarin Chinese, Cantonese Chinese, English, Portuguese, Spanish, Thai, Turkish, and Vietnamese. In addition to the main survey questions, each interview included a screener phase to ensure the eligibility of respondents. The interviews were conducted between June and November 2019.

The survey was piloted in all 10 countries to test the survey instrument in various languages and to identify effective strategies to increase response rates. The lessons from the pilot phase were used to reduce administration time and enhance overall clarity of the survey instrument.

The overall response rate for the survey was 9.3 percent. This response rate is consistent with the current expected range for phone-based business surveys.[21] The main fieldwork of the survey leveraged lessons from empirical research in survey design and administration to implement the strategies described below to ensure high response rates.[22]

Potential respondents were notified by email before the survey. Building on research evidence (Dillman 2000; Lynn, Turner, and Smith 1997), a prenotification email with World Bank Group and International Finance Corporation (IFC) branding was sent to potential respondents to signal that the survey would contribute to important global policy research. The prenotification emails also directed potential respondents to an informational website (www.investorsurvey.net) to obtain additional information about the survey, including a (view-only) copy of the survey questionnaire. These measures aimed to lower information barriers and enhance trust between respondents and interviewers, thereby improving the likelihood of securing an interview with senior executives.

An easy-to-follow survey questionnaire was administered by well-trained professional CATI enumerators. The survey questionnaire, in the country's primary business language, was used to ensure than it could be completed within a reasonable time frame. The online read-only version of the questionnaire was available to be consulted during the interview. The fieldwork managers and CATI enumerators were screened to ensure experience in conducting business and market research, and they underwent specific interviewer training to prepare for this survey. A questionnaire manual with detailed explanations of the questionnaire also served as a reference source while the survey was being administered.

Survey administration arrangements prioritized respondents and constraints on the time of senior executives. Sensitive to variability in typical business hours and local norms around time use,[23] CATI enumerators attempted to establish contact and schedule interviews during conducive time periods. Survey administration arrangements such as timing of calls, language options, repeat follow-up attempts, and scheduled callbacks were implemented to maximize the likelihood of obtaining responses from the contacted sample. In case of initial failure to reach the intended respondent, 5–10 follow-up call attempts were made.

As a token of appreciation, respondents were promised a set of nonmonetary incentives. A key constraint to survey participation is the opportunity cost of time. Business surveys impose a net cost on respondents, requiring executives to apportion productive time away from work. Research largely supports the use of incentives as an effective means to increase response rates (Singer and Ye 2013). To encourage potential respondents to "invest" time in the survey, interviewers (a) emphasized the important policy research that the survey will inform; (b) promised to send respondents a copy of the final research report; (c) promised to send respondents a certificate of appreciation; and (d) noted that a charitable donation would be made to the United Nations Children's Fund (UNICEF) when the target number of surveys was reached.[24]

Data Analysis

Throughout the chapter, tests of the significance of differences are conducted using ordered logistic (for ordinal variables such as ratings for importance) or logistic (for binary variables) regressions. Unless otherwise noted, tests for statistical significance of differences control for sector, a dummy variable for exports constituting over 50 percent of revenues, sector-export interactions, import share of inputs as a continuous variable, sector-import interactions, source country income group, a dummy for employment over 250 employees, a dummy for investment stock over US$10 million, number of years in host country, percentage of foreign ownership, and country fixed effects.

Annex 1B. Country-Level FDI Outlook Trends

TABLE 1B.1 FDI Outlook Trends in Surveyed Countries

Country	*Survey data (share planning to expand investment over next three years)*[a]	*Forecast data (inward FDI value, CAGR 18–21F)*	*Historical data*	
			(inward FDI value, CAGR 13–18)	*(Greenfield FDI project announcements, CAGR 13–18)*
China	17%	−7%	-7%	-6%
Turkey	35%	2%	-1%	8%
Malaysia	40%	8%	-5%	0%
Thailand	43%	−12%	-4%	2%
Mexico	45%	−3%	-5%	−1%
Nigeria	81%	29%	-19%	-4%
Vietnam	46%	6%	12%	11%
Brazil	49%	-5%	3%	-4%
Indonesia	57%	4%	-3%	-9%
India	64%	8%	8%	7%

Sources: 2019 GIC Survey; Economist Intelligence Unit forecast data; World Development Indicators database (historical inward FDI value); and historical greenfield FDI data from fDi Markets, a *Financial Times* dataset (https://www.fdimarkets.com/).
Note: Green shading indicates more growth, while red indicates low or negative growth. CAGR = compound annual growth rate; FDI = foreign direct investment.
a. The interviews were conducted June–November 2019, so the implied three-year time horizon for this question is 2019–22.

Notes

1. "Developing countries" in this report refers to low- and middle-income countries as defined by the World Bank. For the definitions of all income categories and the countries therein, see "World Bank Country and Lending Groups," World Bank Knowledge Base: https://datahelpdesk.worldbank.org/knowledgebase/articles/906519-world-bank-country-and-lending-groups.
2. Although FDI inflows as a share of GDP have declined in most of the surveyed MICs, experiences have varied. For example, from 2008 to 2018, FDI inflows to China fell sharply (from 3.7 percent to 1.5 percent) but increased in Brazil (from 3.0 percent to 4.7 percent). As discussed in the Overview, a mix of economic factors are plausibly shaping global FDI trends, including declining rates of return on FDI, changes in US tax policy, increasingly asset-light forms of international production on the backs of digital technologies, and rising policy uncertainty.
3. Recent projections show remittances exceeding FDI for low- and middle-income countries in 2019, although they are not projected to do so for the 10 surveyed MICs given their

relatively higher FDI compared to remittances (Global Knowledge Partnership on Migration and Development [KNOMAD] database: https://www.knomad.org/data/remittances). Foreign bank lending is also a significant source of private external finance and represents about half of all external liabilities of emerging-market countries (Bräuning and Ivashina 2019).

4. The 2019 GIC Survey covers foreign companies that have invested in the 10 surveyed countries. It does not represent the perceptions and experiences of companies that have never invested in foreign countries or that have invested only in countries other than those surveyed. The results of the survey are not generalizable to all developing countries but are highly relevant because the surveyed countries account for a substantial share of FDI inflows to developing countries (75 percent in 2018).
5. For the various uncertainty indexes, see the Economic Policy Uncertainty index website: https://www.policyuncertainty.com/.
6. For a discussion on the sources of policy uncertainty, see the Overview of this volume.
7. Studying this relationship empirically is particularly challenging using modeling techniques because of the strong assumptions required to measure trade and investment policy uncertainty across heterogeneous firms and the lack of firm-level data on relevant economic outcomes. Several 2019 surveys have attempted to address these limitations by directly asking firms about their investment plans in response to trade tensions and uncertainty. They include the seminannual Survey of Business Uncertainty (SBU) in the United States conducted by the Federal Reserve Bank of Atlanta, Stanford University, and the University of Chicago Booth School of Business (July 2019); the annual US-China Business Council (USCBC) Member Survey of US businesses in China (August 2019); the monthly Reuters Tankan survey of Japanese manufacturers (September 2019); and the quarterly UBS Investor Sentiment survey (March 2019).
8. The "last year" refers to the last financial year preceding the 2019 GIC Survey—that is, a year spanning a 12-month period between January 1, 2018, and September 30, 2019, depending on the country.
9. Throughout the chapter, tests of the significance of differences are done through either ordered logistic (for ordered ordinal variables such as ratings for importance) or logistic (for binary variables) regression analysis. Unless otherwise noted, tests for statistical significance of differences are done via ordered logistic regression of the dependent variable, controlling for a wide variety of company characteristics and country fixed effects. For more details on the analytical methodologies such as modeling techniques and control variables, see annex 1A.
10. The 10 percentage point difference between large and small firms is significant at the $p < 0.10$ level.
11. The interviews were conducted between June and November 2019, so the implied time horizon for this question is 2019–22.
12. The coefficient in the ordered logistic regression is negative and significant at the $p < .10$ level after controlling for firm characteristics and host country fixed effects.
13. In the logistic regression with full controls and country fixed effects, the coefficient on having been adversely affected by policy uncertainty is negative and significant at the $p < .05$ level.
14. Differences are significant at the $p < .01$ level in the ordered logistic regression with full controls.
15. Differences are significant at the $p < .10$ level in the ordered logistic regression with full controls.
16. These differences are statistically significant at the $p < .05$ level in the ordered logistic regression with full controls.
17. Political instability includes high incidence of political turbulence and internal conflicts. Macroeconomic instability includes volatility in inflation and in real exchange rates.
18. Ranking of importance is based on the percentage of investors that rate a factor as "important" or "critically important." Differences in average importance are significant at the $p < .01$ level in the ordered logistic regression with full controls and country fixed effects.
19. Because of sampling frame limitations, the Nigeria sample is 164 respondents (55 manufacturing and 109 services firms).
20. The sample size of 125 respondents per sector per country is greater than the required sample strength for estimates with 7.5 percent precision in 90 percent confidence intervals.
21. The response rate calculation follows the *Response Rate 3* (RR3) methodology outlined in the latest guidance on response rates from The American Association for Public Opinion Research (AAPOR 2016). This approach estimates the proportion of

cases of unknown eligibility that is actually eligible. The response rate was calculated as follows:

- Response rate = Interview / (Interview + Eligible Non-Interview + e (Unknown Eligibility Non-Interview))
- Response rate = (2424) / (2424 + 7309 + 0.38 (42783)) = 9.33 percent
- e = the estimated proportion of cases of unknown eligibility that are eligible.
- e = (Confirmed Eligible) / (Confirmed Eligible + Confirmed Not Eligible)
- e = (2424 + 7309) / (2424 + 7309 + 15818) = 0.38.

The Pew Research Center reported that response rates in 2017 and 2018 telephone surveys fell to 7 percent and 6 percent, respectively, a decline from the prior norm of 9 percent (Kennedy and Hartig 2019). Gallup reported attaining a similar 7 percent average response rate in the Gallup Poll Social Series in 2017 (Marken 2018). The AAPOR reported that response rates from leading survey research firms were about 9 percent for landlines and 7 percent for cell phones in 2015 (AAPOR 2017).

22. For global data collection from formal businesses in developing countries, the use of telephone-based surveys can be advantageous. Compared with face-to-face surveys, telephone surveys take less time and are less expensive, and the near-universal prevalence of telephones supports the generation of representative samples (von der Lippe, Schmich, and Lange 2011). However, this administration mode has unique challenges, including the growing aversion to divulging business information by phone (de Leeuw and Hox 2004) and the proliferation of answering machines and caller ID (Callegaro, McCutcheon, and Ludwig 2010).
23. Local norms include, in some countries, the prevalence of an afternoon break from work or breaks for prayers.
24. A small monetary incentive for respondents was also introduced in China.

References

AAPOR (American Association for Public Opinion Research). 2016. "Standard Definitions: Final Dispositions of Case Codes and Outcome Rates for Surveys." 9th edition. AAPOR, Oakbrook, IL.

AAPOR (American Association for Public Opinion Research). 2017. "The Future of U.S. General Population Telephone Research." Report, AAPOR Task Force, Oakbrook Terrace, IL.

Abel, Andrew B., Avinash K. Dixit, and Janice C. Eberly. 1996. "Options, the Value of Capital, and Investment." *Quarterly Journal of Economics* 111 (3): 753–77.

Abel, Andrew B., and Janice C. Eberly. 1996. "Optimal Investment with Costly Reversibility." *Review of Economic Studies* (63) 4: 581–93.

Aitken, Brian J., and Ann E. Harrison. 1999. "Do Domestic Firms Benefit from Direct Foreign Investment? Evidence from Venezuela." *American Economic Review* 89 (3): 605–18.

Akame, Afuge Junior, Metougue Eric Ekwelle, and George Ndonghandou Njei. 2016. "The Impact of Business Climate on Foreign Direct Investment in the CEMAC Region." *Journal of Economics and Sustainable Development* 7 (22): 66–74.

Anand, Rahul, and Volodymyr Tulin. 2014. "Disentangling India's Investment Slowdown." Working Paper 14/47, International Monetary Fund, Washington, DC.

Arnold, Jens Matthias, and Beata S. Javorcik. 2009. "Gifted Kids or Pushy Parents? Foreign Direct Investment and Plant Productivity in Indonesia." *Journal of International Economics* 79 (1): 42–53.

Asiedu, Elizabeth. 2006. "Foreign Direct Investment in Africa: The Role of Natural Resources, Market Size, Government Policy, Institutions and Political Instability." *World Economy* 29 (1): 63–77.

A.T. Kearney. 2019. "Facing a Growing Paradox: The 2019 A.T. Kearney Foreign Direct Investment Confidence Index." Annual survey report, A.T. Kearney, Chicago.

Baker, Scott R., Nicholas Bloom, and Steven J. Davis. 2013. "Measuring Economic Policy Uncertainty." Working Paper No. 21633, National Bureau of Economic Research, Cambridge, MA.

Baker, Scott R., Nicholas Bloom, and Steven J. Davis. 2019. "The Extraordinary Rise in Trade Policy Uncertainty." *VoxEU*, September 17 (accessed November 7, 2019), https://voxeu.org/article/extraordinary-rise-trade-policy-uncertainty.

Beamish, Paul W., and John C. Banks. 1987. "Equity Joint Ventures and the Theory of the Multinational Enterprise." *Journal of International Business Studies* 18 (2): 1–16.

Bernanke, Benjamin S. 1983. "Irreversibility, Uncertainty, and Cyclical Investment." *Quarterly Journal of Economics* 98 (1): 85–106.

Blanchard, Emily J. 2019. "Trade Wars in the Global Value Chain Era." In *Trade War: The Clash of Economic Systems Endangering Global Prosperity*, edited by Meredith A. Crowley, 57–63. VoxEU.org e-book, CEPR Press.

Bloom, Nicholas. 2009. "The Impact of Uncertainty Shocks." *Econometrica* 77 (3): 623–85.

Bloom, Nicholas. 2014. "Fluctuations in Uncertainty." *Journal of Economic Perspectives* 28 (2): 153–76.

Bloom, Nicholas, Max Floetotto, Nir Jaimovich, Itay Saporta-Eksten, and Stephen J. Terry. 2012. "Really Uncertain Business Cycles." Working Paper No. 18245, National Bureau of Economic Research, Cambridge, MA.

Bonaime, Alice, Huseyin Gulen, and Mihai Ion. 2018. "Does Policy Uncertainty Affect Mergers and Acquisitions?" *Journal of Financial Economics* 129 (3): 531–58.

Bräuning, Falk, and Victoria Ivashina. 2019. "U.S. Monetary Policy and Emerging Market Credit Cycles." *Journal of Monetary Economics*. Published ahead of print, February 22, 2019. doi:10.1016/j.jmoneco.2019.02.005.

Buchanan, Bonnie G., Quan V. Le, and Meenakshi Rishi. 2012. "Foreign Direct Investment and Institutional Quality: Some Empirical Evidence." *International Review of Financial Analysis* 21: 81–89.

Busse, Matthias, and Carsten Hefeker. 2007. "Political Risk, Institutions and Foreign Direct Investment." *European Journal of Political Economy* 23 (2): 397–415.

Caldara, Dario, Matteo Iacoviello, Patrick Molligo, Andrea Prestipino, and Andrea Raffo. 2019. "The Economic Effects of Trade Policy Uncertainty." *Journal of Monetary Economics*. Published ahead of print, November 8, 2019. doi:10.1016/j.jmoneco.2019.11.002.

Callegaro, Mario, Allan L. McCutcheon, and Jack Ludwig. 2010. "Who's Calling? The Impact of Caller ID on Telephone Survey Response." *Field Methods* 22 (2): 175–91.

Cao, Chunfang, Xiaoyang Li, and Guilin Liu. 2017. "Political Uncertainty and Cross-Border Acquisitions." *Review of Finance* 23 (2): 439–70.

Cebreros, Alfonso, Aldo Heffner, and Alejandrina Salcedo. 2019. "Trade Policy Uncertainty and Its Effect on Foreign Direct Investment and Export Participation: Evidence from Mexico." Working Paper, Bank of Mexico, Mexico City.

Chen, Kexin, He Nie, and Zhenyu Ge. 2019. "Policy Uncertainty and FDI: Evidence from National Elections." *Journal of International Trade and Economic Development* 28 (4): 419–28.

Chen, Yu-Fu, and Michael Funke. 2003. "Option Value, Policy Uncertainty, and the Foreign Direct Investment Decision." Discussion Papers 234, Hamburg Institute of International Economics, Hamburg, Germany.

Daude, Christian, and Ernesto Stein. 2007. "The Quality of Institutions and Foreign Direct Investment." *Economics and Politics* 19 (3): 317–44.

de Leeuw, Edith D., and Joop J. Hox. 2004. "I Am Not Selling Anything: 29 Experiments in Telephone Introductions." *International Journal of Public Opinion Research* 16 (4): 464–73.

Dillman, Don A. 2000. *Mail and Internet Surveys.* 2nd ed. Hoboken, NJ: John Wiley & Sons.

Djankov, Simeon, and Bernard Hoekman. 2000. "Foreign Investment and Productivity Growth in Czech Enterprises." *World Bank Economic Review* 14 (1): 49–64.

Freund, Caroline, Mary Hallward-Driemeier, and Bob Rijkers. 2014. "Deals and Delays: Firm-Level Evidence on Corruption and Policy Implementation Times." *The World Bank Economic Review* 30 (2): 354–82.

Gani, Azmat. 2007. "Governance and Foreign Direct Investment Links: Evidence from Panel Data Estimations." *Applied Economics Letters* 14 (10): 753–56.

Ghosal, Vivek, and Prakash Loungani. 2000. "The Differential Impact of Uncertainty on Investment in Small and Large Businesses." *Review of Economics and Statistics* 82 (2): 338–43.

Globerman, Steven, and Daniel Shapiro. 2002. "Global Foreign Direct Investment Flows: The Role of Governance Infrastructure." *World Development* 30 (11): 1899–919.

Gonzalez, Anabel, Christine Zhenwei Qiang, and Peter Kusek. 2018. "Overview." In *2017/2018 Global Investment Competitiveness Report: Foreign Investor Perspectives and Policy Implications*, 1–18. Washington, DC: World Bank.

Gulen, Huseyin, and Mihai Ion. 2016. "Policy Uncertainty and Corporate Investment." *Review of Financial Studies* 29 (3): 523–56.

Hallward-Driemeier, Mary, and Lant Pritchett. 2015. "How Business Is Done in the Developing

World: Deals versus Rules." *Journal of Economic Perspectives* 29 (3): 121–40.

Havránek, Tomáš, and Zuzana Iršová. 2011. "Estimating Vertical Spillovers from FDI: Why Results Vary and What the True Effect Is." *Journal of International Economics* 85 (2): 234–44.

IMF (International Monetary Fund). 2019. "World Economic Outlook Update, July 2019: Still Sluggish Global Growth." IMF, Washington, DC.

IMF (International Monetary Fund). 2020. *World Economic Outlook, April 2020: The Great Lockdown.* Washington, DC: IMF.

Iršová, Zuzana, and Tomáš Havránek. 2013. "Determinants of Horizontal Spillovers from FDI: Evidence from a Large Meta-Analysis." *World Development* 42: 1–15.

Javorcik, Beata Smarzynska. 2004. "Does Foreign Direct Investment Increase the Productivity of Domestic Firms? In Search of Spillovers through Backward Linkages." *American Economic Review* 94 (3): 605–27.

Julio, Brandon, and Youngsuk Yook. 2016. "Policy Uncertainty, Irreversibility, and Cross-Border Flows of Capital." *Journal of International Economics* 103: 13–26.

Jun, Kwang W., and Harinder Singh. 1996. "The Determinants of Foreign Direct Investment in Developing Countries." *Transnational Corporations* 5 (2): 67–105.

Kazmin, Amy. 2019. "India Slashes Corporate Taxes to Give a Boost to Economy." *Financial Times,* September 20.

Kennedy, Courtney, and Hannah Hartig. 2019. "Response Rates in Telephone Surveys Have Resumed Their Decline." *Fact Tank* (online platform) report, February 27, Pew Research Center, Washington, DC.

Knight, Frank H. 1921. *Risk, Uncertainty, and Profit.* Boston: Hart, Schaffner, and Marx; Houghton Mifflin.

Krifa-Schneider, Hadjila, and Iuliana Matei. 2010. "Business Climate, Political Risk and FDI in Developing Countries: Evidence from Panel Data." *International Journal of Economics and Finance* 2 (5): 54–65.

Kusek, Peter, and Andrea Silva. 2018. "What Matters to Investors in Developing Countries: Findings from the Global Investment Competitiveness Survey." In *2017/2018 Global Investment Competitiveness Report: Foreign Investor Perspectives and Policy Implications,* 19–50. Washington, DC: World Bank.

Lin, Ping, and Kamal Saggi. 2005. "Multinational Firms and Backward Linkages: A Critical Survey and a Simple Model." In *Does Foreign Direct Investment Promote Development?* edited by Theodore H. Moran, Edward Graham, and Magnus Blomstrom, 159–74. Washington, DC: Peterson Institute for International Economics and Center for Global Development.

Lynn, P., R. Turner, and P. Smith. 1997. "The Effect of Complexity and Tone of an Advance Letter on Response to an Interview Survey." *Survey Methods Centre Newsletter* 17: 13–17.

Marken, Stephanie. 2018. "Still Listening: The State of Telephone Surveys." *Gallup Methodology Blog,* January 11. https://news.gallup.com/opinion/methodology/225143/listening-state-telephone-surveys.aspx.

Mistura, Fernando, and Caroline Roulet. 2019. "The Determinants of Foreign Direct Investment: Do Statutory Restrictions Matter?" OECD Working Papers on International Investment 2019/01, Organisation for Economic Co-operation and Development, Paris.

Rodrik, Dani. 1991. "Policy Uncertainty and Private Investment in Developing Countries." *Journal of Development Economics* 36 (2): 229–42.

Schneider, Friedrich, and Bruno S. Frey. 1985. "Economic and Political Determinants of Foreign Direct Investment." *World Development* 13 (2): 161–75.

Sekkat, Khalid, and Marie-Ange Veganzones–Varoudakis. 2007. "Openness, Investment Climate, and FDI in Developing Countries." *Review of Development Economics* 11 (4): 607–20.

Singer, Eleanor, and Cong Ye. 2013. "The Use and Effects of Incentives in Surveys." *Annals of the American Academy of Political and Social Science* 645 (1): 112–41.

UNCTAD (United Nations Conference on Trade and Development). 2013. *World Investment Report 2013: Global Value Chains: Investment and Trade for Development.* Geneva: UNCTAD.

UNCTAD (United Nations Conference on Trade and Development). 2016. *World Investment Report 2016: Investor Nationality: Policy Challenges.* Geneva: UNCTAD.

UNCTAD (United Nations Conference on Trade and Development). 2019. *World Investment Report 2019: Special Economic Zones.* New York: UNCTAD.

UNCTAD (United Nations Conference on Trade and Development). 2020. *Investment Policy Monitor* 23. April. UNCTAD.

Vogiatzoglou, Klimis. 2016. "Ease of Doing Business and FDI Inflows in ASEAN." *Journal of Southeast Asian Economies* 33 (3): 343–63.

von der Lippe, Elena, Patrick Schmich, and Cornelia Lange. 2011. "Advance Letters as a Way of Reducing Non-Response in a National Health Telephone Survey: Differences between Listed and Unlisted Numbers." *Survey Research Methods* 5 (3): 103–16.

Walch, Nadja, and Julia Wörz. 2012. "The Impact of Country Risk Ratings and of the Status of EU Integration on FDI Inflows in CESEE Countries." *Focus on European Economic Integration* 3: 8–26.

Wei, Shang Jin. 2000. "How Taxing is Corruption on International Investors?" *Review of Economics and Statistics* 82 (1): 1–11.

Wei, Yingqi, Xiaming Liu, and Chengang Wang. 2008. "Mutual Productivity Spillovers between Foreign and Local Affiliates in China." *Cambridge Journal of Economics* 32 (4): 609–31.

Wernick, David A., Jerry Haar, and Shane Singh. 2009. "Do Governing Institutions Affect Foreign Direct Investment Inflows? New Evidence from Emerging Economies." *International Journal of Economics and Business Research* 1 (3): 317–22.

World Bank. 2019a. *Doing Business 2020: Comparing Business Regulation in 190 Economies*. Washington, DC: World Bank.

World Bank. 2019b. *Global Economic Prospects, June 2019: Heightened Tensions, Subdued Investment*. Washington, DC: World Bank.

World Bank. 2020. *World Development Report 2020: Trading for Development in the Age of Global Value Chains*. Washington, DC: World Bank.

2 How Beneficial Are Foreign Acquisitions of Firms in Developing Countries? Evidence from Six Countries

Alexandros Ragoussis

Key Findings

- **Acquisitions of domestic firms by foreign investors have doubled as a share of FDI in developing countries over the past 10 years.** The acquired firms in developing countries can be diverse. They can be in any sector but more commonly in activities that rely on land and established distribution networks, as well as in sectors where entry is highly regulated. For developing countries, income level and market size are strong predictors of the intensity of "brownfield" investment.
- **This report explores differences in the performance and development impact of brownfield FDI relative to greenfield FDI and domestically owned firms by analyzing a unique set of industrial censuses from six developing countries: China, Côte d'Ivoire, Indonesia, Moldova, Serbia, and Vietnam.** Although FDI's benefits to economic development have been well studied using aggregate statistics and country case studies, this report brings new evidence on the contributions of brownfield FDI to developing countries' competitiveness, productivity, and labor markets.
- **Results show that firms acquired by multinational enterprises not only perform better than the average domestic firm at the time of the acquisition but also improve their performance after acquisition faster than local firms along some of the key dimensions that matter for development.** For example, over the first five years of a firm's operation, a brownfield affiliate is 70–100 percent more likely to export than a domestic firm. Wages in foreign take-overs at the end of the first five years of operations are 40–50 percent higher than in domestic firms.
- **Furthermore, contrary to conventional belief about the potential job-destroying effects of foreign mergers and acquisitions, employment in newly acquired firms tends to grow faster in most countries than employment in domestic firms with similar characteristics.** Specifically, two years after acquisition, the average employment in brownfield affiliates expands by approximately 4 percent, compared with 1.5 percent in domestic firms with similar characteristics. The firms' asset value after the acquisition follows a similar path. In addition, wages in brownfield affiliates tend to increase, compared with relatively stagnant wages in the domestic firms. The experience of the six countries analyzed in this study suggests that foreign acquisitions could be adding more value in markets at the lower end of the development spectrum—that is, in countries where most FDI still takes place through greenfield investment.
- **A policy framework that is supportive of brownfield investment should emphasize (a) streamlining investment screening mechanisms and approval processes, (b) increasing the effectiveness of competition policies to reduce the administrative burden of merger and acquisition controls, and (c) enhancing cooperation between competition and investment authorities.** Although legal safeguards to protect the public interest ought to be preserved, an alleviation of the administrative burden, unpredictability, cost, and time involved in brownfield investment would facilitate the process greatly. Differential treatment of brownfield multinationals with respect to investment incentives should also be avoided.

Introduction

Acquisitions of domestic firms by foreign investors have doubled as a share of total foreign direct investment (FDI) in developing countries over the past 10 years. In the past, foreign investors in developing countries would typically establish new facilities in unused "green fields" rather than investing in established companies in potentially contaminated "brown fields," as the analogy goes. That is still how most FDI takes place outside the industrialized world.

The balance between the two modes of entry, however, is shifting toward more brownfield investment. Upper- and lower-middle-income countries lead the way (figure 2.1). The trend is also discernible in outward investment by upper- and lower-middle-income countries to other developing countries and, notably, to high-income economies.

The rise of foreign acquisitions brings tensions in the investment landscape. The United States and the European Union have enacted strict screenings of foreign acquisitions in response to perceived challenges to national security. Cases of investment withdrawals—either rejected or withdrawn over security concerns—tripled in 2018 alone, often receiving high publicity (UNCTAD 2019). China and South Africa have also changed their FDI screening mechanisms in recent years for the same reasons. Although tensions arise primarily over assets in high-income and large emerging economies, they entail a risk of shaping narratives, policy precedents, and responses beyond their own jurisdictions.

But how beneficial is brownfield FDI for developing countries? Opinions vary. Greenfield FDI adds new elements to the economy: new facilities, new jobs, and additional production capacity. Brownfield investment, by contrast, transforms existing production. Any positive effect would therefore tend to materialize over longer time frames and with varying intensity.

That brownfield investment represents rents to existing assets is the prevailing explanation offered by various empirical studies for the modest effects on aggregate growth (Harms and Meon 2018; Wang and Wong 2009). Narratives likening cross-border mergers and acquisitions (M&A) to "bad cholesterol" or qualifying them as "useless" rely on this evidence to play down their contribution (Beattie 2014; Harms and Meon 2018). These critiques are not new. Following the 1990s surge of acquisitions of state-owned enterprises, the United Nations Conference on Trade and Development (UNCTAD) noted "concerns in political discussions and the media that foreign acquisitions as a mode of entry are less beneficial for economic development, if not positively harmful" (UNCTAD 2000).

For the development community, one complicating factor in discerning the effect of brownfield investment is that most of the evidence comes from high-income countries, where the impact of investment can be different in scope and depth than in developing countries. In addition, much of what captures the public eye tends to focus on macroeconomic growth, overlooking the shift of attention to development outcomes at the level of firms, the jobs they create, or the wages they offer. Little is known about acquired firms in developing countries[1]—what they look like, how they evolve, and whether conventional narratives do justice to their contribution in development terms.

This study uses a unique set of industrial censuses from six developing countries (China, Côte d'Ivoire, Indonesia, Moldova, Serbia, and Vietnam) to shed additional light on these three questions. The discussion that follows shows that acquired firms in developing countries can be diverse. They can be in any sector but are more common in activities that rely on land and established distribution networks, as well as in sectors where entry is highly regulated.

Motivations matter: firm acquisitions are strongly associated with market-seeking and asset-seeking FDI. For developing countries, income and the size of the market are strong

FIGURE 2.1 Brownfield Investment Rose as a Share of Total FDI in Developing Countries, 2010–17

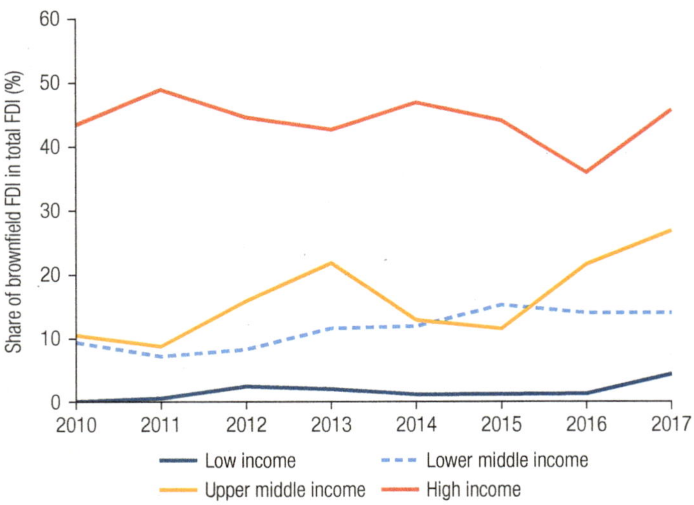

Source: World Bank, based on 2019 United Nations Conference on Trade and Development (UNCTAD) Mergers and Acquisitions (M&A) database, http://www.unctad.org/fdistatistics.
Note: The trend is illustrated using a two-year moving average. All country income categories use 2017 World Bank-defined classifications; "developing" countries refers collectively to low- and middle-income countries. FDI = foreign direct investment.

predictors of the intensity in which acquisitions take place. And while there is a sorting of average outcomes between the three groups—greenfield affiliates doing better than brownfield affiliates, and the latter doing better than domestic firms—brownfield affiliates are shown to develop significant advantages over domestic firms, and those advantages are consolidated in the first five years of their operations. Steeper transformation paths of domestic firms taken over by foreign investors highlight important contributions of brownfield FDI to some key outcomes that matter for development.

Although more evidence would be necessary to establish general conclusions, the experience of the six countries analyzed in this study suggests that foreign acquisitions could be adding more value in markets at the lower end of the development spectrum—that is, in countries where most FDI still takes place through greenfield investment. This study's findings could therefore be more relevant for rapidly growing economies where the share of foreign acquisitions is rising as well as for investment into sectors in which brownfield investment takes place more frequently, such as agriculture or services.

Governments have various means to foster the potential of brownfield ventures in these contexts. Improving the predictability of screening mechanisms; strengthening competition enforcement; ensuring equal applicability of incentives such as tax credits, preferential rates, or subsidies; and facilitating the participation of foreign investors in development of firms can go a long way in that direction. Although legal safeguards to protect the public interest ought to be preserved, an alleviation of the administrative burden, unpredictability, cost, and time involved in the process would facilitate brownfield investment greatly.

The rest of the chapter is organized as follows: *The Choice between Brownfield and Greenfield FDI* reviews existing knowledge on brownfield FDI as the starting point for the investigation. *Characteristics of Markets Affecting Brownfield FDI* describes countries and sectors where brownfield investment grows more rapidly. *Differences between Brownfield Affiliates and Other Firms* delves into the firm-level outcomes, growth, and transformation paths of firms taken over by foreign investors. *Policy Considerations for Brownfield FDI* explores policy options for countries to foster their development potential.

The Choice between Brownfield and Greenfield FDI

There are two main ways for a foreign investor to enter a market: either set up a new firm or acquire existing facilities (box 2.1). The choice between the two depends naturally on which yields the greatest return. The benefits and costs differ substantially by mode of entry.

The value of a firm's assets is the prime driver of brownfield investment. Access to a successful firm's technology, machinery, or brand name represents a future stream of revenues to the acquirer, especially when those assets yield lower returns domestically than

BOX 2.1

Conceptual Overlaps between Mergers, Acquisitions, and Brownfield FDI

"Mergers and acquisitions" (M&A) is a general term used to describe the consolidation of companies or assets through various types of financial transactions. The terms "merger" and "acquisition" are often used interchangeably, although they have slightly different meanings.

In an *acquisition*, a company purchases another entity, partially or entirely, and establishes itself as a new owner. From a legal point of view, the target company does not cease to exist. In other words, acquisitions involve the purchase of an entity's assets without a change in market structure.

In a *merger*, on the other hand, one or several entities involved cease to exist, and a new entity may be created; thus there is a change in market structure. In the case of public firms, the boards of directors of the two companies approve the combination of their assets and seek shareholders' approval. If the purchase of assets takes place without the consent of the board or shareholders of the target company, the operation is called a "hostile take-over." A hostile take-over can also result in a merger, whereby companies' stocks are surrendered, and new company stock is issued in its place.

Depending on the activities exercised by the buyer and seller, M&A can further be classified as (a) *horizontal:* between firms that produce and sell the same products—that is, between competing firms; (b) *vertical:* between firms operating at different stages of the value chain; or (c) *conglomerate:* between firms in unrelated businesses.

"Brownfield foreign direct investment (FDI)" is a broader term for any purchase by a foreign entity of assets that corresponds to more than 10 percent of the total assets of a target company, which is the threshold for a foreign investment to be considered direct (FDI) according to the International Monetary Fund (IMF) and Organisation for Economic Co-operation and Development (OECD).

Ownership of a 10 percent share does not necessarily grant control over the firm. The investor's ability to make independent decisions would require a majority share, although shareholders can significantly influence the firm strategies and managerial decisions at lower thresholds, generally over 30 percent. The purchase can be friendly or unfriendly and result in various combinations of outcomes in terms of creating a new legal entity, including a simple acquisition or a merger. Joint ventures do not fall under the category of brownfield foreign investment because they refer to the establishment of new facilities—greenfield investment—involving a local and a foreign entity.

in international markets. The foundation of the decision to acquire lies in the investor's ability to raise the value of the assets, which often involves a substantial but lower commitment of resources than setting up a subsidiary from scratch. Partly for this reason, brownfield FDI seems to attract less productive investors than greenfield investment, on average.[2]

Fundamentally, there can be two sources of surplus from foreign acquisitions: (a) the efficiency gains due to operational synergies, and (b) the valuation gains associated with the relaxation of the target firm's liquidity constraints. The more credit constrained the target firm, the larger the valuation gains relative to operational synergies.

These sources of surplus can become a relatively more important motive for brownfield investment during financial crises—a situation often referred to as "fire-sale FDI," coined by Paul Krugman to describe the surge in foreign acquisitions of Asian firms during the 1997–98 financial crisis (Krugman 2000). Indeed, a crisis is associated with a 30 percent increase in the probability of a foreign acquisition of a typical target relative to the noncrisis average (Alquist, Mukherjee, and Tesar 2016). But more generally, valuation gains appear to explain an important share of variation in cross-country mergers and acquisitions (M&A): firms in countries whose stock market has increased in value, whose currency has recently appreciated, and that have a relatively high market-to-book value tend to be purchasers, while firms from weaker-performing economies tend to be targets (Erel, Liao, and Weisbach 2011).

The value of the acquired assets is always assessed against the purpose of the investment. If the main objective is to sell in the domestic market—a "market-seeking" investment—then acquiring a company that is already operating is a common way to gain access. Market intelligence is part of that advantage: existing firms know the demand and know the risks, so the investor does not have to start at the bottom of the learning curve. Complementarity between acquired assets and foreign owners' tangible and intangible assets is another factor that often tips the balance in favor of brownfield FDI (Balsvik and Haller 2010; Curran, Lv, and Francesa Spigarelli 2017). In all cases, the average domestic firm in a host country would rarely combine all these qualities, so foreign investors "cherry pick" the more successful, productive, and profitable ones that suit their plans (Almeida 2007; Balsvik and Haller 2010; Bertrand et al. 2012; Guadalupe, Kuzmina, and Thomas 2012).

There are reasons why investors may prefer to set up a new venture rather than acquire an existing firm. Control over precious intellectual property, operations, and management would justify that preference. To secure their property, investors are often willing to bear higher costs of construction and navigate a host country's regulatory system and tax structure, in what consists overall in a longer-term commitment to the market and host country.

The activity of the firm itself matters in the decision to build or buy. Acquisitions do not make equal sense in all sectors of economic activity; they can be more beneficial for the investor in markets where there is higher contractual intensity, higher informational asymmetries among firms as well as between firms and consumers, and greater costs in setting up new facilities. Sectors such as real estate, financial services, or pharmaceuticals are examples (Davies, Desbordes, and Ray 2018). The high cost of setting up a local supply network in a vertically integrated market with strong backward linkages also favors cross-border acquisition relative to greenfield investment (Milliou and Pavlou 2014). In high-income countries, the location, geography, and cultural barriers, together with tariff rates applied on inputs from the origin country, are other factors affecting the attractiveness of acquisitions (Davies, Desbordes, and Ray 2018; di Giovanni 2005; Roberto 2004).

Overall, a variety of factors explain the decision to acquire rather than set up a new venture: the particularities of the sector and the location, the motivation, the level of control over intellectual property, the macroeconomic environment, restrictions to alternative modes such as costly procedures for construction permits, and the length of the commitment wished by the investor.

Impacts of FDI on Acquired Firms and Host Economies

What is perhaps more critical from a development standpoint, however, is the question of the impact of foreign take-overs on acquired firms. Employment tops the list of concerns. In developed economies, both job losses and gains have been documented in acquired firms over time. In developing economies, there are fewer records of effects of acquisitions on employment, but they are generally positive.[3] These findings are consistent with the findings that foreign investment in existing firms improves productivity (Bircan 2019; Conyon et al. 2002; Hale and Xu 2016; Lichtenberg and Siegel 2000; Maksimovic and Phillips 2001; Maksimovic, Phillips, and Prabhala 2008; Schoar 2002), which tends to be associated with larger size. Skill and knowledge transfers, as well as increased labor efficiency are the main channels through which improvements happen. And productivity improvements in turn lead gradually to better wages.

Positive valuation gains are also reported for the acquiring firm when it buys a majority stake in an enterprise in a developing country (Chari, Ouimet, and Tesar 2010). The size of the stock price increase for the buyer is more pronounced when the contracting environment is weak and in industries with high asset intangibility.

When it comes to the contribution of foreign take-overs to the growth of the host economy as whole, the prevailing view is that the growth impact of greenfield investment is stronger than that of acquisitions (Calderón, Loayza, and Servén 2004). The commitment involved in greenfield ventures also makes their impact more lasting (Bandick and Karpaty 2007; Harms and Meon 2018). Greenfield ventures not only raise the production capacity and create jobs but also intensify competition by increasing the number of suppliers, which adds to their appeal (Burger and Ianchovichina 2017; Claeys and Hainz 2007).

Cross-border acquisitions, by contrast, keep the number of market players unchanged. Their effects on market structure thus are often thought to be neutral, if not negative, which is a recurring concern when foreign investors enter by this mode (OECD 2012). In developing countries in particular, newly acquired firms can in principle capitalize on advantages associated with foreign ownership and concentrate market power more easily where competition enforcement is ineffective. Evidence on the general validity of that effect across countries and contexts remains limited.

In the same way that greenfield investment transforms markets, brownfield investment can also bring about job creation, innovation, and competition, but it takes longer for that impact to materialize as the acquired firms gradually improve their position in the host market. Recent evidence from Turkey, for example, indicates that foreign acquisitions increase physical productivity in acquired firms while lowering competitor prices (Bircan 2019). This finding suggests that their procompetitive effects may have been underestimated to date.

A distinct feature of brownfield investment is also that it can *save* jobs and revenue rather than create new ones, by restructuring companies that would otherwise fail to sustain operations (Grzegorz 2014). And although little has been written on the evolution of domestic linkages of foreign take-overs in broader areas like revenue and taxes, there is agreement that, unless they transfer their entire profit to the parent company, brownfield affiliates make a significant contribution to the host economy (Bandick and Karpaty 2007; Beattie 2014).

Feedback loops whereby brownfield investment induces more greenfield investment by reducing informational asymmetries, and greenfield investment induces more brownfield investment, have been studied less and have shown mixed results. In high-income countries, the limited evidence suggests that foreign acquisitions are associated with more greenfield FDI over time, while the reverse has been observed in developing countries: greenfield investment is associated with more brownfield investment over time (Calderón, Loayza, and Servén 2004).

Characteristics of Markets Attracting Brownfield FDI

The decision to set up a firm or acquire one is driven by multiple factors. How does a country's level of development influence that decision? Stronger institutions associated with development enable more effective protection of investors' intellectual property and more reliable contractual arrangements, both of which make brownfield investment more appealing. A market's level of development, moreover, reflects the attractiveness of acquisition targets—the presence of successful firms that require less time and effort to bring returns—as well as structural shifts to services in which brownfield affiliates are more common. But is the relationship between share of acquisitions and level of development linear, and which sectors and firms are more likely to receive foreign investment in developing countries?

Macroeconomic investment data by mode of entry (aggregated from commercial sources) and firm-level microdata from industrial censuses in six developing countries—China, Côte d'Ivoire, Indonesia, Moldova, Serbia, and Vietnam—employed in this study yield a wealth of insights. A few caveats are in order, however. The datasets have imperfections: in all cases they include some transactions that do not strictly fall under the standard definition of FDI. They also have not been thoroughly benchmarked in terms of representativeness and coverage. (See annex 2A for more details on the sources, their contents, and limitations.)

Brownfield investment occurs frequently in developing countries, but more so in some than in others. Income is a strong predictor of both the absolute volume of brownfield investment and its relative intensity. Of the US$313 billion of brownfield investment in developing countries between 2014 and 2017, three-quarters consisted of acquisitions of assets in upper-middle-income countries. The more developed among developing countries also tend to receive higher shares of brownfield investment in total foreign investment (figure 2.2).

Regional concentration is also evident because of, or perhaps in addition to, income. Latin American economies such as Argentina, Chile, Colombia, Mexico, and Peru have disproportionally high shares of brownfield FDI, while in Sub-Saharan Africa, the share of foreign acquisitions in total FDI is very low. The size of the market matters as well. The BRICS (Brazil, the Russian Federation, India, China, and South Africa), Argentina, and Mexico—where larger shares of brownfield investment are recorded—are some of the largest economies in the developing world.

FIGURE 2.2 Higher Shares of Brownfield Investments Occur in More Developed Economies

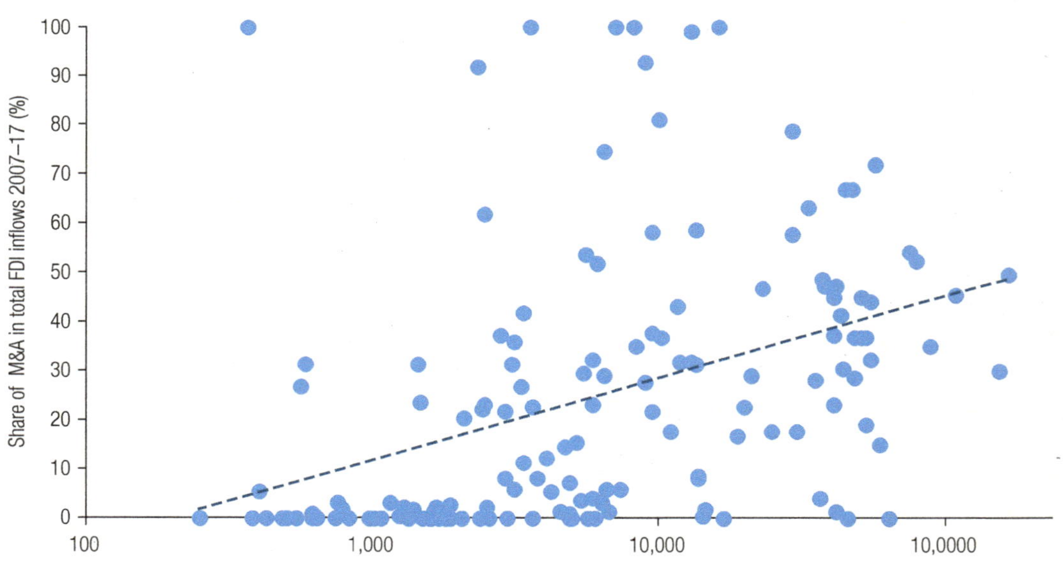

Source: World Bank calculations, based on data from the United Nations Conference on Trade and Development (UNCTAD) Mergers and Acquisitions (M&A) database (http://www.unctad.org/fdistatistics) and fDi Markets, a *Financial Times* dataset (https://www.fdimarkets.com/).
Note: The figure shows investment destination countries with per capita GDP below US$15,000. Data are averages for 2007–17. FDI = foreign direct investment; GDP = gross domestic product; M&A = mergers and acquisitions.

The sectoral composition of these large economies might also lie behind cross-country differences in the intensity of acquisitions. The aggregate data confirm that although brownfield investment can take place in any sector, it occurs more intensely in (a) activities that rely on land (agriculture, mining, and real estate, for example) where access is restricted; (b) activities where distribution and client networks are hard to build from scratch, such as food and beverages, wholesale and retail trade, and health services; and (c) sectors that are highly regulated, such as financial services (figure 2.3). Manufacturing activities with strong backward or forward linkages to these industries—such as food processing, tobacco, or pharmaceuticals—also attract significantly greater shares of brownfield investment.

FIGURE 2.3 Brownfield FDI Is Likelier in Sectors That Rely on Land, Have Established Distribution Networks, or Are Highly Regulated

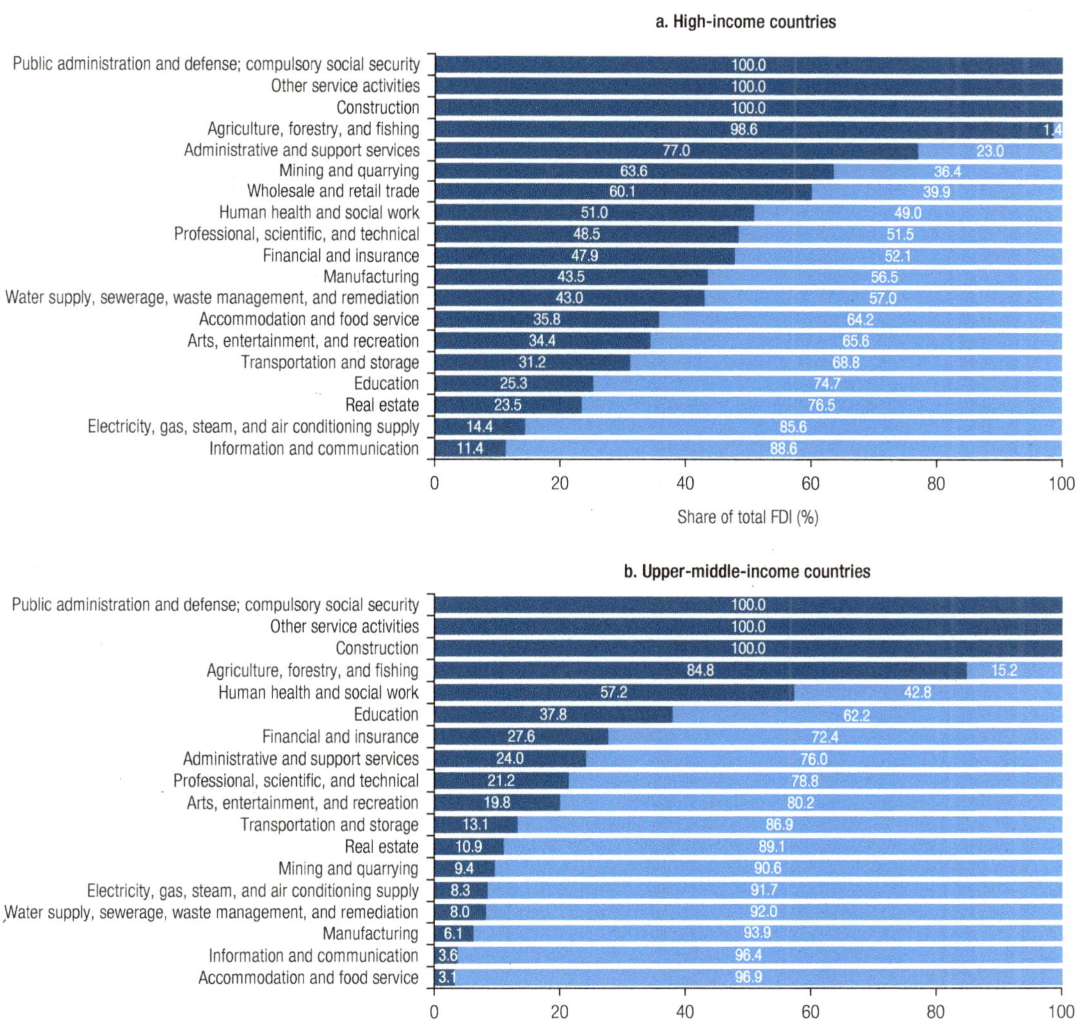

Figure continues next page

FIGURE 2.3 Brownfield FDI Is Likelier in Sectors That Rely on Land, Have Established Distribution Networks, or Are Highly Regulated *(continued)*

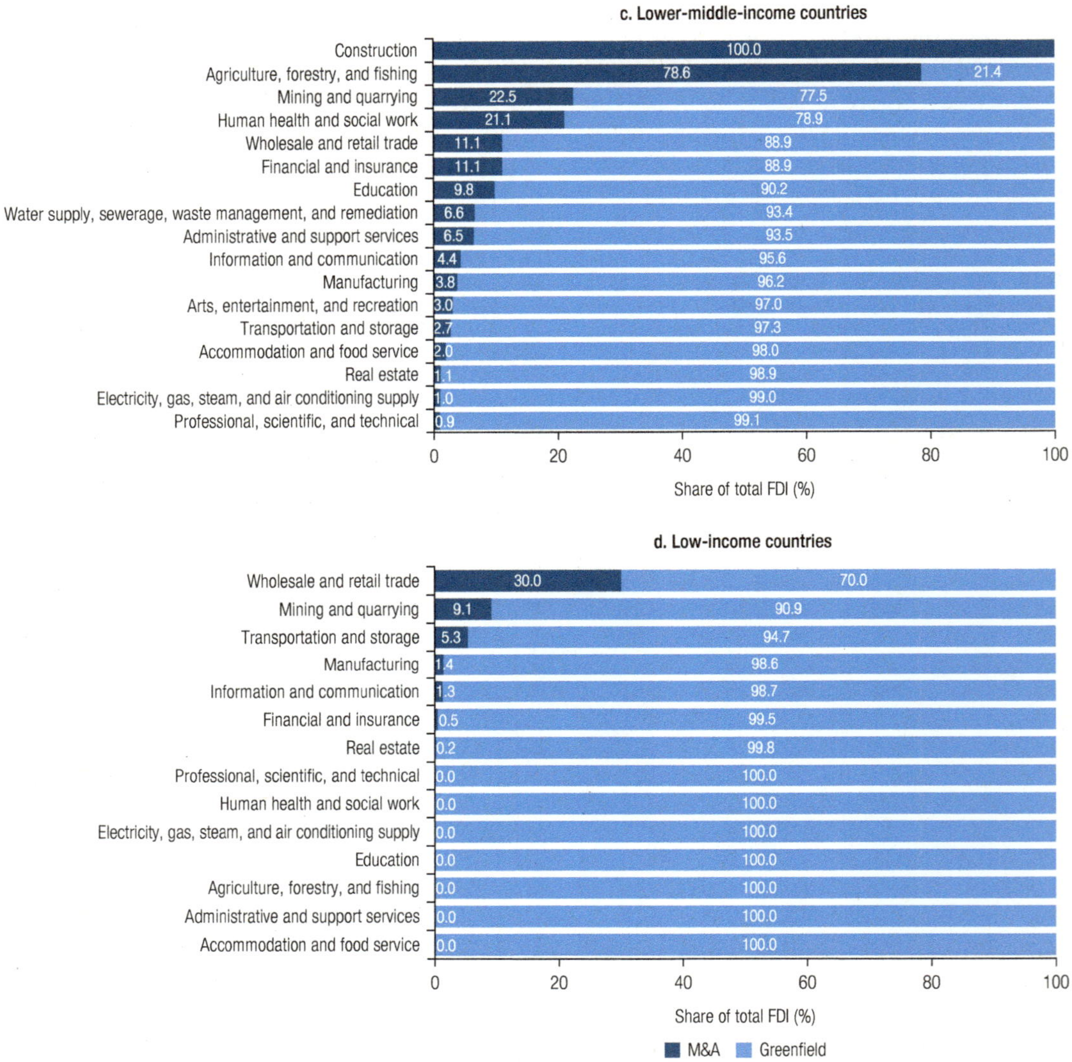

Source: World Bank calculations, based on data from the United Nations Conference on Trade and Development (UNCTAD) Mergers and Acquisitions (M&A) database (http://www.unctad.org/fdistatistics) and fDi Markets, a *Financial Times* dataset (https://www.fdimarkets.com/).
Note: Data are for 2010–17. Volumes are aggregated by country income group, following the World Bank classifications for fiscal year 2017 throughout, to maintain consistency. Only shares of foreign direct investment (FDI) over total industry values exceeding US$20 million are represented in the panels. FDI = foreign direct investment; M&A = mergers and acquisitions.

In upper-middle-income countries, a substantial share of brownfield investment takes place in all these sectors in addition to important volumes in manufacturing. In lower-middle-income countries and low-income countries, by contrast, the volumes remain lower and sectoral concentration is high: brownfield investment tends to take place in agriculture, mining, wholesale trade, and construction. In other words, this mode of entry prevails in industries where foreign investors have few to no alternatives.

More generally, country-specific factors such as the market size, level of development, and quality of institutions explain a much greater share of variation in modes of entry than sectoral characteristics. Firm-level data from six developing countries lend support to this conclusion (see annex 2B, table 2B.1). Although both country-specific factors and sector-specific factors drive the intensity by which foreign investors choose one mode over another, the former explain twice as much of the variation in frequency of foreign acquisition as the latter.

Differences between Brownfield Affiliates and Other Firms

Delving further into how brownfield affiliates differ from the rest of firms in host economies is not simple because of data constraints. Many industrial surveys do not ask firms to report the origin of their capital, whether domestic or foreign. This reduces the number of surveys that can be used for this exercise.

In surveys that do include ownership information, greenfield affiliates can be identified only if a firm's activity is observed in the year it is established, which is rare. Many firms do not report activity figures until several years after entry, which adds a significant margin of error in the estimates. To identify brownfield affiliates, by contrast, information on the time of establishment is not needed. All that is required is a moment when foreign ownership turns positive. The sample of firms where this happens is older and larger; it tells us a lot about the characteristics of firms that foreign investors acquire. But to reliably study differences between greenfield affiliates, brownfield affiliates, and domestic firms, the three samples need to be comparable to avoid attributing age differences to ownership and mode of entry. This requirement constrains this exercise to firms that are younger and smaller.

The six countries used for this study—China, Côte d'Ivoire, Indonesia, Moldova, Serbia, and Vietnam —represent a solid sample for the exercise. Covering various periods from the early 2000s to recently, they contain almost 54,000 observations of multinational firms that have been acquired by foreign investors at some point in their lifetime. Of these, about 16,700 observations are from firms whose time of origin is observed (see annex 2A, table 2A.1).

The countries themselves are quite diverse, spanning three continents and three income levels, with stark differences in terms of market size (ranging from China to Moldova) and varied industrial structures. The regulatory context of the six countries varies as well. With the exceptions of Serbia and Vietnam, the rest fare rather poorly during the period studied in terms of the World Bank's *Doing Business* scores—particularly on the subcomponent dealing with construction permits, which would incentivize modes of entry other than greenfield.[4] The sample overall allows cross-country evidence over multiple dimensions that previous studies have not been able to capture.

Different Outcomes of Brownfield Ventures Relative to Greenfield Ventures or Domestic Firms

A closer examination of the six countries' industrial censuses reveals important differences within the multinational segment by mode of entry, as expected from previous work. The average brownfield affiliate is larger than a greenfield affiliate, measured by workforce size. However, this statistic masks the fact that greenfield affiliates that can be identified in the sample are often younger than the rest of the firms. The bulk of acquisitions takes place within the first 10 years of a firm's lifetime, but that margin makes acquired firms on average older than greenfield affiliates at the time of observation (figure 2.4, panel a).

When accounting for how long firms have been in operation, that is, at a given age, greenfield affiliates are typically larger than brownfield affiliates in all sample countries. In turn, both types of multinational enterprises (MNEs) are significantly larger than their domestic counterparts (figure 2.4, panel b).

FIGURE 2.4 Greenfield Affiliates Typically Have Larger Workforces than Brownfield Affiliates, Considering Age of the Firm

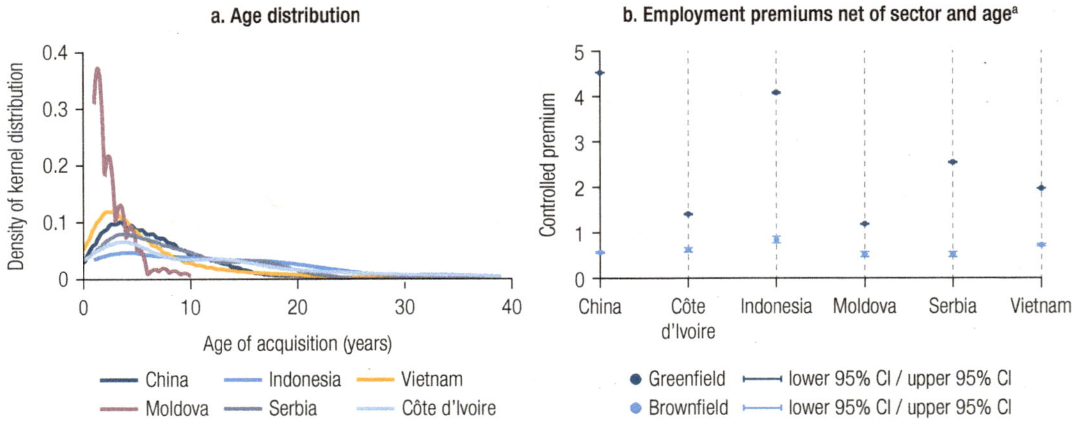

Source: World Bank calculations, based on industrial censuses from six countries.

Note: Industrial census data were analyzed from China, Côte d'Ivoire, Indonesia, Moldova, Serbia, and Vietnam (for data details, see annex 2A). CI = confidence interval.

a. In panel b, the graph shows premia relative to the benchmark of a domestic firm, set at 0. "Domestic" refers to the firms that have not changed their ownership from local to foreign at any point in the observed sample.

Myriad dimensions and layers can be studied under the umbrella of firm-level outcomes. In terms of development impact, more emphasis is placed on impacts that reflect two broad objectives: *competitiveness* (which captures productivity and returns to investment) and *inclusiveness* (the extent to which these returns benefit a broad range of society). These two objectives conceptually track two pillars of sustainable development—economic and social—to which typically a third pillar, environmental, is added. Firm-level data used for this exercise only shed light on the first two, although several hypotheses can be made on the differential effect on the environment of brownfield versus greenfield investment.

The economic and social outcomes of foreign-owned firms differ substantially from those of domestic firms (box 2.2). These differences in turn help shift macroeconomic and social outcomes in host countries, depending on the volume of investment and the presence of complementary conditions that facilitate the absorption of this foreign investment by firms, regions, and countries.

Productivity, the value of the firm's assets, exports, and diversification of production are conventional measures of how competitive a firm is, while the extent to which these returns benefit local workers and suppliers can be measured by wages and imports, respectively.

Starting from competitiveness, both types of multinationals are significantly more productive than the average domestic firm in all six countries observed (figure 2.5). The value of firms' assets is a distinct feature of brownfield affiliates (figure 2.5, panel c); indeed, it is a major motivation for investment. Valuable assets, however, are not reflected in significantly better labor productivity for brownfield affiliates than greenfield affiliates (figure 2.5, panel b): the averages across the two groups of firms are within the margin of error, and in all countries are significantly better than domestic firms. When it comes to internationalization, both brownfield and greenfield affiliates have greater exposure than domestic firms, and comparable levels in exports and imports (figure 2.5, panels d and e), exhibiting closer supply linkages to the domestic market in only one case: Indonesia.

BOX 2.2

The Evidence on Economic and Social Outcomes of Multinational Enterprises

Although foreign direct investment (FDI) is generally associated with positive effects on development, whether these effects will materialize is neither automatic nor monotonic; it varies considerably across various types of enterprises, sectors, regions, and countries, and it is highly dependent on mediating factors and local conditions.

A recent examination of the World Bank Enterprise Surveys highlighted systematic differences between foreign multinational enterprises (MNEs) and domestic firms across 63 countries over 10 dimensions that matter for development. Although there appears to be no striking trade-off between competitiveness and inclusiveness of foreign multinationals, their premiums over domestic firms differ substantially across regions and income groups.

Relative to other regions, foreign MNEs established in eastern Europe and central Asia, for example, exhibit better outcomes than domestic firms on most of the dimensions relating to competitiveness (such as productivity, outward orientation, and innovation) as well as inclusiveness (wages or provision of training). Foreign MNEs established in Latin America stand out in terms of productivity and skills transfer, while in Sub-Saharan Africa, foreign MNEs stand out with respect to job expansion and wages.

The mix appears to be highly specific to the type of multinationals each region attracts, including the industry and investor motivations as well as the host economy conditions. In the Middle East and North Africa, for example, multinationals differ significantly in terms of export propensity and geographical diversification because of the concentration of FDI in natural resource sectors. Multinationals also contribute more to gender empowerment in this region than anywhere else by employing significantly more women in managerial positions than do domestic firms, potentially because of social and cultural differences between the home and host countries.

Differences in some key areas that drive competitiveness (such as productivity, innovation, and skills transfer) appear to increase with income, while premiums in all other areas are greatest in lower-middle-income or low-income markets, highlighting the relevance of foreign multinationals for socioeconomic progress in these contexts.

Outcomes of foreign-owned firms, however, should not be confused with the aggregate development impact of international business; they are one among a number of such drivers that shift the macroeconomic and social outcomes of host countries. The actual aggregate impact of foreign multinationals on host countries remains dependent on the volume of investment and the presence of complementary conditions that facilitate their absorption by firms, regions, and countries. These conditions include the policy environment, quality of local institutions and financial markets, sector characteristics, and spatial colocation of domestic with foreign firms.

Sources: Alfaro 2017; Lejárraga and Ragoussis 2018.

Improvements in the competitiveness of firms acquired by foreign investors, however, pass through only partially to workers. The productivity premiums of both brownfield and greenfield affiliates over domestic firms should translate into broadly similar wage premiums for workers. However, this is not the case: there appears to be a clear sorting between greenfield, brownfield, and domestic firms in terms of wages (figure 2.5, panel a). Both brownfield and greenfield FDI pay their workers better than domestic firms, yet greenfield affiliates pay considerably more.

Why this discrepancy? Greenfield FDI adds production to the economy, so it boosts demand for labor, driving wages up for new hires. Paying "efficiency" wages (those above market clearance) is also to be expected as frontier firms enter new countries. On the other hand, "sticky" wages (those that respond slowly to changes in the performance of a company or the economy) would tend to keep wages of brownfield ventures at

FIGURE 2.5 Brownfield Affiliates and Greenfield Ventures Differ from the Average Domestic Firm

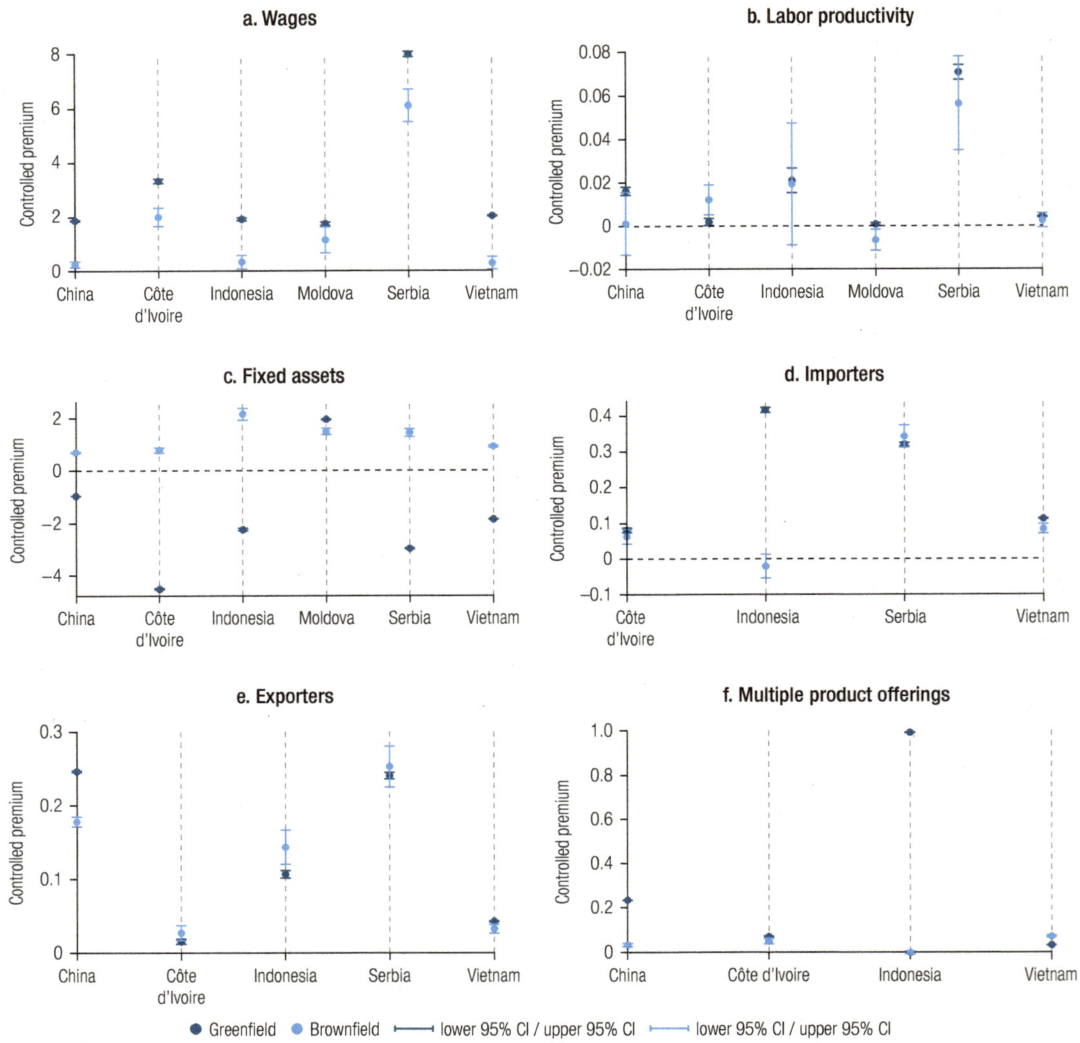

Source: World Bank calculations, based on industrial censuses from six countries.
Note: For this figure, industrial census data were analyzed from China, Côte d'Ivoire, Indonesia, Moldova, Serbia, and Vietnam (further described in annex 2A). The graphs show premia relative to the benchmark of a domestic firm, set at 0. "Domestic" refers to the firms that have not changed their ownership from local to foreign at any point in the observed sample. Vertical bars indicate the confidence interval (CI). Industrial censuses vary in their coverage of different variables, and so some countries are missing from selected panels.

lower levels that persist after the acquisition. In the smaller countries in the sample, such as Côte d'Ivoire, Moldova, and Serbia, these wage premiums of multinational firms are significantly greater than in bigger economies.

As brownfield investment increases in a host country, the characteristics of acquired firms evolve as well in directions that depend on the country context and period of study (see annex 2C). In China, for example, the average size of firms acquired by foreign investors relative to the rest increased over 1998–2007, while the opposite happened in Serbia and Indonesia over 2006–13 and 2009–15, respectively. In both

China and Vietnam, the trend in average productivity over the periods studied has been toward acquisitions of firms that resemble more the rest of firms in the economy, while in Serbia and Indonesia, that has not been the case. General patterns in the evolution of acquired firm characteristics would require study of more country cases over longer periods.

Differences in Growth Paths between Brownfield Affiliates and the Average Domestic Firm

Foreign investors do not target the average domestic firms for acquisition. So questions naturally arise as to whether brownfield affiliates look different from the first day they are established and whether differentiation is the result of (a) growth over their lifetimes, or (b) direct influence of the foreign investor.

By comparing the growth and transformation paths of firms in the different categories over several key outcomes such as employment, labor productivity, wages, and levels of internationalization, the evidence points to a positive answer to both questions, to varying extents. Track records of firms allow observations for only five to seven years after firms enter.[5] A deeper analysis of transformation following acquisition yields insights for only the same number of years. These first years of a firm's life cycle capture important dynamics: whether in developing countries or in mature economies such as the United States, half of start-ups fail within that period.

Growth paths of brownfield affiliates and greenfield ventures. Firms that get acquired by foreign investors look different at origin from firms that do not. They start off larger and more productive from the first year of their operations, and they offer better wages for their workers than the average domestic firm. These differences are not statistically discernible at the very origin but become apparent already within the first year of a firm's lifetime.

Average wages in the three categories of firms are clearly sorted, with brownfield affiliates paying marginally less than greenfield affiliates throughout the first years of their operations. Wages in foreign take-overs at the end of the first five years of operations are 40–50 percent higher than domestic firms, and the gap can reach 70 percent in greenfield affiliates (figure 2.6, panel a).

The same pattern arises when it comes to importer and exporter status: greenfield affiliates are significantly more internationalized than brownfield affiliates, which in turn are significantly more exposed to global markets than domestic firms (figure 2.6, panels e and f). Specifically, over the first five years of the firm's operations, a brownfield affiliate is 70–100 percent more likely to export than domestic firms, while greenfield affiliates are at least three times more likely to export throughout the period. By the fifth year of their operation, brownfield and greenfield affiliates tend to significantly narrow their gap in terms of internationalization.

Overall, much of the growth in the firms' employment takes place within the first three years of their operations. After that time, firm sizes seem to stabilize. Both brownfield and greenfield affiliates begin with more ambitious undertakings, stabilizing at levels that are 15–25 percent larger than the average domestic firm (figure 2.6, panel c). When it comes to product offerings, while all types of firms diversify within the first five years of their operations, greenfield and brownfield affiliates accelerate their diversification more rapidly, and by the fifth year of their lifetimes end up with a profile that includes different activities (figure 2.6, panel d).

Firm transformation after firm acquisition. Growth paths show that acquisition targets start off with above-average potential, which translates into better outcomes in the medium to long term. But is it foreign ownership that improves firm performance, or rather advantages at birth and the ability of firms to grow differently?

This exercise examines changes in outcomes for firms that transition into MNE

FIGURE 2.6 Brownfield and Greenfield FDI Firms Perform Better than Domestic Firms over the First Five Years of Operation

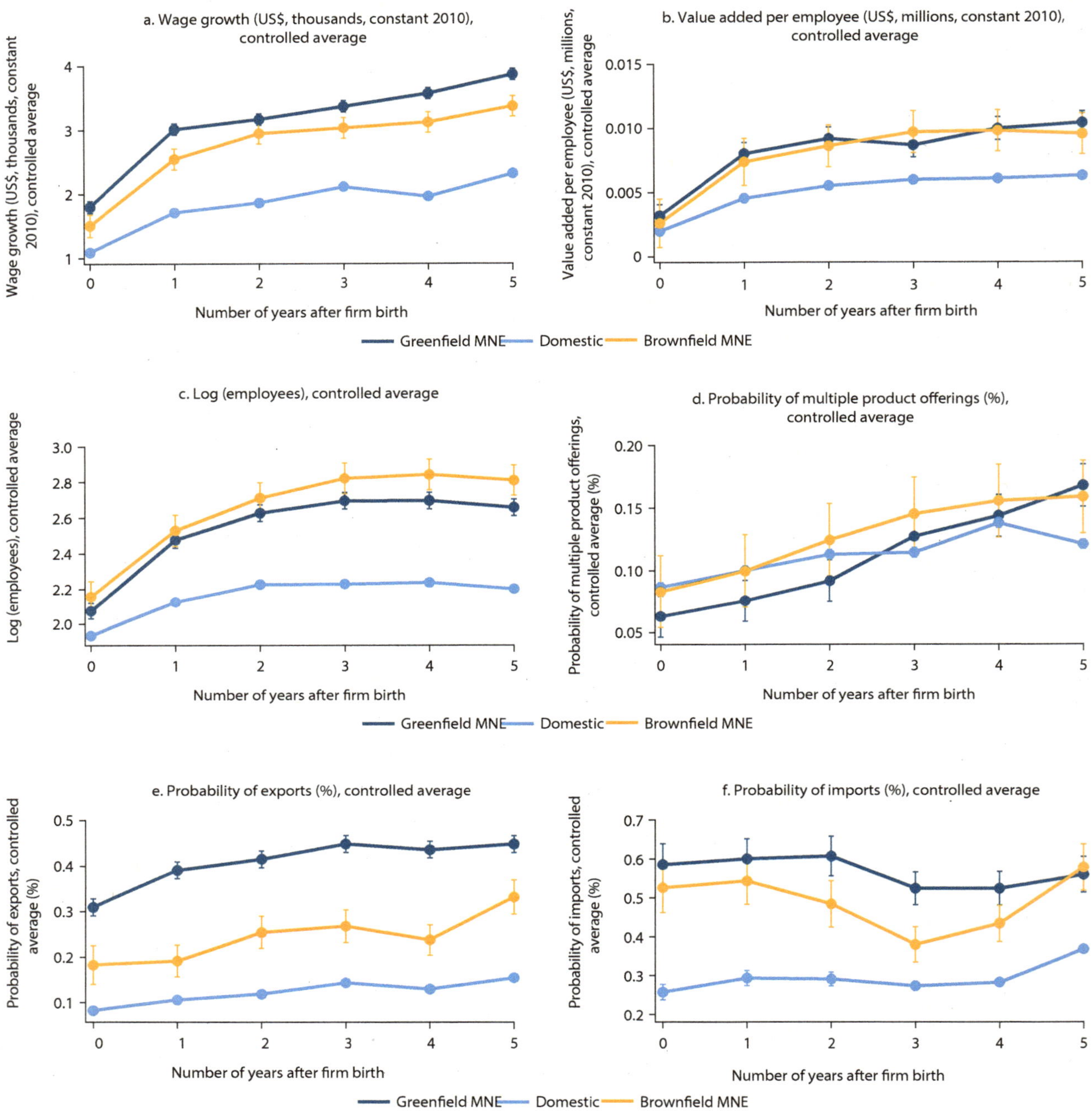

Source: World Bank calculations, based on industrial censuses from six countries.

Note: For this figure, industrial census data were analyzed from China, Côte d'Ivoire, Indonesia, Moldova, Serbia, and Vietnam (as further described in annex 2A). "Domestic" refers to the firms that have not changed their ownership from local to foreign at any point in the observed sample. Growth paths of firm outcomes can be captured in a simple framework using an interaction between indicators of firm group (greenfield, brownfield, domestic) and years after entry in the following specification: $y_{ics} = group_i \boldsymbol{\beta} \cdot d_t + \alpha_{cs} + \delta d_{it_0} + \varepsilon_{ics}$. The sample is restricted to cohorts whose entry is observed. To account for differences that might be driven by country characteristics, sector composition, and macroeconomic trends, the regressions also control for country-sector fixed effects (FE) and cohort fixed effects. Wage growth paths are calculated using constant deflated values in US dollars. Regression includes country FE*2 -digit sector FE as well as cohort start year dummies. Vertical bars indicate the margin of error. FDI = foreign direct investment; MNE = multinational enterprise.

status relative to firms of similar profile that remain domestic. The procedure involves matching every firm acquired by foreign investors to a firm that remains domestic and has similar characteristics (in terms of employment, age, and sector) during the year before the acquisition takes place.[6] Average outcomes in the two groups of firms are then tracked over the years before and after the acquisitions in a framework identical to the growth paths used in the previous section.

Contrary to conventional belief about the potential job-destroying effects of M&A, employment in newly acquired firms grows at similar or often faster rates than the control group of domestic firms for the first few years after acquisition (figure 2.7, panel a). More specifically, two years after acquisition, the average employment in brownfield affiliates expands by approximately 4 percent, compared with 1.5 percent in domestic firms with similar characteristics. The value of firms' assets after the acquisition follows a similar path. In addition, wages in brownfield affiliates appear on average to increase, marginally widening the differences with domestic firms (figure 2.7, panel b).

Transformation paths are highly dependent on the context. The options available to domestic firms of similar characteristics differ across markets, and so do the limitations in foreign owners' decision making—all of which affect the value added from foreign capital. Large upper-middle-income countries (notably, China) offer more growth opportunities to firms independently of the origin of their capital. Indeed, transformation paths in the sample of five smaller or lower-income

FIGURE 2.7 Targeted Firms Improve Their Performance after Acquisition by Foreign Investors

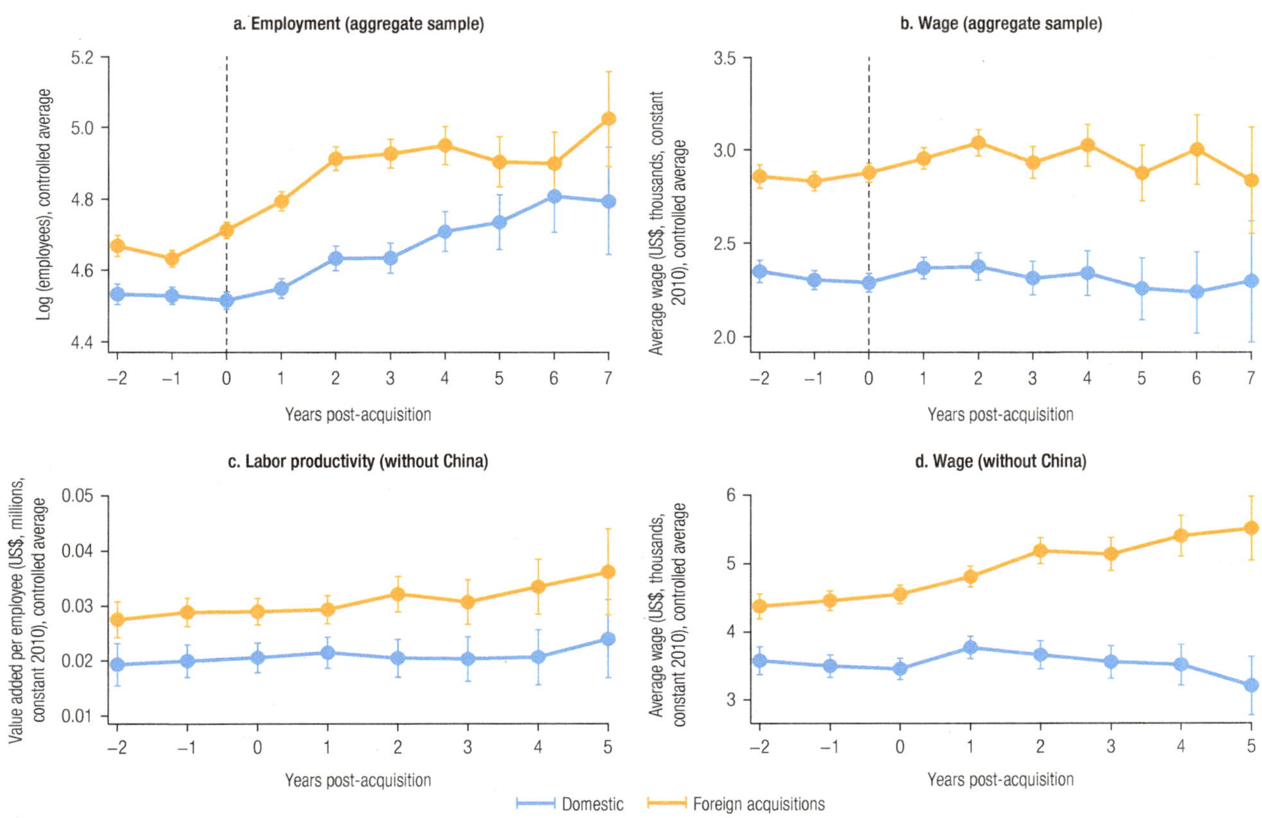

Figure continues next page

FIGURE 2.7 Targeted Firms Improve Their Performance after Acquisition by Foreign Investors *(continued)*

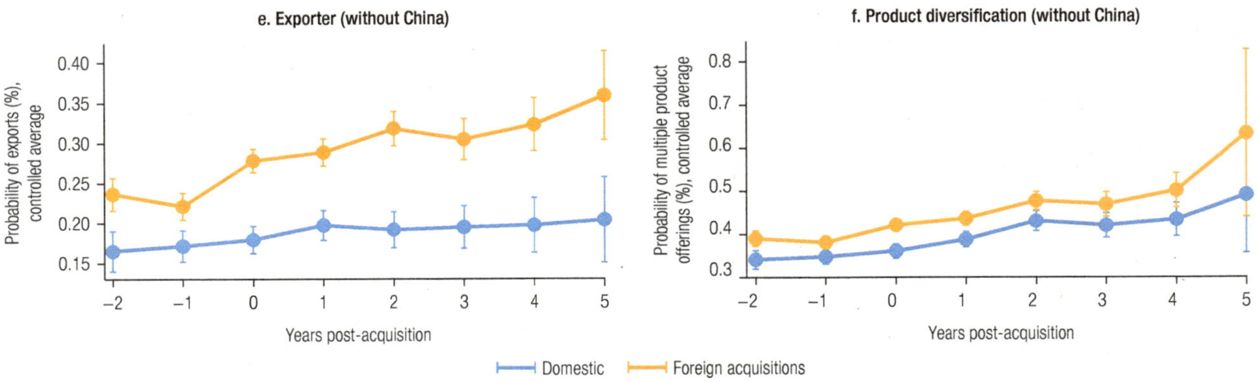

Source: World Bank calculations, based on industrial censuses from six countries.
Note: "Without China" refers to results for five countries: Côte d'Ivoire, Indonesia, Moldova, Serbia. and Vietnam. Industrial census data analyzed for this figure are further described in annex 2A, table 2A.1. "Domestic" refers to the firms that have not changed their ownership from local to foreign at any point in the observed sample. Growth paths of firm outcomes can be captured in a simple framework using an interaction between indicators of firm group (brownfield, domestic) and years after entry in the following specification: $y_{ics} = group_i \beta \cdot d_t + \alpha_{cs} + \delta d_{it_0} + \varepsilon_{ics}$. The sample is restricted to equinumerous groups of brownfield affiliates and domestic firms matched on the basis of employment, age, and sector, in the year before the firm was acquired. To account for differences that might be driven by country characteristics, sector composition, and macroeconomic trends, the regressions also control for country-sector fixed effects (FE) and year fixed effects. Regression includes country FE* 2-digit sector. Vertical bars indicate the margin of error.

countries excluding China (Côte d'Ivoire, Indonesia, Moldova, Serbia, and Vietnam) confirm greater value addition of foreign capital in some dimensions (figure 2.7, panels c–f). Acquired firms in these countries significantly increase their ability to access markets through exports and product diversification, while wages adjust to a higher level than expected. Specifically, by the fifth year following acquisition, the average brownfield affiliate has increased wages by 10–30 percent relative to no adjustment in the wages of domestic firms. The rise in labor remuneration reflects, at least partly, adjustment to a marginally higher level of productivity. These premiums for new brownfield affiliates persist for the observed period following acquisition.

These findings come with caveats. That ownership shares are unobserved dilutes potentially stronger impact in cases in which foreigners gain majority or full control of domestic firms.[7] Moreover, that the reported estimates are conditional on country and sectoral effects conceals important variations of benefits that are specific to these levels. Benefits from greater market access and diversification, for example, are expected to be more pronounced in manufacturing and primary commodities than in services. There are also a number of dimensions—such as liabilities and the skill composition of workforce, or relative measures such as export-to-sales ratio—where differences are less discernible in the sample studied following acquisition.

Overall, and despite important data limitations, the evidence supports a value addition of foreign investors in some key dimensions related to development, such as employment and market access complementing systemic benefits of acquisitions reported from other sources (box 2.3). The evidence also suggests that these advantages are more pronounced in markets that are less developed, smaller, or both, which is a general hypothesis warranting further investigation.

BOX 2.3

Systemic Benefits of Brownfield Foreign Direct Investment: Telecommunication Acquisitions in Africa

Starting in the mid-1990s, state-owned telecommunications operators in Africa were privatized in large numbers, with the vast majority acquired by foreign brownfield investors. Acquirers included global firms in the industry from Europe such as Orange, Vodafone, and Portugal Telecom, but also developing-country multinational firms such as Maroc Telecom, South Africa's MTN, and India's Bharti Airtel. The sector grew rapidly, with a subsequent phase of booming greenfield investment through license acquisitions and a wave of new brownfield investment in existing operators over the past decade.

Firms that were acquired by foreign investors often invested in network expansion and upgrade, especially for mobile and fixed internet access. Following the acquisition of Ghana Telecom, for example, Vodafone invested around US$1 billion in improving the digital infrastructure in the country. There were 400 sites in 2008, increased to more than 2,000 sites within six years.

Employment reductions during an initial restructuring of the acquired firms have not been rare but were often followed by fast growth and subsequent job creation. The acquisition of Burkina Faso's Airtel by Orange in 2016, for example, was associated with a drop of the enterprise's full-time headcount from 291 to 259, followed by a 10 percent average annual increase annually that increased the headcount to 365 by 2019. Jobs offered to local populations by these multinational firms often served as a vehicle for skills upgrade: in 2016, for example, 80 percent of the 20,000 employees of the Middle East and Africa branch of Orange received training averaging 26 hours.

Engagement of the operators in areas outside the strict boundaries of their markets has also been common. Orange funded the Africa Cup of Nations football tournament in 2013 and supported more than 30 rural radio stations in 13 counties by providing them access to free electricity 24 hours a day. In addition, it provided four incubators for entrepreneurs in four countries and six accelerators as well as programs and e-education services for digital skills to schoolchildren, university students, and young professionals in partnership with local ministries of education. Vodafone invested in Healthline in Ghana, the first medical call center in Africa.

The rapid growth has helped boost the economy and employment across Africa. In 2015, mobile technologies and services generated 6.7 percent of Africa's gross domestic product (GDP), or around US$150 billion in economic value. Africa's mobile ecosystem directly supported over 1 million jobs. The expansion of the sector has also supported an additional 2.4 million jobs indirectly through production inputs, wages, public funding, and profits spent in other sectors. This development has strengthened economic activity in other industries through improved information sharing and increased access to data and mobile broadband.

The outcomes of foreign acquisitions have been more spectacular in some countries than in others, with the context making a difference. Gasmi et al. (2013) note poor outcomes of some acquisitions in resource-scarce, landlocked African countries as well as in resource-rich African countries because of weak contractual design, inadequate policy enforcement in the infrastructure sector, and insufficient aggregate demand. The bundling of telecommunications with banking services allowed some incumbents to compete successfully against brownfield ventures in some markets. Sector-specific taxation imposes additional costs to the investor in others. Generally, in the absence of strong state capacity, competition is a necessary complement to foster development outcomes of such investments.

Sources: Estrin and Pelletier 2018; Gasmi et al. 2013; GSMA Intelligence 2016; GSM Association (GSMA) financial statements; Orange 2017; Staff 2015.

Policy Considerations for Brownfield FDI

A policy framework for foreign investment comprises incentives, rules, and restrictions that firms need to comply with through their life cycle. These policy elements are not systematically designed to favor one mode of foreign entry over another. Yet, typically, some are more relevant to investors entering through a particular mode or to sectors where brownfield investment takes place more intensively.

Investment Incentives by Mode of Entry

Investment incentives such as tax credits, preferential rates, or subsidies are commonly made conditional on characteristics of the firm. Most developing countries that grant tax holidays (77 percent) condition them on location requirements within the country (World Bank 2018). Less common is the requirement to export or to sell to exporting firms and engage in research and development (R&D). The mode of entry can be specified—as was done in the Czech Republic, Mozambique, or South Africa, where preferential treatments and concessions are explicitly applicable only to greenfield investments or acquired firms that plan on expanding production capacity—although no widespread discrimination has been reported in the literature over that dimension.[8]

Incentives are not often a deal breaker for foreign investment. They might add an important element to the equation when other, more fundamental components are present. Asset-seeking investment, such as FDI in natural resource sectors, tends to be less responsive to incentives (World Bank 2018), which suggests that any discrimination by mode of entry might be less relevant. But more generally, the signal that some foreign investors are less welcome than others can hurt the growth prospects of countries that would otherwise benefit from brownfield FDI in the medium term.

Sensitivity of Brownfield FDI to Investment Restrictions

Statutory restrictions on foreign investment generally apply to all modes of entry. Thresholds on foreign equity (for example, investment screenings), restrictions on movement of people, or repatriation of profits do not discriminate between newly established firms and brownfield ventures. They apply regardless of whether equity was acquired or created. By contrast, licensing requirements, or limitations on the number of firms in a market segment, are less relevant to firms that are already operating and, by extension, to brownfield investment targeting those firms.

Although most restrictions apply equally to all modes of entry, brownfield investment tends to be more sensitive than greenfield investment to the general severity of restrictions and to certain types of restrictions in particular. Evidence in the literature, while limited, finds that a similar reduction in total investment restrictions is associated with a greater increase in cross-border acquisitions than in greenfield foreign investment, independent of a country's size or level of development (Lee 2016; Mistura and Roulet 2019). This pattern could be partly explained by the greater frequency of acquisitions in services industries, which are also subject to higher restrictions.

Restrictions that are more frequently encountered in sectors where brownfield investment takes place, such as services, could have greater impact on that mode of entry. Restrictions on movement of people and on board nominations are examples that deter investment by hindering participation of foreign investors in development of the firm. This type of restriction can be particularly stringent when investment originates from other developing countries (Borchert, Gootiiz, and Mattoo 2012).

The limited evidence to date confirms that cross-border M&A is highly sensitive to variable requirements that are left to the discretion of authorities, such as investment screenings or economic needs tests (Lee 2016; Mistura and Roulet 2019). These procedures end up being more relevant to brownfield investment because of the prevailing ambiguity over the value this type of investment brings to the host economy. It is on the basis of this evidence that the rest of the policy discussion emphasizes investment screenings and variable requirements.

Investment screenings vary in scope and depth across countries; they tend to include a range of administrative burdens in terms of contracts and can be applied in nontransparent ways. Russia, for example, requires a national security review for foreign investments in more than 40 sectors but provides no criteria for evaluating an application on these grounds. In Tunisia, multiple sectors require preauthorization for foreign acquisitions of a majority share of a company, yet again without specific criteria for review.

Many countries do not screen prospective FDI extensively, although notable recipients of brownfield investment do, including China, India, Malaysia, Mexico, Russia, Tunisia, and Vietnam.[9] Investment screenings, moreover, are significantly on the rise in higher-income economies (UNCTAD 2019). By submitting more sectors or activities to review, lowering the triggering thresholds, or broadening the definition of foreign investment, countries increasingly strengthen these mechanisms. The risk of these policies is that they shape narratives and establish precedents that will likely influence the policy stance of developing countries in the future, either through reciprocity or established practice.

Competition Frameworks: Another Layer of Frictions

Several types of brownfield investment aiming at control or a vertical merger of acquired firms are also the subject to review from competition authorities because of their potential impact on market dynamics. The nexus between foreign investment and competition is loosely delimited in the literature, although there is general agreement that the feedback loops between the two are important.

Competition is typically enforced by an independent authority that has the capacity to detect anticompetitive behavior, such as collusion and abuses of dominance, as well as the power to penalize misbehavior. This authority typically requires notification of prospective M&A, issues approvals on the basis of its reviews of likely effects, and proposes remedies to minimize the anticompetitive effects of market consolidation.

In principle, the absence of proper competition enforcement can deter entry for both greenfield and brownfield investors. Private impediments to acquisitions, such as crossholding or tactical obstacles by incumbents, are common, all falling under the realm of competition barriers (Nolan 2019). These barriers can be addressed through a well-functioning competition authority that limits the ability of incumbents to deter entry.

In practice, the rules and their enforcement often pose additional burden to investors. Although more than 120 countries and regional blocs have relevant legal frameworks, implementation is limited in countries whose competition frameworks or authorities are more recent. In these cases, the administrative burden of information requirements, their cost, and the time they take can be an impediment to an acquisition of a firm. To minimize undue burdens on the investor, many competition authorities conduct two-phase investigations or have a formal simplified notification procedure for certain transactions that allow for fast-track decisions (World Bank 2016). This procedure filters out investments that are less likely to have an impact on competition.

The independent application of competition reviews and investment screenings by different authorities, under different frameworks, can be the source of numerous failures. Of 40 developing economies across regions surveyed by the World Bank in 2016, two-thirds keep the two processes separate.[10]

The frameworks are often disconnected not only in terms of the criteria used to evaluate transactions but also in their procedural requirements. Generally, although competition reviews are often more focused on efficiency considerations and potential market effects, public interest considerations are pervasive in investment assessment frameworks. Therefore, the degree of subjectivity of investment reviews is higher, and so is the uncertainty of the process. The lack of predictability can be potentially discouraging for brownfield investments that qualify for such review.

An alternative proposed by some practitioners is to merge the two processes into one, in a so-called single-review model (Bakhoum and Fox 2019). An example of full convergence on the substantive criteria to review mergers and investment is South Africa, where the investment framework specifically delegates the review to the competition control framework.[11] The adoption of that model remains the exception rather than the rule in practice.

Overall, a policy framework that supports brownfield investment should emphasize the following:

- *Streamline investment screening mechanisms and approvals, focusing on transparency, well-defined criteria, consistency with competition frameworks, reliable time frames for reviews and decisions, and judicial redress for the investor.* Clearly defined methodologies to assess "public interest" could expand the empirical basis underpinning the assessments and increase the efficiency of the process. In addition, a multilateral investment facilitation framework would go a long way toward improving the transparency and predictability of a range of other administrative procedures to deal with investments.[12] International rules for investment facilitation are rare (Polanco Lazo 2018). Only a few international investment agreements cover rules on the facilitation of business activity.
- *Increase the efficiency of competition policies to reduce the administrative burden of controls, strengthen enforcement capacity, and reduce the scope for tactical impediments to foreign acquisitions by incumbents.* The objective here is to both safeguard competition and minimize the burden of administrative procedures on business by using public resources more effectively, ultimately fostering the international exposure of markets. Competition authorities are often ill equipped to deliver these mandates in lower-income countries (Berger, Gsell, and Olekseyuk 2019; World Bank 2016).
- *Enhance cooperation between competition and investment authorities with a view to reducing inconsistencies between different time lines for reviews, different thresholds and considerations triggering review, or their mandatory nature.* This cooperation stands to facilitate both processes without necessarily compromising their content: independent assessments of competition effects are essential to market well-being. A wider application of the single-review model, along with improvements in its design, could potentially prove beneficial in countries where brownfield investment is rising fast.
- *Avoid differential treatment of brownfield multinationals with respect to investment incentives.* Although more information is necessary to assess the extent of discrimination in this area, and its potential cost, eligibility for incentives is an essential element of a supportive framework for brownfield investment. It is also an element that ensures that the right signals are being sent to investors likely to enter in that mode.
- *Address operational barriers to multinationals, such as to movement of people and board nominations, to facilitate participation of foreign investors in development of the firm.* Many of these restrictions are not specific to brownfield investment but are more frequently encountered in sectors where this mode of entry is more intensive, such as services,

and can be particularly stringent with respect to investment originating from other developing countries.

The reasons why brownfield investment is more common in higher-income economies extend beyond the specific considerations already discussed. By engaging actively in the process of improving institutions and laying strong market foundations, governments are supporting brownfield investment without that necessarily being the explicit objective. Stronger institutions ensure the protection of intellectual property, respect of contractual arrangements, and shareholders' minority rights, all of which make this mode of entry more appealing. The growth of viable stock markets and successful firms that are attractive for foreign investment can have the same effect. Causality could go in both directions, as brownfield acquisitions can potentially bring longer-term benefits like stronger corporate governance, which in turn can foster stronger institutions (Bris, Brisley, and Cabolis 2008).

Concluding Remarks

This study documents the characteristics, growth paths, and outcomes of multinational firms established through brownfield investment relative to those established through greenfield investment and domestic firms in six developing countries to shed additional light on their contribution. A key takeaway from this analysis is that brownfield affiliates add value to the development process in ways that do not differ in their essence from those established through greenfield investment.

Although more evidence is necessary to establish general conclusions and macroeconomic effects, the experience of the six countries analyzed in this study suggests that foreign acquisitions could be adding more value in markets at the lower end of the development spectrum—that is, in countries where most FDI still takes place through greenfield investment. The findings reported here could therefore be more relevant for fast growing, lower-middle-income economies where the share of foreign acquisitions is rising. They could also be more relevant for attracting investment into sectors where brownfield investment takes place more frequently, such as agriculture or services. Governments in these contexts have the means to foster the potential of foreign acquisitions by addressing administrative frictions, enhancing the predictability of controls, and safeguarding competition.

Future research should expand the evidence base with analysis of outcomes of acquisitions over longer periods of time and in different country contexts. Additional evidence would also be warranted on the effects of acquisitions of intangible as opposed to tangible assets, as well as on the development effects on the acquiring firm, motivated by the booming outward investment from major developing economies to the rest of the world. All these extensions will allow a more nuanced case to be made for brownfield investment in the development process.

Finally, assessing the extent of "masked effects" of this mode of entry on domestic firms that would otherwise exit the market, saving jobs and revenue, could shed light on the ways that brownfield investment contributes to sustaining economic activity that other modes of foreign entry cannot. Coupled with a systematic mapping of competition and investment screening frameworks, this evidence could improve technical assistance to developing countries and attract more investment that works for development.

Annex 2A. Data Sources

UNCTAD Aggregate Data

Cross-border mergers and acquisitions (M&A) statistical sources from the United Nations Conference on Trade and Development (UNCTAD) are based on information reported by Thomson Reuters. Such M&A conform to the standard definition of foreign direct investment (FDI) as far as the equity share is concerned. However, the data also include purchases via domestic and international capital markets, which should not be considered to be FDI flows. Cases of round-tripping (also known as round-trip transactions) are also considered on the basis of the immediate acquiring country and immediate target country principles.

Data on announced greenfield FDI projects sourced from UNCTAD are based on the information provided by fDI Markets, a service of the *Financial Times* (https://www.fdimarkets.com/). fDI Markets tracks all new investment projects and expansion of existing investments but does not include information on the equity participation by investors. This suggests that the data may include investments that are not qualified as FDI. Joint ventures are also included only where they lead to a new physical operation.

Industrial Censuses

The cross-country microeconomic evidence draws firm and establishment survey or census longitudinal data from the six developing countries investigated in this study: China, Côte d'Ivoire, Indonesia, Moldova, Serbia, and Vietnam. For the growth path analysis, this study analyzed all cohorts of firms whose entry as well as survival for at least five years was observed (table 2A.1).

Cross-country, firm-level data have important limitations. One of the most critical concerns is the issue of comparability of employment and capital measures, which can vary from one survey to another. Harmonization has been undertaken to address this issue. However, the analysis is necessarily constrained by the data available (or not available) in the raw surveys or censuses. In addition, all surveys available for this study record foreign ownership as a binary indicator (yes or no), bundling portfolio investment of less than 10 percent with FDI (>10 percent of total assets) and not allowing a separate treatment of majority-owned affiliated of foreign firms, where effects of acquisitions could be more pronounced.

TABLE 2A.1 Industrial Census Data Used for Cross-Country Analysis

				Full sample				*Sample of firms whose entry is observed*			
					Observations				*Observations*		
Country	*GDP per capita (2017)*	*Time coverage*	*Restrictions*	*Firms*	*Total*	*MNE*	*Brownfield MNE*	*Firms*	*Total*	*MNE*	*Brownfield MNE*
China	8,827	1998–2007	Manufacturing firms (legally independent subsidiaries) with sales ≥ RMB 5 million	570,108	2,048,525	421,544	32,759	292,978	829,869	173,041	10,184
Côte d'Ivoire	1,662	2003–13	Firms in all sectors	40,424	75,326	11,127	7,937	29,380	45,541	6,063	2,290
Indonesia	3,847	2010–15	Manufacturing establishments with at least 20 employees (L ≥ 20)	33,131	169,324	15,985	5,014	6,768	19,097	1,363	712
Moldova	2,290	2004–14	Firms in all sectors	31,591	122,423	12,895	1,566	31,295	120,699	12,874	1,566
Serbia	5,900	2006–16	Firms in all sectors, with at least 6 employees (L ≥ 6)	35,402	159,487	14,029	827	10,698	31,798	3,880	171
Vietnam	2,343	2007–12	Full census of large firms, limited information on small firms	504,916	1,573,373	13,248	5,858	289,779	777,300	2,641	1,797

Source: Data provided by country authorities to the World Bank Group.
Note: GDP = gross domestic product; L = number of employees; MNE = multinational enterprise; RMB = renminbi.

Annex 2B. Relative Importance of Country-Level versus Sectoral Factors in Favoring Greenfield or Brownfield Investment

TABLE 2B.1 Variance Decomposition

Source	Partial SS	Df	F	Prob > F (%)	Contribution to model SS (%)
Model	**1,042.00**	**1,327**	**13.21**	**0.00**	**42.9**
Country	21.38	5	71.96	0.00	2.1
Sector	8.49	86	1.66	0.01	0.8
Year	18.61	17	18.42	0.00	1.8
country*sector	36.16	263	2.31	0.00	3.5
country*year	237.41	31	128.87	0.00	22.8
sector*year	124.35	925	2.26	0.00	11.9

Source: World Bank calculations, based on industrial censuses.
Note: Industrial census data came from six countries: China, Côte d'Ivoire, Indonesia, Moldova, Serbia, and Vietnam (further described in annex 2A). Variance components are estimated on the linear probability of a multinational firm transitioning to foreign ownership from domestic status at some point during the period it is observed; on country, sector, and year fixed effects; and on their two-way interactions. Df = degrees of freedom; F = F-value; SS = sums of squares.

Annex 2C. Evolution of Brownfield MNE Characteristics over Time

FIGURE 2C.1 Evolution of Brownfield MNE Characteristics over Time

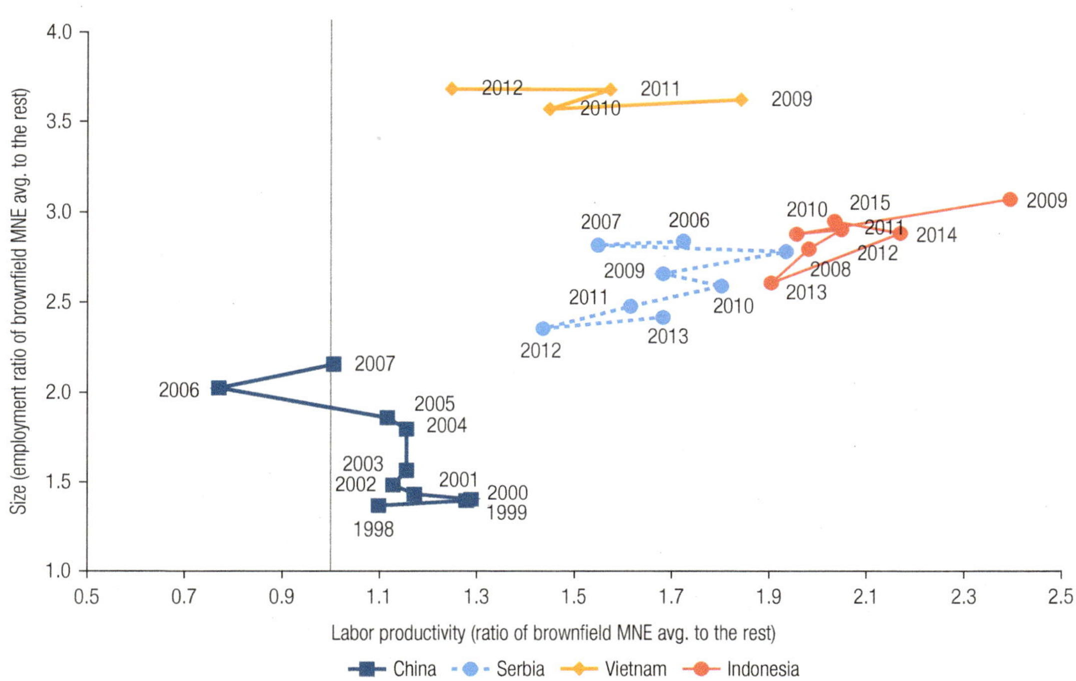

Source: World Bank calculations, based on industrial censuses from four countries.
Note: Industrial census data analyzed for this figure are further described in annex 2A, table 2A.1. MNE = multinational enterprise.

Notes

1. Notable exceptions of research focusing on employment and productivity of acquired firms in the context of a single developing country are Gong, Görg, and Maioli (2007) (China); Arnold and Javorcik (2009) (Indonesia); Lipsey, Sjöholm, and Sun (2013) (Indonesia); and Bircan (2019) (Turkey).
2. Nocke and Yeaple (2008) find this for multinational enterprises (MNEs) making brownfield investments in the United States, while Raff, Ryan, and Stähler (2011) find a similar pattern in Japan.
3. Geluebcke (2015) shows the negative impacts of foreign take-overs on employment in Germany. Bellak, Pfaffermayr, and Wild (2006), Martins and Esteves (2008), and Mattes (2010) find no statistically significant impact of foreign acquisitions on the employment reduction in Austria, Brazil, and Germany, respectively. Yet foreign ownership is found to contribute to formal employment in developing countries like Indonesia (Lipsey, Sjöholm, and Sun 2013) and in Nigeria's manufacturing sector (Inekwe 2013), as well as China (Gong, Görg, and Maioli 2007), in addition to some high-income countries including New Zealand (Fabling and Sanderson 2014), Portugal (Almeida 2007), and Sweden (Bandick and Görg 2010).
4. Data are from the World Bank's *Doing Business* Indicators database (accessed December 2019), https://www.doingbusiness.org/.
5. The growth and evolution of firms continue after the first five years of their operations. However, data constraints allow examination of cohorts of firms through the end of the seventh year without major loss of statistical power. The paths in cohorts with that duration do not differ substantially in any of the dimensions discussed.
6. Propensity score matching for this exercise implements the full Mahalanobis matching based on employment, age, sector, and year to adjust for pretreatment observable differences between a group of firms targeted by foreign investors and firms that remained domestic throughout the observed period. Matching is performed separately for each country, one-to-one with the nearest neighbor the year before acquisition takes place. Weights are not used in the transformation paths.
7. In a seminal contribution 10 years ago, Arnold and Javorcik (2009) reported that foreign acquisitions of more than 20 percent equity had stronger effects in nearly 400 establishments in Indonesia: an average 24 percent increase in employment and 40 percent increase in wages within the first two years following acquisition.
8. In South Africa, for example, the additional investment allowance for industrial policy projects may not exceed R 900 million for any greenfield project with a preferred status, R 550 million for any other greenfield project, R 550 million for any brownfield project with a preferred status, or R 350 million for any other brownfield project.
9. Data on FDI screening come from the World Development Indicators database and the OECD FDI Restrictiveness Index 2017 (https://www.oecd.org/investment/fdiindex.htm).
10. According to a review of country-specific merger control and foreign investment regimes in 40 developing economies in multiple regions in 2016, 86 percent of countries have a predefined merger control framework, and only 70 percent have investment review mechanisms (World Bank 2016). Where investment control frameworks exist, the institutions in charge of the review as well as the regulatory framework applied tend to be both economywide as well as sector specific.
11. The exceptions are certain sectors that require government approval for foreign participation, including energy, mining, banking, insurance, and defense.
12. In 2017, during the 11th World Trade Organization (WTO) Ministerial Conference in Buenos Aires, 70 WTO members adopted a "Joint Statement on Investment Facilitation for Development," announcing discussions toward a multilateral framework on investment facilitation (WTO 2017). The discussions aim primarily at achieving transparency and predictability of investment measures; streamlining and speeding up administrative procedures and requirements; and enhancing international cooperation, information sharing, the exchange of best practices, and relations with relevant stakeholders, including dispute prevention.

References

Alfaro, Laura. 2017. "Gains from Foreign Direct Investment: Macro and Micro Approaches." *The World Bank Economic Review* 30 (Supplement 1): 2–15.

Almeida, Rita. 2007. "The Labor Market Effects of Foreign-Owned Firms." *Journal of International Economics* 72 (1): 75–96.

Alquist, Ron, Rahul Mukherjee, and Linda Tesar. 2016. "Fire-Sale FDI or Business as Usual?" *Journal of International Economics* 98: 93–113.

Arnold, Jens Matthias, and Beata S. Javorcik. 2009. "Gifted Kids or Pushy Parents? Foreign Direct Investment and Plant Productivity in Indonesia." *Journal of International Economics* 79 (1): 42–53.

Bakhoum, Mor, and Eleanor M. Fox. 2019. *Making Markets Work for Africa: Markets, Development, and Competition Law in Sub-Saharan Africa.* Oxford: Oxford University Press.

Balsvik, Ragnhild, and Stefanie A. Haller. 2010. "Picking 'Lemons' or Picking 'Cherries'? Domestic and Foreign Acquisitions in Norwegian Manufacturing." *Scandinavian Journal of Economics* 112 (2): 361–87.

Bandick, Roger, and Holger Görg. 2010. "Foreign Acquisition, Plant Survival, and Employment Growth." *Canadian Journal of Economics* 43 (2): 547–73.

Bandick, Roger, and Patrik Karpaty. 2007. "Foreign Acquisition and Employment Effects in Swedish Manufacturing." Research Paper No. 2007/35, University of Nottingham, U.K.

Beattie, Alan. 2014. "Foreign Direct Investment: It's Not All Good." *Financial Times,* October 22 (accessed March 23, 2019), https://www.ft.com/content/6f71229d-d74d-34fa-a30d-39e4ac07de8b.

Bellak, Christian, Michael Pfaffermayr, and Michael Wild. 2006. "Firm Performance after Ownership Change: A Matching Estimator Approach." *Applied Economics Quarterly* 52 (1): 29–54.

Berger, Axel, Sebastian Gsell, and Zoryana Olekseyuk. 2019. "Investment Facilitation for Development: A New Route to Global Investment Governance." Briefing Paper No. 5/2019, German Development Institute (DIE), Bonn.

Bertrand, Olivier, Katariina Nilsson Hakkala, Pehr-Johan Norbäck, and Lars Persson. 2012. "Should Countries Block Foreign Takeovers of R&D Champions and Promote Greenfield Entry?" *Canadian Journal of Economics* 45 (3): 1083–124.

Bircan, Çağatay. 2019. "Ownership Structure and Productivity of Multinationals." *Journal of International Economics* 116: 125–43.

Borchert, Ingo, Batshur Gootiiz, and Aaditya Mattoo. 2012. "Policy Barriers to International Trade in Services: Evidence from a New Database." Policy Research Working Paper 6109, World Bank, Washington, DC.

Bris, Arturo, Neil Brisley, and Christos Cabolis. 2008. "Adopting Better Corporate Governance: Evidence from Cross-Border Mergers." *Journal of Corporate Finance* 14 (3): 224–40.

Burger, Martijn J., and Elena I. Ianchovichina. 2017. "Surges and Stops in Greenfield and M&A FDI Flows to Developing Countries: Analysis by Mode of Entry." *Review of World Economics* 153 (2): 411–32.

Calderón, Cesar, Norman Loayza, and Luis Servén. 2004. "Greenfield Foreign Direct Investment and Mergers and Acquisitions: Feedback and Macroeconomic Effects." World Bank Policy Research Paper 3192, World Bank, Washington, DC.

Chari, Anusha, Paige P. Ouimet, and Linda Tesar. 2010. "The Value of Control in Emerging Markets." *Review of Financial Studies* 23 (4): 1741–70.

Claeys, Sophie, and Christa Hainz. 2007. "Acquisition versus Greenfield: The Impact of the Mode of Foreign Bank Entry on Information and Bank Lending Rates." Working Paper Series No. 210, Sveriges Riksbank (Central Bank of Sweden), Stockholm.

Conyon, Martin J., Sourafel Girma, Steve Thompson, and Peter W. Wright. 2002. "The Productivity and Wage Effects of Foreign Acquisition in the United Kingdom." *Journal of Industrial Economics* 50 (1): 85–102.

Curran, Louise, Ping Lv, and Francesa Spigarelli. 2017. "Chinese Investment in the EU Renewable Energy Sector: Motives, Synergies and Policy Implications." *Energy Policy* 101: 670–82.

Davies, Ronald B., Rodolphe Desbordes, and Anna Ray. 2018. "Greenfield versus Merger and Acquisition FDI: Same Wine, Different Bottles?" *Canadian Journal of Economics* 51 (4): 1151–90.

di Giovanni, Julian. 2005. "What Drives Capital Flows? The Case of Cross-Border M&A Activity and Financial Deepening." *Journal of International Economics* 65 (1): 127–49.

Erel, Isil, Rose Liao, and Michael Weisbach. 2011. "Determinants of Cross-Border Mergers and Acquisitions." *Journal of Finance* 67 (3): 1045–82.

Estrin, Saul, and Adeline Pelletier. 2018. "Privatization in Developing Countries: What Are the Lessons of Recent Experience?" *The World Bank Research Observer* 33 (1): 65–102.

Fabling, Richard, and Lynda Sanderson. 2014. "Foreign Acquisition and the Performance of New Zealand Firms." *New Zealand Economic Papers* 48 (1): 1–20.

Gasmi, Farid, Alexis Maingard, Paul Noumba Um, and Laura Recuero Virto. 2013. "The Privatization of the Fixed-Line Telecommunications Operator in OECD, Latin America, Asia, and Africa: One Size Does Not Fit All." *World Development* 45: 189–208.

Geluebcke, John P. 2015. "The Impact of Foreign Takeovers: Comparative Evidence from Foreign and Domestic Acquisitions in Germany." *Applied Economics* 47 (7–9): 739–55.

Gong, Yundan, Holger Görg, and Sara Maioli. 2007. "Employment Effects of Privatisation and Foreign Acquisition of Chinese State-Owned Enterprises." *International Journal of the Economics of Business* 14 (2): 197–214.

Grzegorz, Pac. 2014. "Foreign Acquisition and Post-Privatization Exit of State-Owned Firms." *Journal of International Trade & Economic Development* 23 (4): 540–77.

GSMA Intelligence. 2016. "The Mobile Economy: Africa 2016." Report, GSMA Intelligence, GSM Association, London.

Guadalupe, Maria, Olga Kuzmina, and Catherine Thomas. 2012. "Innovation and Foreign Ownership." *American Economic Review* 102 (7): 3594–627.

Hale, Galina, and Mingzhi Xu. 2016. "FDI Effects on the Labor Market of Host Countries." Working Paper 2016-25, Federal Reserve Bank of San Francisco.

Harms, Philipp, and Pierre-Guillaume Meon. 2018. "Good and Useless FDI: The Growth Effects of Greenfield Investment and Mergers and Acquisitions." *Review of International Economics* 26 (1): 37–59.

Inekwe, John Nkwoma. 2013. "FDI, Employment and Economic Growth in Nigeria." *African Development Review* 25 (4): 421–33.

Krugman, Paul. 2000. "Fire-Sale FDI." In *Capital Flows and the Emerging Economies: Theory, Evidence, and Controversies*, edited by Sebastian Edwards, 43–58. Chicago: University of Chicago Press.

Lee, Hyun-Hoon. 2016. "Policy Factors Influencing FDI Inflows to Developing Countries." Background paper for *Asian Economic Integration Report 2016: What Drives Foreign Direct Investment in Asia and the Pacific?* Manila: Asian Development Bank.

Lejárraga, Iza, and Alexandros Ragoussis. 2018. "Beyond Capital: Monitoring Development Outcomes of Multinational Enterprises." Policy Research Working Paper 8686, World Bank, Washington, DC.

Lichtenberg, Frank R., and Donald Siegel. 2000. "Productivity and Changes in Ownership of Manufacturing Plants." In *Innovation, Evolution of Industry and Economic Growth*, edited by David B. Audretsch and Steven Klepper, 322–62. Cheltenham, U.K.: Edward Elgar Publishing.

Lipsey, Robert E., Fredrik Sjöholm, and Jing Sun. 2013. "Foreign Ownership and Employment Growth in a Developing Country." *Journal of Development Studies* 49 (8): 1133–47.

Maksimovic, Vojislav, and Gordon Phillips. 2001. "The Market for Corporate Assets: Who Engages in Mergers and Asset Sales and Are There Efficiency Gains?" *Journal of Finance* 56 (6): 2019–65.

Maksimovic, Vojislav, Gordon Phillips, and Nagpurnanand Prabhala. 2008. "Post-Merger Restructuring and the Boundaries of the Firm." *Journal of Financial Economics* 102 (2): 317–43.

Martins, Pedro S., and Luiz Alberto Esteves. 2008. "Foreign Ownership, Employment and Wages in Brazil: Evidence from Acquisitions, Divestments and Job Movers." Discussion Paper No. 3542, Institute of Labor Economics (IZA), Bonn.

Mattes, Anselm. 2010. "International M&A: Evidence on Effects of Foreign Takeovers." Discussion Paper 60, Institute for Applied Economic Research (IAW), Tübingen, Germany.

Milliou, Chrysovalantou, and Apostolis Pavlou. 2014. "Foreign Direct Investment Modes and Local Backward Linkages." Working Paper Series 4623, CESifo Group, Munich.

Mistura, Fernando, and Caroline Roulet. 2019. "The Determinants of Foreign Direct Investment: Do Statutory Restrictions Matter?" Working Papers on International Investment 2019/01, Organisation for Economic Co-operation and Development (OECD), Paris.

Nocke, Volker, and Stephen Yeaple. 2008. "An Assignment Theory of Foreign Direct Investment." *Review of Economic Studies* 75 (2): 529–57.

Nolan, Marcus. 2019. "Competition Policy and FDI: A Solution in Search of a Problem?" Working Paper No. 99-3, Peterson Institute for International Economics, Washington, DC.

OECD (Organisation for Economic Co-operation and Development). 2012. "Cross-Border Merger Control: Challenges for Developing and Emerging Economies." Competition Policy Roundtable proceedings, DAF/COMP/GF(2011)13, OECD Publishing, Paris.

Orange. 2017. "Orange–Action Statement: Support for Innovative Digital Ecosystems in Middle East and Africa." Note for the Make-IT Alliance, Orange, Paris.

Polanco Lazo, Rodrigo. 2018. "Facilitation 2.0: Investment and Trade in the Digital Age." Paper produced under the RTA Exchange of the International Centre for Trade and Sustainable Development (ICTSD), Geneva; and Inter-American Development Bank (IDB), Washington, DC.

Raff, Horst, Michael Ryan, and Frank Stähler. 2011. "Firm Productivity and the Foreign-Market Entry Decision." Working Paper, Kiel University, Kiel, Germany.

Roberto, Basile. 2004. "Acquisition versus Greenfield Investment: The Location of Foreign Manufacturers in Italy." *Regional Science and Urban Economics* 34 (1): 3–25.

Schoar, Antoinette. 2002. "Effects of Corporate Diversification on Productivity." *Journal of Finance* 57 (6): 2379–403.

Staff, Matthew. 2015. "Ghana Undergoes a Vodafone Transformation." *Africa Outlook* 23/24: 26–41.

UNCTAD (United Nations Conference on Trade and Development). 2000. *World Investment Report 2000: Cross-Border Mergers and Acquisitions and Development.* New York and Geneva: United Nations.

UNCTAD. 2019. *World Investment Report 2019: Special Economic Zones.* New York: United Nations.

Wang, Miao, and Man C. Sunny Wong. 2009. "What Drives Economic Growth? The Case of Cross-Border M&A and Greenfield FDI Activities." *Kyklos* 62 (2): 316–30.

World Bank. 2016. *Breaking Down Barriers: Unlocking Africa's Potential Through Vigorous Competition Policy.* Washington, DC: World Bank.

World Bank. 2018. *Global Investment Competitiveness Report 2017/2018: Foreign Investor Perspectives and Policy Implications.* Washington, DC: World Bank

WTO (World Trade Organization). 2017. "Joint Ministerial Statement on Investment Facilitation for Development." Adopted at the 11th Ministerial Conference, December 13, WTO, Geneva. https://docs.wto.org/dol2fe/Pages/FE_Search/FE_S_S009-DP.aspx?language=E&CatalogueIdList=240870.

3 The Distributional Effects of FDI: Evidence from Ethiopia, Vietnam, and Turkey

Victor Steenbergen and Trang Thu Tran

Key Findings

- **Many countries aim to attract foreign investment to help create jobs and reduce poverty.** Yet empirical evidence on the direct poverty-reducing effects of FDI is surprisingly scarce, especially in developing countries. Little is also known about the aggregate effects of FDI on income distributions.
- **Analysis of unique firm-level and household data from Ethiopia, Vietnam, and Turkey shows that FDI firms create new jobs and pay higher wages than domestic firms.** Workers in sectors and regions with higher foreign-firm presence are generally more likely to be formally employed and receive higher wages. FDI allowed more than 350,000 individuals to enter formal manufacturing employment in Vietnam between 2007 and 2016, and at least 40,000 in Turkey between 2009 and 2016. FDI also raised average manufacturing wages by 32 percent in Ethiopia, 12 percent in Vietnam, and 8 percent in Turkey.
- **Consequently, FDI-induced wage increases helped reduce poverty in all three countries.** Conservative estimates suggest that FDI contributed to lifting at least 35,000 individuals out of poverty in Ethiopia during 2009–14; 24,000 in Vietnam (2007–16); and 15,000 in Turkey (2009–16). Although the FDI-induced wage increases helped improve the incomes of the bottom 40 percent of the population in all three countries, the effects across the entire income distribution differed significantly across countries. In Ethiopia, the benefits of FDI were more concentrated in the bottom 40 percent, while in Vietnam, the welfare gains were evenly distributed across the income distribution. Turkey had the greatest average wage benefits from FDI but also experienced increases in wage inequality.
- **However, FDI can also contribute to inequality by disproportionately benefiting better-educated and higher-skilled workers.** When comparing regions and sectors with higher FDI activity with those with no FDI, higher-skilled workers experience large benefits, while low-skilled workers may see no changes or even experience relative short-term declines in formal employment and wages.
- **The possible adverse effects of FDI on income inequality and on lower-skilled workers emphasize the importance of a country's labor market and education policies.** Key policies include strengthening the absorptive capacity of domestic firms and workers (for example, through programs that foster FDI-supplier linkages and employment training); supporting vulnerable communities (such as lower-skilled workers, youths, and women) with active jobs information, provision, and skills certification; and establishing programs to stimulate labor mobility within countries.

Introduction

Many countries around the world aim to attract foreign investment to help create jobs and reduce poverty. Yet direct empirical evidence on the direct poverty-reducing effects of foreign direct investment (FDI) is surprisingly scarce. Most of the earlier literature focused on the ability of FDI to raise economic growth, which in turn is associated with reductions in poverty (Chen and Ravallion 2007). However, it is notably difficult to estimate the growth effects of FDI precisely (Lipsey 2003). FDI's poverty-alleviating effects may also be greater or less than average because of its direct influence on a country's aggregate employment numbers and average wages (Nunnenkamp, Schweickert, and Wiebelt 2007).

A second generation of literature then argued that FDI helps raise household income because formal firms pay premium wages.[1] While important, this literature focuses on firm-level effects. This can present a biased picture because foreign-owned firms may be "cherry-picking" the most productive workers, possibly leading to labor shifts among firms with no real change in overall employment or household income. Using firm-level data also means that the aggregate effects on labor markets that most policy makers care about (such as creation of formal jobs and growth in average wages) cannot be observed. To better establish the relationship between FDI and development, it is therefore important to consider FDI's effect at the household level. So far, robust economic analysis doing so has been limited.

Little is also known about the aggregate effect of FDI on income distributions. This relationship has become particularly important in recent years, as backlashes against globalization have been attributed to growing concerns around the effects of trade and investment on rising levels of income inequality. This may have played a role in reducing investor confidence and FDI flows in recent years (see Overview).

Recent findings about trade liberalization indeed confirm that some evidence backs such popular sentiments. For higher-income countries, import liberalization may have increased competition in less-skilled, labor-intensive industries while favoring demand for skilled workers (Acemoglu and Autor 2011; Acemoglu and Restrepo 2017; Goldberg and Pavcnik 2007; Maloney and Molina 2016; Michaels, Natraj, and Van Reenen 2014; Pavcnik 2017). Tariff reductions on Chinese products contributed to substantial job losses in US manufacturing in the 1990s and 2000s (Autor, Dorn, and Hanson 2013; Pierce and Schott 2016). Similarly, in Brazil, trade liberalization and import competition strongly affected local labor markets, resulting in wage increases for skilled workers but wage declines for unskilled workers. These effects persisted up to 20 years after import liberalization (Dix-Carneiro and Kovak 2015).

It is important to better understand the role that FDI plays in national income distributions. This could help counter nationalist sentiments around FDI by providing opposing evidence or by stressing the need for complementary interventions that proactively address FDI's impact on income inequality. To do so, it is critical to understand the potential impact that FDI may have across different countries, sectors, and workers with different skill levels.

This study aims to answer two vital questions around the contribution of FDI to development:

- How does the presence of FDI firms influence labor market outcomes (formal employment and wages)?
- What are the effects of FDI firms' presence on poverty and income distributions?

This analysis will help demonstrate the effects of FDI on jobs and offer practical insights into how investment promotion can support inclusive growth. It will investigate the effect of FDI presence on the World Bank Group's twin goals to end extreme poverty and boost shared prosperity.[2]

This report also ties in with the wider discussions around FDI and development and relates to the renewed focus by the United Nations (UN), Organisation for Economic Co-operation and Development (OECD), and others on "Promoting Investment in the Sustainable Development Goals" (UNCTAD 2018).[3]

To examine the effects of FDI, this chapter studies three countries where FDI increased greatly in the past 20 years: Ethiopia, Vietnam, and Turkey (in order of lowest to highest income level). The analysis links firm-level data with household survey data to examine the effect that economic activity from multinational enterprises (MNEs) has on local labor market outcomes (jobs and wages).

The analysis focuses on MNE presence rather than FDI inflows for two reasons: First, FDI inflow data broken down by sector are rarely available across countries. Second, FDI inflows merely measure the amount of cross-border financing, which may or may not materialize into meaningful economic activities. By focusing on the activity of MNEs, this study follows recent research that has increasingly analyzed firm-level operational data to better understand the impact of FDI on host economies (Alfaro and Chauvin, forthcoming; Antràs and Yeaple 2014).

The exercise exploits variations in MNE total sales (as a share of a sector's and region's total output) to compare the formal employment and average wages of workers employed in sectors and regions with higher MNE activity with those with lower MNE activity. To explore the distributional impact of FDI firms, the analysis focuses on the potential skill bias by comparing the effects of MNE activities on labor market outcomes in higher- and lower-skilled sectors and for workers with different education levels. It uses these estimated effects to estimate a simple back-of-the-envelope counterfactual income (without MNE activities). From this, it assesses the aggregate effect of FDI on poverty reduction and shared prosperity (income gain of the bottom 40 percent). Income equality is measured through two metrics: the Gini coefficient and the Palma ratio (the ratio of the richest 10 percent of the population's share of gross national income divided by the poorest 40 percent's share).

The analysis finds that increases in MNE activities have a significant differential effect on formal job creation and wages. Workers in sectors and regions with a higher share of MNE output are more likely to be formally employed and receive higher wages (relative to workers in sectors with a lower share of MNE output). In aggregate, the estimations suggest the following:

- *In Vietnam,* on average, FDI has contributed to more than 350,000 individuals switching from informal to formal manufacturing employment each year between 2007 and 2016. FDI also resulted in 12 percent higher wages in manufacturing and 2 percent higher wages in services.
- *In Turkey,* manufacturing FDI is associated with around 40,000 additional formal jobs from 2009 to 2016 annually and an 8 percent increase in average wages. No effects were identified on formal employment or on average wages in Turkey's services sector.
- *In Ethiopia,* aggregate formal employment effects are insignificant, but FDI contributed to a large increase (32 percent) in manufacturing wages. No information was available for Ethiopia's services.

FDI-induced growth in formal jobs and wages has translated into increased shared prosperity and reduced poverty. The wage benefits from FDI were positive and sizable for all three countries studied. Yet, the distributional effects differ across countries (figure 3.1):

- *In Ethiopia,* the wage effects from low-skilled manufacturing FDI are highly positive but limited in magnitude because of the manufacturing sector's small scale. The income benefits are with the bottom 40 percent and linked to declining income inequality. Wage increases from FDI are

FIGURE 3.1 FDI Has Had Varied Effects on National Income Distributions in Ethiopia, Vietnam, and Turkey

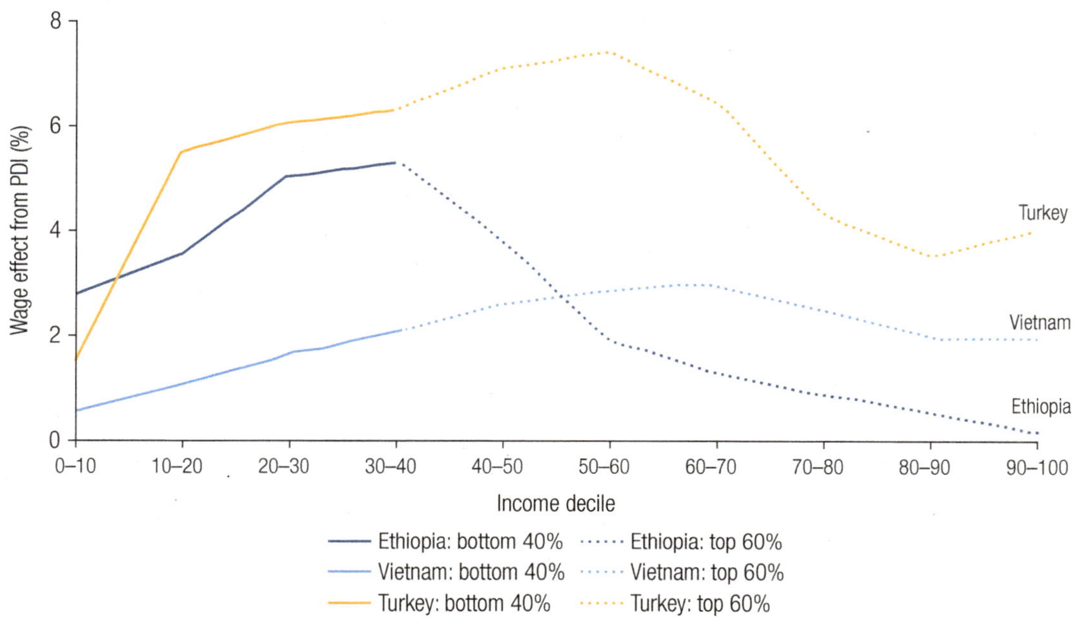

Source: World Bank.
Note: FDI = foreign direct investment.

found to have reduced poverty for at least 35,000 individuals between 2009 and 2014.

- *In Vietnam,* the wage benefits from FDI have also been positive and are the most widespread and evenly distributed across incomes. Corresponding to these effects, FDI has almost no effect on income inequality. These wage increases from FDI contributed to lifting at least 24,000 individuals out of poverty between 2007 and 2016.
- *In Turkey,* FDI had the largest average wage benefits across the three countries. It increased average wage income for the bottom 40 percent and helped reduce poverty for over 15,000 individuals between 2009 and 2016. However, FDI was associated with substantial benefits for high-skilled workers and evidence of displacement and potential wage reductions for the lowest-skilled workers—thus contributing to increased income inequality.

The aggregate FDI effects across the three countries mask significant variations by sectors and workers' education levels (summarized in table 3.1). In general, the average effects of FDI on formal employment and wages are positive for manufacturing and high-skilled services but neutral for extractives and low-skilled services.

There is also evidence of FDI's skill premium. In regions and sectors with higher MNE activity, higher-skilled workers experience large increases, while low-skilled workers may see no changes or relative declines in formal employment and wages (relative to the sectors not receiving FDI). The skill premium is more pronounced in services than in manufacturing.

This analysis suggests that FDI, especially in tradable sectors, can contribute meaningfully to development by stimulating formal job creation, poverty reduction, and shared prosperity. FDI brings about productivity improvements and structural transformation

TABLE 3.1 The Effects of FDI on Labor Markets Vary by Sector and Workers' Skill Levels

Broad sector	*Average effect*	*Low-skilled workers*	*High-skilled workers*
Extractives	No effect	No effect	No effect
Low-skilled manufacturing	Positive	Positive	Positive
High-skilled manufacturing	Positive	Neutral	Positive
Low-skilled services	Neutral	Negative	Positive
High-skilled services	Positive	Negative	Positive

Source: World Bank calculations, summarizing table 3.2.
Note: Low-skilled workers are defined as those with primary education or less, while high-skilled workers have completed at least secondary education. All results are *relative* to workers in sectors with less or no investment by multinational enterprises (MNEs). For all sector- and country-specific data, see annex 3C, table 3C.6. FDI = foreign direct investment.

that boost long-term economic growth. Yet, in some cases, skill-intensive FDI can be associated with a skill premium that increases wage inequality. To maximize FDI's contribution to inclusive growth, countries should therefore complement investment policy and investment promotion efforts with progressive labor market policies to counter FDI's potential effect on any (temporary) declines in employment and increased income inequality. The chapter makes six recommendations (discussed in detail in the concluding "Policy Implications" section):

- *Better align investment promotion strategies* with a country's labor skill base, related sectors, and relevant source countries.
- *Strengthen the absorptive capacity of domestic firms and workers* (for example, through programs supporting FDI-supplier linkages and employment training) to help extend the labor market benefits from FDI.
- *Open up services sectors to foreign investment* to help (indirectly) create new jobs. Governments may wish to combine the promotion of services FDI with progressive labor market interventions to ensure that both high- and low-skilled workers in the services sector benefit.
- *Improve bargaining power and knowledge spillovers* for workers by enforcing sufficient labor standards and supporting labor representation.
- *Support vulnerable communities* (such as lower-skilled workers, youth, and women) by providing active jobs information and skills certification.
- *Establish programs to stimulate internal migration,* which can further help improve access to employment, with important household welfare benefits.

Conceptual Framework: The Link between FDI and Welfare

FDI can affect welfare by both changing individuals' incomes and altering the prices of goods and services available to consumers through three channels (figure 3.2):

- *Employment income:* As FDI brings capital and new technology to a sector, it often raises the overall labor demand and productivity in the sector. This can raise total employment and average wages, leading to higher household incomes.
- *Consumer prices:* The entry of new (and possibly more productive) foreign firms to markets also increases competition. This may lower the price of goods and services, thus raising household purchasing power and consumption possibilities.
- *Producer income:* As foreign firms compete with, buy from, and sell to domestic firms, they may influence the productivity and profitability of these enterprises, increasing or cutting into income for domestic producers.

FIGURE 3.2 FDI Affects Household Incomes through Several Broad Channels

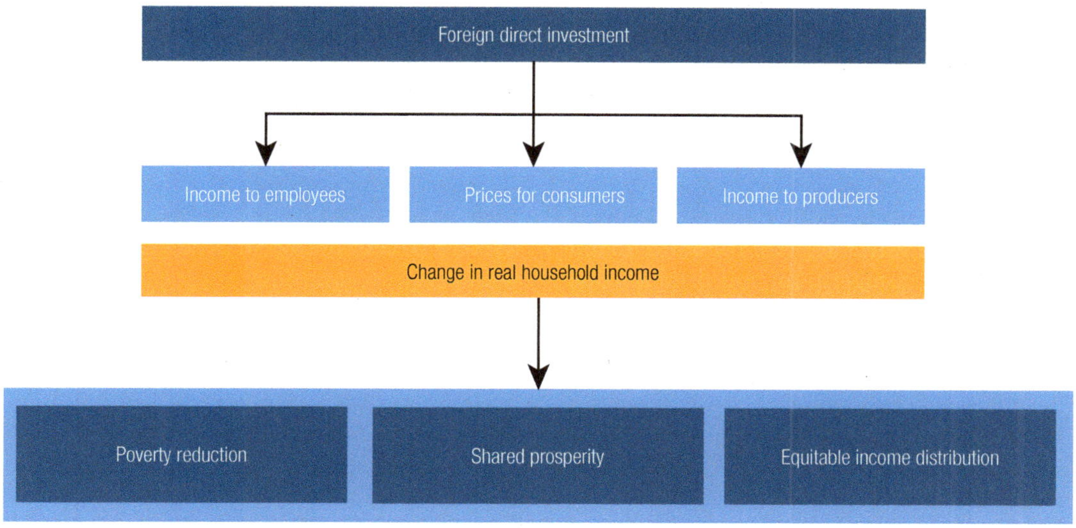

Source: World Bank, based on World Bank and OECD 2017.
Note: FDI = foreign direct investment.

Depending on how important such effects are for individuals along the income distribution, FDI will have different consequences on three welfare goals often considered by policy makers around the world: poverty reduction, shared prosperity, and an equitable income distribution. Poverty is often defined as those households that fall below a minimum basic level of real household income (based on income or consumption patterns). To the extent that FDI raises income for these households, it also helps reduce poverty.

Yet governments often face a parallel challenge to ensure that any general income gains are equitably distributed within the country. This is captured by two different metrics. Shared prosperity has been defined as "expanding the size of the pie continuously and sharing it in such a way that the welfare of those at the lower end of the income distribution rises as quickly as possible" (World Bank 2013). It is measured as income growth of the bottom 40 percent of the income distribution in the population. In some lower-income countries, this goal will coincide with that of reducing poverty.

Finally, metrics of income inequality reflect on a country's overall (wage) income distribution. Recent research suggests that, for many countries, inequality trends are mainly driven at the top and the bottom (with limited shifts in the middle of the income distribution). Such research thus promotes the use of the Palma ratio, which considers the aggregate income share for the top 90 percent versus the bottom 40 percent (Krozer 2015).

This analysis focuses on how FDI affects labor income, which has been shown to be the main channel through which individuals escape poverty. Historically, poverty reduction has been shaped most by growth in labor income rather than by changes in nonlabor income or demographics (Ferreira 2010). Among 21 developing countries, growth in labor income accounts for more than half of the poverty reduction in 12 countries, while it accounts for more than 40 percent of poverty reduction in another 6 countries, Inchauste et al. (2014) find. They note that wage growth (rather than increased employment) contributed most to poverty reduction.

The Effect of FDI on Labor Market Outcomes

The overall labor market impact of FDI is theoretically and empirically ambiguous because of the opposing effects it can have on labor demand for different types of workers (figure 3.3).

Effects on the aggregate demand for labor. Inflows of FDI affect a sector's labor demand through scale, competition, and productivity. Scale effects may take place when the foreign firm produces new or extra goods and services (for example, for export-oriented firms). This often increases overall labor demand. FDI can also take away market share from domestic firms (for example, for domestic products).

The effect this has on employment depends on the relative labor intensity of foreign versus domestic firms. MNE productivity may be reflected in higher employment and workers' compensation. Alternatively, MNEs may adopt labor-saving technologies that could be associated with a net negative employment effect. In addition, there may be labor demand effects from other sectors that supply to MNEs (upstream) or that rely on MNE inputs in producing their goods or services (downstream).

Effects on the demand for skilled versus unskilled labor (skill-biased labor demand). Alongside overall shifts in employment demand, there may also be changes in the employment and remuneration across different types of workers. MNEs often bring in new technology, which requires higher-skilled workers to operate. For that reason, high-skilled workers may be more likely to be employed and could enjoy a wage premium. In contrast, demand for lower-skilled workers might fall. A limited supply of skilled labor in the local economy further helps raise benefits for skilled work by affecting their wage bargaining power, further intensifying the skill bias for FDI.

Effects on Aggregate Labor Demand

Empirically, FDI has often been found to have a positive impact on wages and employment, particularly for lower-income countries. Much of the evidence points to FDI's

FIGURE 3.3 Conceptual Framework: FDI Has Varied Effects on Labor Market Outcomes

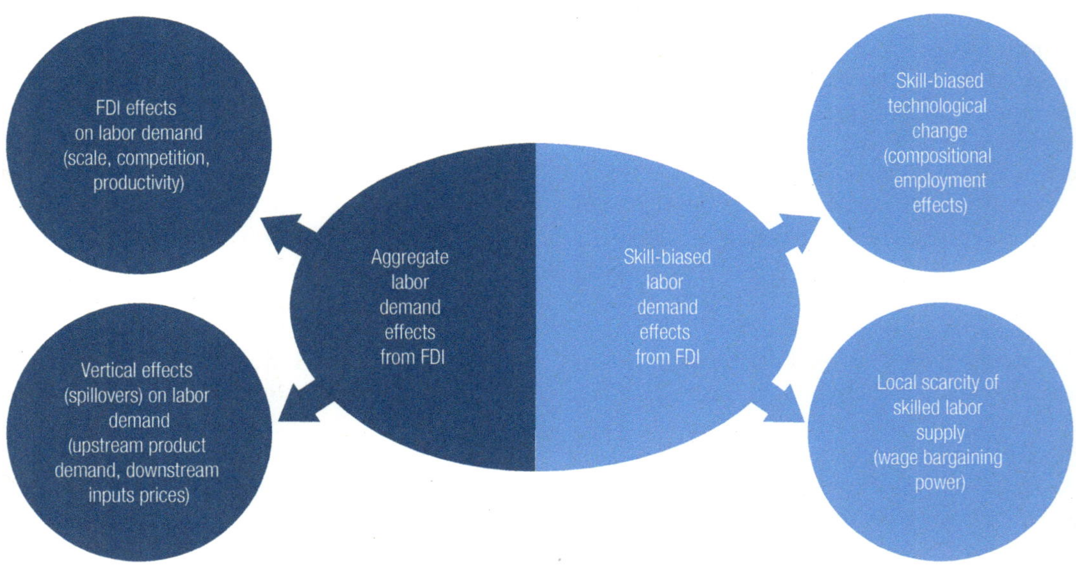

Source: World Bank.
Note: FDI = foreign direct investment.

potential to raise wages, driven primarily by new technology and increased labor productivity (Hale and Xu 2016). In many cases, the literature also finds a positive effect of FDI on aggregate employment. For example, FDI was found to increase the employment rate in China, the Czech Republic, and Uruguay (Dinga and Münich 2010; Karlsson et al. 2009; Peluffo 2015). FDI also had a strong positive employment effect on Mexico's manufacturing FDI, with stronger effects in export-oriented industries (Waldkirch, Nunnenkamp, and Bremont 2009).

However, the evidence is more mixed for higher-income countries. Although manufacturing FDI in Sweden was associated with an increase in employment (Bandick and Karpaty 2011), FDI in central and eastern Europe led to job losses through competitive pressure and introduction of labor-saving technology (Jude and Silaghi 2015). For higher-income countries, FDI may decrease the number of jobs in the short term by introducing labor-saving technology, but it will likely increase job growth in the long term by enhancing labor productivity (Hale and Xu 2016).

There is limited and inconclusive evidence on the effect of FDI's vertical spillovers. The overall effect of FDI on upstream firms that supply inputs to foreign-invested firms is ambiguous. In some cases, product demand rises, and positive technological spillovers may push up employment and the average wage. On the other hand, target firms might switch from domestic to foreign suppliers of intermediate inputs, in which case production, labor demand, and wages of upstream industries will decline (Reyes 2017).

The effect of FDI on downstream firms' wages is similarly unclear. Access to cheaper or higher-quality inputs (such as in business services) can improve domestic firms' productivity, increase output, and raise wages (Arnold et al. 2016; Arnold, Javorcik, and Mattoo 2011; Duggan, Rahardja, and Varela 2013). Yet FDI firms may shift production focus from domestic to international markets, so that the cost of intermediate inputs may increase for domestic downstream firms. This can lead to lower production, lower employment, and possibly lower wages (Hale and Xu 2016). So far, the overall effect is unclear, given that few studies consider the vertical spillovers of FDI to labor market outcomes.

Effects on Skill-Biased Labor Demand

FDI often introduces new technologies that raise the demand for higher-skilled workers and increase the wage gap between skilled and unskilled workers. There is considerable empirical evidence confirming that FDI contributes to rising wage inequality in host countries.

In developing countries, wage inequality increases with stocks of inward FDI, a cross-country study shows (Figini and Görg 2011). A rise in Japanese FDI in developing countries is associated with an increase in nonproduction wages (for more-skilled workers) relative to production wages (for less-skilled workers), according to Head and Ries (2002). Similar effects of foreign investments have been found for firms in Indonesia and Mexico (Feenstra and Hanson 1997; Lee and Wie 2015).

However, technological change is not necessarily biased in favor of skilled workers (Luo 2017). There is an important sector bias in the type of FDI attracted. FDI in some types of low-skilled sectors (such as textiles and food processing) could disproportionally benefit unskilled workers (Cruz et al. 2018; Leamer 1998). For this reason, FDI in labor-intensive manufacturing and infrastructure is associated with declining inequality in Ethiopia, Ghana, and Mozambique (Cornia 2016).

The effects of FDI can be local, at least in the short term. Overall employment in receiving industries tends to increase with FDI. Yet because of these industries' greater reliance on technology that requires complementary skills, a larger presence of foreign firms or affiliates in the region and industry also increases demand for skilled labor. Because the supply of skilled labor is highly inelastic in the short and medium term, this further pushes up the wages of skilled workers in the regions and industries with higher FDI presence (Hale and Xu 2016). Given that most developing countries have considerable restrictions on worker mobility between regions, the effects tend to be rather concentrated in local labor markets (Dix-Carneiro and Kovak 2015; Pavcnik 2017). This also means that FDI can lead to another form of inequality—geographical inequality—as has been found in Bolivia and Vietnam (McLaren and Yoo 2016; Nunnenkamp, Schweickert, and Wiebelt 2007).

Overall, the literature suggests that FDI has positive but unequal effects on host countries' labor markets. FDI is associated with higher aggregate employment and a rise in average wages. Many of these benefits accrue to higher-skilled workers, while lower-skilled workers may experience adverse effects. Yet the literature also suggests that FDI might change local norms about labor conditions (Hale and Xu 2016; Javorcik 2015). Although the increase in inequality resulting from disproportionate growth of demand for skilled labor is a worrying dynamic, this may also induce the labor force, in the long term, to seek additional education and training (Heath and Mobarak 2015).

The Sectoral Impact of FDI on Labor Market Outcomes

> *"FDI flows come in at least three—and probably four—separate forms: FDI in extractive industries, FDI in infrastructure, FDI in manufacturing, plus the underresearched field of FDI in services. Each form presents such distinctive policy challenges for developing-country host authorities, and generates such diverse impacts on the developing host economy, as to undermine the usefulness of any research that does not disaggregate the FDI flows."*
>
> —Theodore H. Moran, *Foreign Direct Investment and Development (2011)*

Depending on a sector's labor and skill content, FDI can have markedly different impacts on employment and wages. Much of the evidence considered so far has either been cross-sectoral or focused only on manufacturing. However, policy makers often must decide which sectors should receive priority in their investment promotion efforts (Javorcik 2004). For that reason, it is important to consider the various impacts of FDI by sector.

Labor Market Impact in the Services Sector

The distributional impact of FDI in the services sector is underresearched but deserves greater policy attention. FDI in services differs from FDI in manufacturing in three important ways.

First, the services sector tends to increase the demand for higher-skilled labor. Many service-oriented firms rely more than manufacturers on intellectual capital and may therefore exhibit larger skill premiums (Kianto, Hurmelinna-Laukkanen, and Ritala 2010). For example, in the Philippines, service liberalization in banking, distribution, and telecommunications created employment opportunities for higher-skilled workers and generated negative impacts on the employment and wages of low-skilled workers (Amoranto, Brooks, and Chun 2010). Greenfield FDI in business support services (for example, professional services, information and communication technology [ICT], and research and development [R&D]) across 17 higher-income countries benefited high-skilled workers at the expense of medium-skilled workers (Davies and Desbordes 2015).

Second, FDI in the services sector is more likely to reduce domestic employment because of labor-saving productivity improvements. Although some services are export-oriented (such as ICT), many operate exclusively within the domestic market. This means that FDI in services often lacks scale effects and instead captures market share from domestic firms, often resulting in little or no aggregate employment effects.

Evidence from China on services liberalization finds that although output increased in almost all services industries, employment losses occurred because of labor-saving improvements in productivity (Li, Wang, and Zhai 2003). Although these job losses could be offset by expansion of overall labor demand in nonservice industries and by long-term growth of aggregate labor demand, these findings suggest that there are important short-term labor adjustment costs from FDI in services sectors.

Third, services sector FDI exerts competitive pressure on smaller businesses. Services sectors in developing countries are more often dominated by small, family-owned businesses (such as retail operations). Unlike manufacturing, which is often dominated by a few large firms, competitive pressures on these smaller businesses might lead to a more regressive impact of FDI. A notable example is the entry of foreign supermarkets in Mexico, which helped lower the cost of living and substantially benefited the average household (Atkin, Faber, and Gonzalez-Navarro 2018)—an effect represented by the consumer price channel in figure 3.2. However, those researchers also find evidence of a sizable reduction in the monthly incomes of workers in traditional retail sectors as well as some decline in the labor incomes of workers in modern retail sectors. In total, the household benefits are positive but regressive.

Labor Market Impact in the Manufacturing Sector

A synthesis of the literature previously discussed suggests that FDI in different sectors has different effects on overall and skill-biased labor demand. FDI in low-skilled manufacturing is expected to have the largest effects on labor demand, with limited skill premiums. Higher-skilled manufacturing is more skill-biased but with some aggregate benefits to labor demand. FDI in low- and high-skilled services has been found to create few jobs but to have notable effects on average wages and skill premiums. As a capital-intensive sector, FDI in extractives is expected to have little overall impact on wage incomes (figure 3.4).

FIGURE 3.4 FDI Has Different Labor Market Outcomes by Sector

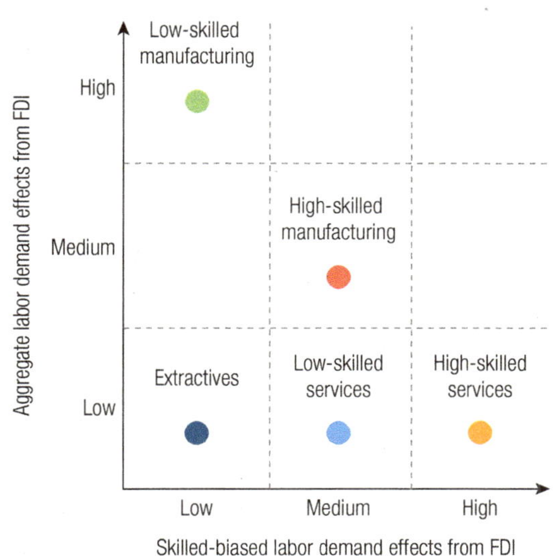

Source: World Bank.
Note: The figure is a stylistic representation based on available literature. Each aggregated sector (manufacturing, services, and extractives) is subdivided based on workers' average education: "high skilled" are those in which at least 50 percent of workers had secondary or postsecondary education; the remainder is considered "low skilled." For more about the subclassification, see annex 3C, table 3C.1. FDI = foreign direct investment.

Finally, it is worth noting that while this chapter focuses on the potential skill bias of FDI, there are other channels through which FDI can have different consequences on income distribution and inclusive growth. One such example comes from gender-specific labor market effects. Although this chapter does not explicitly analyze this issue in the case studies, a discussion on past findings on FDI's impact on women's opportunities is presented in box 3.1.

Country Case Studies: Ethiopia, Vietnam, and Turkey

To examine the effects of FDI, this chapter studies three countries where FDI has taken off significantly in the past 20 years: Ethiopia, Vietnam, and Turkey (figure 3.5).

Turkey's first episode of significant growth was in the early 2000s, when FDI increased twentyfold in the five-year period between 2002 and 2007. Despite the slowdown following the global financial crisis, cumulative inflows in the 15 years between 2003 and 2017 are still almost 13 times higher than total inflows in the preceding 30 years.[4]

In Vietnam, FDI growth has been more gradual but more persistent. FDI there first jumped in 2007–08 and has since steadily increased, leading to inflows matching those of Turkey by 2017.

As the least developed country among the three countries, the FDI takeoff in Ethiopia lags Turkey's and Vietnam's by almost a decade. Nevertheless, acceleration of FDI since 2012 has made Ethiopia one of the largest FDI recipients in Africa (UNCTAD 2019).

These episodes of FDI growth took place when the three countries were at different stages of development. The countries have also had distinct economic structures and supplies of skills.[5] In 2018, Turkey's income per capita was close to US$28,000 (in purchasing

BOX 3.1

FDI's Potential to Improve Women's Economic Opportunities

Through its impacts on labor market outcomes, foreign direct investment (FDI) can notably affect women's economic opportunities (for example, by raising the female participation rate in the country or reducing the gender wage gap).[a] Unfortunately, little evidence currently exists on the gender-specific effects of FDI. What evidence does exist indicates that FDI generally has a positive effect on gender equality, partly by raising the overall demand for all labor and partly through cultural norm transfers from source countries with more gender-equal cultures. Yet much of these benefits ultimately depend on the sectoral FDI type and skill level of women in the host economy.

FDI can increase gender equality by raising labor demand. Women in many developing countries are relatively overrepresented in the informal sector, which is often poorly remunerated. More formal employment opportunities brought by FDI can thus present a significant step up in pay for women relative to informal employment.

Empirical studies from economies in three different parts of the world provide supportive evidence that FDI can help raise women's labor demand. *In Honduras,* FDI inflows were critical in establishing export-oriented manufacturing maquiladoras.[b] Surveys found that women who moved to this kind of employment for the first time earned about 50 percent more than in their previous jobs (Ver Beek 2001). *In China,* the establishment of foreign firms helped raise the female participation rate; female employment rates in such firms were 13 percent higher than for domestic-owned firms (Chen, Li, and Shapiro 2012). *In Madagascar,* FDI generated jobs in export-processing zones (EPZs) that provided women with high-wage jobs relative to their skill level and with similar pay between men and women. Looking at

Box continues next page

BOX 3.1

FDI's Potential to Improve Women's Economic Opportunities *(continued)*

firm-level data from 1995 to 2002, the study found that after three initial years, wage growth for women even outstripped that of men: 35 percent versus 25 percent (Glick and Roubaud 2006).

FDI may also affect cultural norm transfers. Women's position in the labor force may be affected by gender-biased norms and perceptions.[c] Recent evidence suggests multinational firms may be less subject to such gender-biased norms and can help the global diffusion of gender-equal norms. Cross-country analysis for 94 developing countries finds that higher FDI inflows are associated with increases in gender development (including female participation rates) and with declines in gender inequality (including the gender wage gap) (Ouedraogo and Marlet 2018). Similarly, in China, foreign affiliates from countries with a more gender-equal culture are found to employ proportionally more women and appoint more female managers. They also generate cultural spillovers, increasing domestic firms' female labor shares in the same industry or city (Tang and Zhang 2017).

Women's skill level affects the impact of FDI on women's empowerment. In many developing countries, women are relatively unskilled and face lower wages relative to men. These features can be a pull factor for FDI in low-skilled, labor-intensive sectors (such as textiles) and help increase women's access to employment. Yet as countries move toward better technology and higher demand for skilled labor, women's employment and wages may decline or even reverse (Braunstein 2006; Seguino and Grown 2006). Lower-skilled women working within these firms may be disproportionately assigned to low-value-added, low-tech, and low-training tasks in foreign firms, with lower relative wages as a result (Chen, Li, and Shapiro 2012). China provides some evidence of this dynamic effect. Looking at household data from 1995–2002, FDI was found to have positive effects on both female and male wages. At the beginning, women experienced larger wage increases from FDI than men. At the end of the sample period, however, this trend reversed, and men experienced larger wage increases (Braunstein and Brenner 2007).

Finally, the sectoral dimension of FDI also influences its gender impact. The overall skill requirements of labor differ significantly across sectors. FDI's impact on women's employment and wages may therefore depend on FDI's sectoral differences *and* women's skill level. Evidence from this comes from a study in rural Indonesia, which considered the effect of FDI on women's employment in lower-skilled plantation employment and higher-skilled hotel employment. The study found that low wages affected employment in plantations the most, while skills availability was the main determinant for employment in hotels. On the whole, female workers in rural Indonesia were both low waged and low skilled. As a result, relatively more women ended up being employed on plantations, while relatively fewer women ended up working in the new hotels (Siegmann 2007).

a. This box is based in part on Fang, Shamseldin, and Xu (2019) and on extensive inputs from Matthew Stephenson.
b. Maquiladoras are factories producing labor-intensive products with imported goods; a high share of their employment is female.
c. For example, about two-thirds of firms surveyed in Pakistan's Enterprise Survey in 2013 reported gender-discriminatory attitudes as reasons for not hiring women. These reasons include "women should focus on family responsibilities"; "women employees 'disrupt' the workplace"; and "male colleagues/customers are hesitant to interact with women" (Amir et al. 2018).

FIGURE 3.5 FDI Has Increased Significantly in Ethiopia, Vietnam, and Turkey

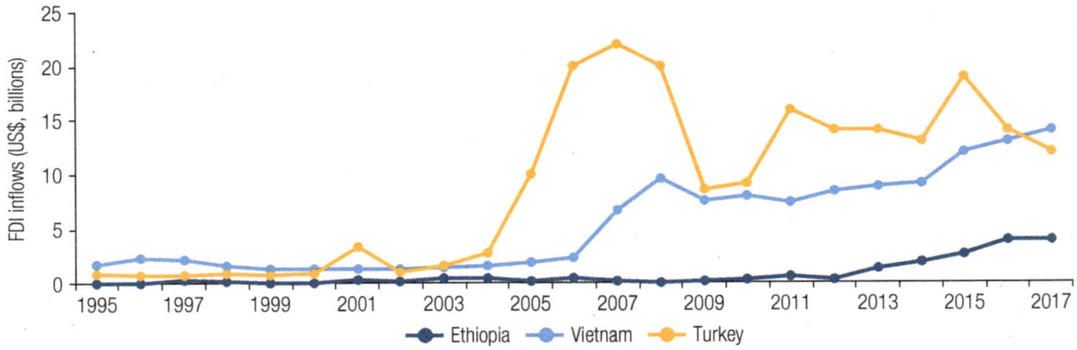

Source: World Development Indicators database.
Note: FDI = foreign direct investment.

power parity terms), more than 3 times that of Vietnam and 14 times that of Ethiopia. The Turkish economy is typical of an upper-middle-income economy, with services contributing 65 percent of gross domestic product (GDP). Vietnam still has a substantial agriculture and industry base (contributing 15 percent and 34 percent of GDP, respectively), while Ethiopia still depends heavily on agriculture (31 percent of GDP). Gaps in educational attainment also remain substantial. In 2017, lower-secondary completion rates were 95 percent and 87 percent for Turkey and Vietnam, respectively, but were only 30 percent in Ethiopia.

Ethiopia, Vietnam, and Turkey have attracted FDI in different types of sectors, reflecting both their current economic structure and educational attainment. Ethiopia has mainly attracted FDI in agroprocessing and manufacturing, notably in the textile and food and beverages sectors (EIC 2017). Vietnam's FDI remains concentrated in manufacturing but with increasing diversification from less-skilled activities (such as textiles/clothing and plastics/rubber) to more sophisticated activities, particularly in the electronics sector. Investments in real estate and retail/wholesale have also increased following the recent opening up of these sectors—these investments reflecting the increased share of output and of employment due to FDI (VFIA 2018). Turkey's FDI inflows have been the most broad based, covering substantial investments in both manufacturing and services. The financial sector has attracted the highest amount of FDI, closely followed by manufacturing, energy, and ICT services (ISPAT 2018).

The differences in economic structure, labor supply composition, and types of investments the countries have attracted provide a rich setting to study the distributional impact of FDI. As discussed earlier, the impact of FDI will depend on the scale of investments as well as the interaction between the labor and skill content of FDI activities and the domestic skills supply. To organize the empirical analysis, the exercise explores these interactions through a sector typology that classifies FDI activities based on their labor content (extractives versus nonextractives); tradability (manufacturing versus services); and skill intensity (high skilled versus low skilled), as detailed in box 3.2 and the next section. Analyzing the labor market impact of FDI based on these characteristics will improve understanding of the channels through which FDI affects aggregate income distributions.

BOX 3.2

A Sector Typology

To better understand the sectoral dynamics of foreign direct investment (FDI), this study uses a typology that clusters various sectors as grouped by the International Standard Industrial Classification of All Economic Activities (ISIC) at the two-digit level (ISIC2), based on their general classification (extractives, manufacturing, or services) combined with their average workers' skill intensity (low skilled or high skilled). The analysis focuses only on these sectors (and excludes others, such as agriculture, utilities, and personal recreation) because these are easier to analyze using firm- and household-level data, and they jointly make up around 87 percent of global FDI (with almost all other FDI going to the utilities sector).[a]

The subsectoral classification is broadly based on Hallward-Driemeier and Nayyar (2017). To provide additional detail at the ISIC2 level, the exercise divided up the low- and high-skilled sectors based on the average education profile of that sector's workers in Vietnam's and Turkey's household surveys. If at least 50 percent of workers had secondary or postsecondary education, the sector was classified as "high skilled." Otherwise, it was considered "low skilled." The exact subclassification is provided in annex 3C, table 3C.1.

a. Share of global FDI from World Bank calculations of 2010–15 global FDI, based on greenfield FDI announcements from fDi Markets, a *Financial Times* dataset (https://www.fdimarkets.com/) and Thomson Reuters's Mergers & Acquisitions database (https://www.refinitiv.com/).

A breakdown of foreign firms' investments across the five sectors (extractives, high-skilled manufacturing, low-skilled manufacturing, high-skilled services, and low-skilled services) shows that the three countries differ substantially in the type of FDI they have attracted (figure 3.6). Given the varying skill content and potential tradability of sectors receiving FDI in the three countries, the labor market outcomes will also likely differ significantly.

Ethiopia's FDI is heavily concentrated in low-skilled manufacturing activities, with very little FDI going to other sectors. Vietnam has had sizable increases in both low-skilled and high-skilled manufacturing as well as small but consistent increases in extractives and both types of services. Turkey has had the highest growth of investment in high-skilled manufacturing (driven by pharmaceuticals, motor vehicles, and chemicals) and low-skilled service activities (driven by employment services or activities). FDI in low-skilled manufacturing is also significant (driven mainly by tobacco).

Empirical Strategy

The significant takeoff of FDI in different sectors experienced by Ethiopia, Vietnam, and Turkey creates an ideal setting to study the impact of MNEs' presence on labor market outcomes. The analysis links household survey data with firm-level data to examine the relationship between individual workers' exposure to multinational activities and their employment and wages in each country.

The main data source for individual labor market outcomes is the World Bank's International Income Distribution Database (I2D2), supplemented with the countries' Labor Force Surveys. Firm-level data come from various sources, including the Large and Medium Manufacturing Survey (Ethiopia), Enterprise Census (Vietnam), and Enterprise Information System (Turkey). The period of analysis is limited by the overlap of household and firm-level data. Nevertheless, the analysis still captures periods with significant FDI growth in all three countries: Ethiopia (2009–14), Vietnam

FIGURE 3.6 Ethiopia, Vietnam, and Turkey Have Attracted Different Types of FDI

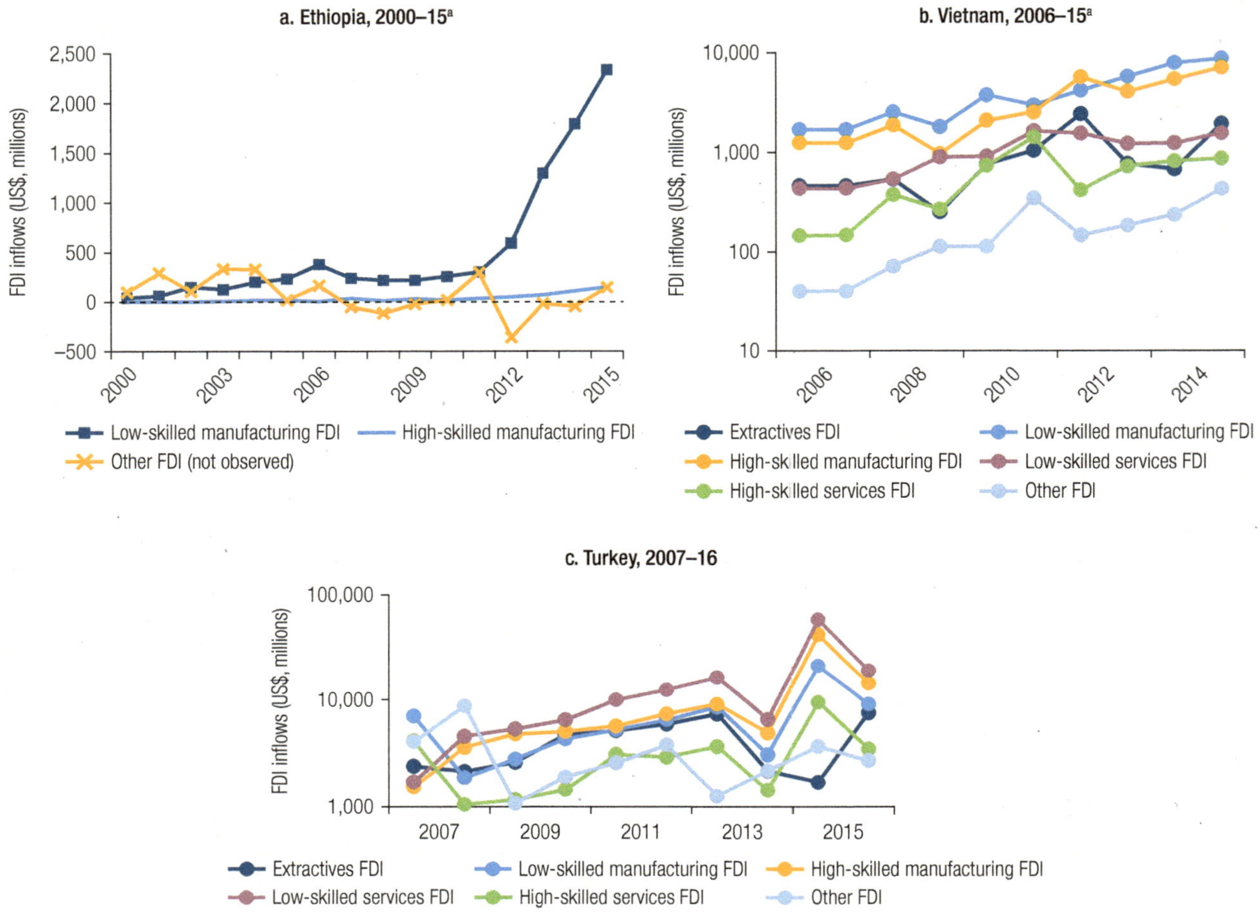

Source: World Bank calculations based on the World Development Indicators database, Ethiopia's Large and Medium Manufacturing Survey, Turkey's Enterprise Information System data, and Vietnam's Enterprise Census.

Note: Total foreign direct investment (FDI) inflow is calculated as the total investments in assets made by all foreign companies in the data. Sectors (extractives, manufacturing, or services) are aggregated based on International Standard Industrial Classification (ISIC) two-digit classification. Each is subdivided based on workers' average education: "high skilled" are those in which at least 50 percent of workers had secondary or postsecondary education; the remainder is considered "low skilled." For more about the subclassification, see annex 3C, table 3C.1.

a. Breakdown for Ethiopia includes only manufacturing FDI because very little of the country's FDI goes to other sectors.

(2007–16), and Turkey (2009–16). For further details on data, see annex 3A.

To study the direct impact of FDI, the analysis looks at different cohorts of workers over time in each country and compares labor market outcomes for workers who are employed in sectors *and* regions with higher versus lower MNE activity. It focuses on two main outcomes: formal employment and wages.[6] To proxy for MNE activity, it uses the share of foreign firms' revenue in the total output of a sector and region within a country. This approach takes the sector and region as the relevant labor market, as in Dix-Carneiro and Kovak (2015) and Cruz et al. (2018). The hypothesis is that FDI inflows into a sector have two potential opposing effects on the local (regional) labor market: Increased MNE activities create higher labor demand, which results in an increase in formal employment and wages. At the same time, FDI can compete away market share from domestic firms, reducing their labor demand. If, for example, foreign firms are more efficient, the net effect on employment could be negative.

Increased FDI in upstream (selling) and downstream (buying) sectors can also affect labor demand.[7] To examine this vertical impact of FDI, the exercise analyzes how workers' outcomes vary with the total amount of MNE activity in their upstream or downstream sectors as well as the strength of linkages between them. More specifically, this variable is calculated as the sum of FDI firms' output shares—the share of revenue (employment) by foreign firms in total output (employment)—in all upstream or downstream sectors, weighted by how much those sell to or buy from a workers' own sector (see annex 3B).

The main empirical challenge is to separate the impact of FDI from other unobserved changes in policies or market trends that can affect the labor markets at the same time. For example, infrastructure spending can attract FDI as well as other domestic investments that boost employment and wages. MNEs in certain sectors can also choose to locate in low-wage regions because of cost considerations, in which case higher FDI activity might appear to be associated with lower wages. As a result, a simple correlation between FDI activity and labor market outcomes can either inflate or underestimate the true impact of FDI. To account for this potential bias, lagged global FDI growth was used as an instrument to capture supply-side changes that affect FDI inflows and eventually MNE presence but are unlikely to be correlated with other domestic shocks. Operationally, the instrument is the growth in global FDI (greenfield FDI and mergers and acquisitions [M&A]) interacted with a region's original shares of FDI per ISIC2 sector.[8]

Beyond the average impact, how FDI affects the distribution of income will depend on what types of workers benefit most from these investments. The exercise attempts to answer this question from one main angle: how the skill content of the sector receiving FDI interacts with workers' skills. That is, the impact of FDI on labor market outcomes is compared for high- versus low-skilled sectors and for workers with different education levels. If FDI concentrates more in skill-intensive sectors, then the more-educated workers will likely benefit the most, potentially increasing inequality. If FDI concentrates in less-skilled sectors, then it has the potential to improve employment and wage outcomes for those at the lower end of the income distribution.

Finally, the estimated average impact of FDI is used to calculate the aggregate impact on (wage) income in a simple back-of-the-envelope counterfactual exercise. To compare the actual (wage) income distribution to the hypothetical case without FDI presence, the exercise assumes that there is a constant effect of FDI on all workers that is equal to the estimated average effect. The counterfactual (wage) income is then equal to the actual wage minus the estimated average income gain (loss) due to FDI. From these two income distributions, estimates are made of FDI's aggregate contributions to poverty reduction, shared prosperity (other income gains within the bottom 40 percent), and income equality—the latter measured through the Gini coefficient and the Palma ratio, which considers the aggregate income share for the top 90 percent versus the bottom 40 percent (Krozer 2015).[9] Annex 3B discusses these different empirical specifications in more detail.

Results

This section discusses results on the average impact of FDI and its implications for aggregate poverty, shared prosperity, and inequality. As discussed, results using ordinary least squares (OLS) can either underestimate or overestimate the true impact of FDI; this exercise finds indication of both types of biases across different countries and sectors. For the sake of brevity, only the results from the instrumental variables (IV) estimations are presented. A full comparison and discussion of results can be found in the online appendix.[10]

FDI in Manufacturing Has Been Most Effective in Shifting Employment toward the Formal Sector and Increasing Wages

On average, increases in MNE activities are associated with increased formal employment in manufacturing but not in services. In annex 3C, table 3C.2 presents the second-stage IV results from the baseline specification (see annex 3B, equation [3B.1]), estimated separately for manufacturing and services. The results suggest that a worker's relative probability of formal employment (versus informal employment in that sector) tends to increase with the output share of MNEs in the worker's sector and region.[11] However, this effect is significant only for manufacturing FDI (with positive average effects in Turkey and Vietnam). The estimated average effect of MNE presence in services is both smaller in magnitude and statistically imprecise.

Based on the coefficient estimates, the total impact of FDI activity was calculated as a population-weighted average effect.[12] These calculations suggest that in the sample period, manufacturing FDI has created around 350,000 additional formal jobs in Vietnam and around 40,000 new formal jobs in Turkey each year.[13] Aggregate employment effects are minimal for Ethiopia because both baseline manufacturing employment and FDI activities have been relatively small.

The effects on average wages also vary by sector and by country. In annex 3C, table 3C.2 shows that increases in MNE presence in Vietnam were associated with very large, significant average wage increases in both manufacturing (12 percent nationwide) and services (2 percent across the country). In Turkey, average wages increased in manufacturing (nearly 8 percent), but there was no significant effect on services. In Ethiopia, large increases in manufacturing wages (almost 32 percent) were identified; no information was available for services.

FDI Resulted in a Skill Premium, Especially in Services Sectors

The effects from FDI presence on labor markets vary significantly across the broad sectors and workers' education levels. In annex 3C, tables 3C.3, 3C.4, and 3C.5 present the FDI labor markets effects across the five broad sectors and by workers' education for Ethiopia, Vietnam, and Turkey, respectively (see annex 3B, equation [3B.2]). To get a better sense of the magnitude of FDI's effects, annex 3C, table 3C.6 presents the overall population-weighted average effects for each of the three countries, across the five broad sectors. These are further summarized stylistically in table 3.2.

Overall, there is considerable evidence of FDI's skill premium in Turkey and Vietnam. Although higher-skilled (more educated) workers benefit—enjoying greater formal employment opportunities and higher average wages—the effects of FDI on low-skilled (less-educated) workers are less positive. For them, there is either no effect or their probability of employment and wages decline relatively in regions with higher services FDI. As expected, the skill premium seems to be stronger in services than in manufacturing (annex 3C, tables 3C.4 and 3C.5). These results are broadly consistent with previous findings, as summarized in figure 3.4.

The exercise also finds considerable differences in the total effect of FDI across the five broad sectors.

Extractives. *FDI in the extractives sector has little impact on household income, as expected of a capital-intensive sector.* Few households are employed in this sector, and no significant effects from FDI on wage growth or formal employment were identified in Turkey or Vietnam, except among workers with primary education in Vietnam.

Low-skilled manufacturing. *Benefits on employment and wages are positive.* Low-skilled manufacturing FDI has the highest average effect in Ethiopia (+5 percent in formal jobs, +24 percent in average wages) but also has positive effects on Vietnam (+5 percent in formal jobs, +12 percent in average wages) and Turkey (+0.8 percent formal jobs, +6 percent in average wages).

Interestingly, the beneficiaries from these gains differ significantly across the three countries: In Ethiopia, FDI has primarily benefited those with no education or only

TABLE 3.2 The Relative Effects of FDI on Labor Markets (Formal Employment and Wages) in Ethiopia, Vietnam, and Turkey, by Broad Sector and Worker Skill Level

Country	*Broad sector*	*Average effect*	*Low-skilled workers*	*High-skilled workers*
Ethiopia[a]	Low-skilled manufacturing	Positive	Positive	No effect
	High-skilled manufacturing	Positive	Positive	No effect
Vietnam	Extractives	No effect	No effect	No effect
	Low-skilled manufacturing	Positive	Positive	Positive
	High-skilled manufacturing	Positive	Positive	Positive
	Low-skilled services	Neutral	Negative	Positive
	High-skilled services	Positive	Negative	Positive
Turkey	Extractives	No effect	No effect	No effect
	Low-skilled manufacturing	Positive	Positive	Positive
	High-skilled manufacturing	Positive	Positive	Positive
	Low-skilled services	Neutral	Negative	Positive
	High-skilled services	Positive	Negative	Positive

Source: World Bank summary, based on annex 3C, table 3C.6.
Note: Low-skilled workers are defined as those with primary education or less, while high-skilled workers have completed at least secondary education. All results are *relative* to workers in sectors with less or no multinational enterprise (MNE) involvement. Sectors (extractives, manufacturing, or services) are aggregated based on International Standard Industrial Classification (ISIC) two-digit classification. For more about the subclassification, see annex 3C, table 3C.1.
a. No data were available on foreign direct investment (FDI) in extractives or services for Ethiopia.

primary education (reflecting low-skilled factory work). In Turkey, those with primary or secondary education benefited most. In Vietnam, the total average effects are concentrated and similar among those with primary education.

High-skilled manufacturing. *FDI in high-skilled manufacturing sectors results in the highest average benefits for Vietnam (+5 percent in formal employment, +14 percent in average wages).* For Turkey and Vietnam, the benefits from this sector are concentrated among those with primary or secondary education. Turkey also had notable positive average effects in employment (+1.3 percent in formal jobs) and wages (+10.8 percent in average wages). Although Ethiopia saw some benefits in high-skilled manufacturing (+0.3 percent in formal jobs, +23 percent in average wages), few were affected given that the whole sector employed fewer than 25,000 individuals, on average.

Low-skilled services. *FDI in low-skilled services results in significant wage dispersion.* In Vietnam, wages increase relatively for workers with postsecondary education (+5.5 percent), while workers with no education or only primary education both experience a relative decline in wages (–6.6 percent and –4.1 percent, respectively).

In Turkey, the effects differ even more strongly by education. Workers with secondary and postsecondary education enjoy both formal employment benefits (+2 percent for workers with secondary education, +3 percent for postsecondary education) and sizable wage benefits (+12 percent and +18 percent, respectively). In contrast, low-skilled workers experience sizable relative declines in their probability of formal employment and wages. This applies particularly for those with no education (–10 percent probability of formal employment, –49 percent in average wages) as well as for those with primary education, but to a much lesser extent (–2 percent in formal employment, no significant change in wages, respectively).

High-skilled services. *FDI in high-skilled services also results in significant wage dispersion.* FDI in this sector has the biggest average effects in Turkey, with positive effects on formal employment (+1.2 percent) and wages (+12.9 percent), concentrated among workers with secondary and postsecondary education. Yet effects are negative for the small group of workers with no education working in these sectors, who are most likely to be displaced (with very high reductions in wages as a result). In Vietnam, the result is neutral in terms of employment but positive in terms of average wage effect (+4.9 percent), driven entirely by workers with postsecondary education (+11.1 percent).

The Vertical Spillover Effects of FDI Are Mixed

When controlling for FDI's direct effects, the results in other sectors (vertical labor market spillovers) are less conclusive. Findings are mixed across the three countries. The results from the second-stage IV (specifications in annex 3B, equation [3B.2]) are presented in annex 3C, table 3C.7. These present sector-region coefficients that interact FDI output share with intensity of a vertical sector's engagement with FDI. The magnitude can be hard to interpret. To aid interpretation, this table also includes the population-weighted average effects from each regression.

Ethiopia. *No significant effect is found on either backward or forward linkages.* This could indicate that relatively few domestic firms are currently supplying MNEs in Ethiopia. Another possibility is that the overall manufacturing sector is too small for any statistically significant results to appear.

Vietnam. *The FDI backward link appears to be the most important channel.* When FDI in upstream (selling) sectors increases, wages go up in the services sector (+5 percent), and formal employment in both manufacturing and services increases (+4.2 percent and +1.7 percent, respectively). Both types of increase may be the result of productivity increases linked to labor market benefits from accessing cheaper or higher-quality inputs (such as MNE producers of intermediate inputs, or in business services).

Turkey. *The effect of FDI's forward linkages is negative in manufacturing and has no effect on services.* Increased FDI in downstream (buying) sectors is associated with a reduction in both formal manufacturing employment (–5 percent) and wages (–36 percent).[14] One potential explanation is that MNEs are switching from domestic to foreign suppliers of intermediate inputs, prompting a decline in domestic production, labor demand, and wages of sectors with forward links to FDI. Such a finding would warrant additional analysis to better understand potential constraints between MNEs and domestic suppliers.

FDI's Aggregate Effects on Poverty, Shared Prosperity, and Inequality Vary Notably among the Sample Countries

The aggregate effects of FDI on poverty, shared prosperity, and income inequality were estimated by comparing the observed income distribution against a counterfactual distribution with no FDI presence. This calculation combines the estimated direct effects from FDI activity in manufacturing in the case of Ethiopia and from FDI activity across extractives, manufacturing, and services in the cases of Turkey and Vietnam. The counterfactual income distribution is assumed to be the predicted wage income where foreign firms' revenue share is set to zero.

Undoubtedly, deriving counterfactual predictions from estimated differential responses across regions or sectors might lead to underestimation or overestimation of the true total effects (see Adão, Arkolakis, and Esposito [2019] for a discussion). Nevertheless, these estimates provide for a rough approximation as a useful first step to gauge the potential aggregate effect of FDI.

Ethiopia. In Ethiopia, the effects from FDI are highly positive, with noticeable effects on poverty reduction and shared prosperity, but they are limited in magnitude. The FDI wage benefits accruing to low-skilled workers have an important pro-poor effect, concentrating the FDI benefits in the bottom 40 percent (figure 3.7, panel b). Consequently, FDI is associated with a lower average Palma ratio and Gini coefficient—that is, a *decline* in

FIGURE 3.7 Ethiopia: FDI Effects on Poverty, Shared Prosperity, and Inequality

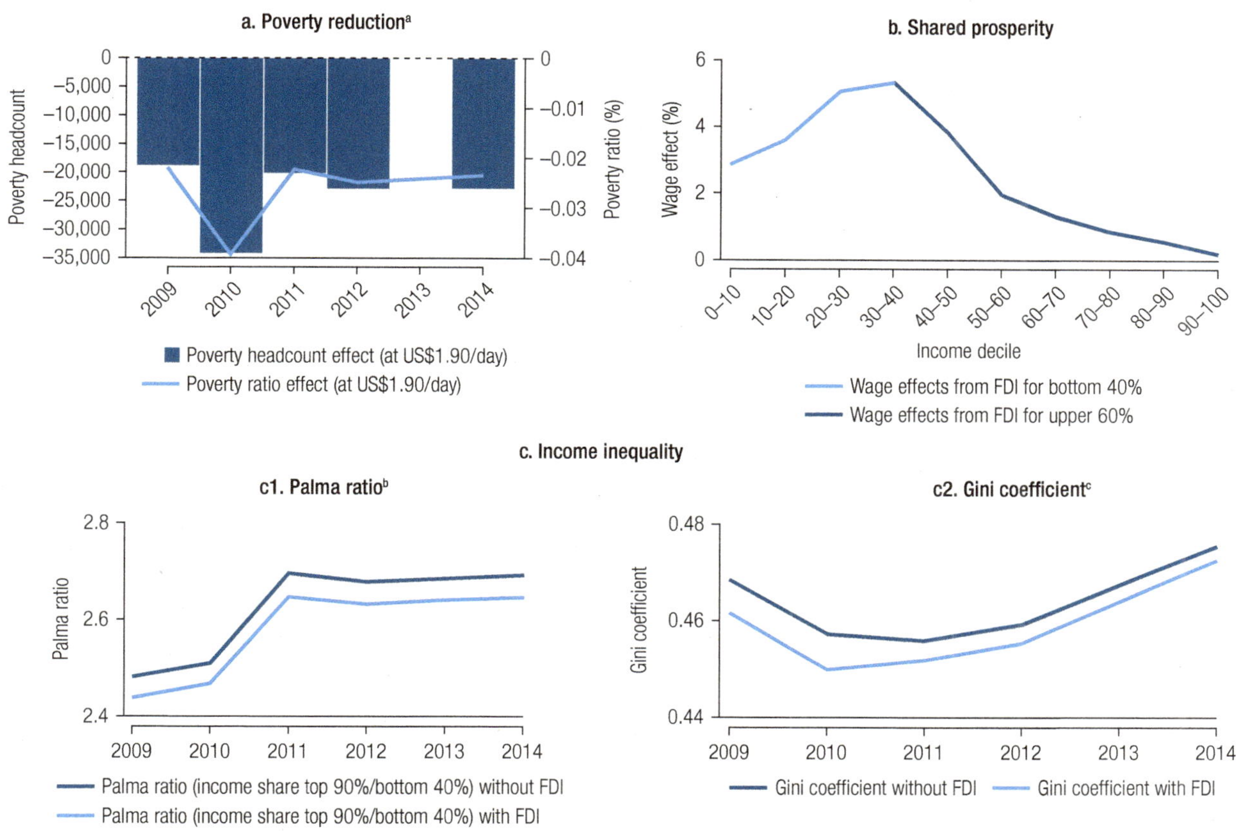

Source: World Bank calculations.

Note: Estimates of the effect on poverty headcount, Palma ratio, and Gini coefficients for 2013 are not available because firm-level data are not available for that year; FDI = foreign direct investment.

a. The poverty headcount effect is the effect of multinational enterprises (MNEs) on raising workers' income above the poverty headcount (at US$1.90/day).

b. The Palma ratio is the ratio of the richest 10 percent of the population's share of gross national income (GNI) divided by the poorest 40 percent's share.

c. The Gini coefficient summarizes the dispersion of income across the entire income distribution. It ranges from 0 (indicating perfect equality, where everyone receives an equal share) to 1 (perfect inequality, where only one recipient or group of recipients receives all the income).

income inequality (figure 3.7, panel c). However, given that relatively few households are employed in the manufacturing sector, the effects apply to only a small share of the population.

Wage increases from FDI are found to have reduced poverty for only around 35,000 individuals in 2010 (0.04 percent of the population) (figure 3.7, panel a). This suggests that although FDI can offer a powerful tool for poverty reduction, a greater focus on investment promotion is needed to extend the benefits to a wider share of the population.

Vietnam. In Vietnam, effects from FDI are positive for poverty reduction and shared prosperity, but they are minimal on income inequality. The wage increases from FDI have helped lift almost 24,000 individuals out of poverty each year between 2007 and 2016, on average (figure 3.8, panel a). The wage income benefits from FDI are positive for all workers along the income distribution. While the largest wage increases are in the middle of the distribution, increases in income are also significant for the bottom 40 percent (figure 3.8, panel b). Given the fairly evenly distributed wage benefits, the effects from FDI on income inequality are minimal, with almost no changes in the Palma ratio and very small increases of the Gini coefficients over time, with and without FDI (figure 3.8, panel c).

Turkey. In Turkey, FDI has had the most pronounced distributional effects. Although manufacturing FDI helped raise wages for lower-skilled workers, there is evidence of displacement for lower-skilled workers from services FDI. In total, FDI provided minor benefits to poverty reduction (affecting at most 15,000 individuals, or around 0.02 percent of Turkey's population) (figure 3.9, panel a). In contrast, higher-skilled workers enjoyed strong rises in their income when FDI flowed in, thus presenting evidence of skill premiums leading to wage dispersion. Overall, FDI has contributed to shared prosperity (with positive effects for both the bottom 40 percent and top 60 percent) (figure 3.9, panel b), but it did structurally contribute to income inequality (as identified by the Palma ratio and Gini coefficient) (figure 3.9, panel c).

FIGURE 3.8 Vietnam: FDI Effects on Poverty, Shared Prosperity, and Inequality

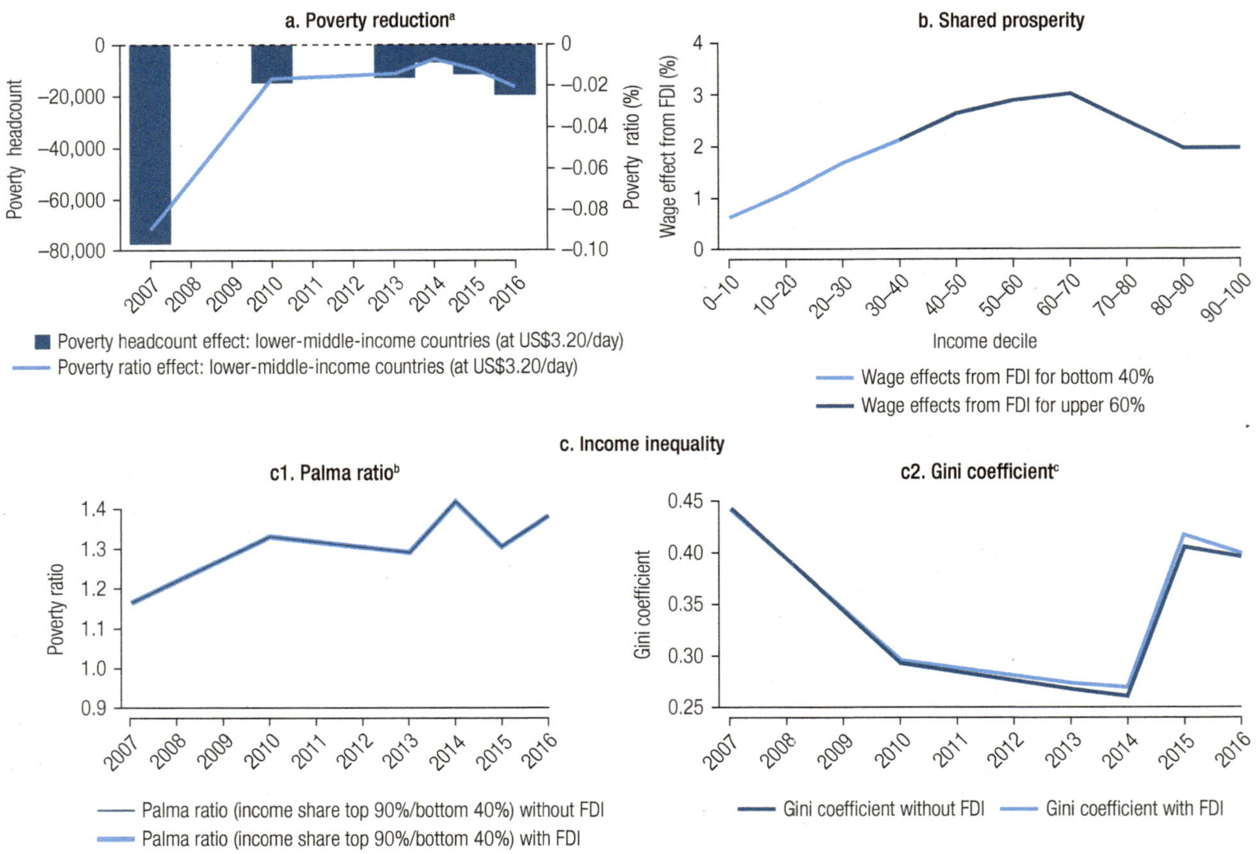

Source: World Bank calculations.

Note: Estimates of the effect on poverty headcount, Palma ratio, and Gini coefficients for 2008, 2009, 2011, and 2012 are not available because firm-level data are not available for those years. FDI = foreign direct investment.

a. The poverty headcount effect is the effect of multinational enterprises (MNEs) on raising workers' income above the poverty headcount (at US$3.20/day).

b. The Palma ratio is the ratio of the richest 10 percent of the population's share of gross national income (GNI) divided by the poorest 40 percent's share.

c. The Gini coefficient summarizes the dispersion of income across the entire income distribution. It ranges from 0 (indicating perfect equality, where everyone receives an equal share) to 1 (perfect inequality, where only one recipient or group of recipients receives all the income).

FIGURE 3.9 Turkey: FDI Effects on Poverty, Shared Prosperity, and Inequality

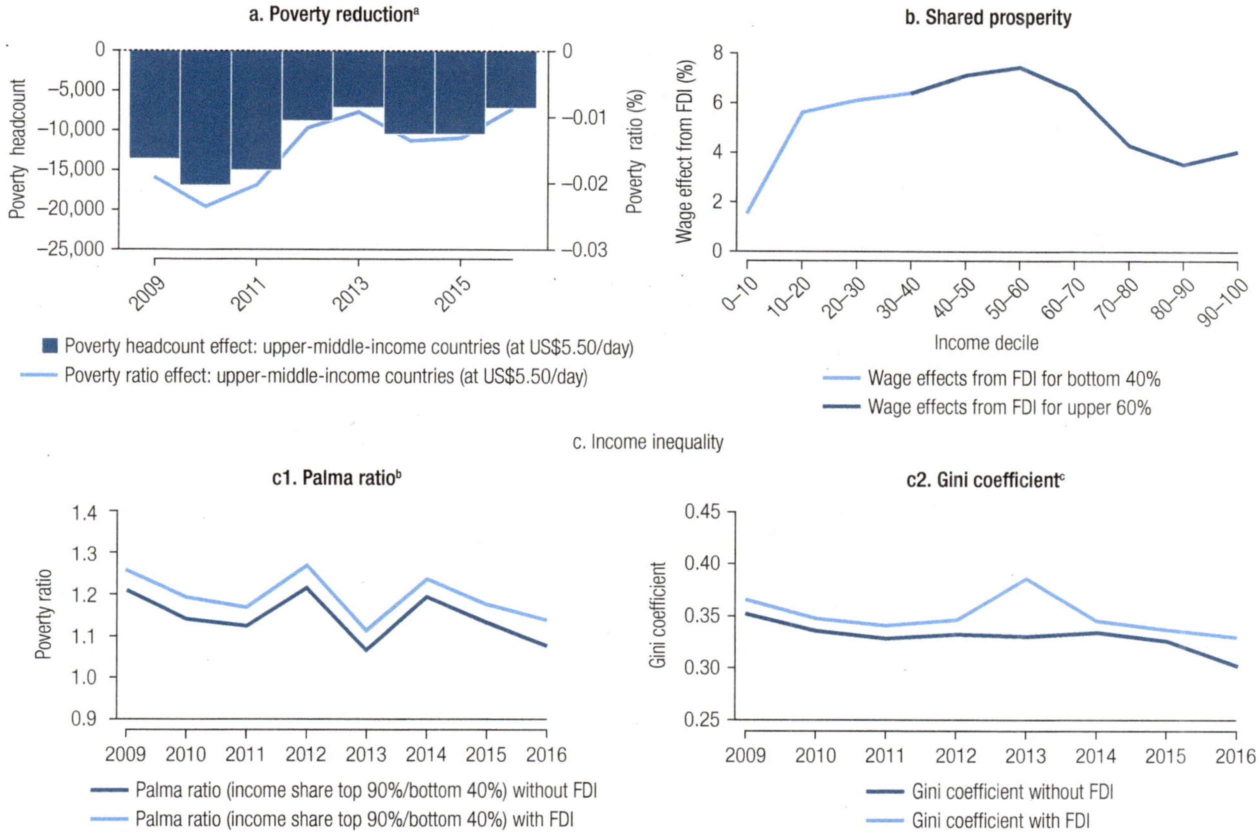

Source: World Bank calculations.
Note: FDI = foreign direct investment.
a. The poverty headcount effect is the effect of multinational enterprises (MNEs) on raising workers' income above the poverty headcount (at US$5.50/day).
b. The Palma ratio is the ratio of the richest 10 percent of the population's share of gross national income (GNI) divided by the poorest 40 percent's share.
c. The Gini coefficient summarizes the dispersion of income across the entire income distribution. It ranges from 0 (indicating perfect equality, where everyone receives an equal share) to 1 (perfect inequality, where only one recipient or group of recipients receives all the income).

Policy Implications

The evidence in this chapter so far has shown that FDI plays an important role in shaping labor markets, affecting both aggregate labor demand and skill-biased employment and wage dynamics. The three countries examined in more detail (Ethiopia, Vietnam, and Turkey) further confirm the varied impact that FDI can have across different types of sectors and by workers' education levels. Although all three countries have been relatively successful at attracting FDI, all have experienced notably different effects on poverty reduction, shared prosperity, and income inequality. In general, FDI in lower-skilled, tradable, labor-intensive sectors have had the most significant pro-poor impact. FDI in higher-skilled, less tradable sectors tend to benefit the more-educated workers at the expense of those at the lower end of the income distribution.

This section extracts lessons from the experience of the analyzed countries and incorporates other empirical evidence to suggest which complementary policies can enhance FDI's contribution to poverty reduction and inclusive growth. Specific recommendations to help improve the developmental impact of FDI fall into two areas: (a) investment policy and promotion efforts, and (b) labor market policies.

Investment Policy and Promotion for Development

Recommendation 1: Align investment promotion with a country's labor skill base, related sectors, and relevant source countries.

Not all FDI will have the same impact on an economy. Thus, investment promotion officials may wish to target FDI that is most likely to bring the impact they seek (Javorcik 2004). For the purposes of designing investment promotion strategies and adopting investment promotion measures, officials may wish to consider targeting based on the country's *skill base*, *related sectors,* and *relevant source countries.*

The case studies showed that FDI has the biggest effect on inclusive income growth when it is aligned with a country's skill base. While FDI in low-skilled manufacturing resulted in the highest average welfare benefits for Ethiopia and Vietnam, Turkey benefited most from FDI in higher-skilled manufacturing. In addition, Turkey was the only country in the sample where benefits from higher-skilled services increased significantly, on average. A likely reason is that Turkey's population is higher-skilled on average, making it easier to employ domestic workers and absorb knowledge transfers from MNEs.

In practical terms, this suggests that to best use FDI for household income growth, investment promotion strategies should start with an assessment of the country's labor skill base (possibly through a jobs diagnostic).[15] Sectors to be targeted may then be those in which the host economy has some skill endowment and in which it wishes to develop greater capacity when considering its national development strategy.

A country's skill base may also have implications for relevant FDI source countries. Source economies to be targeted may be those that have firms with capacity in these sectors, and especially at a level of technology that is complementary to the host economy. If the technology gap between foreign and domestic firms is too wide, it will be difficult for domestic firms to benefit from direct knowledge transfer or spillovers, limiting the developmental impact of the FDI on inclusive growth (Perea and Stephenson 2018).

Recommendation 2: Strengthen the absorptive capacity of domestic firms and workers (such as through programs fostering FDI-supplier linkages and employment training) to help extend the labor market benefits from FDI.

Host governments may wish to increase the level of absorptive capacity of their economy to increase the potential benefit of FDI. The results on vertical spillovers illustrated the potential impact that FDI-supplier linkages can have on household income. In the case of Ethiopia, the study found evidence that FDI in forward-linked areas has a positive effect on employment and wages (likely capturing the broader demand effects from manufacturing FDI on their suppliers). However, in the case of Turkey, the study found a negative effect on forward-linked FDI, suggesting that MNEs are switching from domestic to foreign suppliers of intermediate inputs, in which case production, labor demand, and wages of sectors forward linked to FDI can decline.

These two cases suggest that absorptive capacity is *relative to the type of FDI attracted.* Turkey's domestic suppliers likely have higher absorptive capacity than Ethiopia's suppliers, yet Turkey's MNEs are also involved in more-complex production (placing additional demands on Turkey's suppliers). To better improve FDI-supplier linkages would therefore warrant additional analysis to better understand potential constraints between MNEs and domestic suppliers in Turkey.

Policy makers have a role to play in helping develop the hard infrastructure and soft skills needed for domestic firms to assimilate knowledge and technology brought by foreign firms when MNEs invest in the economy (Amann and Virmani 2014). As seen in the empirical evidence, skill level can make the difference between being locked into a low-income, low-skill cycle of FDI or moving up to a high-income, high-skill cycle of FDI (Te Velde and Xenogiani 2007). Measures to consider include promoting firm linkages, boosting R&D expenditures, increasing R&D employment, providing training programs, building business networks, establishing institutional partnerships, creating national infrastructure, helping to diffuse information, and designing appropriate school curricula. The specific type of relevant policy will depend in large part on a country's economy and stage of development. What is most critical is an approach of continuous learning and adaptation for domestic firms and the domestic economy to maximize the benefits of FDI.

Policy makers' interventions to boost absorptive capacity should be considered at the national level. Absorptive capacity can be measured at the levels of the firm and the economy. To provide the most transformational benefits for the country from FDI, it is most important to adopt the necessary horizontal measures that can boost the absorptive capacity of the economy as whole rather than try to boost the absorptive capacity of individual firms (Perea and Stephenson 2018).

Recommendation 3: Opening up services sectors to foreign investment can (indirectly) create new jobs. Governments may wish to combine the promotion of services FDI with progressive labor market interventions to ensure that both high- and low-skilled workers in the services sector benefit.

The three case studies suggest that FDI in services has little direct effect on aggregate (formal) job creation. Although FDI in high-skilled services led to a minor increase in formal employment for Turkey, FDI in lower-skilled services led to a decline (Turkey) or no effect on employment (Vietnam). A possible reason for this is that most services firms operate exclusively within the domestic market. FDI in services can thus capture market share from domestic firms, resulting in little or no aggregate employment effects. Negative employment effects possibly indicate the use of labor-saving technology.

However, liberalization of services can also stimulate long-term economic development by raising an economy's overall total factor productivity (the efficiency with which societies combine labor, capital, and technology) (Van der Marel 2012). For 86 developing countries from 1985 to 1999, those that opened up their financial and telecommunications sectors grew, on average, 1.5 percentage points faster than countries that did not open up these sectors (Mattoo, Rathindran, and Subramanian 2006). Similarly, for 20 transition economies from 1990 to 2004, enabling entry of FDI in select services (finance, power, transport, and telecommunications) was associated with large new investments and provided statistically significant explanatory variables for their economic performance after 1990 (Eschenbach and Hoekman 2006). This suggests that services FDI may have important *dynamic* effects in stimulating household income growth.

Removing restrictions on foreign equity in the services sector is also known to improve productivity in other sectors and can therefore improve *indirect* job creation. Evidence from the Czech Republic, India, and Indonesia shows that opening up services to foreign investors improves the productivity of domestic firms in manufacturing, which may raise average wages in this sector (Arnold et al. 2016; Arnold, Javorcik, and Mattoo 2011; Duggan, Rahardja, and Varela 2013). This chapter found evidence that in Vietnam, FDI in backward-linked sectors (such as professional business services) led to higher employment in manufacturing and to higher wages in the service sector. This suggests that services liberalization can assist *indirectly* in creating jobs.

To limit the potential increase in wage inequality from services FDI in the short run, governments can prioritize promoting service sectors that are export oriented or that most affect (export-oriented) manufacturing.

The case studies showed that FDI in services is associated with the largest increases in wage inequality because lower-skilled workers are displaced in favor of higher-skilled workers. As shown in the conceptual framework, FDI is most associated with wage inequality in services sectors that are (a) *more skill intensive* (see the broad sectoral classification in box 3.2 and annex 3C, table 3C.1); (b) *domestically oriented* (such as construction and security services) rather than export oriented (such as tourism, ICT, and business process outsourcing); and (c) *dominated by small, family-owned businesses* (such as retail).

For that reason, it can make sense to prioritize promoting services in areas that are either export oriented or that strongly affect export-oriented manufacturing (such as logistics, transport, and wholesale trade) and adopt robust social safety net policies to compensate for potential losers, as discussed below.

Progressive Labor Market Policies

Progressive labor market policies can be important complements to counter FDI's effect on any (temporary) declines in formal employment and increases in income inequality. This chapter shows that FDI is associated with skill premiums that can increase wage inequality (as seen in Turkey). Yet evidence also suggests that FDI can bring about productivity improvements and structural transformation that boost long-term growth. Hence, rather than undermine FDI flows, the best way to ensure inclusive growth is to *complement* investment policy with progressive labor market policies.[16]

Recent evidence suggests that some active labor market policies, including vocational training and employment subsidies, are not cost-effective (box 3.3). However, that does not mean that government policy cannot improve labor market outcomes. Three types of labor market policies have had the most beneficial effect on labor markets: (a) improving labor standards and labor representation; (b) providing labor market information and skills certification to vulnerable communities; and (c) stimulating internal labor mobility. These are discussed in Recommendations 4–6.

Recommendation 4: Improve bargaining power and knowledge spillovers for workers by enforcing sufficient labor standards and supporting labor representation.

BOX 3.3

The Limited Effectiveness of Traditional Active Labor Market Policies

A systematic survey of 24 randomized control trials of active labor market programs in 10 developing countries found that "these programs have at best modest impact in most circumstances" (McKenzie 2017).

Vocational training programs were found to have modest effects on employment. "For every 100 people offered vocational training, fewer than 3 will find a job they would not have otherwise found" (McKenzie 2017). The study finds that the cost of employing one additional person ranged from approximately US$17,000 to US$60,000.

Employment subsidies are also not effective, especially when firms had to formally register workers, the literature suggests. In the one study, initial positive results disappeared quickly once the subsidy ended. No study identified any long-term impact on employment from subsidies (McKenzie 2017). Such evidence from developing countries is consistent with findings of ineffective active labor market policies in developed countries (Crépon and van den Berg 2016).

While FDI may be job creating, FDI benefits in terms of creating "good" jobs are not automatic. The OECD defines job quality based on three dimensions: wages, labor market security, and the working environment (Cazes, Hijzen, and Saint-Martin 2015). Although this study finds that FDI has an impact on wages, evidence regarding FDI and labor market security and the quality of the working environment is mixed (Hijzen et al. 2013). Some studies have found that foreign firms adapt to local labor practices rather than export the labor practices of their home economy (Almond and Ferner 2006). Others have argued that governments have been tempted to lower labor standards to attract FDI, resulting in an international "race to the bottom" (Bernard and Jensen 2007; Bernard and Sjöholm 2003). Yet, in many cases, such policy is misguided, given that efficiency-seeking firms care about low *unit labor costs* (the average cost of labor per unit of output) rather than the lowest employment costs overall. Government-enforced labor standards may raise labor costs but can also reduce unit labor costs by reducing turnover.

One way to reduce labor turnover is to improve safety standards—in turn creating better opportunities for knowledge spillovers to workers and increasing labor productivity for firms. Many of the manufacturing jobs associated with FDI in low-income countries are associated with significant health risks. Blattman and Dercon (2018) find that, in Ethiopia, chances of a chronic health issue went up 1 percentage point for every month someone works in an industrial firm (associated with chemical use and dirty air). Combined with extremely low pay, this situation meant that worker turnover was very high, and 77 percent of workers quit within their first year. Other estimates also find evidence of extreme annual turnover in Ethiopia, ranging from 60 percent to 120 percent (with complete turnover of more than one cohort occurring in some years) (Barrett and Baumann-Pauly 2019). When workers are employed for such a short period, they have little opportunity to learn on the job or receive knowledge spillovers from MNEs. This leads to low labor efficiency for the firm and little in productivity-linked wage benefits for the workers.[17] Government can play a role by enforcing labor standards throughout an industry, which is likely to reduce turnover, raise employee health benefits, and give firms a reason to invest in training their workers.

Better labor representation can also reduce wage inequality, but more research is needed on ways to balance the costs and benefits of labor laws (Blattman and Dercon 2018). There is considerable evidence from developed countries that unions can reduce wage inequality (see, for example, Dinardo and Lemieux 1997; Lemieux 1993) and that differences in the rate of deunionization are correlated with differences in the growth of inequality (Card, Lemieux, and Riddell 2004, 2018; Gosling and Lemieux 2004). This evidence has led some experts to argue that labor law reforms should be part of any policy response to rising inequality (see, for example, Stiglitz 2012). Yet regulation also risks raising labor costs (which could scare off FDI in the country) and risks benefiting insiders (union members) at the expense of outsiders (those without employment).

More research is needed in this area. A key example comes from labor standards campaigns in Indonesia, which led to large real wage increases in targeted firms, with some costs (falling profits) but no adverse employment effects (Harrison and Scorse 2010). In the absence of union representation (which takes time to establish), governments can also foster workers' councils to grant employees a voice and a venue to air grievances (Barrett and Baumann-Pauly 2019).

Recommendation 5: Support vulnerable communities (such as lower-skilled workers, youth, and women) by providing jobs information and skills certification.

Governments can also help vulnerable communities by lowering search costs in the labor market by offering public information about jobs and organization of job fairs.

Providing job seekers with information about the labor market can help improve employment. In rural India, informing young women about urban ICT jobs and helping them with the application process meant that these women were 4.6 percentage points more likely than others to work in ICT jobs (Jensen 2012). In Ethiopia, providing job seekers with bus fares to search for vacancies or attend job interviews improved labor market outcomes (Abebe et al. 2017). Finally, in the Philippines, a job fair also allowed attendees to learn about their labor market prospects, increasing the probability of working in a formal job by 11 percentage points (compared with the control group) (Beam 2016).

Recent experimental evidence also shows that programs that certify existing skills can also help job seekers find better jobs. In Ethiopia, workers who attended job application workshops that provided skill certificates as well as training on résumés, cover letters, and job interviews had 20 percent higher earnings than comparable workers in the control group. These gains were concentrated among those with the least education and experience (Abebe et al. 2018). In Uganda, certificates of soft skills led employed workers to earn 11 percent more in the two years after the intervention (Bassi and Nansamba 2018). Certificates work best when they focus on general skills rather than apprenticeships, which focus on firm-specific skills that are harder to certify and were valued less by other firms in the market (Alfonsi et al. 2017). In sum, reducing information gaps can increase employment quality and earnings for job seekers in vulnerable communities (Caria and Lessing 2019).

Recommendation 6: Establish programs to stimulate internal migration.

Regulatory changes and support programs to stimulate internal migration can further help improve access to employment, with important welfare benefits (Newman et al. 2016). FDI often creates more jobs close by, which often means that large wage benefits are restricted to urban areas. Stimulating urbanization can help expand some of these benefits to the wider population. Yet moving is costly, and informal insurance in the form of relying on families and communities means that individuals rarely move (Munshi and Rosenzweig 2016).

Some of the most successful labor market interventions are those that helped workers access job opportunities in a different location (Jensen 2012) or subsidized job searches in different parts of the city (Abebe et al. 2016; Franklin 2015).[18] More striking evidence comes from Bryan, Chowdhury, and Mobarak (2014), who show that a small subsidy equal to the cost of a bus ticket spurred new seasonal migration in Bangladesh, which improved employment opportunities and increased household consumption (analogous to income) by 30–35 percent.

Overall, this report calls for an integrated approach that combines (a) *proactive investment policy and promotion* (including targeting FDI, tackling absorptive capacity, and liberalizing services with the best prospects for employment and wage increases) with (b) *progressive labor market policies* (including support for workers' labor standards and labor representation, active provision of information to vulnerable job seekers, and support programs to stimulate internal migration). Policies that can align these different elements have the best chance of ensuring that FDI will bring benefits to the host economy, stimulate poverty reduction, promote shared prosperity, and produce inclusive growth.

Annex 3A. Data Description

The analysis links household survey data with firm-level data. The main source of household data comes from the World Bank's International Income Distribution Database (I2D2). The I2D2 is a harmonized dataset covering more than 900 nationally representative household surveys from more than 160 countries.[19] The data include the industry of employment, which can be harmonized in all countries to two-digit ISIC (rev. 4) industries. In addition, it includes information on workers' characteristics (gender, age, education) and geographic location (region). The analysis uses this sector and location information to match with the variable of interest concerning MNE activities. For Ethiopia, this resulted in five surveys between 2009 and 2014. For Vietnam, to increase overlap with the firm-level data, the I2D2 was supplemented with Labor Force Surveys for 2013–16. For Turkey, household surveys recorded two-digit industrial sectors only from 2009 onward (previously, it was one-digit).

Various firm-level datasets in each country were used to match with the household-level data. For Vietnam and Turkey, the analysis relies on information from the Enterprise Census and Enterprise Information System, respectively. Both include information on firms from all sectors in the economy. For Ethiopia, a census of all manufacturing establishments with 10 or more employees, the Large and Medium Manufacturing Survey, was used.

From firm-level data, the share of revenue (employment) by foreign firms in total output (employment) was calculated as a proxy for FDI activity. This MNE output share is estimated annually, across each region and ISIC two-digit sector. In Vietnam and Turkey, the data include information on firms in all sectors. In Ethiopia, the survey covers manufacturing activity only. As a result, the analysis in Ethiopia is restricted to FDI in the manufacturing sector, which nevertheless captures 70–89 percent of annual FDI inflows since 2007 (EIC 2017). The analysis covers the periods with significant FDI growth in Ethiopia (2009–14), Vietnam (2007–16), and Turkey (2009–16).

Before conducting the analysis, all the datasets were restricted to only working-age individuals (ages 15–65). The focus is on employed individuals. Two main outcomes were constructed: an indicator for whether a worker is formally employed and the worker's wage level. Because of differences in the household survey, the definition of formal employment varies slightly across the three countries. In Ethiopia and Vietnam, this indicator takes a value of 1 if a worker is either a paid employee or employer, and 0 if the individual is a nonpaid employee or self-employed. In Turkey, this indicator takes a value of 1 if a worker contributes to social security (a common indicator of formal employment), and 0 otherwise. The measure of wages was normalized to monthly payments in constant 2010 terms.

The main variable of interest is defined as the share of FDI firms' revenue in a sector and region. Because of differing data availability, there are some variations in how this variable is measured across the three sample countries. In all countries, a region is defined as a level-2 administrative region (NUTS2 in the case of Turkey, and province in the case of Ethiopia and Vietnam), which results in 11 regions in Ethiopia, 26 in Turkey, and 64 in Vietnam. Foreign firms are defined as those with at least 10 percent foreign ownership in Ethiopia and Turkey. In Vietnam, foreign firms are those identified as having any positive foreign shares, given the lack of data on shareholders in some years. Nevertheless, when this variable is available, a high correlation is found between the two definitions.

Annex 3B. Empirical Specifications

The analysis is performed separately for each of the three country case studies. The baseline model estimates the following:

$$y_{isrt} = \beta \times FDI_{srt-1} + \delta X_{irst} + \gamma * tariff_{st} + d_s + d_{rt} + \varepsilon_{irst}, \quad (3B.1)$$

where, y denotes formal employment or (log) wages, i is the specific individual, s is the two-digit sector, r is the region within a country, and t is the year. FDI_{srt-1} denotes lagged FDI activity, calculated as the share of foreign firms' revenue in the total output of a sector and region within a country. β is the main coefficient of interest, which measures the change in the probability of formal employment or the percentage change in wages associated with a unit change in FDI activity.

Implicitly, this specification assumes that the relevant labor market is within a sector and region. There is an adjustment cost to move between sectors and regions, so there are differences in individual employment and wages due to differences in FDI activities. The analysis controls for a set of individual characteristics in X_{irst}, including age, gender, and education level to account for potential selection of workers into regions and sectors with higher FDI. The sectoral fixed effects, d_s, control for inherent differences in sectoral labor demand that could be correlated with FDI attractiveness.

Equation (3B.1) is estimated using an instrumental variable, where FDI_{srt} is instrumented for by growth in global FDI (greenfield and M&A) in sector s in year t-4, interacted with the original shares of FDI in region sector rs (that is, the shares at the beginning of the sample period). A quadratic term is included of the instrument to capture potential nonlinear effects between the instrument and the variable of interest. For example, agglomeration effects might imply that the original shares of FDI would have an exponential effect on FDI activities in later years.

Including another excluded instrument also allows the analysis to formally test for the exogeneity of the instruments and the error terms. Global FDI captures supply shocks that are unlikely to be correlated with other domestic changes. Nevertheless, this instrument is not exogenous if regional shocks occur that affect both the labor markets and FDI shares. To account for this, the model also controls for a set of region-year fixed effects. Finally, for all nonservices sectors, the model also controls for average tariff in the sector to separate out the potential impact of FDI from trade liberalization, given that FDI reforms are often accompanied by trade liberalization.

The effect of vertical FDI is estimated using the following specification:

$$\begin{aligned} y_{isrt} = {} & \beta_{fw} \times \sum{}_j FDI_{j\rightarrow s,srt} + \beta_{fw} \\ & \times \sum{}_k FDI_{j\rightarrow k,srt} + \delta X_{irst}\gamma * \\ & tariff_{st} + d_s + d_{rt} + \varepsilon_{irst}, \end{aligned} \tag{3B.2}$$

where $\Sigma_j FDI_{j\rightarrow s,srt}$ and $\Sigma_k FDI_{s\rightarrow k,srt}$ denote the weighted sum of FDI output shares in all sectors supplying to or buying from sector s, where the weights are the technical coefficients in the input-output table for each country, to capture the degree of linkages between sectors.

Intuitively, this specification examines the extent to which labor demand in a sector is affected by backward and forward linkages with other foreign-invested sectors. The instrument is the weighted sum of the original instrument for FDI in each sector and region.

To understand the distribution impact of FDI, the following specification is estimated:

$$\begin{aligned} y_{isrt} = {} & \beta FDI_{rst} + nFDI_{rst} \times Edu_{isrt} + \delta X_{irst} \\ & + \gamma * tariff_{st} + d_s + d_{rt} + \varepsilon_{irst}. \end{aligned} \tag{3B.3}$$

Here, the interactions between FDI and workers' education is included to capture how worker outcomes vary with their education levels. In aggregate, the total effect will also depend on the types of sectors receiving FDI and the nature of FDI (low skill versus high skill, tradable versus nontradable, labor intensive versus capital intensive).

The impact of FDI on the income distribution is then aggregated using estimates from equation (3B.3). For each individual, the counterfactual wage *without* FDI is predicted assuming a zero FDI value. The aggregate poverty level, total income of the bottom 40 percent, and the inequality indicators (Palma ratio and Gini coefficient) are estimated for the actual and this counterfactual (wage) income distribution. The contribution of FDI to poverty reduction, shared prosperity, and inequality are then calculated as the differences between these numbers.

Annex 3C. Additional Tables

TABLE 3C.1 Broad Sectoral Classification and Their Subsectors

Broad sector	*Subsectors*
Extractives	Mining of coal and lignite
	Extraction of crude petroleum and natural gas
	Mining of metal ores
	Other mining and quarrying
	Mining support service activities
Low-skilled manufacturing	Food, beverages, and tobacco products
	Wood and wood products
	Other nonmetallic mineral products
	Fabricated metal
	Paper and paper products; printing and publishing
	Rubber and plastics products
	Basic metals
	Textiles, wearing apparel, and leather products
	Furniture; manufacturing n.e.c. (not specified)
High-skilled manufacturing	Coke and refined petroleum products
	Chemicals and chemical products
	Machinery and equipment n.e.c. (not specified)
	Transport equipment
	Electrical machinery and equipment
	Computer, electronics, and optical equipment
	Pharmaceutical products
Low-skilled services	Construction
	Wholesale and retail trade; repair of motor vehicles and motorcycles
	Transportation and storage (land, warehousing)
	Accommodation and food service activities
	Security, landscape, and employment activities
High-skilled services	Transportation and storage (water, air, postal)
	Information and communication
	Financial and insurance activities
	Professional, scientific, and technical activities
	Travel agencies and tour operators
	Office administration and other business support activities

Source: World Bank, based on Hallward-Driemeier and Nayyar 2017.
Note: Based on International Standard Industrial Classification (ISIC) rev. 4 classification. Extractives follows ISIC 05–09. Low-skilled manufacturing covers ISIC 10–18, 22–24, 31–32. High-skilled manufacturing covers ISIC 19–21, 25–30, 33. Low-skilled services covers ISIC 41–49, 52, 55–56, 68, 77–78, 80, 81. High-skilled services covers ISIC 50–51, 53, 58–66, 69–75, 79, 82. n.e.c. = not elsewhere classified.

TABLE 3C.2 FDI Labor Market Effects: All Countries (Second-Stage IV Results)

	Vietnam				Turkey				Ethiopia	
	(1)	(2)	(3)	(4)	(5)	(6)	(7)	(8)	(9)	(10)
Outcome Variables	*Wages (LN)*	*Wages (LN)*	*Formal Employment*	*Formal Employment*	*Wages (LN)*	*Wages (LN)*	*Formal Employment*	*Formal Employment*	*Wages (LN)*	*Formal Employment*
Household Sample	*Manu-facturing*	*Services*	*Manu-facturing*	*Services*	*Manu-facturing*	*Services*	*Manu-facturing*	*Services*	*Manu-facturing*	*Manu-facturing*
MNE output share (lagged Y1)	0.340*** (2.78)	0.577** (2.20)	0.141** (2.45)	−0.0200 (−0.16)	1.054*** (0.356)	1.033 (1.247)	0.122*** (0.045)	−0.010 (0.168)	1.156* (0.654)	0.124 (0.100)
Additional controls	Education, Gender, Age	Education, Gender, Age	Education, Gender, Age	Education, Gender, Age	Education, Gender, Age	Education, Gender, Age	Education, Gender, Age	Education, Gender, Age	Education, Gender, Age	Education, Gender, Age
Sectoral tariffs	Yes	No	Yes	No	Yes	No	Yes	No	Yes	Yes
Region × year fixed effects	Yes	Yes	Yes	Yes	Yes	Yes	Yes	Yes	Yes	Yes
ISIC2 sector fixed effects	Yes	Yes	Yes	Yes	Yes	Yes	Yes	Yes	Yes	Yes
Observations	265,335	489,660	393,905	885,941	202,855	392,785	211,900	418,975	10,683	11,084
R-squared	0.405	0.342	0.260	0.296	0.050	0.049	0.053	0.049	0.120	0.082
Hansen J statistic (p-value)	0.222	0.168	0.000	0.061	0.7107	0.6907	0.9815	0.3867	0.2904	0.2700
Kleibergen-Paap LM test (test)	107.6	34.8	115.9	37.2	42.4	25.3	42.4	25.1	11.4	11.6
Kleibergen-Paap LM test (p-value)	4.21e-24	2.83e-08	6.91e-26	8.42e-09	0.0000	0.0000	0.0000	0.0000	0.0033	0.0030
Kleibergen-Paap Wald rk F statistic	68.39	35.28	88.94	34.56	142.44	24.11	139.64	23.17	10.36	10.93
Total average effects (%)	12.0	2.0	5.2	0	7.7	0	0.9	0	31.5	0

Source: World Bank.
Note: FDI = foreign direct investment; IV = instrumental variables; ISIC2 = International Standard Industrial Classification of All Economic Activities two-digit code; LM = Lagrange Multiplier; LN = natural logarithm; MNE = multinational enterprise; Y1 = Year 1.
Standard errors are clustered at the region*sector level: *** $p < 0.01$ ** $p < 0.05$ * $p < 0.10$

TABLE 3C.3 FDI Labor Market Effects by Broad Sector and Education Level: Ethiopia (Second-Stage IV Results)

	(1)	(2)	(3)	(4)	(5)	(6)
Outcome variables	*Wages (LN)*	*Wages (LN)*	*Wages (LN)*	*Formal Emp.*	*Formal Emp.*	*Formal Emp.*
Household sample	*Manufacturing*	*Low-skilled manufacturing*	*High-skilled manufacturing*	*Manufacturing*	*Low-skilled manufacturing*	*High-skilled manufacturing*
MNE output share (lagged Y1)*no education	1.810***	1.793***	17.20***	0.239**	0.233**	2.295***
	(0.637)	(0.643)	(3.780)	(0.104)	(0.107)	(0.484)
MNE output share (lagged Y1)*primary education	1.595**	1.913**	1.108	0.199*	0.235**	0.0983
	(0.729)	(0.781)	(1.177)	(0.109)	(0.117)	(0.145)
MNE output share (lagged Y1)*secondary education	2.741	2.750	—	0.332	0.198	—
	(2.672)	(3.143)	(.)	(0.400)	(0.467)	(.)
MNE output share (lagged Y1)*postsecondary education	−0.772	−0.847	1.255	−0.246	−0.260	0.0120
	(1.225)	(1.609)	(1.408)	(0.171)	(0.225)	(0.196)
Additional controls	Education, Gender, Age	Education, Gender, Age	Education, Gender, Age	Education, Gender, Age	Education, Gender, Age	Education, Gender, Age
Sectoral tariffs	Yes	Yes	Yes	Yes	Yes	Yes
Region-year fixed effects	Yes	Yes	Yes	Yes	Yes	Yes
ISIC2 sector fixed effects	Yes	Yes	Yes	Yes	Yes	Yes
Observations	10,683	10,024	659	11,084	10,411	673
R-squared	0.112	0.106	−0.082	0.071	0.069	−0.182

Source: World Bank.
Note: See first-stage results in the supplementary appendix; FDI = foreign direct investment; ISIC2 = International Standard Industrial Classification of All Economic Activities two-digit code; IV = instrumental variables; LN = natural logarithm; MNE = multinational enterprise; Y1 = Year 1. Both the dash and (.) mean that there were insufficient observations for this, and so no results were identified.
Standard errors are clustered at the region*sector level: *** $p < 0.01$ ** $p < 0.05$ * $p < 0.10$

TABLE 3C.4 FDI Labor Market Effects by Broad Sector and Education Level: Vietnam (Second-Stage IV Results)

	(1)	(2)	(3)	(4)	(5)	(6)	(7)	(8)	(9)	(10)	(11)	(12)	(13)	(14)
Outcome variables	*Wages (LN)*	*Wages (LN)*	*Wages (LN)*	*Wages (LN)*	*Wages (LN)*	*Wages (LN)*	*Wages (LN)*	*Formal Emp.*	*Formal Emp.*	*Formal Emp.*	*Formal Emp.*	*Formal Emp.*	*Formal Emp.*	*Formal Emp.*
Household sample	*Extractives*	*Manu-facturing*	*Low-skilled manuf.*	*High-skilled manuf.*	*Services*	*Low-skilled services*	*High-skilled services*	*Extractives*	*Manu-facturing*	*Low-skilled manuf.*	*High-skilled manuf.*	*Services*	*Low-skilled services*	*High-skilled services*
MNE output share (lagged Y1)* no education	1.560***	0.627	0.836	−0.217	-3.791**	-3.995**	4.230	−0.514***	0.372***	0.443***	0.223*	−0.401	−0.457	1.242
	(9.48)	(1.48)	(1.58)	(−0.75)	(-2.30)	(-2.22)	(1.40)	(0.16)	(2.70)	(2.72)	(1.77)	(−0.79)	(−0.79)	(1.60)
MNE output share (lagged Y1)* primary education	−1.418	0.356**	0.445***	−0.005	-1.57**	-1.838**	0.425	−0.750***	0.259***	0.329***	0.043	−0.422	−0.509	−0.048
	(2.48)	(2.42)	(2.62)	(−0.03)	(-2.13)	(-1.99)	(0.49)	(0.32)	(3.83)	(4.17)	(0.69)	(−1.38)	(−1.28)	(−0.31)
MNE output share (lagged Y1)* secondary education	0.783	0.319**	0.368**	−0.108	0.478	0.853*	0.028	0.029	0.149**	0.226***	−0.035	0.185	0.352*	0.004
	(0.51)	(2.43)	(2.40)	(−0.83)	(1.21)	(1.72)	(0.10)	(0.14)	(2.57)	(3.25)	(−0.64)	(1.31)	(1.89)	(0.02)
MNE output share (lagged Y1)* postsecondary education	0.370	0.348***	0.969***	−0.166	0.837***	1.115**	0.211	−0.096	−0.103*	−0.052	−0.199***	−0.162	−0.120	0.072
	(0.44)	(2.64)	(3.33)	(−1.28)	(2.95)	(2.22)	(0.97)	(0.14)	(−1.65)	(−0.56)	(−3.46)	(−1.16)	(−0.64)	(0.59)
Additional controls	Education, Gender, Age	Education, Gender, Age	Education, Gender, Age	Education, Gender, Age	Education, Gender, Age	Education, Gender, Age	Education, Gender, Age	Education, Gender, Age	Education, Gender, Age	Education, Gender, Age	Education, Gender, Age	Education, Gender, Age	Education, Gender, Age	Education, Gender, Age
Sectoral tariffs	Yes	Yes	Yes	Yes	No	No	No	Yes	Yes	Yes	Yes	No	No	No
Region-year fixed effects	Yes	Yes	Yes	Yes	Yes	Yes	Yes	Yes	Yes	Yes	Yes	Yes	Yes	Yes
ISIC2 sector fixed effects	Yes	Yes	Yes	Yes	Yes	Yes	Yes	Yes	Yes	Yes	Yes	Yes	Yes	Yes
Observations	11,436	265,325	215,664	49,661	489,641	446,685	42,956	17,450	393,895	324,270	69,625	885,922	826,071	59,851
R-squared	0.0339	0.0221	0.0121	0.0329	0.0140	0.0122	0.0534	−0.0284	0.0667	0.0654	0.0202	0.0944	0.0923	0.0956

Source: World Bank.
Note: See first-stage results in the supplementary appendix. FDI = foreign direct investment; ISIC2 = International Standard Industrial Classification two-digit code; IV = instrumental variables; LN = natural logarithm; MNE = multinational enterprise; Y1 = Year 1.
Standard errors are clustered at the region*sector level: *** $p < 0.01$ ** $p < 0.05$ * $p < 0.10$

TABLE 3C.5 FDI Labor Market Effects by Broad Sector and Education Level: Turkey (Second-Stage IV Results)

	(1)	(2)	(3)	(4)	(5)	(6)	(7)	(8)	(9)	(10)	(11)	(12)	(13)	(14)
Outcome variables	*Wages (LN)*	*Wages (LN)*	*Wages (LN)*	*Wages (LN)*	*Wages (LN)*	*Wages (LN)*	*Wages (LN)*	*Formal Emp.*	*Formal Emp.*	*Formal Emp.*	*Formal Emp.*	*Formal Emp.*	*Formal Emp.*	*Formal Emp.*
Household sample	*Extractives*	*Manu-facturing*	*Low-skilled manuf.*	*High-skilled manuf.*	*Services*	*Low-skilled services*	*High-skilled services*	*Extractives*	*Manu-facturing*	*Low-skilled manuf.*	*High-skilled manuf.*	*Services*	*Low-skilled services*	*High-skilled services*
MNE output share (lagged Y1)*no education	0.119 (1.070)	0.189 (1.145)	0.155 (1.372)	0.546 (0.763)	−11.690*** (2.377)	−11.040*** (2.558)	−2.772 (1.725)	−0.510 (0.488)	0.260** (0.122)	0.290* (0.148)	0.075 (0.092)	−2.344*** (0.381)	−2.324*** (0.404)	−0.316 (0.203)
MNE output share (lagged Y1)*primary education	0.184 (0.326)	1.424*** (0.414)	1.902*** (0.571)	0.571* (0.312)	−1.859 (1.167)	−0.762 (1.433)	−1.989 (1.243)	0.007 (0.013)	0.174*** (0.052)	0.236*** (0.073)	0.053 (0.039)	−0.467*** (0.158)	−0.353* (0.191)	−0.204 (0.153)
MNE output share (lagged Y1)* secondary education	−0.512 (0.730)	0.813*** (0.307)	1.099** (0.509)	0.232 (0.245)	3.269*** (1.018)	5.469*** (1.346)	−0.191 (0.967)	0.016 (0.015)	0.076** (0.038)	0.087 (0.063)	0.021 (0.031)	0.363*** (0.133)	0.610*** (0.176)	−0.075 (0.109)
MNE output share (lagged Y1)* postsecondary education	0.322 (0.489)	0.431 (0.317)	0.550 (0.522)	0.024 (0.280)	4.037*** (1.245)	2.505 (1.600)	1.412 (1.256)	0.007 (0.019)	0.041 (0.039)	0.031 (0.063)	0.009 (0.034)	0.690*** (0.186)	0.712*** (0.240)	0.089 (0.142)
Additional controls	Education, Gender, Age	Education, Gender, Age	Education, Gender, Age	Education, Gender, Age	Education, Gender, Age	Education, Gender, Age	Education, Gender, Age	Education, Gender, Age	Education, Gender, Age	Education, Gender, Age	Education, Gender, Age	Education, Gender, Age	Education, Gender, Age	Education, Gender, Age
Sectoral tariffs	Yes	Yes	Yes	Yes	No	No	No	Yes	Yes	Yes	Yes	No	No	No
Region-year fixed effects	Yes	Yes	Yes	Yes	Yes	Yes	Yes	Yes	Yes	Yes	Yes	Yes	Yes	Yes
ISIC2 sector fixed effects	Yes	Yes	Yes	Yes	Yes	Yes	Yes	Yes	Yes	Yes	Yes	Yes	Yes	Yes
Observations	5,948	202,855	153,448	49,407	444,774	392,785	51,989	6,102	211,900	159,955	51,945	475,068	418,975	56,093
R-squared	0.021	0.050	0.061	0.025	0.042	0.048	0.012	−0.004	0.053	0.066	0.022	0.039	0.046	0.027

Source: World Bank.
Note: See first-stage results in the supplementary appendix; FDI = foreign direct investment; ISIC2 = International Standard Industrial Classification two-digit code; IV = instrumental variables; LN = natural logarithm; MNE = multinational enterprise; Y1 = Year 1.
Standard errors are clustered at the region*sector level: *** $p < 0.01$ ** $p < 0.05$ * $p < 0.10$

TABLE 3C.6 FDI Labor Market Effects by Broad Sector and Education Level: All Countries (Population Weighted, Total Average Effects)

	a. Ethiopia									
	(1)	(2)	(3)	(4)	(5)	(6)	(7)	(8)	(9)	(10)
Outcome variables	Wages (LN)	Wages (LN)	Wages (LN)	Wages (LN)	Wages (LN)	Formal Emp.	Formal Emp.	Formal Emp.	Formal Emp.	Formal Emp.
Household sample	Extractives	Low-skilled manufacturing	High-skilled manufacturing	Low-skilled services	High-skilled services	Extractives	Low-skilled manufacturing	High-skilled manufacturing	Low-skilled services	High-skilled services
Total average effects (%)										
FDI effect: average	—	37.1	23.5	—	—	—	4.7	0.3	—	—
FDI effect: no education	—	53.1	29.4	—	—	—	6.9	4.0	—	—
FDI effect: primary education	—	51.4	0	—	—	—	6.3	0	—	—
FDI effect: secondary education	—	0	0	—	—	—	0	0	—	—
FDI effect: postsecondary education	—	0	0	—	—	—	0	0	—	—

	b. Vietnam									
	(1)	(2)	(3)	(4)	(5)	(6)	(7)	(8)	(9)	(10)
Outcome variables	Wages (LN)	Wages (LN)	Wages (LN)	Wages (LN)	Wages (LN)	Formal Emp.	Formal Emp.	Formal Emp.	Formal Emp.	Formal Emp.
Household sample	Extractives	Low-skilled manufacturing	High-skilled manufacturing	Low-skilled services	High-skilled services	Extractives	Low-skilled manufacturing	High-skilled manufacturing	Low-skilled services	High-skilled services
Total average effects (%)										
FDI effect: average	0.2	11.6	14.4	-0.8	4.9	-0.8	5.1	5.5	0	0
FDI effect: no education	11.2	0	0	-6.6	-27.3	9.8	13.6	0	0	0
FDI effect: primary education	0	12.6	13.0	−4.1	−18.2	−4.0	5.3	5.4	0	0
FDI effect secondary education	0	11.4	14.1	0	0	0	5.3	6.6	0	0
FDI effect: postsecondary education	0	11.9	17.6	5.5	11.1	0	0	0	0	0

table continues next page

TABLE 3C.6 FDI Labor Market Effects by Broad Sector and Education Level: All Countries (Population Weighted, Total Average Effects) *(continued)*

	c. Turkey									
Outcome variables	*(1) Wages (LN)*	*(2) Wages (LN)*	*(3) Wages (LN)*	*(4) Wages (LN)*	*(5) Wages (LN)*	*(6) Formal Emp.*	*(7) Formal Emp.*	*(8) Formal Emp.*	*(9) Formal Emp.*	*(10) Formal Emp.*
Household sample	*Extractives*	*Low-skilled manufacturing*	*High-skilled manufacturing*	*Low-skilled services*	*High-skilled services*	*Extractives*	*Low-skilled manufacturing*	*High-skilled manufacturing*	*Low-skilled services*	*High-skilled services*
Total average effects (%)										
FDI effect average	0	6.0	10.8	5.1	12.9	0	0.8	1.3	−0.7	1.2
FDI effect: no education	0	0	0	−49.3	−116.0	0	1.1	2.0	−9.8	−23.0
FDI effect: primary education	0	7.5	14.7	0	0	0	0.9	1.8	−2.2	−4.2
FDI effect: secondary education	0	5.5	11.4	18.0	20.0	0	0.5	1.1	2.1	2.3
FDI effect: postsecondary education	0	0	0	22.4	14.3	0	0	0	3.8	2.4

Source: World Bank.
Note: Based on population-weighted, total average effects in the country, using regression coefficients from tables 3C.3 through 3C.5. FDI = foreign direct investment; LN = natural logarithm; — = not available.

TABLE 3C.7 Vertical Spillovers Effect of FDI on Labor Market Outcomes: All Countries (Second-Stage IV Results)

	Vietnam				*Turkey*				*Ethiopia*	
	(1)	*(2)*	*(3)*	*(4)*	*(5)*	*(6)*	*(7)*	*(8)*	*(9)*	*(10)*
Outcome variables	*Wages (LN)*	*Wages (LN)*	*Formal Emp.*	*Formal Emp.*	*Wages (LN)*	*Wages (LN)*	*Formal Emp.*	*Formal Emp.*	*Wages (LN)*	*Formal Emp.*
Household sample	*Manuf.*	*Services*	*Manuf.*	*Services*	*Manuf.*	*Services*	*Manuf.*	*Services*	*Manuf.*	*Manuf.*
MNE output share (lagged Y1)	0.307*** (0.116)	0.141*** (0.052)	0.201*** (0.030)	−0.089 (0.130)	1.036*** (0.378)	0.760 (0.895)	0.119** (0.048)	0.032 (0.123)	1.237* (0.679)	0.135 (0.104)
MNE output share (lagged Y1)*backward intensity (backward link)	0.829 (0.559)	0.452** (0.212)	0.415*** (0.066)	0.169** (0.084)	2.761 (2.251)	−0.194 (0.666)	0.409 (0.309)	−0.080 (0.119)	0.323 (3.648)	−0.015 (0.487)
MNE output share (lagged Y1)*forward intensity (forward link)	−0.515 (0.628)	0.146 (0.266)	0.205*** (0.063)	−0.024 (0.087)	−6.793*** (2.112)	0.056 (0.571)	−0.945*** (0.282)	0.076 (0.088)	3.337 (2.794)	0.471 (0.411)
Additional controls	Education, Gender, Age	Education, Gender, Age	Education, Gender, Age	Education, Gender, Age	Education, Gender, Age	Education, Gender, Age	Education, Gender, Age	Education, Gender, Age	Education, Gender, Age	Education, Gender, Age
Sectoral tariffs	Yes	No	Yes	No	Yes	No	Yes	No	Yes	Yes
Region-year fixed effects	Yes	Yes	Yes	Yes	Yes	Yes	Yes	Yes	Yes	Yes
ISIC2 sector fixed effects	Yes	Yes	Yes	Yes	Yes	Yes	Yes	Yes	Yes	Yes
Observations	265,335	393,905	489,660	885,941	202,855	444,774	211,900	475,068	10,683	11,084
R-squared	0.404	0.260	0.342	0.296	0.048	0.043	0.050	0.044	0.117	0.078
	(1)	*(2)*	*(3)*	*(4)*	*(5)*	*(6)*	*(7)*	*(8)*	*(9)*	*(10)*
Total average effects (%)										
MNE output share (lagged Y1)	10.8	5.0	0.9	0.0	8.4	0	1.0	0	33.8	0
MNE output share (lagged Y1)*backward intensity (backward link)	0	5.0	4.2	1.7	0	0	0	0	0	0
MNE output share (lagged Y1)*forward intensity (forward link)	0	0	1.7	0.0	-35.7	0	-4.9	0	0	0

Source: World Bank.
Note: See first-stage results in the supplementary appendix; FDI = foreign direct investment; ISIC2 = International Standard Industrial Classification two-digit code; IV = instrumental variable; LN = natural logarithm; MNE = multinational enterprise; Y1 = Year 1.
Standard errors are clustered at the region*sector level: *** $p < 0.01$ ** $p < 0.05$ * $p < 0.10$

Notes

1. For an overview of the general literature on FDI and firm dynamics, see Iršová and Havránek (2013) and Javorcik (2015). For examples from Africa, see El Badaoui, Strobl, and Walsh (2008) and Söderbom and Teal (2004). Other examples include Bernard, Robertson, and Schott (2010); Feenstra and Hanson (1997); and Verhoogen (2008).
2. More specifically, the goals are to reduce extreme poverty in the world to less than 3 percent by 2030 and to foster income growth of the bottom 40 percent of the population in each country (World Bank 2015).
3. The UN estimates the gap in financing to achieve the Sustainable Development Goals (SDGs) at US$2.5 trillion per year in developing countries alone (UNCTAD 2014). Although governments and the public sector

will continue to play a key financing role, there is greater scope for the private sector to engage in financing many areas of the SDGs to help close the gap (UNCTAD 2018). Out of the 17 SDGs, this chapter focuses on the link between FDI and three of the SDGs in particular: (a) SDG 1: End poverty in all its forms everywhere; (b) SDG 8: Promote inclusive and sustainable economic growth and decent work for all; and (c) SDG 10: Reduce inequalities within and among countries.

4. "FDI in Turkey," Investment Office, Presidency of the Republic of Turkey website: http://www.invest.gov.tr/en-US/investmentguide/investorsguide/Pages/FDIinTurkey.aspx.
5. Data for the following discussion come from World Bank's various World Development Indicator (WDI) statistical tables: http://wdi.worldbank.org/tables.
6. Ideally, one would examine how FDI in a sector where an individual was *previously* employed affects their *subsequent* labor market outcomes. However, a lack of panel household data precludes the analysis from following individuals over time. As a result, the analysis cannot observe when a worker transitions between employment and unemployment and through different jobs.
7. An example of an upstream effect comes from a car parts manufacturer increasing sales to an MNE auto manufacturer. An example of a downstream transaction may be professional services (such as lawyers and accountants) that are used for an MNE's bookkeeping.
8. Data for sectoral greenfield FDI come from public announcements recorded by the *Financial Times*'s fDi Markets dataset (https://www.fdimarkets.com/), while M&A data capture public announcements recorded by Thomson Reuters.
9. The Gini coefficient uses the Lorenz curve to define the income distribution, with a number ranging from perfect equality (0) to perfect inequality (1). This analysis includes both the Gini coefficient and Palma ratio because the Gini coefficient is oversensitive to the middle of the distribution, and undersensitive to the tails, and thus might underestimate inequality for most countries today (Krozer 2015).
10. For the full results of the empirical analysis, see the online appendix accessible through the report website: http://www.worldbank.org/gicreport
11. Note that the effects estimated in this chapter capture relative effects of FDI (as proxied for by MNEs' output share) across regions and sectors experiencing a higher or lower share of MNE activities, not aggregate national effects. Dix-Caneiro and Kovak (2015) raise a similar point in their study on trade liberalization in Brazil.
12. To identify aggregate effects on formal employment, the regression coefficients from annex 3C, table 3C.1, are used and multiplied by the total yearly number of workers in manufacturing in the country using sampling weights. The results are averaged over time.
13. Similar findings on FDI for Turkey's manufacturing employment were identified by Kalemli-Ozcan, Sánchez-Martín, and Thirion (2016).
14. The aggregate regressions (annex 3C, table 3C.3) find that Turkey's manufacturing FDI is positively though insignificantly associated with manufacturing wages and employment. This suggests that any negative vertical effect is undone by the positive direct effects.
15. For more details on the World Bank's Jobs Diagnostics, see Hallward-Driemeier (2015) and Merotto, Weber, and Aterido (2018).
16. Similar arguments could be made for social policy (including unemployment and disability benefits) to complement FDI and temporarily accommodate labor market adjustment. Yet such policies are often not within the fiscal space of developing countries, which is why this section focuses on labor market policies.
17. More research is needed to better understand why firms do not try to combat high turnover (for example, through efficiency wages or self-enforced standards). It is possible that firms are poorly managed or constrained in unobserved ways. But it is also possible that high turnover at very low wages, where only those workers with the poorest outside options remain, is the firm's profit-maximizing choice (Blattman and Dercon 2018). Given the positive externalities associated with workers' knowledge transfer, this would call for government intervention.
18. One notable exception comes from countries that have seen high internal migration patterns (such as in the Middle East, where some countries experienced a large inflow of refugees in a short period). Because it takes time for labor markets to adapt to such labor supply shocks, in such cases, there may be limited benefits (or possible harm) from furthering internal migration.

19. As the World Bank's repository of household surveys, I2D2 harmonizes nationally representative household surveys—both welfare and labor force surveys—from around the world, presenting data using the same variables and coding in each country and survey.

References

Abebe, Girum, Stefano Caria, Marcel Fafchamps, Paolo Falco, Simon Franklin, and Simon Quinn. 2016. "Anonymity or Distance? Experimental Evidence on Obstacles to Youth Employment Opportunities." Unpublished research study, Stanford University, Stanford, CA.

Abebe, Girum, Stefano Caria, Marcel Fafchamps, Paolo Falco, Simon Franklin, and Simon Quinn. 2018. "Anonymity or Distance? Job Search and Labour Market Exclusion in a Growing African City." Discussion Paper 13136, Centre for Economic Policy Research, London.

Abebe, Girum, Stefano Caria, Marcel Fafchamps, Paolo Falco, Simon Franklin, Simon Quinn, and Forhad Shilpi. 2017. "Job Fairs: Matching Firms and Workers in a Field Experiment in Ethiopia." Policy Research Working Paper 8092, World Bank, Washington, DC.

Acemoglu, Daron, and David Autor. 2011. "Skills, Tasks and Technologies: Implications for Employment and Earnings." In *Handbook of Labor Economics*, Volume 4B, edited by Orley Ashenfelter and David Card, 1043–171. San Diego, CA, and Amsterdam: North Holland.

Acemoglu, Daron, and Pascual Restrepo. 2017. "Robots and Jobs: Evidence from US Labor Markets." Working Paper 23285, National Bureau of Economic Research, Cambridge, MA.

Adão, Rodrigo, Costas Arkolakis, and Federico Esposito. 2019. "Spatial Linkages, Global Shocks, and Local Labor Markets: Theory and Evidence." Working Paper No. 2019-10, Becker Friedman Institute for Economics, University of Chicago.

Alfaro, Laura, and Jasmina Chauvin. Forthcoming. "Foreign Direct Investment, Finance, and Economic Development." In *Encyclopedia of International Economics and Global Trade, Vol. 3: Foreign Direct Investment and the Multinational Enterprise*, edited by Mariana Spatareanu, 1–32. Singapore: World Scientific.

Alfonsi, Livia, Oriana Bandiera, Vittorio Bassi, Robin Burgess, Imran Rasul, Munshi Sulaiman, and Anna Vitali. 2017. "Tackling Youth Unemployment: Evidence from a Labour Market Experiment in Uganda." Development Economics Papers No. 64, Suntory and Toyota International Centres for Economics and Related Disciplines, London School of Economics.

Almond, Phil, and Anthony Ferner, eds. 2006. *American Multinationals in Europe*. Oxford: Oxford University Press.

Amann, Edmund, and Swati Virmani. 2014. "Foreign Direct Investment and Reverse Technology Spillovers: The Effect on Total Factor Productivity." *OECD Journal: Economic Studies* 2014 (1): 129–53.

Amir, Saman, Aphichoke Kotikula, Rohini P. Pande, Laurent Loic Yves Bossavie, and Upasana Khadka. 2018. "Female Labor Force Participation in Pakistan: What Do We Know?" Note for the Pakistan Gender and Social Inclusion Platform and Social Protection and Jobs Teams, World Bank, Washington, DC.

Amoranto, Glenita, Douglas H. Brooks, and Natalie Chun. 2010. "Services Liberalization and Wage Inequality in the Philippines." Working Paper 239, Asian Development Bank, Manila.

Antràs, Pol, and Stephen R. Yeaple. 2014. "Multinational Firms and the Structure of International Trade." In *Handbook of International Economics*, Volume 4, edited by Gita Gopinath, Elhanan Helpman, and Kenneth Rogoff, 55–130. Oxford and Amsterdam: North-Holland

Arnold, Jens Matthias, Beata Javorcik, Molly Lipscomb, and Aaditya Mattoo. 2016. "Services Reform and Manufacturing Performance: Evidence from India." *The Economic Journal* 126 (590): 1–39.

Arnold, Jens M., Beata S. Javorcik, and Aaditya Mattoo. 2011. "Does Services Liberalization Benefit Manufacturing Firms? Evidence from the Czech Republic." *Journal of International Economics* 85 (1): 136–46.

Atkin, David, Benjamin Faber, and Marco Gonzalez-Navarro. 2018. "Retail Globalization and Household Welfare: Evidence from Mexico." *Journal of Political Economy* 126 (1): 1–73.

Autor, David H., David Dorn, and Gordon H. Hanson. 2013. "The China Syndrome: Local Labor Market Effects of Import Competition in the United States." *American Economic Review* 103 (6): 2121–68.

Bandick, Roger, and Patrik Karpaty. 2011. "Employment Effects of Foreign Acquisition." *International Review of Economics & Finance* 20 (2): 211–24.

Barrett, Paul M., and Dorothée Baumann-Pauly. 2019. "Made in Ethiopia: Challenges in the Garment Industry's New Frontier." Report, NYU Stern Center for Business and Human Rights, New York.

Bassi, Vittorio, and Aisha Nansamba. 2018. "Screening and Signaling Non-Cognitive Skills: Experimental Evidence from Uganda." Research Paper No. 19-08, University College London.

Beam, Emily A. 2016. "Do Job Fairs Matter? Experimental Evidence on the Impact of Job-Fair Attendance." *Journal of Development Economics* 120: 32–40.

Bernard, Andrew B., and J. Bradford Jensen. 2007. "Firm Structure, Multinationals, and Manufacturing Plant Deaths." *Review of Economics and Statistics* 89 (2): 193–204.

Bernard, Andrew B., Raymond Robertson, and Peter K. Schott. 2010. "Is Mexico a Lumpy Country?" *Review of International Economics* 18 (5): 937–50.

Bernard, Andrew B., and Fredrik Sjöholm. 2003. "Foreign Owners and Plant Survival." Working Paper 10039, National Bureau of Economic Research, Cambridge, MA.

Blattman, Christopher, and Stefan Dercon. 2018. "The Impacts of Industrial and Entrepreneurial Work on Income and Health: Experimental Evidence from Ethiopia." *American Economic Journal: Applied Economics* 10 (3): 1–38.

Braunstein, Elissa. 2006. *Foreign Direct Investment, Development and Gender Equity: A Review of Research and Policy.* Geneva: United Nations Research Institute for Social Development.

Braunstein, Elissa, and Mark Brenner. 2007. "Foreign Direct Investment and Gendered Wages in Urban China." *Feminist Economics* 13 (3–4): 231–37.

Bryan, Gharad, Shyamal Chowdhury, and Ahmed Mushfiq Mobarak. 2014. "Underinvestment in a Profitable Technology: The Case of Seasonal Migration in Bangladesh." *Econometrica* 82 (5): 1671–748.

Card, David, Thomas Lemieux, and W. Craig Riddell. 2004. "Unions and Wage Inequality." *Journal of Labor Research* 25 (4): 519–62.

Card, David, Thomas Lemieux, and W. Craig Riddell. 2018. "Unions and Wage Inequality: The Roles of Gender, Skill and Public Sector Employment." Working Paper 25313, National Bureau of Economic Research, Cambridge, MA.

Caria, Stefano, and Theres Lessing. 2019. "Filling the Gap: How Information Can Help Jobseekers." Growth Brief, International Growth Centre, London.

Cazes, Sandrine, Alexander Hijzen, and Anne Saint-Martin. 2015. "Measuring and Assessing Job Quality: The OECD Job Quality Framework." Social, Employment and Migration Working Paper 174, Organisation of Economic Co-operation and Development, Paris.

Chen, Shaohua, and Martin Ravallion. 2007. "Absolute Poverty Measures for the Developing World, 1981–2004." *Proceedings of the National Academy of Sciences* 104 (43): 16757–62.

Chen, V. Zitian, Jing Li, and Daniel M. Shapiro. 2012. "International Reverse Spillover Effects on Parent Firms: Evidences from Emerging-Market MNES in Developed Markets." *European Management Journal 30* (3): 204–18.

Cornia, Giovanni Andrea. 2016. "An Econometric Analysis of the Bifurcation of Within-Country Inequality Trends in Sub-Saharan Africa, 1990–2011." Africa Report 267781, United Nations Development Programme, New York.

Crépon, Bruno, and Gerard J. van den Berg. 2016. "Active Labor Market Policies." *Annual Review of Economics* 8 (1): 521–46.

Cruz, Marcio, Gaurav Nayyar, Gerhard Toews, and Pierre-Louis Vézina. 2018. "FDI and the Skill Premium: Evidence from Emerging Economies." Policy Research Working Paper 8613, World Bank, Washington, DC.

Davies, Ronald B., and Rodolphe Desbordes. 2015. "Greenfield FDI and Skill Upgrading: A Polarized Issue." *Canadian Journal of Economics* 48 (1): 207–44.

Dinardo, John, and Thomas Lemieux. 1997. "Diverging Male Wage Inequality in the United States and Canada, 1981–1988: Do Institutions Explain the Difference?" *ILR Review* 50 (4): 629–51.

Dinga, Marián, and Daniel Münich. 2010. "The Impact of Territorially Concentrated FDI on Local Labor Markets: Evidence from the Czech Republic." *Labour Economics* 17 (2): 354–67.

Dix-Carneiro, Rafael, and Brian K. Kovak. 2015. "Trade Liberalization and the Skill Premium: A Local Labor Markets Approach." *American Economic Review* 105 (5): 551–57.

Duggan, Victor, Sjamsu Rahardja, and Gonzalo Varela. 2013. "Service Sector Reform and Manufacturing Productivity: Evidence from Indonesia." Policy Research Working Paper 6349, World Bank, Washington, DC.

EIC (Ethiopia Investment Commission). 2017. "Ethiopian Investment Report 2017." EIC, Addis Ababa. http://www.investethiopia.gov.et/images/pdf/EIC%202017%20Report%20.pdf.

El Badaoui, Eliane, Eric Strobl, and Frank Walsh. 2008. "Is There an Informal Employment Wage Penalty? Evidence from South Africa." *Economic Development and Cultural Change* 56 (3): 683–710.

Eschenbach, Felix, and Bernard Hoekman. 2006. "Services Policy Reform and Economic Growth in Transition Economies." *Review of World Economics* 142 (4): 746–64.

Fang, Sheng, Heba M. M. Shamseldin, and L. Colin Xu. 2019. "Foreign Direct Investment and Female Entrepreneurship." Policy Research Working Paper 9083, World Bank, Washington, DC.

Feenstra, Robert C., and Gordon H. Hanson. 1997. "Foreign Direct Investment and Relative Wages: Evidence from Mexico's Maquiladoras." *Journal of International Economics* 42 (3–4): 371–93.

Ferreira, Francisco. 2010. "Distributions in Motion: Economic Growth, Inequality, and Poverty Dynamics." Policy Research Working Paper 5424, World Bank, Washington, DC.

Figini, Paolo, and Holger Görg. 2011. "Does Foreign Direct Investment Affect Wage Inequality? An Empirical Investigation." *The World Economy* 34 (9): 1455–75.

Franklin, Simon. 2015. "Location, Search Costs and Youth Unemployment: A Randomized Trial of Transport Subsidies in Ethiopia." Working Paper WPS/2015-11, Centre for the Study of African Economies, University of Oxford.

Glick, Peter, and François Roubaud. 2006. "Export Processing Zone Expansion in Madagascar: What Are the Labour Market and Gender Impacts?" *Journal of African Economies* 15 (4): 722–56.

Goldberg, Pinelopi Koujianou, and Nina Pavcnik. 2007. "Distributional Effects of Globalization in Development Countries." Working Paper 12885, National Bureau of Economic Research, Cambridge, MA.

Gosling, Amanda, and Thomas Lemieux. 2004. "Labor Market Reforms and Changes in Wage Inequality in the United Kingdom and the United States." In *Seeking a Premier Economy: The Economic Effects of British Economic Reforms, 1980–2000*, edited by David Card, Richard Blundell, and Richard B. Freeman, 275–312. Chicago: University of Chicago Press.

Hale, Galina, and Mingzhi Xu. 2016. "FDI Effects on the Labor Market of Host Countries." Working Paper 2016-25, Federal Reserve Bank of San Francisco.

Hallward-Driemeier, Mary C. 2015. "Jobs Diagnostics Guidance: Why, What, and How?" Working Paper No. 96328, World Bank, Washington, DC.

Hallward-Driemeier, Mary, and Gaurav Nayyar. 2017. *Trouble in the Making? The Future of Manufacturing-Led Development*. Washington, DC: World Bank.

Harrison, Ann, and Jason Scorse. 2010. "Multinationals and Anti-Sweatshop Activism." *American Economic Review* 100 (1): 247–73.

Head, Keith, and John Ries. 2002. "Offshore Production and Skill Upgrading by Japanese Manufacturing Firms." *Journal of International Economics* 58 (1): 81–105.

Heath, Rachel, and A. Mushfiq Mobarak. 2015. "Manufacturing Growth and the Lives of Bangladeshi Women." *Journal of Development Economics* 115: 1–15.

Hijzen, Alexander, Pedro S. Martins, Thorsten Schank, and Richard Upward. 2013. "Foreign-Owned Firms around the World: A Comparative Analysis of Wages and Employment at the Micro-Level." *European Economic Review* 60: 170–88.

Inchauste, Gabriela, João Pedro Azevedo, B. Essama-Nssah, Sergio Olivieri, Trang Van Nguyen, Jaime Saavedra-Chanduvi, and Hernan Winkler. 2014. *Understanding Changes in Poverty*. Directions in Development Series. Washington, DC: World Bank.

Iršová, Zuzana, and Tomáš Havránek. 2013. "Determinants of Horizontal Spillovers from FDI: Evidence from a Large Meta-Analysis." *World Development* 42: 1–15.

ISPAT (Investment Office of the Presidency of the Republic of Turkey). 2018. "FDI in Turkey." Online statistical report, ISPAT website: http://www.invest.gov.tr/en-US/investmentguide/investorsguide/Pages/FDIinTurkey.aspx.

Javorcik, Beata Smarzynska. 2004. "Does Foreign Direct Investment Increase the Productivity of Domestic Firms? In Search of Spillovers through Backward Linkages." *American Economic Review* 94 (3): 605–27.

Javorcik, Beata S. 2015. "Does FDI Bring Good Jobs to Host Countries?" *World Bank Research Observer* 30 (1): 74–94.

Jensen, Robert. 2012. "Do Labor Market Opportunities Affect Young Women's Work and Family Decisions? Experimental Evidence from India." *Quarterly Journal of Economics* 127 (2): 753–92.

Jude, Cristina, and Monica Ioana Pop Silaghi. 2015. "Employment Effects of Foreign Direct Investment: New Evidence from Central and Eastern European Countries." *International Economics* 145: 32–49.

Kalemli-Ozcan, Sebnem, Miguel Eduardo Sánchez-Martín, and Gilles Thirion. 2016. "A Difficult Relationship: Declining (but Productive) FDI Inflows in Turkey." Policy Research Working Paper 7919, World Bank, Washington, DC.

Karlsson, Sune, Nannan Lundin, Fredrik Sjöholm, and Ping He. 2009. "Foreign Firms and Chinese Employment." *The World Economy* 32 (1): 178–201.

Kianto, Aino, Pia Hurmelinna-Laukkanen, and Paavo Ritala. 2010. "Intellectual Capital in Service- and Product-Oriented Companies." *Journal of Intellectual Capital* 11 (3): 305–25.

Krozer, Alice. 2015. "The Inequality We Want: How Much Is Too Much?" Working Paper 2015/015, UNU-WIDER (United Nations University World Institute for Development Economics Research), Helsinki.

Leamer, Edward E. 1998. "In Search of Stolper-Samuelson Effects on U.S. Wages." In *Exports, Imports and the American Worker*, edited by Susan M. Collins, 141–214. Washington, DC: Brookings Institution Press.

Lee, Jong-Wha, and Dainn Wie. 2015. "Technological Change, Skill Demand, and Wage Inequality: Evidence from Indonesia." *World Development* 67: 238–50.

Lemieux, Thomas. 1993. "Unions and Wage Inequality in Canada and the United States." In *Small Differences that Matter: Labor Markets and Income Maintenance in Canada and the United States*, edited by David Card and Richard B. Freeman, 69–108. Chicago: University of Chicago Press.

Li, Shantong, Yan Wang, and Fan Zhai. 2003. "Impact of Service Sector Liberalization on Employment and Output: A CGE Analysis." Paper for the Joint Senior Policy Seminar, "China's Service Sector in the Post-WTO Era," National Development and Reform Commission and World Bank, Beijing, September 22–24.

Lipsey, Robert E. 2003. "Foreign Direct Investment, Growth, and Competitiveness in Developing Countries." In *The Global Competitiveness Report 2002/2003*, edited by P. K. Cornelius. New York: Oxford University Press.

Luo, Rui. 2017. "Skill Premium and Technological Change in the Very Long Run: 1300–1914." Discussion Papers in Economics 17/09, University of Leicester, U.K.

Maloney, William F., and Carlos A. Molina. 2016. "Are Automation and Trade Polarizing Developing Country Labor Markets, Too?" Policy Research Working Paper 7922, World Bank, Washington, DC.

Mattoo, Aaditya, Randeep Rathindran, and Arvind Subramanian. 2006. "Measuring Services Trade Liberalization and Its Impact on Economic Growth: An Illustration." *Journal of Economic Integration* 21 (1): 64–98.

McKenzie, David J. 2017. "How Effective Are Active Labor Market Policies in Developing Countries? A Critical Review of Recent Evidence." Policy Research Working Paper 8011, World Bank, Washington, DC.

McLaren, John, and Myunghwan Yoo. 2016. "FDI and Inequality in Vietnam: An Approach with Census Data." Working Paper 22930, National Bureau of Economic Research, Cambridge, MA.

Merotto, Dino, Michael Weber, and Reyes Aterido. 2018. "Pathways to Better Jobs in IDA Countries: Findings from Jobs Diagnostics." Jobs Series Issue No. 14, World Bank, Washington, DC.

Michaels, Guy, Ashwini Natraj, and John Van Reenen. 2014. "Has ICT Polarized Skill Demand? Evidence from Eleven Countries over Twenty-Five Years." *Review of Economics and Statistics* 96 (1): 60–77.

Moran, Theodore H. 2011. *Foreign Direct Investment and Development: Launching a Second Generation of Policy Research: Avoiding the Mistakes of the First, Reevaluating Policies for Developed and Developing Countries*. Washington, DC: Peterson Institute for International Economics.

Munshi, Kaivan, and Mark Rosenzweig. 2016. "Networks and Misallocation: Insurance, Migration, and the Rural-Urban Wage Gap." *American Economic Review* 106 (1): 46–98.

Newman, Carol, John Page, John Rand, Abebe Shimeles, Måns Söderbom, and Finn Tarp. 2016. *Made in Africa: Learning to Compete in Industry*. Washington, DC: Brookings Institution Press.

Nunnenkamp, Peter, Rainer Schweickert, and Manfred Wiebelt. 2007. "Distributional Effects of FDI: How the Interaction of FDI and Economic Policy Affects Poor Households in Bolivia." *Development Policy Review* 25 (4): 429–50.

Ouedraogo, Rasmané, and Elodie Marlet. 2018. "Foreign Direct Investment and Women Empowerment: New Evidence on Developing Countries." Working Paper No. 18/25, International Monetary Fund, Washington, DC.

Pavcnik, Nina. 2017. "The Impact of Trade on Inequality in Developing Countries." Working Paper 23878, National Bureau of Economic Research, Cambridge, MA.

Peluffo, Adriana. 2015. "Foreign Direct Investment, Productivity, Demand for Skilled Labour and Wage Inequality: An Analysis of Uruguay." *World Economy* 38 (6): 962–83.

Perea, Jose Ramon, and Matthew Stephenson. 2018. "Outward FDI from Developing Countries." In *Global Investment Competitiveness Report 2017/2018*, 101–34. Washington, DC: World Bank Group.

Pierce, Justin R., and Peter K. Schott. 2016. "The Surprisingly Swift Decline of US Manufacturing Employment." *American Economic Review* 106 (7): 1632–62.

Reyes, Jose Daniel. 2017. "FDI Spillovers and High-Growth Firms in Developing Countries." Policy Research Working Paper 8243, World Bank, Washington, DC.

Seguino, Stephanie, and Caren Grown. 2006. "Gender Equity and Globalization: Macroeconomic Policy for Developing Countries." *Journal of International Development* 18 (8): 1081–104.

Siegmann, Karin Astrid. 2007. "Globalisation, Gender, and Equity: Effects of Foreign Direct Investment on Labour Markets in Rural Indonesia." Proceedings of the German Development Economics Conference, Göttingen 2007, Verein für Socialpolitik, Research Committee Development Economics, No. 30.

Söderbom, Måns, and Francis Teal. 2004. "Size and Efficiency in African Manufacturing Firms: Evidence from Firm-Level Panel Data." *Journal of Development Economics* 73 (1): 369–94.

Stiglitz, Joseph. 2012. *The Price of Inequality*. New York: W.W. Norton.

Tang, Heiwai, and Yifan Zhang. 2017. "Do Multinationals Transfer Culture? Evidence on Female Employment in China." Working Paper No. 6295, CESifo Group, Munich.

Te Velde, Dirk Willem, and Theodora Xenogiani. 2007. "Foreign Direct Investment and International Skill Inequality." *Oxford Development Studies* 35 (1): 83–104.

UNCTAD (United Nations Conference on Trade and Development). 2014. *World Investment Report 2014. Investing in the SDGs: An Action Plan*. New York and Geneva: United Nations.

UNCTAD (United Nations Conference on Trade and Development). 2018. "Promoting Investment in the Sustainable Development Goals." Investment Advisory Series, Series A, No. 8, United Nations, Geneva.

UNCTAD (United Nations Conference on Trade and Development). 2019. *World Investment Report 2019: Special Economic Zones*. New York and Geneva: United Nations. doi:10.18356/8a8d05f9-en.

Van der Marel, Erik. 2012. "Trade in Services and TFP: The Role of Regulation." *The World Economy* 35 (11): 1387–429.

Ver Beek, Kurt Alan. 2001. "Maquiladoras: Exploitation or Emancipation? An Overview of the Situation of Maquiladora Workers in Honduras." *World Development* 29 (9): 1553–67.

Verhoogen, Eric A. 2008. "Trade, Quality Upgrading, and Wage Inequality in the Mexican Manufacturing Sector." *Quarterly Journal of Economics* 123 (2): 489–530.

VFIA (Vietnam Foreign Investment Agency). 2018. "Investments in Vietnam 2018." [In Vietnamese.] Online statistical report, VFIA website: http://fia.mpi.gov.vn/tinbai/6110/Tinh-hinh-thu-hut-Dau-tu-nuoc-ngoai-nam-2018.

Waldkirch, Andreas, Peter Nunnenkamp, and Jose Eduardo Alatorre Bremont. 2009. "Employment Effects of FDI in Mexico's Non-Maquiladora Manufacturing." *Journal of Development Studies* 45 (7): 1165–83.

World Bank. 2013. "Shared Prosperity Links to Growth, Inequality, and Inequality of Opportunity." Policy Research Working Paper 6649, World Bank, Washington, DC.

World Bank. 2015. *A Measured Approach to Ending Poverty and Boosting Shared Prosperity: Concepts, Data, and the Twin Goals*. Washington, DC: World Bank.

World Bank Group and OECD (Organisation for Economic Co-operation and Development). 2017. *A Step Ahead: Competition Policy for Shared Prosperity and Inclusive Growth*. Washington, DC: World Bank and OECD.

4 | Regulatory Risk and FDI

Sarah Hebous, Priyanka Kher, and Trang Thu Tran

Key Findings

- **This report presents a new global database on the content of legal instruments and a quantitative measure of regulatory risk, focused on transparency, investment protection, and recourse.** It evaluates (a) transparency and predictability in the content as well as in the process of making laws and regulations that apply to investors; (b) legal protection of investors against arbitrary and nontransparent government interference; and (c) investor access to effective mechanisms for recourse, including grievance management and dispute settlement.
- **Evidence from this database, which analyzes laws affecting investment, shows that investor confidence and FDI flows increase with regulatory transparency, investment protection, and effective recourse.** The constructed measure of regulatory risk is predictive of investment risk premium. Lower regulatory risk is associated with higher investment, in regressions using a global dataset of over 14,000 parent companies investing in nearly 28,000 FDI greenfield and expansion projects across 168 host countries.
- **The effect of regulatory risk on FDI is sizable and comparable in magnitude to the investment-enhancing effects of trade openness in the same regression models.** In fact, in some of the models, the effect of regulatory risk on FDI exceeds that of trade openness, showing that a 1 point reduction in regulatory risk increases the likelihood of an investor entering or expanding in a host country by 0.5–2 percentage points. In contrast, a 1 percentage point increase in the host country's trade-GDP ratio is associated with a 0.3–0.6 percentage point increase in an investor's likelihood to enter or expand.
- **Business survey results confirm the importance of transparent, predictable regulatory environments to investors.** Investors rank countries' legal and regulatory environments as one of the top three factors shaping investment decisions, along with political and macroeconomic stability. Exposure to regulatory risks in host countries triggers existing investors to consider withdrawing investments or canceling planned investment. Moreover, results of the 2019 Global Investment Competitiveness (GIC) Survey show that complex administrative procedures are a further obstacle for nearly two-thirds of investors.
- **To enhance investor confidence and reduce regulatory risk, governments need to remain committed to creating open and predictable environments for FDI.** Given that sources of policy uncertainty that erode investor confidence are both international and domestic, solutions at both levels are needed. Governments can reduce risks for investors by improving transparency and predictability in policy making and implementation, reducing room for bureaucratic discretion, aligning domestic rules with international legal frameworks, and facilitating access to a wide range of dispute settlement mechanisms, including mechanisms to prevent disputes by early detection and resolution of investor grievances.

Introduction

Investors in a country rely on its legal and regulatory framework to recognize their property rights and enforce those rights in a predictable and efficient manner. Economic theory suggests that when investors incur fixed and irreversible setup costs, uncertainty about the local conditions—especially policy uncertainty—will have a dampening effect that reduces investment response to new investment opportunities (Bernanke 1983; Bloom 2009; Dixit 1989).

Among studies that look at developed countries, Baker, Bloom, and Davis (2016) construct a news-based index of United States economic policy uncertainty and document that the most frequent references to perceived policy uncertainty are related to macroeconomic and regulatory policy. Their empirical analysis indicates that aggregate investment and output decline as uncertainty in the United States surges. Among the studies that specifically look at developing countries, Alfaro, Kalemli-Ozcan, and Volosovych (2008) find that low institutional quality, a source of uncertainty, is a major deterrent for foreign capital flows into low-income countries. A similar effect has been documented for components of institutional quality including corruption (Wei 2000); government transparency (Gelos and Wei 2005); predictability of laws, regulations, and policies (Daude and Stein 2007); and property rights protection (Papaioannou 2009).

With the global rise in protectionism in response to nationalist sentiments and economic security considerations, policy uncertainty has once again become a key concern for investors. Cross-country evidence documents the highest share of newly introduced restrictive measures against foreign direct investment (FDI) in high-income countries in the past two years (UNCTAD 2019d). Further uncertainty over the development of the international policy frameworks for trade and investment is likely to erode investor confidence. The Global Investment Competitiveness (GIC) Surveys in 2017 (World Bank 2018) and 2019 (see chapter 1) suggest that two-thirds of investors consider policy uncertainty as "important" or "critically important" to their investment decisions. Further, they confirm that political stability and a country's legal and regulatory framework are the two most important factors for firms' decision to invest in developing countries. As FDI to developing countries has been slowing, competition between developing countries for investments has only intensified.

A Regulatory Framework to Reduce Risk and Boost Investor Confidence

Even though the shift toward more protectionist policies has so far concentrated in large economies, it is vital for all governments to improve the regulatory framework to reduce risk and help restore investor confidence for several reasons. First, country risk is difficult to manage from the firm standpoint. In a survey of chief financial officers across the globe, only 15 percent of respondents state that they use political risk insurance,[1] and nearly half avoid investing in a risky country altogether (Giambona, Graham, and Harvey 2017).

Second, the risk profile in each country will influence the types of firms that enter its markets because multinational enterprises (MNEs) vary systematically in their vulnerability to and ability to manage different risks. A joint survey by the Multilateral Insurance Guarantee Agency and the Economist Intelligence Unit (MIGA 2013) finds that firms that outperformed their competitors paid significantly more attention to assessing and taking measures to manage political risk. Better-performing companies, with better capabilities to assess political risk, also experienced fewer cases of expropriation, default of government payments, cancellation of import/export licenses, or restrictions on currency transfer than other firms. More recently, using a new measure of firm-level political risk, Hassan et al. (2019) find that a large share of the variation in political risk appears to play out at the firm level and is significantly associated with investment and hiring decisions. Moreover, they find that dispersion in firm-level risk often increases with aggregate risk level. This result suggests that reducing country-level risk can improve macroeconomic outcomes through an additional channel—by lowering the distortion of resource allocation across firms as they respond to varying levels of risk.

Finally, a country's attractiveness for FDI can suffer in the long term from a bad track record of government conduct. From a signaling perspective, it is important to reduce not only actual risk but also perceived levels of risk.

A New Regulatory Risk Measure

An important response by countries to the increasing policy uncertainty and associated risks is to create supportive, predictable legal and regulatory regimes to de-risk investments. The question is: How is the role of government action reflected in country risk ratings? Relating government actions to the measurement of risks is key to informing policy makers. Attracting FDI requires improving investors' perception about uncertainty in the economy, which in turn requires an effective signal and government actions to boost confidence in its overall policy. Yet country risk ratings often include a wide range of measures, from quantitative macroeconomic indicators to qualitative expert perception of political and investment risk. These qualitative measures are often beyond the influence of or have no direct relationships with government actions.

To fill in this gap, this study develops a quantitative measure of regulatory risk—a subset of political risk—that is linked directly to specific legal and regulatory provisions. Regulatory risk, as defined here, is related to select features of countries' regulatory framework that can reduce risks for investors and limit the potential for unexpected losses due to arbitrary government conduct. Specifically, the new regulatory risk measure examines (a) whether there is transparency in both the content and process of making laws and regulations that apply to investors; (b) the extent of legal protection provided to investors against arbitrary, unpredictable, and nontransparent government interference; and (c) whether investors have access to effective mechanisms for recourse. The regulatory risk measure developed in this study, therefore, serves as a tool to help countries identify specific areas for further improvement.

This study draws on existing indicators and collects new data, including on the content of legal instruments, that cover several regulatory areas: investment laws and treaties, public procurement, property registration, and other cross-cutting regulatory governance measures. Importantly, and in contrast to other risk ratings, the constructed measure of regulatory risk does not rely on inputs based on perception.

The underlying data are organized into three dimensions: transparency, protection, and recourse. For each of these dimensions, two aggregate scores are calculated from individual data points using a simple average and a weighted average, where weights are derived from a principal component analysis (PCA). Because of limited data overlap, two different sets of the overall regulatory risk measure are developed: (a) a panel version including data between 2014 and 2017, and (b) a cross-sectional version that includes richer data but is available only for 2017.

This study finds that these constructed measures carry meaningful signals of risk for investors. The measures show that countries differ substantially in regulatory risk. While many countries' risk levels have stayed relatively stable, some have experienced significant changes in their risk levels over time. Countries with higher regulatory risk in this framework tend to have a higher expropriation risk premium (that is, higher prices to ensure against expropriation risk) and tend to be considered as riskier in other ratings such as the International Country Risk Guide's (ICRG) investment risk profile indicators.

Notably, higher regulatory risk appears to be associated with a more restrictive FDI regulatory framework. Although restrictiveness per se does not necessarily constitute risks for investors, it can increase uncertainty where rules are imprecise or unclear, leaving room for discretion in implementation. This result lends empirical support to the concern about growing protectionism and further highlights the need for countries to manage their regulatory frameworks to restore investor confidence.

How Regulatory Risk Affects FDI

Importantly, regulatory risk matters for investments. This study finds that lower risk is associated with higher FDI inflows. Consistent with this result, estimations from a model of investor location choices suggests that regulatory risk can deter the decisions of MNEs to enter or expand in a host country. This effect is of meaningful magnitude: if the median country improves its performance to the level of a top 25th percentile performer, investors will be 5.5–22 percentage points more likely to locate in the country. To put this result in further perspective, in the same model, the effect of the regulatory risk measure on investment decision making is comparable in magnitude to trade openness: a 1 standard deviation increase in trade openness is associated with a 28 percentage point increase in the likelihood of investor entry, on average. In comparison, a 1 standard deviation decrease in regulatory risk is associated with a 9 percentage point increase in likelihood of investor entry.

To summarize, these results suggest that the legal provisions and other regulatory features selected and scored in this study can provide a meaningful framework for government actions and reforms to reduce regulatory risk. Country case studies suggest that the regulatory risk measure can capture significant changes in line with changing government policy despite the limited number of regulatory areas that can be covered because of the lack of cross-country data. Across countries, performance on the three dimensions of regulatory risk measured—transparency, protection, and recourse—is often correlated. Yet statistically, they all appear to have some predictive power concerning investor behavior, suggesting that it is important for countries to pay attention to all three aspects in their regulatory framework. The constructed risk measure and the underlying data can provide a starting point to help guide further research, diagnostics, and more specific policy recommendations to reduce risk for investors.

Analytical Framework

Measuring risk and uncertainty is inherently challenging. Research has often relied on some measures of volatility or dispersion as proxies of uncertainty, which might or might not be tightly linked to true underlying economic uncertainty (Jurado, Ludvigson, and Ng 2015). A growing literature attempts to quantify policy uncertainty and political risk based on the frequency that "keywords" related to "risk" or "uncertainty" appear in news publications or corporate disclosures (Baker, Bloom, and Davis 2016; Hassan et al. 2019). These proxies are useful to track the movements of risk and to study their consequences on market participants. However, they are not intended to provide a direct link to specific government actions that cause such movements in risk. In addition, because of the nature of the data and textual analysis required, these proxies are not easily expanded or comparable across countries.

In contrast, the risk measure in this study aims to capture risk as implied by policy and regulatory choices. It bears some similarities to other popular risk ratings, such as the ICRG's political risk rating; the Economist

Intelligence Unit's (EIU) legal and regulatory policy risk rating; and the country risk classification of the Organisation of Economic Co-operation and Development (OECD), which allows for a cross-country risk comparison (table 4.1). These risk ratings typically include a mix of quantitative macroeconomic indicators, business environment indicators, and qualitative expert assessment based on political events. The model to arrive at the final rating is often proprietary. In summary, they assess risk as follows:

- *The EIU legal and regulatory policy risk rating* is a component of its operational risk model, ranging from 0 (low risk) to 100 (high risk). It is the (rescaled) simple average of various subindicators, which are scored on a 0–4 scale by the EIU's analysts working in regional teams using open and closed sources (EIU 2017).
- *The ICRG political risk rating* is a composite risk rating of 12 components, including government stability, investment profile, and conflict.[2] It ranges from 0 (low confidence, high risk) to 100 (high confidence, low risk). The scores are determined by political risk experts and editorial staff.
- *The OECD country risk classification* forms the basis for minimum risk premium categories for many official export credit agencies. It is a measure of transfer and convertibility risk and cases of force majeure, and it relies on both quantitative inputs and expert opinions.[3]

Other characteristics of these risk ratings are summarized in table 4.1. Among other factors, these commercially available risk ratings often inform investors' opinions on countries' investment attractiveness. Yet despite the importance of risk rating for investment decisions, the methodology often

TABLE 4.1 Several Popular Cross-Country Risk Ratings Do Not Clearly Link Risk Levels to Specific Government Actions and Rely on Perception-Based Inputs

Characteristic	*ICRG political risk rating*	*EIU legal and regulatory policy risk rating*	*OECD country risk classification*
Objective	To assess the political stability of the country	To assess the risk that the legal system will fail to safeguard investment	To provide country risk classification, encompassing transfer and convertibility risk and cases of force majeure (such as war, expropriation, revolution, civil disturbance, floods, and earthquakes)
Type of analysis	Subjective (perception-based) analysis only	Subjective (perception-based) analysis only	Objective data and subjective (perception-based) analysis
Underlying data	Twelve components, including government stability, investment profile, corruption, and external and internal conflict Scored on a scale from 4 (very low risk) to 1 (very high risk) by political risk experts and editorial staff	Ten questions, including "How vulnerable is the legal process to interference or distortion to serve particular interests?" and "What is the risk that business financial statements are inconsistent or misleading?" Answered on a scale from 0 (very little risk) to 4 (very high risk) by expert opinion of analysts in the regions	*Objective data:* macroeconomic indicators on the country's financial and economic situation *Subjective analysis:* qualitative assessment to integrate information not fully taken into account by quantitative data Answered by country risk experts from export credit agencies
Aggregation methodology	Simple average of individual components	Simple average of individual components	Model-based: two-step procedure, including a quantitative model with possible adjustments through qualitative assessment

Source: World Bank.
Note: EIU = Economist Intelligence Unit; ICRG = International Country Risk Guide; OECD = Organisation for Economic Co-operation and Development.

does not clearly link the level of risk to specific government actions.

This study's measure of regulatory risk contrasts with other risk ratings by measuring regulatory risk without relying on inputs based on perception. It is also narrower in scope and excludes other sources of risks, such as macroeconomic uncertainty or political violence. It captures sources of regulatory risk solely through quantitative indicators that are linked directly to specific, actionable legal and regulatory provisions. It is therefore intended to help identify concrete weaknesses, give specific policy recommendations, and trace real changes in the regulatory environment.

Capturing Sources of Regulatory Risk

Regulatory risk, in this study's definition, is related to selected features of the legal and regulatory framework that might affect the expected profitability of a business. In the same vein that political risk reflects the variability in economic returns that stems from uncertainty about political events, the concept here is closely related to uncertainty about laws and regulations.[4] Given that sources of regulatory risk can be extremely heterogeneous and new risks will continue to emerge, the measure in this study does not include specific regulatory changes. Rather, the analysis aims to capture features of countries' regulatory frameworks that can limit the potential for unexpected losses due to arbitrary government conduct that generates uncertainty for investors.

Three Questions to Assess Risk

The study uses three analytical questions to assess how the legal and regulatory framework affects risk for investors:

- Is there *transparency* regarding the content as well as the process of making laws and regulations that apply to investors?
- What is the extent of legal *protection* provided to investors against arbitrary and unpredictable, or nontransparent, government actions?
- Do investors have access to effective mechanisms for *recourse* in case of grievances or disputes?

These questions allow for a systematic way to think about dimensions of the regulatory framework that countries can influence to improve perceived and actual levels of risk. They also serve as a guide to organize the data sources used (box 4.1).

By improving *transparency* and reducing room for discretionary behavior of regulators, countries help reduce risks for investors as entry and operating costs become more predictable ex ante. De jure *protection* of rights (that is, protection based on legal provisions) provides guarantees for investors against unexpected interferences. An effective *recourse* mechanism can help minimize the ex post costs of disputes for investors and provide "teeth" for the protection guarantees by making it costlier for governments to violate them. In other words, it provides a way to sanction deviating behavior and determine the credibility of legal promises.

Accordingly, even though the analysis measures regulatory risk through these three dimensions, their effectiveness is dependent on one another. In fact, as will be shown later, countries that perform better on one dimension are often better performers in other dimensions of the regulatory risk measure as well.

The analysis combines existing indicators and collects new data sources, including the content of legal instruments, to measure countries' regulatory risk, guided by the three analytical questions. To ensure cross-country availability, the data focus on a few regulatory areas that apply to investors, both foreign and domestic, or in some cases, only one of them (for example, international investment agreements [IIAs]). The areas covered are investment (specifically, investment laws and treaties); public procurement;

BOX 4.1

Data Sources for the Regulatory Risk Measure

This study's measure of regulatory risk relies on both primary and secondary data that cover cross-cutting regulatory governance as well as specific regulatory areas: investment, public procurement, and property registration. In annex 4A, table 4A.1 lists the full set of seven data sources, the scale of the raw values for each variable, and which of the three pillars they belong to.

Because the data sources differ in their geographical and time coverage, the constructed risk measure includes two different versions. The "panel version" of regulatory risk data maximizes comparability over time (using 2014–17 data), covering up to 167 countries. Its data sources include the following:

- A database of 2,103 international investment agreements (IIAs)[a] includes those that were in force between 2014 and 2017, whose content is mapped by the United Nations Conference on Trade and Development (UNCTAD).[b] The IIA provisions are scored using principles similar to those applied to the investment laws database (used in the "cross-sectional" version described below). The IIAs are publicly available from UNCTAD's online Investment Policy Hub.
- A panel database was compiled of members of the Convention on the Recognition and Enforcement of Foreign Arbitral Awards (the New York Convention) and Convention on the Settlement of Investment Disputes between States and Nationals of Other States (the ICSID Convention) for the universe of all countries.
- World Bank *Doing Business* subindicators are used that were available from 2014 onward and thus define the time coverage for the panel index.

The "cross-sectional" version of the regulatory risk data maximizes the number of underlying variables but only for a single year (2017 data only), covering 86 countries. In addition to the information used in the panel version, its data sources include the following:

- A new investment laws database, compiled for this study, codifies the content of publicly available investment laws of 102 countries.[c] A framework of 162 questions was developed to assess the content of the laws and create a database that includes a series of 0–1 indicators, depending on whether the laws include specific provisions. Only those investment laws that are currently in force are included. Thus, investment law scores are included only in the cross-sectional indicator for 2017 and not in the panel version.
- The World Bank's Benchmarking Public Procurement (BPP) database is used to create a score for public procurement.
- Subindicators from the World Bank's Global Indicators of Regulatory Governance (GIRG) cover virtually all countries (more than 186).

a. The UNCTAD Investment Policy Hub database (https://investmentpolicy.unctad.org/) includes bilateral investment treaties (BITs) as well as other treaties with investment provisions.

b. The measure does not include survival clauses that extend the application of a treaty to a certain number of years beyond its termination. Although BITs between members of the European Union (EU) were included in the analysis, they are expected to terminate over the coming months. On January 15, 2019, EU member states endorsed a political declaration to terminate their intra-EU BITs by December 6, 2019. This followed a recent decision by the European Court of Justice (Achmea v. Slovak Republic), which ruled that investor-state arbitration provisions in BITs between EU member states are not compatible with EU law.

c. In total, the database includes investment laws for 102 countries (as of this writing) that are publicly available on UNCTAD's Investment Policy Hub or that were received directly from government counterparts.

property registration; and other cross-cutting regulatory governance measures.

An important criterion for including data sources is that they can be linked to specific regulatory provisions that lend themselves to government action. The measure covers select aspects of these distinct regulatory areas that fit into one of the three pillars (transparency and predictability, investment protection, and recourse). The legal provisions included across all these data sources are "scored" based on how they increase transparency, protection, and access to recourse through a specific set of principles, as shown below.

The dimension of *transparency* includes three elements: (a) systematic publication of and consultation on laws and regulations;

(b) availability of portals and similar mechanisms that enable investors to find information about relevant laws and regulations; and (c) to a more limited extent, the specificity and clarity of legal provisions on the applicable administrative procedures (to increase predictability and reduce chances of abuse of discretion).[5]

The standards of *protection* are selected based on the importance of the protections to investment operations, especially in the context of unpredictable or nontransparent government actions. These include provisions on expropriation, fair and equitable treatment (FET), and transfer of funds.[6] Further, the focus is on standards that are "absolute" in nature.[7]

For the *recourse* pillar, investors' access to investor-state dispute settlement (ISDS) is reviewed as well as proxies for overall quality of domestic dispute resolution, including the quality of land dispute resolution and the judicial processes.

Figure 4.1 summarizes the three pillars of the regulatory risk measure and the key principles for evaluating the legal provisions under each pillar. For further details on how these principles translate into specific provisions selected and the rationale for such selection, see the first section of annex 4A.

This analytical framework, including the three pillars and areas of regulations covered, is rooted in the legal and international political economy literature. It aims to capture characteristics of the overall regulatory environment and instruments such as investment laws and treaties that governments often adopt to limit the risk to outside investors.

Substantively, protection from unpredictable government conduct is generally one of the core purposes of IIAs and investment laws. They present the fundamental principles of investment protection within a country's investment policy regime. Some evidence suggests that IIAs can work as either a commitment device that protects investors covered by the relevant IIAs or as a signal that countries have laws and policies in place that protect all foreign investment. (For a review of the evidence, see Bonnitcha, Skovgaard Poulsen, and Waibel 2017.) Importantly, IIAs appear to matter more for investments that entail high sunk costs—such as infrastructure (Bauerle Danzman 2016) or fixed capital investments (Kerner and Lawrence 2014)—or that are capital intensive (Colen, Persyn, and Guariso 2016).

Further, it has been argued that it is not the ratification of IIAs per se but the treaty "strength" (including dispute provisions) that is important for FDI inflows. For example, Dixon and Haslam (2016) find a positive association between the strength of protection

FIGURE 4.1 Three Pillars of Regulatory Risk Frame the Analysis

Pillar 1: Transparency

Is there *transparency* regarding the content as well as the process of making laws and regulations that apply to investors?

- Systematic publication of and consultation on laws and regulations
- Registries or ICT platforms, and similar mechanisms to allow investors to find information about relevant laws and regulations
- Specificity and clarity of legal provisions (to reduce space for discretion)

Pillar 2: Protection

What is the extent of legal *protection* provided to investors against arbitrary, unpredictable, or nontransparent government actions?

- Absolute treatment standards
- Protection guarantees against direct and indirect appropriation
- Provisions on transfers of funds and fair and equitable treatment (FET)

Pillar 3: Recourse

Do investors have access to effective mechanisms for *recourse*, in case of grievances or disputes?

- Investor-state dispute settlement and prevention
- Land dispute resolution
- Quality of judicial processes

Source: World Bank.
Note: ICT = information and communication technology.

clauses in bilateral investment treaties (BITs) and FDI inflows. Frenkel and Walter (2019) find that stronger international dispute settlement provisions in BITs are associated with positive effects on FDI activity.

Because of various empirical challenges, evidence about the impact of IIAs remains mixed. One common finding, however, is that IIAs act as complements rather than substitutes for local property rights and that countries must have the necessary domestic institutions in place to make these international commitments credible and valuable to investors (Hallward-Driemeier 2003; Tobin and Rose-Ackerman 2011). As such, the framework in this study aims to cover regulatory aspects that apply to foreign investors but also serve as proxies for the overall domestic regulatory environment.

Caveats in the Regulatory Risk Measure

Although these pillars provide a useful framework to guide government actions to reduce regulatory risk, the regulatory risk measure carries some caveats:

- First, it focuses heavily on de jure legal provisions. Because of lack of data, the study does not review important implementation aspects that can affect regulatory risk, such as the quality of day-to-day functioning of all regulatory bodies and variations in the interpretation and application of laws and regulations.
- Second, although the measure considers whether there is consultation with stakeholders during the rulemaking process, existing data cannot capture how widely or how well such consultation occurs and the extent to which comments have led to changes in laws and regulations.
- Third, even though regulations often vary by sector, given the limited availability of cross-country information on sectoral regulatory frameworks, the regulatory risk measure does not cover this dimension. Both primary and secondary data used for this research are available at the economywide level only. Relatedly, the focus is on a few select legal instruments such as IIAs and investment laws—again, driven by limitation of cross-country comparable data.[8]

Finally, an important caveat is that the framework sidesteps the issue of the "right to regulate," given its varied and unsettled implications. There have been growing concerns around limitations on the sovereign right to regulate and increased vulnerability to investor-state disputes. As a result, states have started including provisions in IIAs to clarify their right to regulate. This is being done in a few ways, such as by defining terms like "indirect expropriation" and "fair and equitable treatment" to limit the scope of interpretation of these terms. In other cases, carve-outs and exceptions are included—for example, to limit the application of provisions on expropriation and transfer of currency for legitimate regulatory measures,[9] or adjustments are made to secure states' right to regulate through jurisdictional exclusion of regulatory disputes. For example, the Comprehensive and Progressive Agreement for Trans-Pacific Partnership (Article 29.5) allows states to revoke the benefit of ISDS with respect to claims challenging a state's measures to control tobacco.

Indeed, provisions clarifying the right to regulate give arbitral tribunals and courts the option to fully weigh them against investor protection guarantees, and carve-outs allow for nonapplication of guarantees. Arguably, such provisions enable greater regulatory flexibility and consequently can also generate uncertainty for investors. Yet they also provide predictability regarding the situations where exceptions can apply. Given the variation in how "right to regulate" provisions are drafted, the high subjectivity in their interpretation, and their multidimensional impact on investors and states, these provisions have not been scored for the purpose of this study.

Constructing a Composite Measure of Regulatory Risk

Based on the three pillars in the analytical framework, individual data sources are combined into the three component scores as well as a composite risk score. The process to construct the composite regulatory risk score requires choices regarding how to normalize original data—which often have different measurement units—and how to aggregate the rescaled data. This study's choices are guided by previous literature on composite indicator methodology (Filmer and Prichett 2001; Gelman and Stanig 2016; Kaufman, Kraay, and Mastruzzi 2011; OECD 2008), taking into account the following criteria:

- *Comparability over time and across countries:* The index should allow for assessing progress of countries over time and relative to one another.
- *Maximized information content:* The index should consider the correlation structure among different variables.
- *Transparency:* The construction method should be simple enough to allow for an understanding of how individual variables contribute to the composite index.

Because of the varying time and country coverage of the different data sources (as described in box 4.1), the study faces a trade-off between maximizing the information content (number of variables used) and maximizing the size of the cross-section and time dimension. In addition, to allow for the inherent trade-off between maximizing information content and transparency, the study tests for two different aggregation choices to allow for an understanding of how individual variables contribute to the composite score: First, both the component scores and the composite score are calculated as a simple average of the underlying (normalized) variables. Second, the component scores are calculated as a weighted average of individual data sources, where weights are given as the first components in a PCA (annex 4A, table 4A.2). The second approach has the advantage of considering the correlation structure of the individual variables, but it is less transparent in how they contribute to the overall index.[10]

Given these criteria and trade-offs, the analysis ends up with two different sets of the overall regulatory risk measure: the panel version (including the 2014–17 data) and the cross-sectional version (richer data but available for 2017 only). In addition, within each version, the robustness of results is tested with the inclusion (exclusion) of certain variables and two different aggregation methods discussed. One caveat of the methodology is that it does not calculate a range of uncertainty, such as in Kaufmann, Kraay, and Mastruzzi (2011). Uncertainty makes comparison of adjacent points less credible (Høyland, Moene, and Willumsen 2012). For this and other reasons—particularly, limited available cross-country data—caution should be taken in comparing countries that are closer to one another in the constructed risk score. For further methodology details, see Data Normalization and Aggregation in annex 4A. The data for all the subcomponents are available in the online supplementary appendix.[11]

Characteristics of the Constructed Measure of Regulatory Risk

The results show high correlations of the constructed risk measure across different aggregation methods and inclusions of different data sources (see annex 4A, figure 4A.1). Therefore, for brevity throughout the chapter, unless indicated otherwise, results using the panel version of the composite risk score are reported.

The constructed score suggests that countries differ substantially in the types and extent of regulatory risk, and some have made regulatory changes that significantly affect the level of risk over time.

FIGURE 4.2 Regulatory Risk Levels Vary Significantly across Countries and Change Substantially for Some Countries over Time

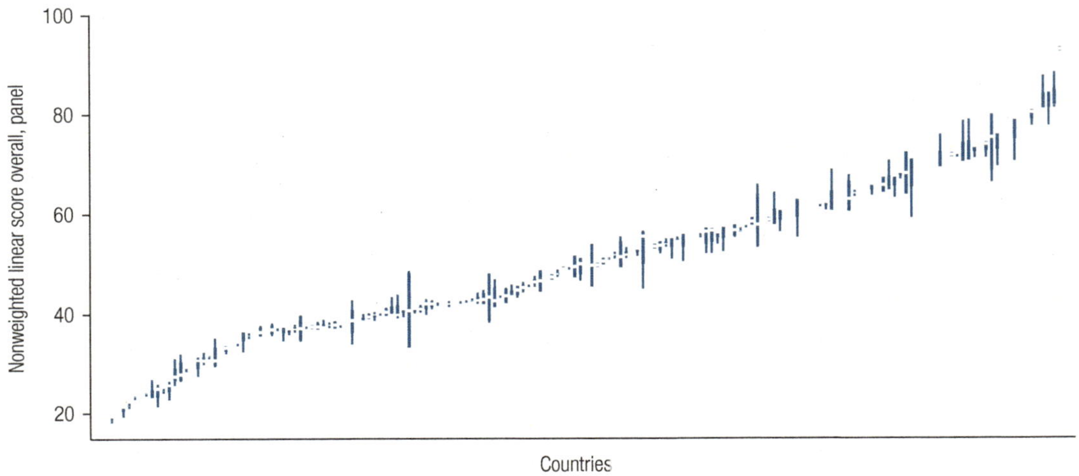

Source: World Bank.
Note: Each bar is a boxplot of the regulatory risk measure (panel version) for one country during the sample period (2014–17), covering 167 countries. The bars are ordered by the average of the countries' regulatory risk score (ranging from 0 to 100) during the sample period. The farther a bar is situated to the left (right), the lower (higher) is the country's average regulatory risk. The bigger (smaller) a bar's height, the bigger (smaller) is the country's change in regulatory risk over time. For the full list and descriptions of data sources used to calculate aggregate scores, see annex 4A.

Figure 4.2 plots the distribution of risk by country as well as the range of changes in each country between 2014 and 2017. On average, the risk scores vary between 20 for the lowest risk score and 95 for the highest risk score (out of a 0–100 range). While many countries have fairly small changes over time, some have experienced significant changes, especially those with a higher average risk level.

Importantly, the results show that regulatory risk, as measured in the framework, can explain perception of investment risk. This is reflected in the correlation of regulatory risk with the risk premium and other risk ratings. Figure 4.3, panel a, presents the variations in the constructed regulatory risk across countries, based on the category of "expropriation and government action" risk insurance premium (that is, risk insurance prices) evaluated by Credendo, a major risk insurance group.[12] It shows that although there is some overlap in regulatory risk for countries across different risk premium categories, in general, for countries with more expensive risk premiums, the median as well as the 25th and 75th percentiles of regulatory risk also tend to be higher. Figure 4.3, panel b, shows the correlations of the regulatory risk measures with the ICRG investment risk rating.[13] In general, the riskier countries in the framework are also rated as riskier in the ICRG rating.

In addition, higher regulatory risk appears to be associated with a more restrictive FDI regulatory framework. Figure 4.4 shows this result for a subset of 69 countries where statutory restrictions to FDI, such as screening or equity restrictions, are captured by the OECD FDI Restrictiveness Index. Although restrictiveness per se does not necessarily constitute risks for investors, it can increase uncertainty through higher chances for abuse of discretion when regulations are imprecise or unclear. Growing protectionism over the past few years has exacerbated policy and regulatory uncertainty. The results here lend empirical support to this concern and further

FIGURE 4.3 Higher Regulatory Risk Is Associated with Higher Expropriation Risk Insurance Premiums and Investment Risk Ratings

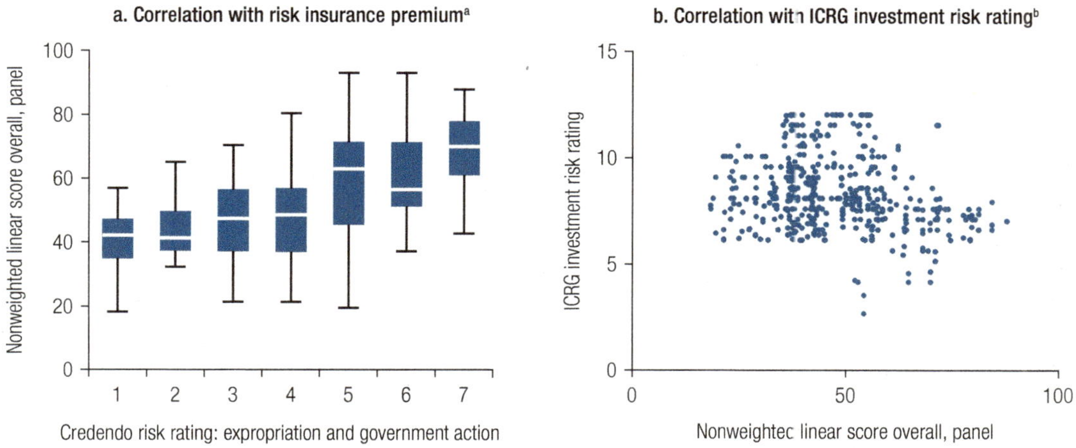

Sources: Panel a: World Bank and Credendo; panel b: World Bank and ICRG.

Note: The "nonweighted linear score overall, panel" refers to the "panel version" of the regulatory risk score (0–100), calculated from 2014–17 data, covering 167 countries. For the full list and descriptions of data sources used to calculate aggregate scores, see annex 4A. See additional results on the correlation of the cross-sectional version in annex 4A, figure 4A.4.

a. Figure is a boxplot of regulatory risk score (panel version) over the seven risk premium categories of "expropriation and government action risk." The country risk rating categories data come from Credendo, a major credit insurance group. The higher (lower) the risk premium, the higher (lower) the risk. The correlation coefficient between Credendo's risk premium rating and regulatory risk is 0.52 (significant at 1% level).

b. Figure is a scatterplot of regulatory risk score (panel version) on the x-axis and International Country Risk Guide (ICRG) investment profile rating on the y-axis. ICRG investment risk is measured on a scale from 1 (low confidence, high risk) to 12 (high confidence, low risk). The correlation coefficient between ICRG investment risk and regulatory risk is -0.24 (significant at 1% level).

FIGURE 4.4 Higher Regulatory Risk Is Associated with More Restrictive FDI Regulations

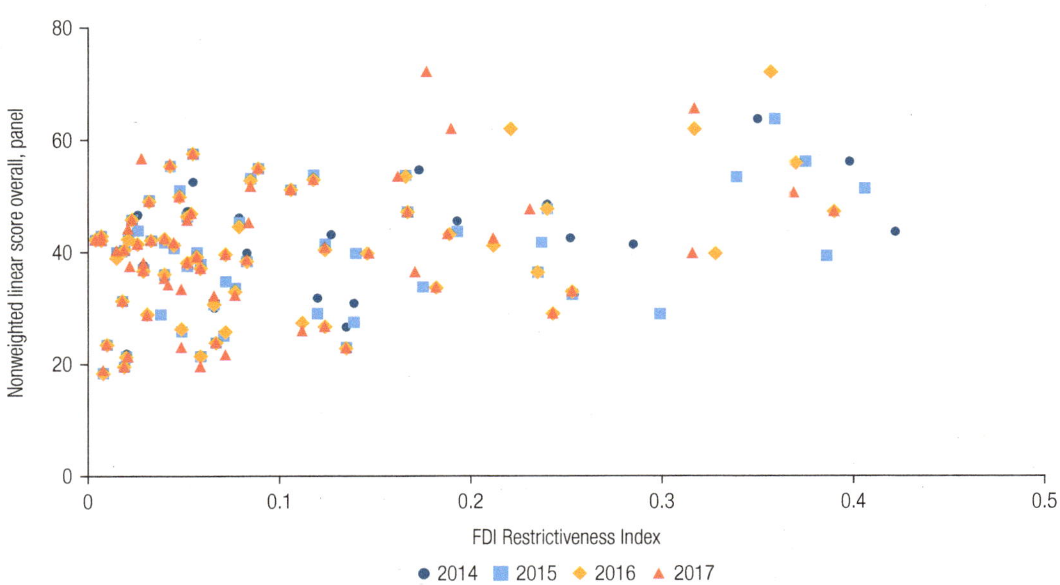

Sources: World Bank and Organisation for Economic Co-operation and Development (OECD) FDI Regulatory Restrictiveness Index, https://www.oecd.org/investment/fdiindex.htm.

Note: Foreign direct investment (FDI) restrictiveness is measured by the OECD FDI Restrictiveness Index, which measures statutory restrictions on FDI in 22 economic sectors across 69 countries, including all OECD and Group of Twenty (G-20) countries. The correlation between the OECD FDI Restrictiveness Index and this study's regulatory risk score is 0.33 (significant at 1% level). The "nonweighted linear score overall, panel" refers to the "panel version" of this study's regulatory risk score (0–100), calculated from 2014–17 data. For the full list and descriptions of data sources used to calculate the panel aggregate scores, see annex 4A.

highlight the need for countries to manage the regulatory framework to restore investor confidence.

In summary, these results suggest that the legal and regulatory provisions selected and scored in the framework carry meaningful signals of risk for investors. With these results in mind, the next section examines whether the regulatory risk measure can predict FDI inflows and other investor decisions.

Regulatory Risk and FDI

At the Country Level, Lower Regulatory Risk Is Associated with Higher FDI

On average, total FDI inflows to a country are negatively correlated with the level of regulatory risk as measured in the framework. Figure 4.5 depicts this relationship, using a log transformation of real net FDI inflows.[14] The model controls for gross domestic product (GDP) per capita, trade openness, and country fixed effects (where appropriate). This relationship is robust to the choice of different index versions: panel a shows the panel index, while panel b shows the cross-section version.

In addition, results using bilateral FDI data (where the source countries can be identified) hold that FDI inflows decrease as a host country's regulatory risk increases. Arguably, aggregate FDI inflows mask heterogeneity in the individual composition of a host country's FDI. By using a newly constructed panel dataset of bilateral FDI inflows, the model is able to consider both home and host countries' characteristics.[15]

In this model, regulatory risk also has a significant and negative impact on bilateral FDI inflows. Moreover, conditional on the destination country's risk, there appears to be a negative correlation (though statistically not significant) between FDI inflows and the difference in risk levels between the destination and source countries (see annex 4A, table 4A.3). It suggests not only

FIGURE 4.5 FDI Inflows Are Higher in Countries with Lower Regulatory Risk

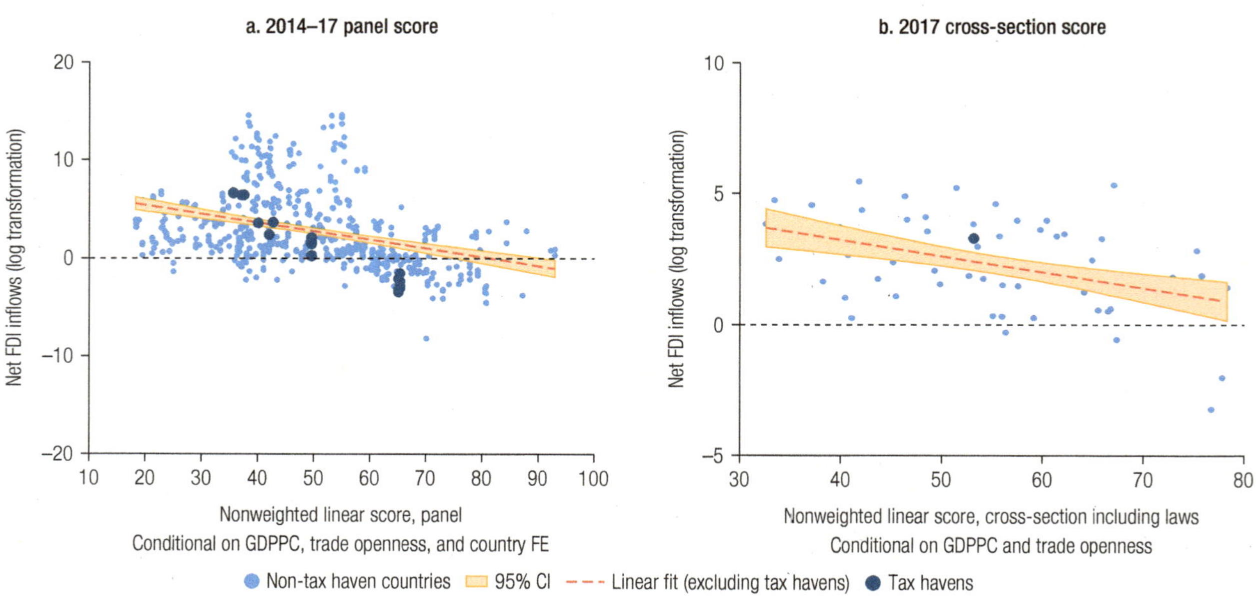

Source: World Bank calculations, from the World Development Indicators database.
Note: The scatterplots show the correlation between net FDI inflows and regulatory risk index. Panel a uses a 2014–17 panel score; panel b uses a 2017 cross-section score. CI = confidence interval; FDI = foreign direct investment; FE = fixed effects; GDPPC = GDP per capita.

that the destination country's risk matters but also that investors from a lower-risk country might be affected more disproportionally.

To focus on the interaction between risk and irreversibility of investments, the analysis examines activities of existing investors that are subject to some adjustment costs. These include the total amount of capital invested that is illiquid or employment expansion. Aggregate data from the US Bureau of Economic Analysis on activity of foreign affiliates are used, including expenditure on fixed capital, research and development (R&D) expenditure, and number of employees. For established MNEs, the correlation between regulatory risk and investment and hiring activities is negative. However, the correlation is not statistically significant, conditional on the host country's GDP per capita, trade openness, and country fixed effects—possibly driven by a small sample size. (See the full regression results in annex 4A, table 4A.4.)

Increased Likelihood that MNEs Will Invest in Locations with Lower Regulatory Risk

Investor-level data lend microfoundation support to the negative relationship found between risk and aggregate FDI. The analysis uses a dataset of 14,335 parent companies investing in 27,886 FDI greenfield or expansion projects across 159 host countries between 2014 and 2016. This dataset enables the exercise to test the relationship between a host country's regulatory risk and MNE-level investment size using an investor decision model (box 4.2).

The analysis confirms that regulatory risk deters investor entry and expansion. This result is robust to the inclusion of host country controls. Figure 4.6 depicts the estimated coefficients for the different models tested, showing that higher regulatory risk has a negative impact on the likelihood that foreign investors will enter or expand

BOX 4.2

Examining How Regulatory Risk Affects Investor Location Decisions

Models of determinants of aggregate FDI suffer from many potential biases, driven by the difficulty in accounting for unobservable country characteristics and characteristics of investment types that can drive investment flows. An alternative approach is to study individual investors' location choices, especially in the context where investors' decisions are observed over time. In such a setting, the assumption that location choices are driven by location characteristics tends to be a less restrictive assumption when investor fixed effects (and hence investor heterogeneity) can be accounted for.

To look for more rigorous evidence on the relationship between regulatory risk and foreign direct investment (FDI), this chapter takes advantage of data from fDi Markets, a *Financial Times* dataset of greenfield FDI transactions that allows identification of the parent company and sector information not typically available in aggregate FDI inflows data.[a] The fDi Markets transaction data are transformed into an investor-level dataset, and a conditional logit model is estimated to investigate the determinants of multinational enterprises' (MNEs) location choices. A random utility model is assumed (McFadden 1974) whereby an investor chooses one location among other alternatives. It can be thought of as a profit-maximizing problem in which investors enter the country with the highest expected profit, where expected profits depend on regulatory risk and other country characteristics, as follows:

$$Pr^{\circ}(invest_{ijt}) = \Phi(\beta_0 + \beta_1 risk_{jt} + X'_{jt}\gamma + \delta_t + \varepsilon_{ijt}), \quad \text{(B4.2.1)}$$

where $Pr^{\circ}(invest_{ijt})$ represents the probability of firm i investing in country j; $\Phi()$ is the logistic cumulative distribution function; $risk_{jt}$ denotes regulatory risk; x'_{jt} is a vector of other host-country characteristics; δ_i denotes firm fixed effects; and the error term ε_{ijt} captures residuals.

Note: Previous studies of the location choices of multinationals using this approach include Chen and Moore (2010) and Joyez (2015).

a. For more on the fDi Markets dataset, see https://www.fdimarkets.com/.

FIGURE 4.6 Higher Regulatory Risk Has a Negative Impact on Investors' Likelihood of Entering or Expanding in a Host Country

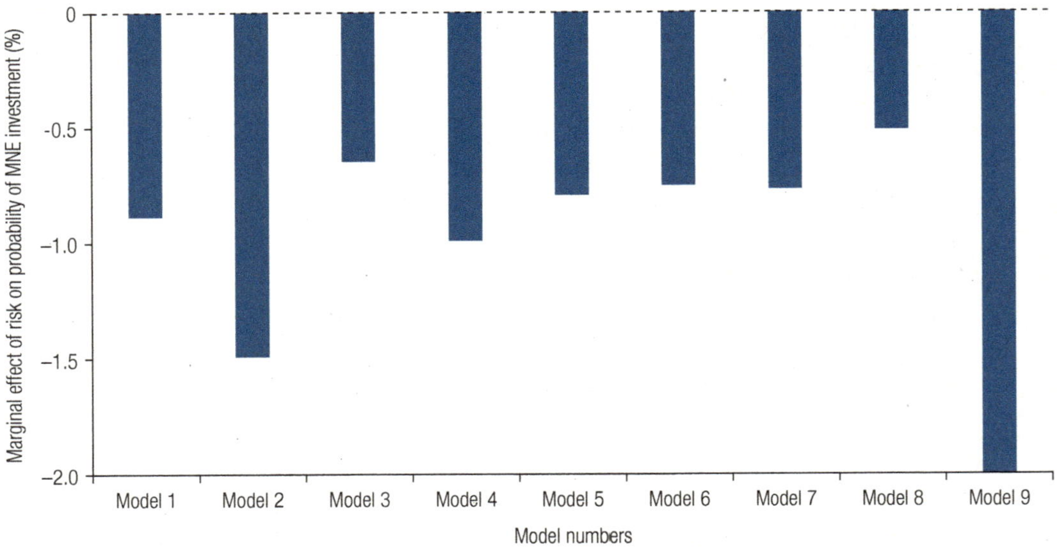

Sources: World Bank, using data from fDi Markets, a *Financial Times* dataset (https://www.fdimarkets.com/).
Note: The figure presents coefficient estimates on regulatory risk from a discrete location choice model using fDi Markets data. All models control for ln(population), ln(GDP per capita), GDP growth (annual %), and trade openness. In addition, models 2–9 include one of the following variables in this order: lower secondary completion rate; bank deposits (% GDP); top combined corporate income tax rate (%); World Governance Indicators (WGI) regulatory quality; Polity IV democracy measure; volatility of GDP per capita growth; exchange rate volatility: and Fitch Sovereign Rating (categorical variables). GDP = gross domestic product; MNE = multinational enterprise. For more detailed model explanations, see box 4.2. For all coefficients, by model, see annex 4A, table 4A.5.

in a host country. All specifications control for economic fundamentals. Furthermore, different measures of a country's institutional environment or other indicators of macro or sovereign risks are included. All results are in the same direction and are statistically significant at the 1 percent level.

The effect of regulatory risk—or, conceived more positively, certainty—on MNEs' investment is of meaningful magnitude. The results across different specifications suggest that, on average, a 1 percent reduction in regulatory risk increases the likelihood of an investor entering or expanding in a host country by 0.5–2 percentage points. In other words, all else equal, if the median country improves its performance (reduces regulatory risk) to the level of the top 25th percentile performer, investors will be 5.5–22 percentage points more likely to locate in the country.

To put this result in further perspective, in the same model, the explanatory power of the regulatory risk score on FDI is comparable in magnitude to trade openness. When controlling for both variables at the same time, a 1 percent increase in the host country's trade-GDP ratio is associated with a 0.3–0.6 percentage point increase in an investor's likelihood to enter or expand.[16] That is, a 1 standard deviation increase in trade openness is associated with a 28 percentage point increase in likelihood of investor entry, on average. In comparison, a 1 standard deviation decrease in regulatory risk is associated with a 9 percentage point increase in likelihood of investor entry.

How Elements of the Regulatory Framework Matter for Investment

The three dimensions of the regulatory risk measure—transparency, protection, and recourse—are not independent of one another. Countries with better protection also tend to have higher measured quality of recourse mechanisms and regulatory transparency (see annex 4A, figure 4A.3, panel a). Nevertheless, most countries still have markedly different performances across the three pillars (see annex 4A, figure 4A.3, panel b). That is, they tend to perform substantially better in one pillar than in others, implying the potential to improve the overall level of risk by focusing on certain pillars. Consequently, the analysis also finds that each of the three risk pillars still has a positive effect on investor entry decision, conditional on other dimensions of the regulatory framework (figure 4.7).

Finally, the econometric evidence that regulatory risk matters for investor decisions is consistent with investor perception as documented in the 2019 GIC Survey: First, investors, especially large investors, consider a host country's legal and regulatory environment to be one of the most important factors shaping their parent firm's decision to invest in the country. Second, exposure to political risk in host countries triggers existing investors to consider withdrawing investments or canceling planned investment. Third, for investors that experienced an adverse political risk event, both the quality of rules and their implementation appear to be a major obstacle in such cases. (See box 4.3 for more detailed survey results and chapter 1 of the report for the survey's methodology and sample.) These findings are also consistent with other surveys, which consistently identify political risk and regulatory uncertainty as major concerns for foreign businesses.[17]

FIGURE 4.7 Different Dimensions of the Regulatory Framework (Transparency, Protection, and Recourse) Matter for Investment

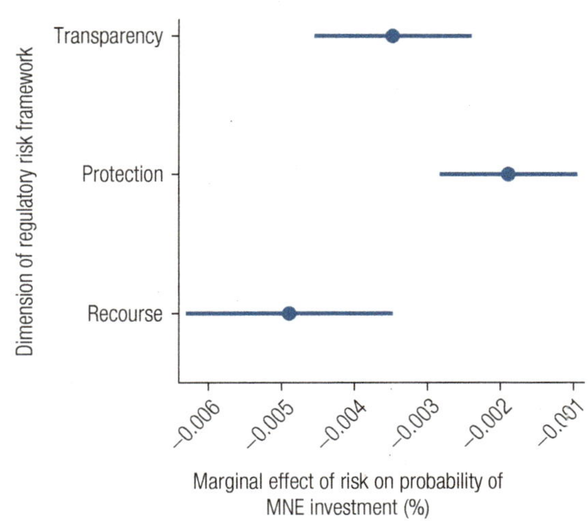

Sources: World Bank, using data from fDi Markets, a *Financial Times* dataset (https://www.fdimarkets.com/).
Note: The figure presents results from a discrete location choice model using fDi Markets data, controlling for ln(population), ln(GDP per capita), GDP growth (annual %), trade openness, WGI (World Governance Index) regulatory quality, and volatility of GDP per capita growth. The plot shows coefficient estimates and 95% confidence intervals of the three components of regulatory risk. GDP = gross domestic product; MNE = multinational enterprise.

BOX 4.3

Importance of Political Risk and a Stable Regulatory Framework for Investment Decisions: Confirmation from the 2019 GIC Survey

Legal and Regulatory Environment

Besides political and macroeconomic stability, investors consider the legal and regulatory environment to be one of the most important factors shaping their investment entry decisions. In the 2019 Global Investment Competitiveness (GIC) Survey, 42 percent of respondents consider it a "critically important" factor in their investment decisions (figure B4.3.1).

Further, countries' legal and regulatory environments are especially important for larger firms. On average, large firms (those with more than 250 employees) rank the legal and regulatory environment as their top investment consideration, while small and medium enterprises (SMEs) consider it to be only the fourth most important consideration. (Ranking of importance is based on the percentage of investors who rate a factor as "important" or "critically important.") These differences may be driven by the presence of restrictions that are applicable only to larger firms and the greater regulatory scrutiny that large companies tend to experience.

Political Risk

Most (two-thirds) of existing investors would consider withdrawing investments or canceling planned investment in the face of political risk exposure in host countries (figure B4.3.2). This result is in line with the finding that more than 70 percent of existing investors consider investment protection guarantees (against political risk) to be "important" or "critically important" for investment decisions (figure B4.3.1).

FIGURE B4.3.1 Legal and Regulatory Environment Is the Third Most-Cited Investment Decision Factor

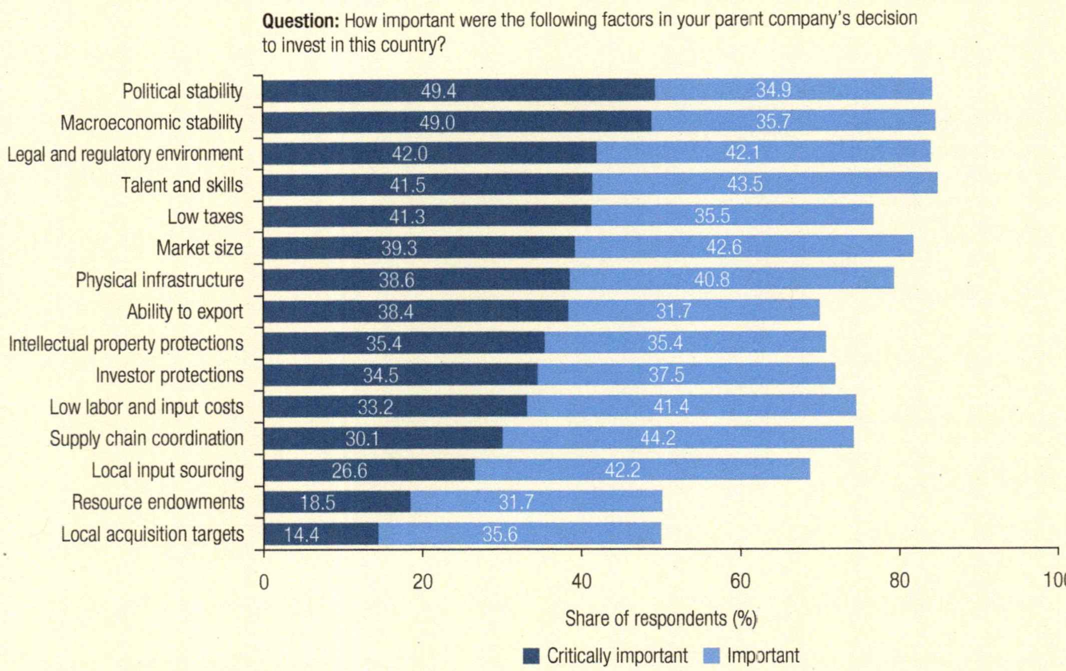

Source: Computation based on 2019 GIC Survey.

Note: Affiliates of multinational enterprises were surveyed in 10 middle-income countries: Brazil, China, India, Indonesia, Malaysia, Mexico, Nigeria, Thailand, Turkey, and Vietnam. "Political stability" is ranked ahead of "macroeconomic stability" because 49.4 percent of respondents cited it as "critically important," versus 49.0 percent for macroeconomic stability.

Box continues next page

BOX 4.3

Importance of Political Risk and a Stable Regulatory Framework for Investment Decisions: Confirmation from the 2019 GIC Survey (*continued*)

FIGURE B4.3.2 Expropriation and Breach of Contract Are the Most Likely to Affect Investments Adversely

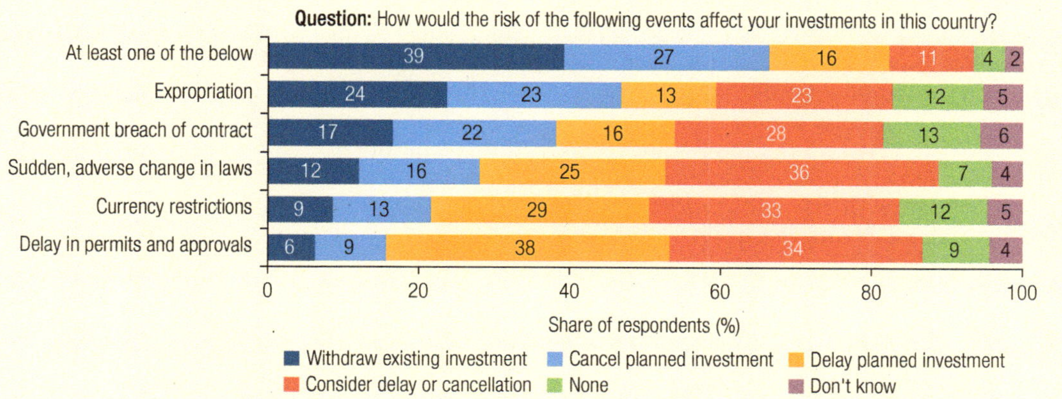

Source: Calculations based on the 2019 GIC Survey.
Note: Affiliates of multinational enterprises were surveyed in 10 middle-income countries: Brazil, China, India, Indonesia, Malaysia, Mexico, Nigeria, Thailand, Turkey, and Vietnam.

FIGURE B4.3.3 Investors Perceive the Quality of Rules and Their Implementation as Obstacles

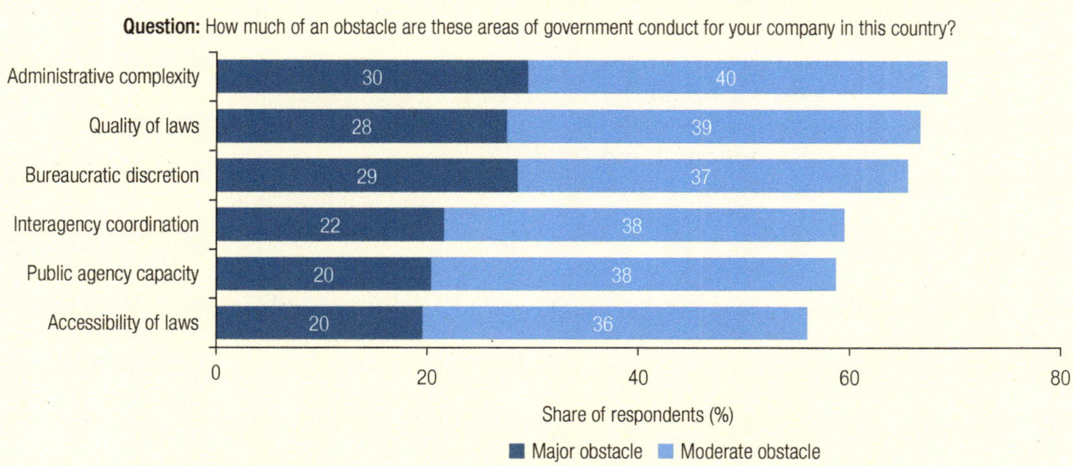

Source: Calculations based on the 2019 GIC Survey.
Note: Affiliates of multinational enterprises were surveyed in 10 middle-income countries: Brazil, China, India, Indonesia, Malaysia, Mexico, Nigeria, Thailand, Turkey, and Vietnam.

Box continues next page

BOX 4.3

Importance of Political Risk and a Stable Regulatory Framework for Investment Decisions: Confirmation from the 2019 GIC Survey (*continued*)

Risks of expropriation and government breach of contract evoke particularly negative investment reactions. Experiencing such events would cause about 50 percent and 40 percent of investors, respectively, to consider withdrawing existing investments or canceling planned ones. Sudden legal changes, currency restrictions, and delays in obtaining permits and approvals elicit less severe reactions. Such risks are more likely to cause investors to delay investments rather than to cancel or withdraw investments completely.

Quality of Rules and Their Implementation

Finally, the quality of rules and their implementation contributes to investors' exposure to political risk. Among respondents who reported having experienced exposure to political risk, the top three obstacles related to government conduct are de jure factors (the complexity of administrative procedures, quality of laws) as well as discretion on the part of bureaucrats who apply these laws or procedures in practice (figure B4.3.3).

Country Case Studies

The primary differentiating feature of this study's constructed regulatory risk measure is the link to specific actionable policy and regulatory levers. As a result, low performance on the measure—under any of the three pillars—can in most cases be influenced by taking specific policy actions.

To illustrate the policy and operational implications of the regulatory risk measure, the discussion that follows presents cases of countries that (a) significantly improved over the sample period (Senegal); (b) significantly declined (Indonesia); and (c) maintained consistently high performance (Kazakhstan).

Substantial Improvement: Senegal

Senegal's score on the regulatory risk measure improved from 2014 to 2017, driven mainly by improvements on the transparency pillar. On the World Bank's *Doing Business* Communication of Tariffs and Tariff Changes Index (within the "Getting Electricity" topic), Senegal substantially outperformed other Sub-Saharan African countries.[18] It made registering property easier in 2016 by increasing the transparency of its land registry and cadaster and thus also improved on the *Doing Business* Transparency of Information Index (within the "Registering Property" topic). Finally, Senegal's bilateral investment treaty (BIT) with Canada, with strong transparency provisions, came into force in 2016.

The improvements documented in the data for Senegal reflect part of a broader package of reforms initiated under the country's Plan for an Emerging Senegal, adopted in 2014 (Republic of Senegal 2014). The plan targets making Senegal an emerging market by 2035, attaining GDP growth of 7–8 percent, creating 600,000 formal jobs, and reaching GDP per capita of US$1,500. It is based on three pillars:

- *Structural transformation of the economy* by consolidating current engines of growth and developing new sectors with a strong capacity to export and attract investment to create wealth, jobs, and social inclusion
- *Promoting human capital* by improving the well-being of the population
- *Enabling good governance* in order to strengthen security, stability, protection of rights and liberties, and consolidation of the rule of law to create better conditions for social peace.

This period of reforms coincides with an increase in investment inflows. FDI inflows to Senegal increased from US$409 million in 2015 to US$587 million in 2017 (UNCTAD 2019b). Six countries steadily increased investment during the period: China, the Republic of Korea, Luxembourg, Morocco, Poland, and Turkey.[19]

Consistent Decline: Indonesia

Indonesia's score on all the three pillars fell substantially from 2014 to 2017, reflecting an increase in risk levels. One main driver was the termination of its IIAs.[20] The content of IIAs is covered under all three pillars of the regulatory risk measure, and therefore their termination affects performance on all. The number of IIAs in force fell from 41 (mapped) in 2014 to 21 in 2018. All but one were unilaterally denounced. IIA scores for Indonesia across all three pillars declined consistently, with the largest decline in 2016—also the year when most of the unilateral terminations took place. FDI declined from US$16.641 billion in 2015 to US$3.921 billion in 2016 (UNCTAD 2019a).

Indonesia's decision to terminate its BITs came at a time when other countries also started expressing concerns about IIAs (including BITs) and the ISDS regime. Indeed, there are legitimate concerns around expansive or inconsistent interpretations of treaty provisions; the qualifications and independence of arbitrators; treaty shopping; lack of transparency; and high costs of dispute settlement. As the broader IIA regime undergoes reform, the challenge for developing countries is in making adequate adjustments to address shortcomings yet ensuring that IIAs remain an effective risk mitigation tool for the country.

More specifically, most of Indonesia's BITs were signed in the 1990s, when the realities of the country were very different from today:[21] it was not a Group of Twenty (G-20) member, was relatively unstable, and was not a capital exporter. The global economic landscape and political economy has changed substantially since then.

Around the time of the terminations, Indonesia also became a respondent to a controversial, high-stakes investment arbitration case. Churchill Mining PLC (a British company) and Planet Mining Pty Ltd. (an Australian company) filed arbitration cases against Indonesia, claiming over US$1 billion in damages.[22] In February 2014, the two cases were consolidated, and the tribunal found that it had jurisdiction to decide on the case, negating Indonesia's arguments opposing jurisdiction.[23] The case was ultimately decided in favor of Indonesia, and the claimants were ordered to pay costs and arbitration fees of nearly US$9.5 million.[24] Nonetheless, from the experience of the Churchill case, the government perhaps also realized the value of having clear treaty language to safeguard against claims based on conduct that was unlawful or contrary to international public policy.[25]

Indonesia's performance on the regulatory risk measure aligns with investment climate assessments indicating that regulatory uncertainty and lack of transparency are key factors that impede operations of investors (US Department of State 2017, 2019b). Investors report that draft laws and regulations are selectively published for public comment,[26] regulations are often vague and leave much room for interpretation, and drafts can take years to become law. Indonesia's significantly decentralized framework on lawmaking creates further uncertainties.[27]

Indeed, political risk and regulatory uncertainty remain critical issues for investors. In the 2019 GIC Survey, more than 90 percent of respondents in Indonesia consider investment protection against political risk to be "important" or "critically important." To address the issue of regulatory uncertainty, Indonesia has made specific efforts since 2017. For example, Presidential Instruction No. 7/2017 was issued, requiring ministries to coordinate before issuing regulations, to conduct regulatory impact assessment, and to provide opportunity for public consultation. Further, Presidential Regulation No. 95/2018 on e-government was issued, requiring that all levels of government (central, provincial, and municipal) implement online governance tools to improve overall transparency. These initiatives happened after the period covered in the regulatory risk measure.

As Indonesia progresses with its IIA reform efforts, key aspects that it may consider are (a) clarifying the definitions of investment, FET, and indirect expropriation; (b) including reasonable and limited exceptions and carve-outs to ensure regulatory space for states; and (c) refining the scope of ISDS.[28]

Notably, countries are also exploring institutional mechanisms to prevent disputes by ensuring better implementation of core investment protection obligations (similar to what Vietnam is setting up, for example).[29] Such mechanisms are part of the regulatory risk framework, and thus Indonesia's performance can be improved by putting them in place. In addition, this may also be an opportunity for Indonesia to ensure greater harmonization between all of its IIAs-BITs, and regional free trade agreements (FTAs). Finally, it is important that Indonesia not only adjust its IIAs but also harmonize its domestic legal framework to ensure consistency in its legal framework and its implementation.

Strong Performance: Kazakhstan

Kazakhstan's performance on the overall risk measure has been strong. Over the past few years, Kazakhstan has consistently improved on various indexes based on de jure legal and regulatory provisions. For example, in 2019, Kazakhstan came 28th out of 190 countries in the World Bank's *Doing Business* rankings. It ranks 4th on the "Enforcing Contracts" topic, 18th on the "Registering Property" topic, and 36th on the "Starting a Business" topic. Kazakhstan also performs well on the OECD FDI Regulatory Restrictiveness Index, with a score similar to Austria's.[30] All these indicators suggest consistent improvement on de jure measures.

This is a result of Kazakhstan's efforts in several areas: the importance of attracting more FDI as a tool to advance productivity and growth is recognized by the country's political leadership. Providing impetus toward this goal is Kazakhstan's strategic location along China's Belt and Road Initiative. And after joining the World Trade Organization (WTO) in 2015, Kazakhstan made several reforms in its regulatory framework (such as eliminating local content requirements).

Despite institutional and legal improvements, investment climate assessments indicate that challenges remain relating to continued corruption, inefficient bureaucracy, and arbitrary law enforcement, especially at the regional and municipal levels (US Department of State 2019a). Other reported areas of concerns are the government's tendency to challenge contractual rights, unannounced tax audits, imposition of high and ad hoc fines, and other interventions in companies' operations. On paper, the government has obligations to publish draft legislations. However, investment climate assessments indicate that the legal and regulatory processes are largely opaque. Draft bills are available for public comment, but the process occurs without notice, and some bills are excluded altogether.

From these investor perceptions reported in investment climate assessments, it appears that the real challenge in Kazakhstan is the lack of enforcement of the legal framework. There is also lack of trust in the court systems—the main avenue for seeking enforcement.

Lack of enforcement of the legal framework is also reflected in Kazakhstan's investor-state disputes. It has had 19 investor-state disputes (based on publicly available information), of which 5 were decided in favor of investors, 5 were decided in favor of the state, and the remaining are either pending or settled.[31] In all cases decided in favor of the investors, the publicly available information indicates, the tribunals found violation of FET or expropriation provisions—both of which are core legal guarantees provided in Kazakhstan's legal framework.

In 2017, the government adopted the 2018–22 National Investment Strategy with the aim of increasing FDI by 25 percent by 2022

(US Department of State 2019c). Priority areas identified in the strategy include investment climate improvements, privatization, and greater economic diversification. Mineral extraction continues to dominate Kazakhstan's economy, with 75 percent of its FDI stock in the extractives sectors.[32] Diversification has consistently been identified as one of the country's priority areas. As Kazakhstan bolsters its efforts to attract a more diverse range of FDI, ensuring effective implementation of its laws and regulations and minimizing risks will be key—indeed, manufacturing and services sector investors tend to be more mobile.

In addition to strengthening the level of regulatory enforcement, Kazakhstan's performance on the measure also indicates certain de jure areas that it can further improve. Figure 4.8 benchmarks Kazakhstan's performance on each risk pillar relative to its neighboring countries in Central Asia and other comparators. It suggests that Kazakhstan could focus on improving the transparency pillar, in which it lags the furthest relative to all comparator countries except Poland and Turkey.

More specifically, Kazakhstan does not include a negative list (which would clarify the sectors and activities that are prohibited or restricted for FDI) either in its Investment Law of 2003 or any other instruments. However, it continues to maintain restrictions on foreign ownership (such as a ceiling on foreign ownership of media). In addition, foreign investors report that new laws and decrees are passed that impose penalties for periods before the laws or decrees came into force—without "grandfathering" existing investments (US Department of State 2019c). Notably, Kazakhstan's investment law does not include a provision to address this aspect.

Kazakhstan's strong performance on the regulatory risk measure also raises the question of why higher-income countries are *not* the highest performers on the regulatory risk measure. The measure is linked to specific legal and regulatory instruments, and some countries lack these instruments—in some cases because they might not be required, given the other laws and regulations of the country. For example, the analysis finds that

FIGURE 4.8 Kazakhstan's Scores on the Three Pillars of the FDI Regulatory Risk Measure

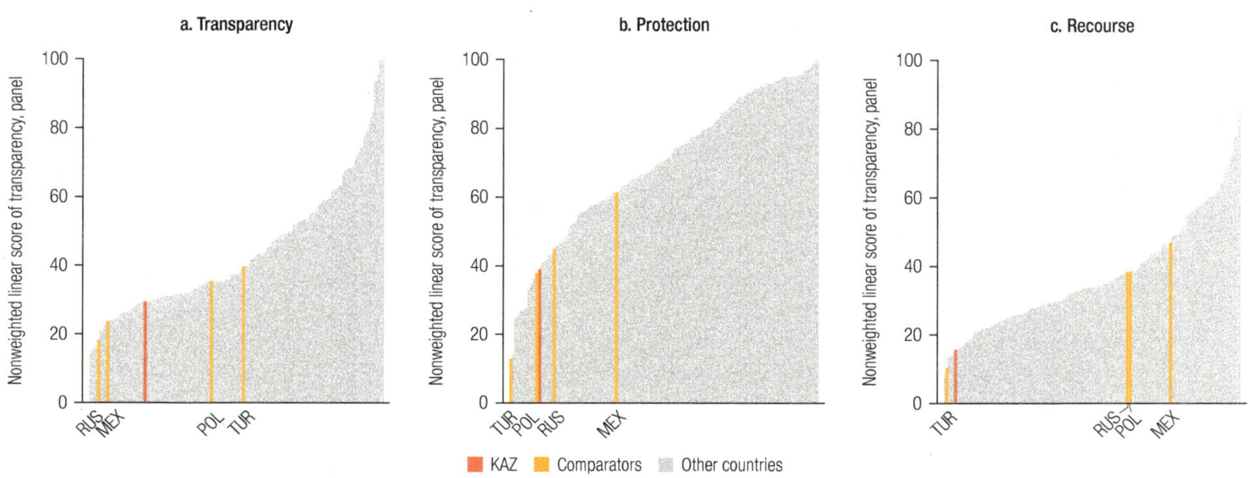

Source: World Bank.
Note: "Other comparators" refers to Mexico, Poland, Turkey, and the Russian Federation. The "nonweighted linear score, panel" refers to the "panel version" of this study's regulatory risk score (0–100), calculated from 2014–17 data. For the full list and descriptions of data sources used to calculate the panel scores, see annex 4A. FDI = foreign direct investment; KAZ = Kazakhstan.

fewer countries with high GDP per capita tend to have an investment law. Arguably, countries with a relatively higher GDP have invested more heavily in creating comprehensive legal frameworks and in building institutional capacity to ensure implementation. Therefore, lesser reliance may be placed on instruments like investment laws, which are often used as signaling devices to generate investor confidence. The dataset on investment laws shows that countries that perform better on *Doing Business* tend not to have an investment law.

Nonetheless, investment laws continue to be a powerful instrument leveraged by countries for different purposes.[33] They serve as an important risk mitigation tool. This is also confirmed in the dataset, which indicates that countries with higher political risk ratings tend to have investment laws.

Concluding Remarks

Growing protectionism has exacerbated policy and regulatory uncertainty—with countries adopting a variety of new measures to protect national security or for other public purposes. With the global decline in FDI over the past few years, competition between developing countries to attract it has only intensified. Attracting FDI will require effective government actions to reduce real *and* perceived risk for investors. Existing risk indicators often help inform investors' decisions, yet those indicators often rely heavily on perception and do not have a direct link to what governments can do or have done to affect risk. Relating specific government actions to the measurement of risks is one potential avenue to inform policy makers in their quest to reduce investment risks.

This chapter has presented a new framework to measure regulatory risk that is linked directly to specific legal and regulatory provisions, drawing on existing indicators and newly constructed data on the content of selected legal instruments. It shows that regulatory risk, as captured in this framework, carries meaningful signals of risk for investors. The evidence at both the country and investor levels suggests that regulatory risk matters for investment attraction and retention. Further, the chapter has demonstrated that the overall risk measure and underlying data sources can be used as a starting point to detect broad areas of weakness in a country and guide further research and diagnostics.

The primary differentiating feature of the risk measure is the link to specific actionable policy and regulatory levers. As a result, low performance on the measure, under any of the three pillars, can in most cases be influenced by taking specific policy actions.

Performance on the transparency pillar. Transparency can be strengthened through actions that improve (a) systematic publication of and consultation on laws and regulations; (b) the availability of portals and other similar mechanisms enabling investors to find information about relevant laws and regulations; and (c) the specificity and clarity of specific provisions.

Countries can adopt specific legal provisions to mandate publication of laws, regulations, and regulatory plans as well as consultations on proposed regulations. In addition, they can clearly publish information on sectors in which there are investment restrictions. To increase the accessibility of legal and regulatory information, countries can set up an online portal or other unified website.

To improve overall predictability, specific actions can be taken on precise drafting of administrative procedures. For example, where an investment approval is required under the investment law, countries can improve their performance by specifying the criteria on which approval would be granted and periods within which such approval should be granted. In the area of procurement, countries can improve their performance on the transparency pillar by ensuring that tendering documents include criteria for evaluation of bids as well as the main terms of the contract and payment schedule.

Performance on the protection pillar. Protection guarantees for investors can be strengthened largely by improving select legal provisions in a country's investment law or IIAs, in accordance with relatively well-established good practices. For example, legal provisions should protect against both direct and indirect expropriation and should mandate timely and adequate compensation. Legal provisions that guarantee the investors' ability to transfer funds in convertible currency in a timely manner can also improve performance on this pillar. Of course, drafting of any legal provisions will entail not only consideration of well-established principles of investor protection but also the country's overall context, legal traditions, and political economy realities (including flexibilities that need to be provided to reflect the right to regulate).

Performance on the recourse pillar. Recourse for investors can be improved by allowing access to a wide range of dispute settlement mechanisms, including state-state as well as investor-state arbitration. Membership in the New York Convention, which can facilitate enforcement of awards, can also improve performance. In addition, countries can consider setting up an institutional mechanism to systematically prevent investor-state disputes.[34] Overall strengthening of judicial processes—through availability of specialized commercial courts, stipulation of time periods for judicial processes, and implementation of case management systems—can also improve performance on this pillar.

This chapter sets the foundation for further research on several related aspects. A major limitation of the current framework is the relatively small number of regulatory areas that can be evaluated because of a lack of comparable data across countries. In using this measure, important caveats discussed earlier in this chapter—including the current focus on de jure legal provisions and coverage of a relatively limited set of regulatory areas—should be kept in mind. To improve the predictive power of the risk measure, additional regulatory areas may be incorporated, such as trade regulations. As data availability improves (by regulatory areas, time period, and geographical coverage), additional research can be undertaken to better understand the impact of regulatory risk on different types of investors as well as which components of risk matter most for investors.

Annex 4A. Construction and Characteristics of the Composite Regulatory Risk Score

Selection and Scoring of Legal and Regulatory Provisions

The selection of the specific legal and regulatory provisions to be included in the risk score, and how to evaluate their contribution to risk, is an inherently subjective exercise. This section details the decision rules used in the study, based on the analytical framework and data availability, within three pillars: transparency, protection, and recourse.

Pillar 1: Is there *transparency* regarding the content as well as the process of making laws and regulations that apply to investors? Here transparency includes three dimensions: (a) systematic publication of and consultation on laws and regulations; (b) availability of portals and other similar mechanisms, to allow investors to find information about relevant laws and regulations; and (c) to a limited extent, the specificity and clarity of legal provisions to increase transparency on the applicable administrative procedures (to increase predictability and reduce chances of abuse of discretion).

The measure covers

- Whether states have an obligation to publish laws and regulations affecting investment, and whether they do publish laws and regulations either on a unified website or in an official gazette;[35]
- Whether countries publish their negative or positive lists either in their investment law or elsewhere in the legal and policy framework;[36]

- Whether international investment agreements (IIAs) contain provisions concerning any mechanisms for technical cooperation (including for provision of information to the private sector);
- Whether procurement laws and regulations, notices of calls for tender, tender documents, notices of award, and minutes of bids are made publicly available; and
- Whether bids are opened electronically and whether minutes of bid processes are published online.

It incorporates the World Bank's *Doing Business* indicators to measure

- Whether information on land ownership, documentation requirements for land registration,[37] fee schedules, and electricity tariffs were made publicly available and changes notified;[38] and
- Whether requirements for obtaining a building permit are clearly specified in the building regulations or on any accessible website, brochure, or pamphlet as well as whether building laws and regulations were publicly accessible.[39]

Indeed, the degree of specificity and clarity of drafting of legal and regulatory provisions determines the room regulators have to exercise discretion—and thus affects regulatory risk. The measure covers this aspect to a limited extent, largely focusing on a few specific administrative processes affecting foreign direct investment (FDI). For example, it covers whether, in cases where foreign investors need to obtain an investment approval to invest in a country, the criteria and time frames for granting such approvals are stipulated in the law.

On procurement, the measure covers whether procedures for acceptance of completed works and termination of contracts are specified in the law.[40] Further, it covers whether tender notices and documents include specific criteria for the evaluation of bids, main terms of the contract, and payment schedule. It also considers whether grandfather clauses are included.[41]

To measure the extent to which countries ensure transparency in the rulemaking process (before the final law or regulation is approved), the measure covers whether states have an obligation under investment laws or IIAs to publish and consult on proposed laws and regulations, and whether there is a period set by law during which the text of the proposed regulations should be made publicly available.[42] It also covers whether regulatory plans are published,[43] public consultation is undertaken on proposed regulations (not yet passed), and reports are issued on the consultation process.[44]

Pillar 2: What is the extent of legal *protection* provided to investors against arbitrary, unpredictable, or nontransparent government actions? For the purpose of this study, the standards of protection reviewed were selected based on the centrality of the protections to investment operations;[45] their particular relevance in the context of arbitrary, unpredictable, and nontransparent government conduct; and whether they are "absolute" in nature.[46] The standard of protection available to investors was measured on the basis of the quality of provisions on expropriation, transfer of funds, fair and equitable treatment (FET), and nonderogation. Indeed, variations may exist in the interpretation of various provisions and jurisprudence; however, as discussed earlier in the chapter, because of lack of availability of cross-country comparable data, such variations are not included in the measure.

The measure covers whether protection is explicitly provided against both direct and indirect expropriation[47] and whether several key elements are included to ensure the legality of expropriation:[48] that expropriation is done (a) only for public purpose; (b) in a nondiscriminatory manner; (c) following due process; and (d) against payment of prompt, adequate, and effective compensation. These specific conditions for expropriation constitute a widely accepted legal standard. The measure also covers whether investors are guaranteed the ability to freely transfer funds in a timely manner and in a freely convertible or freely usable currency.[49]

Further, the measure covers whether a specific FET provision is included. FET is a composite or a bundle of rights available to investors. Although the FET standard is generally not precisely defined in IIAs, it has been clarified through various decisions of arbitral tribunals. These interpretations indicate that FET is an obligation on states to act in a transparent, consistent, reasonable, and proportional manner and to respect legitimate expectations of investors generated from written commitments. Investors have often used the FET standard to seek regulatory stability.[50] The FET provision may either be "qualified" (with reference to international law or to a list of underlying obligations) or "unqualified."[51]

Finally, the protection measure covers whether, if the legal instruments conflict with other legal norms (other laws, regulations, and IIAs), the more favorable rules apply to investors.

Pillar 3: Do investors have access to effective *recourse* mechanisms in case of grievances or disputes? The measure covers

- Whether investors have recourse to investor-state dispute settlement (ISDS)[52] and the full scope of such a right;[53]
- Whether investors could submit an investment dispute under the ICSID Convention and United Nations Commission on International Trade Law (UNCITRAL) rules;[54]
- Whether investors had recourse to other types of alternate dispute resolution mechanisms, such as mediation or conciliation, either voluntarily or as a mandatory procedure before any adjudicatory procedures (such as arbitration) can begin;
- Whether investors had access to domestic courts either as an option alongside other ISDS forums or as a mandatory step before submitting a claim to investor-state arbitration;
- Whether state-state dispute settlement is available;
- Whether domestic investment laws provide access to any alternate institutional mechanisms to address investor issues before they escalate into legal disputes; and
- Whether countries are members of the ICSID and the New York Convention.[55] ICSID membership allows investors to pursue arbitration proceedings against the host state under the ICSID Convention,[56] which requires automatic recognition and enforcement of the pecuniary aspects of awards by all member states.[57]

The World Bank's *Doing Business* indicators were incorporated to measure

- Whether countries have adopted good practices in their court system in four areas[58]—court structure and proceedings, case management, court automation, and alternative dispute resolution—including aspects such as law regulating the number of adjournments allowed, availability of a case management system and electronic filings, and availability of commercial courts; and
- Whether countries have adopted good practices in ensuring accessibility to land dispute resolution mechanisms,[59] including availability of out-of-court compensation mechanisms and databases to verify accuracy of government-issued identity documents.

Table 4A.1 lists the underlying variables of the three index components, indicating the *original* scale of the raw variables.

Data Normalization and Aggregation

The process to construct the composite regulatory risk measure is described below.

Normalization

To preserve comparability of the constructed scores over time and cross-country, a min-max aggregation approach was chosen, whereby all individual variables will be rescaled as (Max–Min)/Range of (possible) values. Each underlying variable is transformed to a scale from 0–100, where 0 indicates the best possible outcome and 100 the worst—reflecting that the constructed regulatory risk measure is an index of risk. Some data sources, such as

TABLE 4A.1 Underlying Variables of the Regulatory Risk Measure, by Dimension and Subindicators

Pillar 1: Transparency	*Pillar 2: Protection*	*Pillar 3: Recourse*
UNCTAD IIA mapping: Provisions on transparency and technical cooperation (0–100)	*UNCTAD IIA mapping:* Provisions on fair and equitable treatment, expropriation, transfers (0–100)	*UNCTAD IIA mapping:* Dispute settlement provisions (0–100)
Doing Business *(World Bank):* • "Registering Property": Transparency of Information Index (0–6) • "Getting Electricity": Communication of Tariffs and Tariff Changes Index (0–1) • "Dealing with Construction Permits": Quality of Building Regulations Index (0–2)		Doing Business *(World Bank):* • "Enforcing Contracts": Quality of Judicial Processes Index (0–18) • "Registering Property": Land Dispute Resolution Index (0–8)
Global Indicators of Regulatory Governance (World Bank): Laws are publicly available; regulatory plans are published; public consultation is conducted on proposed regulations; results of consultation process are reported (0–4)		*Global Indicators of Regulatory Governance (World Bank):* Challenging regulations (0–1)
Investment laws: Provisions on sector restrictions, screening/approval/notifications, access to laws, transparency, and grandfathering (0–100)	*Investment laws:* Provisions on expropriation, transfers, and fair and equitable treatment (0–100)	*Investment laws:* Provisions on dispute settlement and dispute prevention (0–100)
Benchmarking Public Procurement (World Bank): Transparency, clarity, access to information (0–100)		
		Membership in ICSID: (0-1)
		Membership in the New York Convention: (0–1)

Source: World Bank.
Note: IIA = international investor agreement; ICSID = International Centre for Settlement of Investment Disputes (World Bank Group); UNCTAD = United Nations Conference on Trade and Development. The "New York Convention" refers to the United Nations Convention on the Recognition and Enforcement of Foreign Arbitral Awards.

the World Bank's *Doing Business* and Global Indicators of Regulatory Governance (GIRG) subindicators as well as convention membership dummy variables, which are numerical values at the country level, only require this straightforward transformation to a common scale and direction.

Box 4A.1 describes how legal texts (IIAs, investment laws, and public procurement regulations) are transformed into scores. For each of the three pillars, provisions of interest are identified. The legal texts are broken down into a number of simple, mostly yes/no, questions. Responses to questions relevant to provisions of interest are chosen and converted into scores. Scores for the questions/answers were then aggregated and normalized to a [0,1] score for each provision. All relevant provisions for a given pillar are then aggregated and normalized to the pillar level.

BOX 4A.1

Scoring and Aggregating Rules for IIAs

Step 1: Scoring the transparency, protection, and recourse pillars

- Each provision is scored using a set of more detailed 1/0 (yes/no) questions.
- The scores for each question are then added up and normalized to a scale [0–1] for each provision.

Step 2: Aggregating provisions to treaty level

- For each law or treaty, the total score of all provisions is taken as a simple average of all provisions. A higher score indicates lower risk.
- Scores are meant to be on an ordinal scale.

Step 3: Aggregating scores to the country level

- The "relevant" treaty for a country pair is determined, considering the network of available treaties (figure B4A.1.1):
- The weighted average of country pair scores is taken, where weights are the partner country's share in world gross domestic product (GDP). Underlying assumptions are that the pool of potential investors increases with the size of the international investment agreement (IIA) network and the partner's economy.
- The scores are aggregated as in the following notation:

$$p_i = \sum_{j \in IIA_{ij}\ w/o\ MFN} w_j \times \max_t \{p_{ijt}\} + \sum_{j \in IIA_{ij}\ with\ MFN} wj \times \max_k \{p_{ik}\}, \tag{B4A.1.1}$$

where p_i presents the score for each pillar (transparency, protection, and recourse) at the country level; w_j presents the weights; and and p_{ijt} presents the score of the IIA for the country pair.

FIGURE B4A.1.1 Model of a Country with Multiple Treaty Relationships

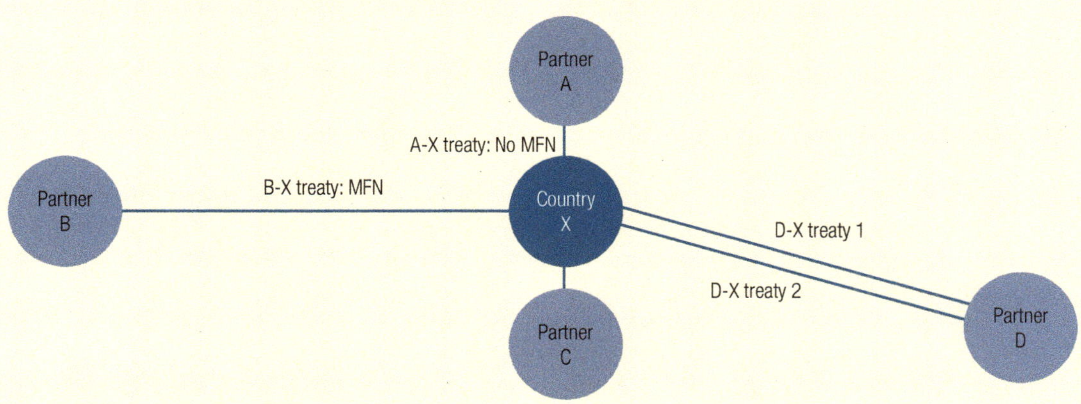

Note: MFN = most-favored nation.

For example, a relevant provision for the transparency score of investment laws is "access to laws." This is scored based on one question: "Does the act guarantee accessibility of laws, regulations, and other legal instruments to investors?" If the answer is yes, a score of 1 is assigned; otherwise, a score of 0 is assigned. This provision as well as four others are used to construct the overall transparency score for investment laws. Other provisions are more complicated to score and require various questions (and legal know-how).

However, in the case of IIAs, this leaves a score at the treaty level rather than the country level. To obtain a country score for each of the pillars, the relevant treaty is first identified at the country pair level. If a pair of countries has more than one treaty at the same time, the better score is considered the relevant one. Furthermore, if a treaty between a pair of countries has a most-favored nation (MFN) provision, then the best score out of all host country scores is assigned.[60]

In a second step, these country-pair scores are collapsed to the host country level by calculating the partner country gross domestic product (GDP) weighted average. This weighting reflects the following assumptions: all else equal, the level of protection increases with (a) the number of IIA partners; and (b) the size of the partners' economies.

There are opposing views in the literature about the marginal effects of additional IIAs in attracting FDI. On the one hand, if investment treaties are pure signaling devices about a host country's commitment to protect investors, then additional treaties have decreasing returns (Bubb and Rose-Ackermann 2007). On the other hand, as Montt (2009) argues, IIAs can have increasing returns because investors could expect a more predictable and efficient jurisprudence to evolve with the size of the treaty network. Given these possible opposing effects, a simple rule was followed in which the level of protection increases linearly with the number of partner countries.

Aggregation of the Composite Score

In combining different data sources, a trade-off arises between maximizing the number of (informative) variables used to construct the index and maximizing the size of the cross-section and time dimension. Thus, two versions of the index were constructed: (a) *a panel version* of comparable data for 2014–17, which excludes some data sources not available for the full period (an investment law database constructed for this study and the World Bank's Benchmarking Public Procurement [BPP] and GIRG databases); and (b) *a cross-section version* with more variables (from the aforementioned sources) for a single data year (2017). (See box 4.1 for a more detailed description of the two versions.)

In addition, the two versions were tested including different data sources. The overall score is robust to the inclusion (or exclusion) of the investment law database, as shown by high correlations of the scores constructed using different sets of data (figure 4A.1, panel a).

The overall index of regulatory risk is the simple average of the three component scores. Each component score (transparency, protection, and recourse) is a composite score of its underlying variables. Two methods were tested to aggregate individual variables into the component scores: a simple average and a weighted average where weights are given by the first component from a principal component analysis (PCA). Table 4A.2 shows the weights for the cross-section version of the risk measure, derived using PCA for each of the three pillars—transparency, protection, and recourse. It suggests that none of the variables included in the framework has an outsize influence on the overall risk components.

The two aggregation methods yield very high correlations (figure 4A.1, panel b). This chapter refers to the simple average version when referring to the index.

Characteristics of the Regulatory Risk Measure: Additional Results

Additional results are presented in figures 4A.2, 4A.3, and 4A.4, in addition to tables 4A.3, 4A.4, and 4A.5.

FIGURE 4A.1 The Regulatory Risk Measure Is Highly Correlated across Varying Data Sources and Aggregation Methods

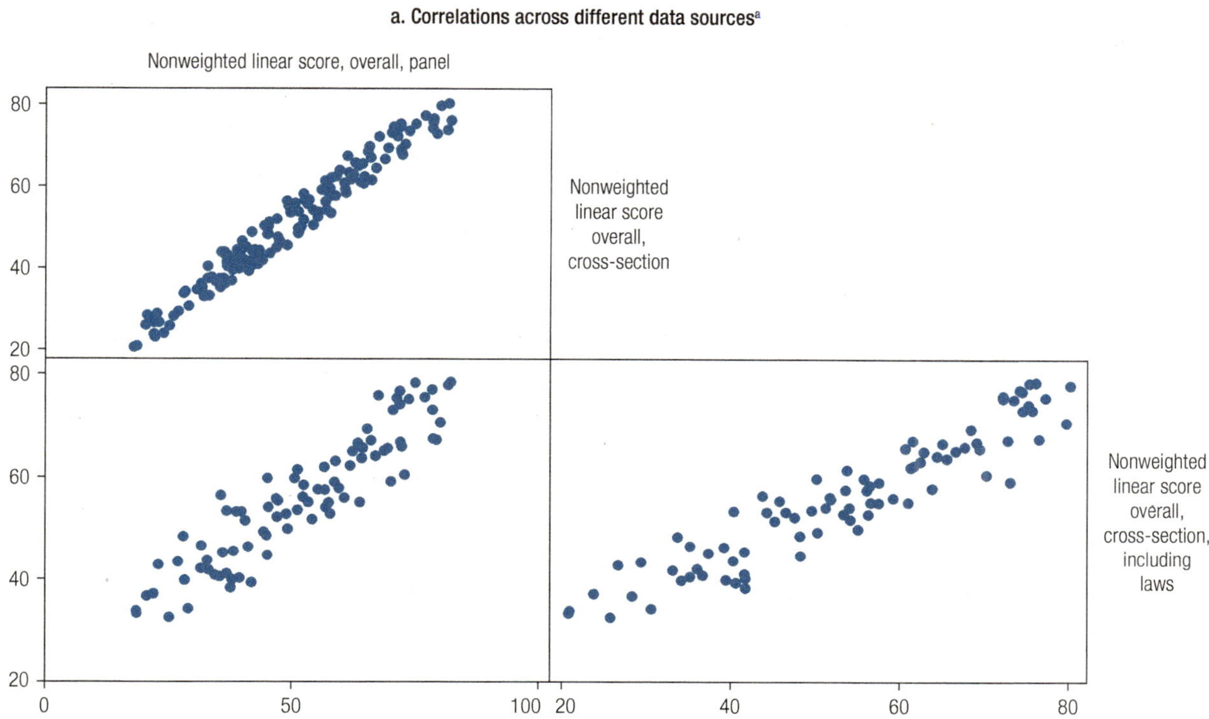

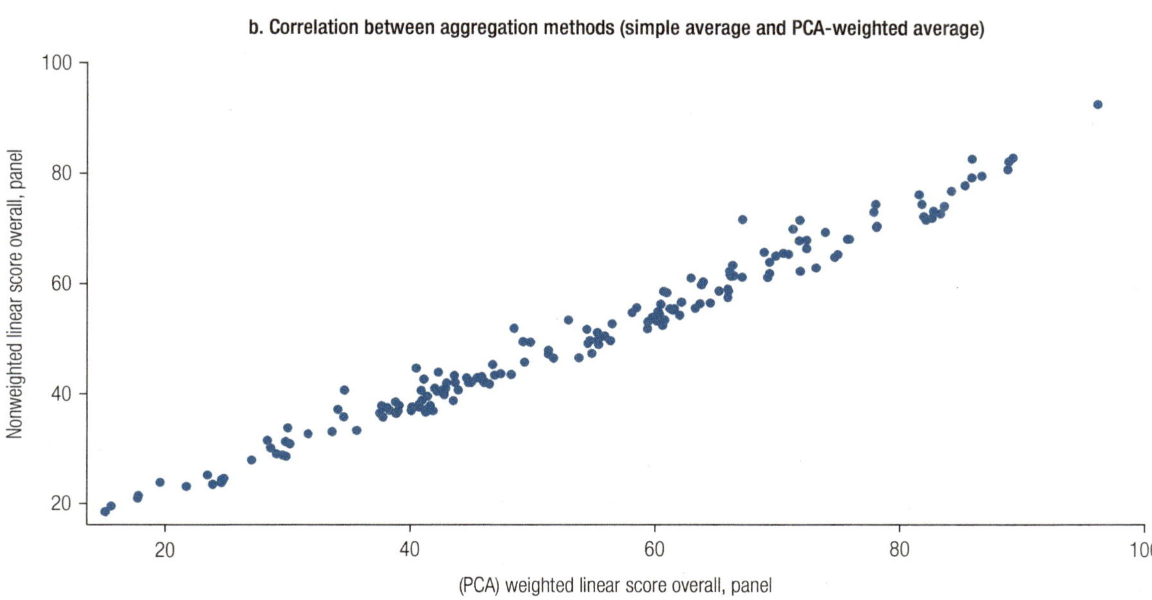

Source: World Bank.
Note: "Nonweighted [or weighted] linear score overall, panel" refers to the "panel version" of this study's regulatory risk score (0–100), calculated from 2014–17 data. "Nonweighted linear score overall, cross-section" refers to the "cross-section version" of the risk score (0–100), calculated from 2017 data. For the full list and descriptions of data sources used to calculate the panel aggregate scores, see annex 4A. PCA = principal component analysis.
a. The correlation matrix plots between different versions of the risk measure—panel version and cross-section version—with additional underlying variables.

TABLE 4A.2 Principal Component Analysis (PCA) Weights

Pillar	*Variable*	*PCA weights*
Transparency	*IIAs:* Provisions on transparency and technical cooperation	0.183
	Investment laws: Provisions on sector restrictions, screening/approval/notifications, access to laws, transparency, and grandfathering	0.026
	GIRG: Laws publicly available, regulatory plans published, public consulted on proposed regulations, consultation results reported	0.207
	BPP: Transparency, clarity, and access to information	0.088
	DB: "Registering Property": Transparency of Information Index	0.216
	DB: "Getting Electricity": Communication of Tariffs and Tariff Changes Index	0.142
	DB: "Dealing with Construction Permits": Quality of Building Regulations Index	0.139
Protection	*IIAs:* Provisions on FET, expropriation, transfers	0.500
	Investment laws: Provisions on FET, expropriation, transfers	0.500
Recourse	*IIAs:* Dispute settlement provisions	0.221
	Investment laws: Dispute settlement provisions	0.041
	GIRG: Challenging regulations	0.086
	ICSID membership	0.084
	New York Convention membership	0.142
	DB: "Enforcing Contracts": Quality of Judicial Processes Index	0.221
	DB: "Registering Property": Land Dispute Resolution Index	0.204

Source: World Bank.
Note: Weights have been normalized to sum up to 1. "New York Convention" refers to the Convention on the Recognition and Enforcement of Foreign Arbitral Awards. BPP = Benchmarking Public Procurement (World Bank); DB = *Doing Business* (World Bank); FET = fair and equitable treatment; GIRG = Global Indicators of Regulatory Governance (World Bank); ICSID = International Centre for Settlement of Investment Disputes; IIAs = international investment agreements.

FIGURE 4A.2 Regulatory Risk Varies across Countries

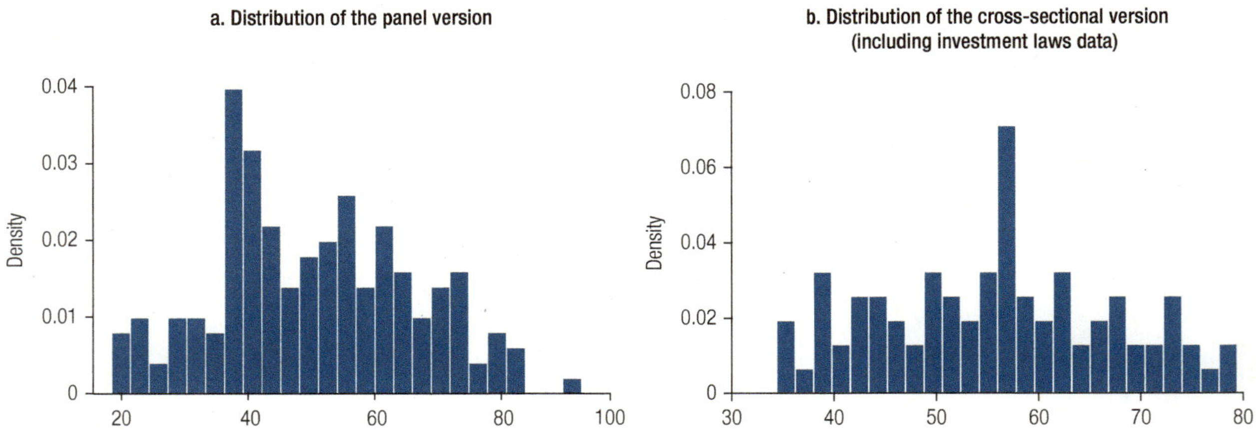

Source: World Bank.
Note: Histograms show distribution of the panel version (panel a), and the cross-sectional version of the regulatory risk measure, including investment laws data (panel b). The "panel version" of the regulatory risk score (0–100) is calculated from 2014–17 data. The "cross-section version" is calculated from 2017 data. For the full list and descriptions of data sources used to calculate the panel aggregate scores, see annex 4A.

FIGURE 4A.3 Countries That Perform Better in One Pillar Often Perform Better in Other Pillars of Regulatory Risk

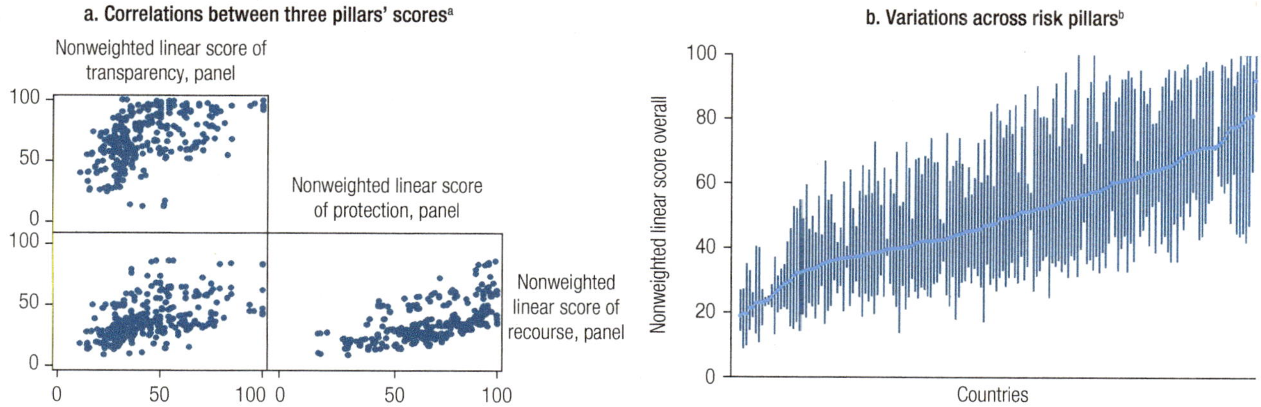

Source: World Bank.

a. "Nonweighted linear score . . . , panel" refers to the "panel version" of the regulatory risk score (0–100), calculated from 2014–17 data. For the full list and descriptions of data sources used to calculate the panel aggregate scores, see annex 4A.

b. In panel b, the blue dots present the overall regulatory risk scores for 2017 (average of the three risk pillars), cover ng 166 countries. The bars present the variations by the three pillars (that is, they denote the range determined by the two pillars with the lowest and the highest scores).

FIGURE 4A.4 Higher Regulatory Risk Is Associated with Higher Expropriation Risk Insurance Premium

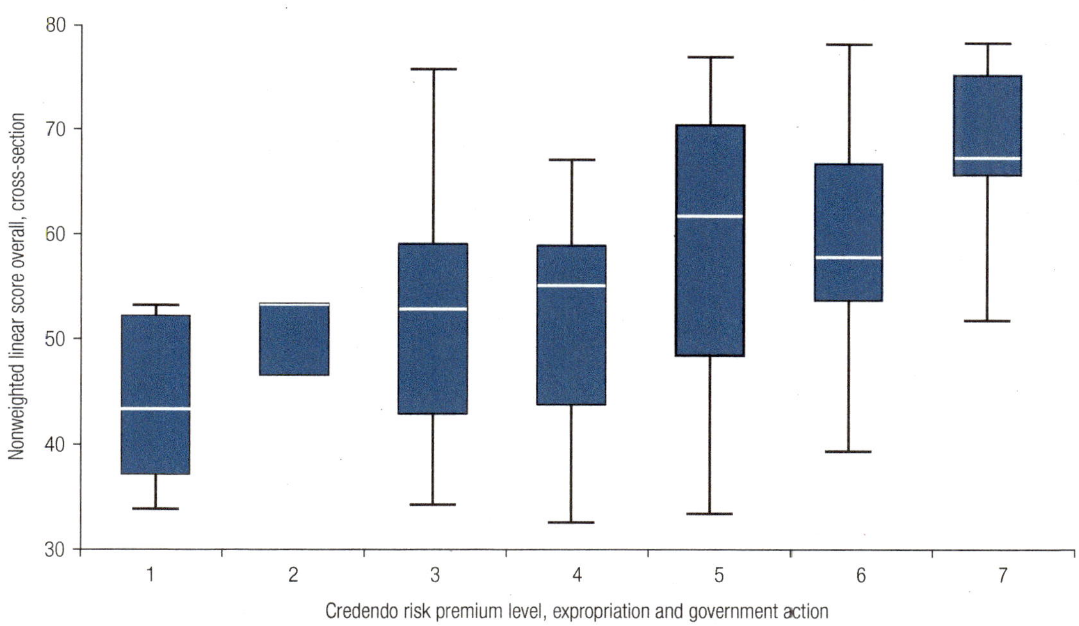

Source: World Bank and Credendo.

Note: Figure is a boxplot of the regulatory risk score (cross-sectional version) over the seven categories of Credendo's "expropriation and government action risk premium." The higher (lower) the risk premium, the higher (lower) the risk. The "Nonweighted linear score overall, cross-section" refers to the cross-sectional version of the regulatory risk score (0–100), calculated from 2017 data. For the full list and descriptions of data sources used to calculate aggregate scores, see annex 4A.

TABLE 4A.3 A Gravity Model of Bilateral FDI Inflows, 2014–16

	(1)	(2)	(3)	(4)
Regulatory risk (panel index, not including dispute data)	−0.0501**	−0.0308		
	(0.0225)	(0.0354)		
Regulatory risk (panel index, including dispute data)			−0.0705***	−0.0560*
			(0.0255)	(0.0335)
Difference between destination and origin countries' regulatory risk		−0.0199		−0.0155
		(0.0298)		(0.0239)
Market size (GDP)	0.240	0.255*	0.241	0.256*
	(0.147)	(0.148)	(0.147)	(0.148)
Difference in income per capita	−0.141**	−0.153**	−0.142**	−0.154**
	(0.0598)	(0.0607)	(0.0599)	(0.0608)
Ln(distant)	−0.503***	−0.529***	−0.502***	−0.529***
	(0.0933)	(0.0950)	(0.0932)	(0.0950)
Contiguity	−0.0321	−0.0541	−0.0302	−0.0518
	(0.386)	(0.383)	(0.385)	(0.382)
A language is spoken by at least 9% of the population in both countries	0.429*	0.415*	0.428*	0.413*
	(0.245)	(0.246)	(0.245)	(0.246)
Ever in colonial relationship	−0.0349	−0.0138	−0.0346	−0.0134
	(0.234)	(0.233)	(0.233)	(0.232)
Common colonizer post-1945	−0.00605	−0.0128	−0.00519	−0.0119
	(0.414)	(0.414)	(0.414)	(0.414)
Constant	5.416	4.289	6.319	5.406
	(4.653)	(4.587)	(4.524)	(4.477)
Observations	68,086	61,396	68,086	61,396

Source: World Bank.
Note: FDI = foreign direct investment; GDP = gross domestic product.
Robust standard errors in parentheses: *** $p < 0.01$ ** $p < 0.05$ * $p < 0.10$

TABLE 4A.4 Regulatory Risk and Activities of Affiliates of US MNEs

	Total employment	*CAPEX*	*R&D expenditures*
Regulatory risk (panel index, not including dispute data)	−0.101	−104.449	−7.594
	(1.599)	(113.909)	(17.580)
GDP per capita (constant 2010 US$)	0.000	−0.163**	0.048***
	(0.000)	(0.067)	(0.006)
Trade openness (trade as % of GDP)	0.025	6.411	−3.536
	(0.116)	(14.091)	(2.536)
Constant	241.723***	11,666.918**	71.836
	−77.31	−5,481.32	−732.201
Country fixed effects	Yes	Yes	Yes
Number of observations	105	100	101
Adjusted R2	−0.027	0.049	0.120

Source: World Bank.
Note: Data on employment, CAPEX (capital expenditure), and R&D (research and development) expenditures are from the US Bureau of Economic Analysis (BEA) on activity of foreign affiliates. GDP = gross domestic product; MNE = multinational enterprise.
Robust standard errors in parentheses: * $p < .10$ ** $p < .05$ *** $p < .01$

TABLE 4A.5 A Discrete Choice Model of Global Investment Location, 2014–16

	Model 1	*Model 2*	*Model 3*	*Model 4*	*Model 5*	*Model 6*	*Model 7*	*Model 8*	*Model 9*
Regulatory risk (panel index, not including dispute data)	−0.00887*** (0.000595)	−0.0149*** (0.000828)	−0.00645*** (0.000629)	−0.00989*** (0.000619)	−0.00793*** (0.000624)	−0.00751*** (0.000606)	−0.00767*** (0.000607)	−0.00511*** (0.000716)	−0.0200*** (0.000852)
ln(GDP per capita)	0.756*** (0.00571)	0.678*** (0.00783)	0.803*** (0.00647)	0.738*** (0.00593)	0.305*** (0.0111)	0.743*** (0.00617)	0.745*** (0.00574)	0.748*** (0.00697)	0.424*** (0.0144)
ln(population)	0.808*** (0.00461)	0.836*** (0.00665)	0.932*** (0.00598)	0.792*** (0.00487)	0.824*** (0.00471)	0.827*** (0.00499)	0.782*** (0.00480)	0.824*** (0.00529)	0.798*** (0.00676)
GDP growth (annual %)	0.0373*** (0.00205)	0.0447*** (0.00244)	0.0290*** (0.00210)	0.0404*** (0.00210)	0.0313*** (0.00226)	0.0319*** (0.00210)	0.0428*** (0.00221)	0.0238*** (0.00241)	0.0476*** (0.00287)
Trade openness (trade as % of GDP)	0.00499*** (9.73e-05)	0.00578*** (0.000123)	0.00861*** (0.000130)	0.00511*** (9.95e-05)	0.00344*** (0.000100)	0.00610*** (0.000126)	0.00493*** (9.68e-05)	0.00457*** (0.000105)	0.00388*** (0.000111)
Lower secondary completion rate, total (% of relevant age group)		−0.0124*** (0.000524)							
Bank deposits (% GDP)			−0.00536*** (0.000165)						
Top Combined CIT Rate (%)				0.00822*** (0.000904)					
WGI Regulatory Quality					0.733*** (0.0162)				
Polity IV: Institutionalized Democracy						0.00391*** (0.00138)			
Volatility of GDP per capita growth							−0.110*** (0.00663)		
Exchange rate volatility								−6.239*** (0.290)	
Fitch Sovereign Rating dummies									YES
Observations	2,825,609	1,349,349	2,308,090	2,564,859	2,825,609	2,563,529	2,825,609	1,641,111	1,805,949

Source: World Bank.
Note: Results from discrete choice model as described in box 4.2, where investors choose to invest a location based on its characteristics relative to other locations. Investors are identified from parent company information from transaction data of fDI Markets, a *Financial Times* dataset (https://www.fdimarkets.com). CIT = corporate income tax; IV = instrumental variable. Standard errors in parentheses. * p < .10 ** p < .05 *** p < .01

Notes

1. In any case, political risk insurance generally does not cover the entire spectrum of a state's conduct that can generate regulatory risks for investors.
2. The ICRG model, created in 1980 and produced since 1992 by investment risk company PRS Group, issues ratings comprising 22 variables in three subcategories of risk: political, financial, and economic. For more information, see "The International Country Risk Guide (ICRG)," PRS Group website: https://www.prsgroup.com/explore-our-products/international-country-risk-guide/.
3. For more information, see "Country Risk Classification," OECD website: http://www.oecd.org/trade/topics/export-credits/arrangement-and-sector-understandings/financing-terms-and-conditions/country-risk-classification/.
4. For a discussion of uncertainty about political events and political risk, see Kobrin (1979).

5. This principle concerns, for example, whether in cases where foreign investors need to obtain an investment approval to invest in a country, the criterion and time frames for granting such approvals are stipulated in a legal instrument.
6. Expropriation, inability to transfer funds outside the host country, and instability in policy and regulatory environment have consistently been identified as critical factors affecting investor decisions to stay and potentially expand operations in a country. (See World Bank [2018] as well as the 2019 GIC Survey, which is covered in chapter 1 of this report and also discussed later in this study.) Breach of these standards has led to most international investor-state disputes. Also see the UNCTAD online Investment Policy Hub: http://investmentpolicyhub.unctad.org.
7. In contrast, the "national treatment" standard is a relative standard of treatment under which treatment of foreign investors and investments is assessed relative to the treatment accorded to domestic investors and investment.
8. Nonetheless, IIAs and investment laws are relatively standardized legal instruments where comparable (text) data are available across all countries.
9. Transfer of funds can be restricted temporarily in a nondiscriminatory manner and in good faith in cases of a balance of payments crisis or on legitimate application of certain national laws—specifically, those relating to bankruptcy, insolvency, or the protection of the rights of creditors; issuing or trading in securities and other stock market instruments; criminal offenses; compliance with orders or judgments in judicial or administrative proceedings; and compliance with labor or tax obligations.
10. Intuitively, the first principal component of a set of variables is the linear index of all the variables, which captures the largest amount of information that is common to all the variables (Filmer and Pritchett 2001). While different in purpose, results from a PCA in practice often closely approximate factor analysis, which is often used to estimate an underlying structure of (a) latent variable(s) (Jolliffe 2002). As such, this aggregation methodology resembles results from the noise extraction approach used in Kaufmann, Kraay, and Mastruzzi (2011), where individual variables are assumed to be noisy measures of a "true" underlying (latent) governance indicator, as estimated by an unobserved components model.
11. To access the online appendix, see www.worldbank.org/gicreport.
12. Credendo is a European credit insurance group that covers risk worldwide. In financial year 2017, the value of transactions insured by Credendo amounted to €85 billion.
13. The correlation patterns suggest that the regulatory risk measure appears to distinguish well between countries with very high or low level of risks, but not the countries with very low risk. This is likely because the measure largely includes de jure measures. For countries that already have "good" rules on the book, additional information on implementation would be needed to distinguish high and low performers.
14. A common log transformation is used to preserve negative and zero values of net FDI inflows: the natural logarithm of 1 plus the absolute value of FDI, multiplied by (–1) if the original FDI variable is negative.
15. The bilateral FDI data are constructed from various sources, including the OECD bilateral FDI database and the International Monetary Fund (IMF) balance-of-payments International Investment Position (IIP) data. (A forthcoming publication on the bilateral FDI database will provide further details.) A basic gravity model is estimated where host and source country fixed effects are used to control for the multilateral resistance term. The model is estimated using the Poisson pseudo maximum likelihood and has the limitation that observations with negative FDI inflows are omitted.
16. Using the same model, the regulatory risk measure has less predictive power than other risk ratings, such as the ICRG's political risk rating and the EIU's legal and regulatory policy risk rating. This suggests that investor perception plays an important role, which the measure presented in this chapter is not well equipped to capture fully.
17. For example, political risk ranks second among nine categories of possible impediments to FDI, according to the MIGA-EIU Political Risk Survey 2013 (MIGA 2013); political risk and uncertainty is ranked 15th among 69 organizational risks, according to

the Aon Global Risk Management Survey 2019 (Aon 2019); and political risks and regulatory uncertainty is ranked 4th among 12 risks, according to the Association for Financial Professionals and Risk Survey 2019 (AFP 2019).

18. For all *Doing Business* data, see https://www.doingbusiness.org/en/data.
19. This list is generated using the database of bilateral FDI; see discussion in the "Regulatory Risk and FDI" section.
20. Indonesia's decision does not immediately affect all foreign investors. Several of the treaties terminated or being renegotiated have sunset clauses allowing for continued application of the treaty for a specific period. Indonesia continues to be a party to other multilateral treaties—in particular, the treaties of the Association of Southeast Asian Nations (ASEAN)—and foreign investors can avail these to seek protection. For the purpose of this study's constructed regulatory risk measure, not all ASEAN treaties in force could be included because they are not mapped in the UNCTAD database. Further, Indonesia's national Law Concerning Investment, 2007, also provides protection guarantees but limited recourse.
21. For a comprehensive historical account of foreign investment and property rights in Indonesia, see Wells and Rafik (2007).
22. ICSID Case No. ARB/12/14 and ICSID Case No. ARB/12/40.
23. The companies, in collaboration with local Indonesian companies (Ridlatama companies), invested in the East Kutai Coal Project (EKCP) in the Regent of East Kutai. In 2010, the Regent of East Kutai revoked the licenses (for activities such as survey and exploration) related to the EKCP, alleging that they were forged. The claimants first filed domestic legal proceedings against the revocation, alleging that they had obtained the licenses lawfully through their partnership with the local companies. The tribunal ultimately decided in favor of Indonesia, stating that the claims were "based on documents forged to implement a fraud aimed at obtaining mining rights" and thus were inadmissible. The tribunal indicated that the local business partner of the claimants was likely the source of the fraudulent conduct but that the claimants failed to exercise sufficient due diligence in carrying out their investment.
24. In March 2017, the claimants applied for annulment at ICSID. On March 18, 2019, the ICSID Annulment Committee dismissed the claimants' application to annul the award.
25. Notably, the tribunal observed that, although generally BITs do not contain provisions on the consequences of unlawful conduct by investors, arbitral decisions have clarified that general principles exist independent of specific treaty language.
26. Law No. 12/2011 on the Development of Laws and Regulations and its implementing government regulation 87/204 allow public comment on draft laws and regulations.
27. See Law No. 23 of 2014 on Regional Government. In June 2016, the central government, exercising its authority under Law No. 23 of 2014, repealed more than 3,000 regional bylaws that were overlapping with other laws and regulations. However, the Constitutional Court in its Decision No. 56/PUU-XIV/2016 limited the central government's authority to repeal these local regulations and allowed local governments to appeal the decision. See Butt (2017).
28. Refining the scope includes reform of the ISDS process. The EU's free trade agreements (such as with Canada, Singapore, and Vietnam) include a standing investment court system, which includes an appellate tribunal. Other FTAs have either excluded ISDS provisions or diluted its scope, such as in Brazil's Cooperation and Facilitation Investment Agreements and the United States–Mexico–Canada Agreement.
29. The World Bank Group has been helping client countries to set up institutional mechanisms to enable them to better detect and resolve investor problems or grievances, which can potentially escalate in investor-state legal disputes (Echandi and Kher 2014; World Bank 2019).
30. For more on the OECD FDI Regulatory Restrictiveness Index, see https://www.oecd.org/investment/fdiindex.htm.
31. Investor-state dispute data from the UNCTAD Investment Policy Hub, https://investmentpolicy.unctad.org/investment-dispute-settlement.
32. Data from "Direct Investment Statistic according to the Directional Principle,"

External Sector Statistics, National Bank of Kazakhstan: https://nationalbank.kz/?docid=469&switch=english.

33. First, as a single instrument capturing all the most important guarantees for foreign investors, an investment law may have an important signaling effect on the country's openness to investment and reform. Second, it can substantively complement the standards of treatment already available under the country's existing legal framework. Third, it can serve as an opportunity to reflect, in a country's domestic legislation, its core international commitments under its IIAs. Fourth, it can be an opportunity to level the playing field between all investors ensuring that all are equally protected. Finally, it can also allow for unifying a country's legal and regulatory framework, consolidating a diverse set of legal instruments currently in force.
34. The World Bank Group has been supporting client countries to set up institutional mechanisms to enable them to better detect and resolve investor problems or grievances that can potentially escalate into investor-state legal disputes (Echandi and Kher 2014; World Bank 2019).
35. "Accessing Laws and Regulations," Global Indicators of Regulatory Governance, World Bank: https://rulemaking.worldbank.org/en/data/comparedata/accessibility.
36. Countries list sectors and activities that are prohibited or restricted for FDI in their negative list. Sectors and activities not listed on the negative list are open to FDI. Alternatively, countries may choose to follow a positive list approach, wherein they list the sectors and activities that are open to FDI.
37. "Registering Property": Transparency of Information Index, World Bank *Doing Business* indicators: https://www.doingbusiness.org/en/data/exploretopics/registering-property.
38. "Getting Electricity": Communication of Tariffs and Tariff Changes Index, World Bank *Doing Business* indicators: https://www.doingbusiness.org/en/data/exploretopics/getting-electricity.
39. "Dealing with Construction Permits": Quality of Building Regulations Index, World Bank *Doing Business* indicators: https://www.doingbusiness.org/en/data/exploretopics/dealing-with-construction-permits.
40. Other areas that were reviewed were whether the law specifies the method to determine the amount of performance guarantee and whether it also specifies that the procuring entity cannot request more than a certain percentage of the contract value as a bid security amount.
41. A grandfather clause would exempt application of a new law due to conditions that were in place before the new law was implemented. In a sense, it provides continuity and predictability for existing investments.
42. "Proposed regulation" means any draft rule affecting business activities proposed by a government's executive authority, ministry, or regulatory agency that, if finalized, is intended to bind any individuals or companies covered by it. This includes subordinated legislation, administrative formalities, decrees, circulars, and directives. The term also includes rules proposed by the government that require final approval by the parliament, other legislative body, or head of state. See "Transparency of Rulemaking," Global Indicators of Regulatory Governance, World Bank: https://rulemaking.worldbank.org/en/data/comparedata/transparency.
43. This refers to forward regulatory plans—that is, a public list of anticipated regulatory changes or proposals intended to be adopted *or* implemented within a specified time frame.
44. See "Transparency in Rulemaking," Global Indicators of Regulatory Governance, World Bank: https://rulemaking.worldbank.org/en/data/comparedata/transparency.
45. Expropriation, inability to transfer funds outside the host country, and instability in policy and regulatory environment have consistently been identified as critical factors affecting investors' decisions to stay and potentially expand operations in a country (World Bank 2018). Breach of these standards has led to most international investor-state disputes (see UNCTAD's online Investment Policy Hub: http://investmentpolicyhub.unctad.org/ISDSn).
46. Absolute standards of treatment—such as protection from expropriation, and fair and equitable treatment (FET)—are to be guaranteed to all investors, irrespective of their nationality or other characteristics. On the other hand, the "national treatment" standard is a relative standard under which treatment of foreign investors or investments is assessed relative to the treatment of domestic investors or investment.

47. "Direct" expropriation refers to the direct seizure or taking of property. "Indirect" expropriation refers to cases where actions (such as regulatory measures) of the government may be tantamount to or have an effect equivalent to taking of the property.
48. The aspect of the legality of expropriation is covered only in investment laws because of the lack of availability of comparable data based on other legal instruments.
49. "Freely usable" currency means a currency determined by the International Monetary Fund (IMF) under the IMF Articles of Agreement [Article XXX(f)] to be a currency that is, in fact, widely used to make payments for international transactions and widely traded in the principal exchange markets. The US dollar, Japanese yen, British pound, euro, and Chinese renminbi are currently determined to be freely usable currencies.
50. In some cases, investors have argued that the FET standard encompasses the obligation to maintain a stable and predictable legal framework (Bayindir v. Pakistan, ICSID Case No. ARB/03/29; CMS v Argentina, ICSID Case No. ARB/01/8), while in others, they have argued that the stability of a legal framework is essential to meet investors' legitimate expectations (Occidental v. Ecuador I, LCIA Case No UN3467). A recent review of arbitral decisions on this topic indicates that tribunals have recognized either a strict or soft regulatory stability obligation of states under the FET standard. In the first case, a mere change in the regulatory framework applicable to investment can trigger a FET violation, while in the other, procedural fairness and substantive reasonableness need to be considered to determine whether a FET violation has occurred. Although the obligation to provide a stable legal and regulatory framework is fairly settled, tribunals have had mixed views on the scope of the obligation (Ortino 2018).
51. In terms of the IIA's text per se, an "unqualified" FET provision provides wider protection because its interpretation is not confined—for example, to specifically enumerated rights or other principles (depending on text of the IIA). The general rules of interpretation (under Article 31 of the Vienna Convention on the Law of Treaties or Article 38 of the Statute of International Court of Justice) continue to apply.
52. Disputes emerging from commercial transactions between enterprises are considered commercial disputes, and those arising from intergovernmental relations are considered state-state disputes. Investor-state disputes are disputes between foreign investors and host states. Such disputes are a relatively unique feature of international investment law.
53. This criterion concerns whether, for example, investors are allowed access to ISDS for (a) *any* disputes relating to investment; (b) only those disputes involving specific bases for claims other than the treaty such as investment contracts and investment authorizations; or (c) only those disputes involving alleged breach of the treaty. The first case allows investors to submit a very broad range of disputes to ISDS, while the latter two cases progressively limit the types of disputes that can be submitted to ISDS.
54. This question focuses on the ease of access to various recourse mechanisms for enforcement of investment protection guarantees in a relatively cost-effective and neutral manner. Therefore, although the extensively documented shortcomings of ISDS are well recognized and noted—in particular, on transparency of the process—this study has not delved into this issue in detail. For further information on ISDS, see "ICSID Rules and Regulations Amendment Process" (https://icsid.worldbank.org/en/amendments); UNCTAD 2019c; and "Working Group III: Investor-State Dispute Settlement Reform," UNCITRAL (https://uncitral.un.org/en/working_groups/3/investor-state).
55. The 1958 Convention for Recognition and Enforcement of Foreign Arbitral Awards (referred to as the New York Convention) requires the courts of a member state to recognize and enforce an award rendered in another member state. It also limits the grounds on which courts of member states may refuse recognition and enforcement of foreign arbitral awards. Under Article V, the following are some of the grounds: incapacity of the parties to the arbitration agreement; invalidity of the arbitration agreement; natural justice grounds; arbitral authority or procedure was not in accordance with the agreement of the parties; the subject matter of the arbitration cannot be referred to arbitration under the national law of the enforcing country; and contrary to public policy of

the enforcing country. These exceptions are not easy to establish. Therefore, countries can rarely use them, making the New York Convention a fairly effective means of ensuring enforcement of awards. On the other hand, enforcement of foreign court judgments is available when states have passed a specific law allowing reciprocal enforcement of foreign judgments.

56. Nonmember states can also pursue arbitral proceedings against host states under ICSID's Additional Facility Rules, although without the benefit of automatic recognition and enforcement of the arbitral awards. However, Article 19 of the Additional Facility Rules requires that arbitration proceedings conducted under the rules be held only in states that are parties to the New York Convention. Therefore, in these cases, the regime under the New York Convention will apply.
57. This implies that ICSID awards are generally not subject to any review process by local courts in host states and are automatically enforced. Under Article 53(1) of the ICSID Convention, an arbitral award of the tribunal is binding on all parties to the proceeding. In case of a failure by a party to comply with an award, then under Article 54(1), the other party may seek to have the pecuniary obligations recognized and enforced in the courts of any ICSID member state as though it were a final judgment of that state's courts. Typically, if a party informs the ICSID Secretariat about nonenforcement by another party, the Secretariat contacts the noncomplying party to request information on the steps taken to ensure compliance. See "ICSID Convention Arbitration Rules," ICSID Documents, ICSID website: https://icsid.worldbank.org/en/Pages/icsiddocs/ICSID-Convention-Arbitration-Rules.aspx.
58. "Enforcing Contracts": Quality of Judicial Processes Index, World Bank *Doing Business* indicators: https://www.doingbusiness.org/en/data/exploretopics/enforcing-contracts.
59. "Registering Property": Land Dispute Resolution Index, World Bank *Doing Business* indicators: https://www.doingbusiness.org/en/data/exploretopics/registering-property.
60. Multinationals can also make use of different treaties through investing from a third country. We sidestep this issue because not all investors can take advantage of restructuring to the same extent. Further, the scoring only considers inclusion of an MFN provision and not any specific exceptions regarding regional integration agreements, ISDS procedural provisions, or phase of application that may be included in treaties and may change the applicable treatment on a case-by-case basis.

References

AFP (Association for Financial Professionals). 2019. "2019 AFP Risk Survey Report: The Evolving Treasury Ecosystem." Survey report, AFP, Bethesda, MD.

Alfaro, Laura, Sebnem Kalemli-Ozcan, and Vadym Volosovych. 2008. "Why Doesn't Capital Flow from Rich to Poor Countries? An Empirical Investigation." *Review of Economics and Statistics* 90 (2): 347–68.

Aon. 2019. "Global Risk Management Survey 2019." Survey report, Aon, London.

Baker, Scott R., Nicholas Bloom, and Steven J. Davis. 2016. "Measuring Economic Policy Uncertainty." *Quarterly Journal of Economics* 131 (4): 1593–636.

Bauerle Danzman, Sarah. 2016. "Contracting with Whom? The Differential Effects of Investment Treaties on FDI." *International Interactions* 42 (3): 452–78.

Bernanke, Benjamin S. 1983. "Irreversibility, Uncertainty, and Cyclical Investment." *Quarterly Journal of Economics* 98 (1): 85–106.

Bloom, Nicholas. 2009. "The Impact of Uncertainty Shocks." *Econometrica* 77 (3): 623–85.

Bonnitcha, Jonathan, Lauge N. Skovgaard Poulsen, and Michael Waibel. 2017. *The Political Economy of the Investment Treaty Regime*. Oxford: Oxford University Press.

Bubb, Ryan J., and Susan Rose-Ackerman. 2007. "BITs and Bargains: Strategic Aspects of Bilateral and Multilateral Regulation of Foreign Investment." *International Review of Law and Economics* 27 (3): 291–311.

Butt, Simon. 2017. "Constitutional Court Lets Local Governments Off the Leash." *Indonesia at Melbourne* (blog), July 4. https://indonesiaatmelbourne.unimelb.edu.au/constitutional-court-lets-local-governments-off-the-leash/.

Chen, Maggie Xiaoyang, and Michael O. Moore. 2010. "Location Decision of Heterogeneous Multinational Firms." *Journal of International Economics* 80 (2): 188–99.

Colen, Liesbeth, Damiaan Persyn, and Andrea Guariso. 2016. "Bilateral Investment Treaties and FDI: Does the Sector Matter?" *World Development* 83: 193–206.

Daude, Christian, and Ernesto Stein. 2007. "The Quality of Institutions and Foreign Direct Investment." *Economics and Politics* 19 (3): 317–44.

Dixit, Avinash. 1989. "Entry and Exit Decisions under Uncertainty." *Journal of Political Economy* 97 (3): 620–38.

Dixon, Jay, and Paul Alexander Haslam. 2016. "Does the Quality of Investment Protection Affect FDI Flows to Developing Countries? Evidence from Latin America." *The World Economy* 39 (8): 1080–108.

Echandi, Roberto, and Priyanka Kher. 2014. "Can International Investor-State Disputes Be Prevented? Empirical Evidence from Settlements in ICSID Arbitration." *ICSID Review Foreign Investment Law Journal* 29 (1): 41–65

EIU. 2017. "World Risk: Alert—Guide to Risk Briefing Methodology." Risk briefing, ViewsWire online analytical service, EIU, August 18.

Filmer, Deon, and Lant H. Pritchett. 2001. "Estimating Wealth Effects without Expenditure Data—or Tears: An Application to Educational Enrollments in States of India." *Demography* 38 (1): 115–32.

Frenkel, Michael, and Benedikt Walter. 2019. "Do Bilateral Investment Treaties Attract Foreign Direct Investment? The Role of International Dispute Settlement Provisions." *The World Economy* 42 (5): 1316–42.

Gelman, Andrew, and Piero Stanig. 2016. "Corruption Perceptions Index 2016: Technical Methodology Note." Transparency International, Berlin.

Gelos, R. Gaston, and Shang-Jin Wei. 2005. "Transparency and International Portfolio Holdings." *Journal of Finance* 60 (6): 2987–3020.

Giambona, Erasmo, John R. Graham, and Campbell R. Harvey. 2017. "The Management of Political Risk." *Journal of International Business Studies* 48 (4): 523–33.

Hallward-Driemeier, Mary. 2003. "Do Bilateral Investment Treaties Attract Foreign Direct Investment? Only a Bit … and They Could Bite." Policy Research Working Paper 3121, World Bank, Washington, DC.

Hassan, Tarek A., Stephan Hollander, Laurence van Lent, and Ahmed Tahoun. 2019. "Firm-Level Political Risk: Measurement and Effects." *Quarterly Journal of Economics* 134 (4): 2135–202.

Høyland, Bjørn, Karl Moene, and Fredrik Willumsen. 2012. "The Tyranny of International Index Rankings." *Journal of Development Economics* 97 (1): 1–14.

Jolliffe, I. T. 2002. *Principal Component Analysis*. 2nd ed. New York: Springer Verlag.

Joyez, Charlie. 2015. "Location Choices and Foreign Direct Investment Motives of Heterogeneous Firms." Unpublished paper. https://www.etsg.org/ETSG2015/Papers/144.pdf.

Jurado, Kyle, Sydney C. Ludvigson, and Serena Ng. 2015. "Measuring Uncertainty." *American Economic Review 105* (3): 1177–216.

Kaufmann, Daniel, Aart Kraay, and Massimo Mastruzzi. 2011. "The Worldwide Governance Indicators: Methodology and Analytical Issues." *Hague Journal on the Rule of Law* 3 (2): 220–46.

Kerner, Andrew, and Jane Lawrence. 2014. "What's the Risk? Bilateral Investment Treaties, Political Risk and Fixed Capital Accumulation." *British Journal of Political Science* 44 (1): 107–21.

Kobrin, Stephen J. 1979. "Political Risk: A Review and Reconsideration." *Journal of International Business Studies* 10 (1): 67–80.

McFadden, Daniel. 1974. "Conditional Logit Analysis of Qualitative Choice Behavior." In *Frontiers in Econometrics*, edited by Paul Zarembka. New York: Academic Press.

MIGA (Multilateral Investment Guarantee Agency). 2013. *World Investment and Political Risk 2013*. Washington, DC: World Bank.

Montt, Santiago. 2009. *State Liability in Investment Treaty Arbitration: Global Constitutional and Administrative Law in the BIT Generation*. Portland, OR: Hart Publishing.

OECD (Organisation for Economic Co-operation and Development). 2008. *Handbook on Constructing Composite Indicators: Methodology and User Guide*. Paris: OECD.

Ortino, Federico. 2018. "The Obligation of Regulatory Stability in the Fair and Equitable Treatment Standard." *Journal of International Economic Law* 21 (4): 845–65.

Papaioannou, Elias. 2009. "What Drives International Financial Flows? Politics, Institutions and Other Determinants." *Journal of Development Economics* 88 (2): 269–81.

Republic of Senegal. 2014. “Plan Sénégal Emergent.” Strategy document, Republic of Senegal, Dakar.

Tobin, Jennifer L., and Susan Rose-Ackerman. 2011. “When BITs Have Some Bite: The Political-Economic Environment for Bilateral Investment Treaties.” *Review of International Organizations* 6 (1): 1–32.

UNCTAD (United Nations Conference on Trade and Development). 2019a. “Country Fact Sheet: Indonesia.” Country FDI data sheet, compiled from *World Investment Report 2019: Special Economic Zones*. New York and Geneva: United Nations. https://unctad.org/sections/dite_dir/docs/wir2019/wir19_fs_id_en.pdf.

UNCTAD. 2019b. “Country Fact Sheet: Senegal.” Country FDI data sheet, compiled from *World Investment Report 2019: Special Economic Zones*. New York and Geneva: United Nations. https://unctad.org/sections/dite_dir/docs/wir2019/wir19_fs_sn_en.pdf.

UNCTAD. 2019c. “Reforming Investment Dispute Settlement: A Stocktaking.” IIA Issues Note, Issue 1, UNCTAD, Geneva.

UNCTAD. 2019d. *World Investment Report 2019: Special Economic Zones*. New York and Geneva: United Nations.

US Department of State. 2017. “2017 Investment Climate Statements: Indonesia.” Annual country statement, US Department of State, Washington, DC. https://www.state.gov/reports/2017-investment-climate-statements/indonesia/

US Department of State. 2019a. “2019 Investment Climate Statements.” Annual business climate report, US Department of State, Washington, DC. https://www.state.gov/reports/2019-investment-climate-statements/.

US Department of State. 2019b. “2019 Investment Climate Statements: Indonesia.” Annual country statement, US Department of State, Washington, DC. https://www.state.gov/reports/2019-investment-climate-statements/indonesia/

US Department of State. 2019c. “2019 Investment Climate Statements: Kazakhstan.” Annual country statement, US Department of State, Washington, DC. https://www.state.gov/reports/2019-investment-climate-statements/kazakhstan/

Wei, Shang Jin. 2000. “How Taxing Is Corruption on International Investors?” *Review of Economics and Statistics* 82 (1): 1–11.

Wells, Louis T., and Rafik Ahmed. 2007. *Making Foreign Investment Safe: Property Rights and National Sovereignty*. Oxford: Oxford University Press.

World Bank. 2018. *Global Investment Competitiveness Report 2017/2018: Foreign Investor Perspectives and Policy Implications*. Washington, DC: World Bank.

World Bank. 2019. “Retention and Expansion of Foreign Direct Investment: Political Risk and Policy Responses.” Working paper, Report No. 144312, World Bank, Washington, DC.

5 Increasing the Development Impact of Investment Promotion Agencies

Armando Heilbron and Hania Kronfol

Key Findings

- **Investment promotion agencies (IPAs) can help increase FDI inflows, attract higher quality FDI, and transform the economies of their home countries.** Estimates of the magnitude of these effects vary in the literature, including a preliminary cost-benefit analysis indicating that US$1 spent on investment promotion yields US$189 in FDI inflows and that spending a relatively modest US$78 in investment promotion creates one additional job in the promoted sectors.
- **The number of IPAs has proliferated over the past two decades—including at national and subnational levels—and evidence shows they can play a significant role in attracting, retaining, and growing investment.** The contributions of IPAs are more pronounced in developing countries, where investors may know less about the location, struggle to obtain reliable information, find the regulatory environments more challenging, and encounter further obstacles stemming from institutional and cultural differences between the investors' home and host markets.
- **Many IPAs are struggling to reach their full potential: they are not nimble enough to respond to new market realities; they lack strategic focus; and they do not adequately provide services most valued by investors, such as advocating for improvements in business climate.** Foreign investors appreciate IPA services offered across their investment life cycle—not just during the investment attraction and entry/establishment stages. For example, about two-thirds of surveyed investors consider IPA assistance with business operational issues to be "important" or "critically important."
- **IPAs can increase their impact by sharpening their strategic focus, building a coherent institutional framework, and strengthening their delivery of investor services.** Specifically, IPAs should (a) focus on a limited number of mandates and target segments; (b) adopt institutional features common to private companies; and (c) offer relevant and high-quality investor services across the investment life cycle. These elements should help IPAs to rapidly adapt to sudden changes in the FDI landscape, such as those presented by the COVID-19 pandemic, and to respond with relevant services to investors.
- **To maximize IPA's impact, policy makers should (a) provide high-level government support (from the president or prime minister); (b) foster strong strategic focus and alignment; (c) grant a clear, uncontested mandate for investment promotion and a high degree of autonomy; (d) facilitate collaboration with governments' other investment institutions; and (e) provide sufficient and sustained financial resources.**

Introduction

Investment promotion agencies (IPAs) are national or subnational institutions mandated to attract and grow investment—usually foreign direct investment (FDI).[1] IPAs (also known as investment promotion intermediaries, IPIs) can play a significant role in fostering economic development in their countries. They can generate larger FDI inflows, attract quality FDI, deepen integration into global value chains (GVCs), and even transform the economies of their home countries.

However, although IPAs have proliferated over the past two decades, their success stories are not as widespread and are especially scarce in developing countries.[2] Many IPAs are stretched across many mandates and target more sectors than they can properly handle, while not providing the key services that investors expect. At the same time, IPAs do not seem to be evolving as dynamically as needed to align with changes in the FDI landscape as well as more sophisticated investor requirements. The current literature, combined with additional research and more than 30 years of World Bank Group operational experience, suggests that IPAs can have much greater impact if they refine their strategic focus, adopt institutional features that prioritize the investor, and improve investor service delivery throughout the investment life cycle (box 5.1).

Given that IPAs are mostly financed by public funds, a reasonable question to ask is whether they provide a good return on such funds. Do they work for development? And if so, what can policy makers do to maximize their impact? Currently, research on IPAs and their impact—primarily considered in terms of FDI inflows generated and direct jobs created (see annex 5A)—is highly dispersed across different academic fields and has yielded few clear findings on the role of IPAs. It remains limited in addressing global trends and themes, particularly in the context of developing countries.

This chapter aims to advance research in the field of investment promotion by consolidating evidence and World Bank Group operational experience, presenting recent global data on IPA characteristics and on investor perceptions about their services, assessing the evolution of IPAs over more than a decade, and recommending new frameworks for these agencies to improve their development impact.

Bringing together different data sources and country experiences, the chapter addresses the role that IPAs can play in fostering FDI inflows and development impact, examines the challenges they face, and presents recommendations to improve their effectiveness. To do so, the sections are organized as follows: "Do IPAs Foster Development Impact?" draws on a literature review to discuss the potential contribution that IPAs can make to economic development and to identify agency characteristics that contribute best to achieving this impact. "Are IPAs Delivering Good Value to Investors? What Challenges Do They Face?" analyzes results from the 2019 Global Investment Competitiveness (GIC) Survey of multinational enterprises (MNEs) to discuss the investment landscape and what investors value from IPAs. The section then compares IPA characteristic surveys over time—from 2005 to 2017/18—to assess the extent to which IPAs have evolved in line with FDI trends and investor needs. "What Can Governments Do to Improve the Development Impact of Their IPAs?" consolidates key findings, insights from World Bank Group operational experience, and examples of country experiences to provide a framework and policy guidelines for governments to improve the impact of their IPAs, focusing on three core areas: strategic alignment and focus, coherent institutional framework, and strong delivery of investor services. "Conclusions and Future Research" summarizes high-level policies governments may consider to support their IPAs and increase their impact, and suggests areas for further research.

BOX 5.1

The Investment Life Cycle

The investment life cycle refers primarily to the investor's journey from project planning to site exploration and selection; investment entry and establishment; operation; expansion, diversification, and linkages; and finally to transition or exit. To successfully attract foreign direct investment (FDI) and foster its growth, the World Bank Group proposes that a host location and its investment promotion agency (IPA) mirror the cycle with a coherent investment policy and promotion offering that can be summarized across four key stages: attraction; entry and establishment; retention and expansion; and linkages and spillovers (figure B5.1.1).

FIGURE B5.1.1 The Investment Life Cycle from Investor and Host Country Perspectives

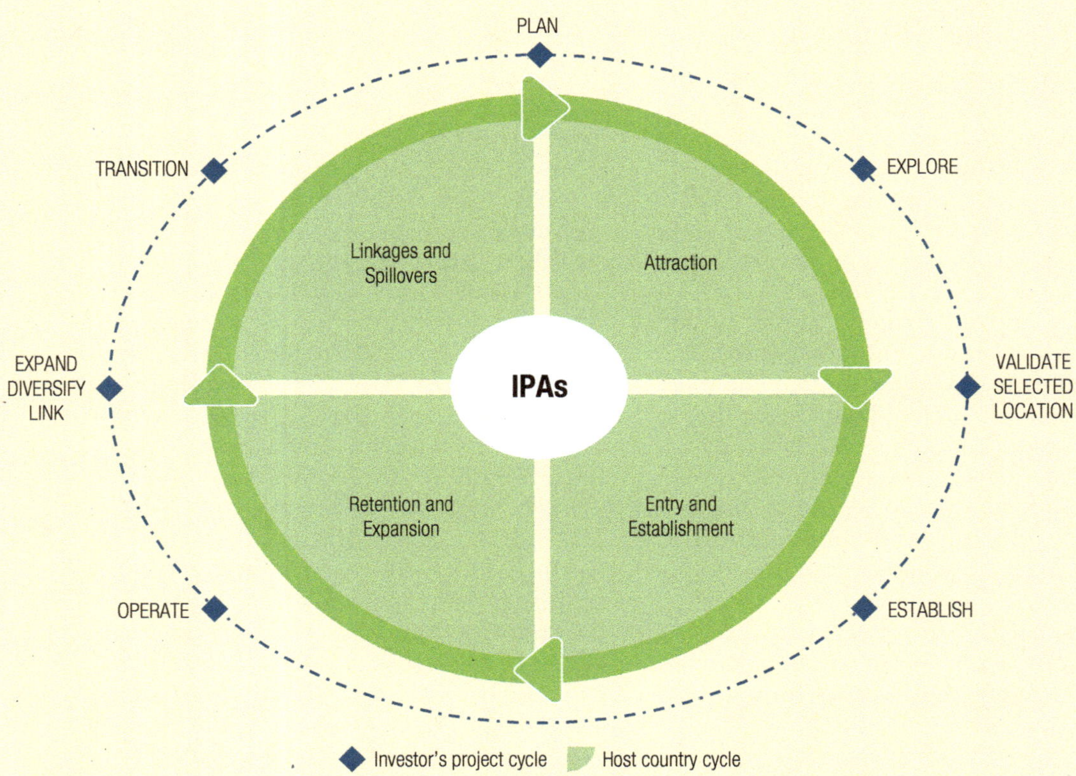

Source: World Bank.
Note: IPAs = investment promotion agencies.

Do IPAs Foster Development Impact?

Economists, researchers, economic development specialists, and policy makers started taking a stronger interest in the field of investment promotion around 20 years ago, when the World Bank Group's Foreign Investment Advisory Service (FIAS) published "Marketing a Country: Promotion as a Tool for Attracting Foreign Investment" (Wells and Wint 2000).[3] IPAs have proliferated since then (Harding and Javorcik 2011). Between 2002 and 2018, the number of national and subnational IPAs registered in the World Association of Investment Promotion Agencies (WAIPA) grew from 112 to 170.[4]

The 2000 FIAS publication and other empirical evidence have shown that IPAs can help generate larger FDI inflows, attract quality FDI, deepen connections to GVCs, and transform economies.[5] Several studies indicate that IPAs increase FDI inflows to their home economies (Cho 2003; Crescenzi, Di Cataldo, and Giua 2019a; Morisset and Andrews-Johnson 2004; Pietersen and Bezuidenhout 2015).[6] Some estimate the magnitude of this FDI increase to be 29.7–45.3 percent (Morisset and Andrews-Johnson 2004; Wells and Wint 2000). Another study finds 155 percent higher FDI inflows and 68 percent greater employment in targeted sectors versus nontargeted sectors (Harding and Javorcik 2011). It also reveals a preliminary cost-benefit analysis: US$1 spent on investment promotion yields US$189 in FDI inflows and a relatively modest US$78 spent on investment promotion creates one additional job in the promoted sectors.

The contribution of IPAs is more pronounced in developing countries, where (a) investors may know less about the location and struggle to obtain good data (because of information asymmetries); (b) regulatory environments are more challenging (as reflected by poor ratings based on the World Bank Group's *Doing Business* indicators); and (c) cultural distance from the United States is greater (Harding and Javorcik 2011, 2012).[7]

IPAs can also bolster the quality of FDI that comes into their economies (Moran et al. 2018), including knowledge-intensive FDI (Crescenzi, Di Cataldo, and Giua 2019b; Monge-González and Tacsir 2014). For example, research points to the essential role of the Costa Rican Investment Promotion Agency (CINDE) in attracting Intel in 1996 and this firm's overwhelmingly positive impact on the country's economic development (MIGA 2006a; Nelson 1999, 2000, 2005, 2009; Spar 1998).[8] The attraction of Intel generated a strong signaling effect that helped boost FDI inflows, diversify exports from mostly fruit commodities to advanced manufacturing, encourage deeper integration into GVCs, and upgrade to higher-value activities.

IPAs can also foster economic transformation (Freund and Moran 2017) and help link economies to GVCs through FDI (World Bank 2020). Developing country examples include Costa Rica, Malaysia, and Morocco, where policies supporting macroeconomic stability, skills development, and strong IPAs contributed to attracting a few large, efficiency-seeking MNEs,[9] which in turn boosted the countries' revealed comparative advantage (Freund and Moran 2017) and their integration into GVCs.

Strategic Focus Matters

IPAs are more likely to succeed when they focus strategically on promoting specific sectors or business activities (Crescenzi, Di Cataldo, and Giua 2019a; ECORYS 2013; Loewendahl 2001; Miškinis and Byrka 2014). (See box 5.2.) One study focusing on OECD countries finds that IPAs targeting industries increased FDI inflows into those targeted industries by 41 percent (Charlton and Davis 2007). Good examples of countries engaging in targeted promotion are Brazil, Chile, and Costa Rica, which developed well-targeted, responsive, and sustained strategies that attracted nontraditional FDI (Nelson 2005). All IPAs that belong to member countries of the Organization for Economic Co-operation and Development (OECD), with the exception of France, prioritize sectors (OECD 2018).

Mandate clustering—adding or merging other policy or economic development functions to the IPA—is a controversial topic in the investment promotion literature. Some suggest that IPAs focus exclusively on investment promotion, while others recommend that economic development agencies pursue multiple mandates, including investment promotion. For example, merging investment and trade promotion may hinder promotion results if done only as a budget-cutting measure. Some countries have achieved synergies by merging mandates under a GVC-focused strategy. Other areas that could be merged are administration, research, image building, and foreign offices (UNCTAD 2013). Recent research, however, finds a negative association between FDI results and combining mandates of investment promotion with trade or with outward investment (Lim 2018). Adding regulatory and other responsibilities to an IPA can prevent the agency from focusing on the already demanding role of catering to investors, as shown in figure 5.1 (Whyte, Ortega, and Griffin 2011).

IPAs with Private Sector-Like Institutional Characteristics are More Successful

Most national IPAs are purely public bodies (around 80 percent, according to the 2017 World Bank Group Global IPA Survey).[10] While this may help with country branding and advocacy, public bodies may need to operate under civil service rules. Traditional civil service recruitment and pay policies typically hamper an IPA's potential to recruit qualified, specialized staff with the required private sector background, international exposure, language skills, and marketing and services skills (Nelson 2009). Without the right staff, IPAs underperform because of the highly competitive nature of attracting FDI—which differs significantly from the role of typical government agencies.

Certain institutional characteristics seem to be linked to better IPA performance, especially in the developing world:

- *Strong support from the topmost levels of government,* sometimes linked to a high institutional status, hierarchy, or attachment to upper ministry levels (Lim 2018; Morisset and Andrews-Johnson 2004; Volpe Martincus and Sztajerowska 2019)
- *Autonomy and operational independence* (ECORYS 2013; Lim 2018; Loewendahl 2001; Nelson 2009; UNCTAD 1997; Wells and Wint 2000), which allow IPAs to receive consistent support even during periods of political transition, attain better understanding of investor needs, and work more effectively alongside private sector actors (Bauerle Danzman and Gertz, forthcoming)[11]
- *Sufficient and sustained financial resources* over periods of three years or longer, given the long cycle of investment promotion (Morisset and Andrews-Johnson 2004; Volpe Martincus and Sztajerowska 2019)

FIGURE 5.1 The Best IPAs Tend to Be Dedicated Promoters

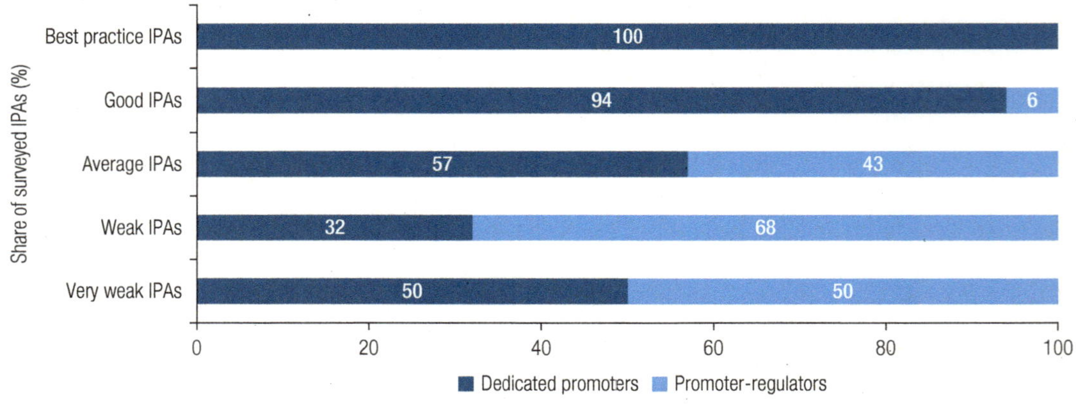

Source: Whyte, Ortega, and Griffin 2011.
Note: The level of investment promotion agency (IPA) performance was proxied by the score in the World Bank Group's "Global Investment Promotion Benchmarking 2009" report. A parallel internal World Bank Group survey of IPAs, deployed in 2009, provided the information as to whether an IPA was a dedicated promoter or promoter-regulator.

- *Management and staff with private sector experience* to develop investor-minded, service-oriented, and consultancy-like organizations (ECORYS 2013; Nelson 2009; UNCTAD 1997; Wells and Wint 2000) with a private sector culture (Ortega and Griffin 2009) and a transnational learning capacity that better understands the private sector and anticipates investor needs (Nelson 2009)[12]
- *Staff with international exposure and an egalitarian and democratic organizational culture* to foster transnational learning capacity (Nelson 2009)
- *Private sector board representatives* (ECORYS 2013; Miškinis and Byrka 2014)
- *Strong institutional collaboration* (Miškinis and Byrka 2014)
- *Longer IPA experience, more staff, and greater overseas presence* (Anderson and Sutherland 2015; Lim 2018; Volpe Martincus and Sztajerowska 2019)
- *Use of digitalization and emerging technologies* to reach target investors more efficiently (DCI 2017; WAIPA 2019).

Quality Services Are Linked to FDI Performance

The quality of IPA information delivery is linked to FDI performance. As shown in figure 5.2, an IPA's score in the World Bank Group's *Global Investment Promotion Best Practices (GIPB) 2012* report on information services (such as website information and inquiry handling) is positively correlated with FDI inflows, and a one-unit increase in the GIPB score is shown to be associated with a 1.5 percent increase in FDI inflows (Harding and Javorcik 2012).

IPA activities have been traditionally clustered under promotion, marketing, or targeting; facilitation; servicing; one-stop-shop (OSS); and aftercare programs (FIAS 2011; Loewendahl 2001; MIGA 2001; Ortega and Griffin 2009; UNCTAD 2007). However, many IPAs lack a service orientation or investor service continuity throughout the investment life cycle, given that most IPAs are staffed by government officials who tend to focus more on either carrying out investment events or providing a regulatory service, sometimes in an OSS. IPAs need staff with private sector experience, service skills, and deep business knowledge (including understanding of investor needs, motivations, challenges, and concerns but also sector terminology and trends) as well as internal systems such as customer relationship management (CRM) systems to improve service and FDI performance (Ortega and Griffin 2009).

For a long time, IPAs have been considered intermediaries between investors and policy makers (Crescenzi 2018), possessing firsthand investor feedback that can be extremely useful to influence policy making. While 76 percent of IPAs include policy advocacy as part of their mandates, 35 percent recognize that they fail to engage in that activity (WAIPA 2019). Moreover, according to the World Bank's 2017 GIC Survey,[13] IPA services were most appreciated by investors during the establishment, retention, and expansion stages, including hands-on assistance with issues during registration, setting up the business, and operation as well as advocacy to improve the business environment (World Bank 2018).

Are IPAs Delivering Good Value to Investors? What Challenges Do They Face?

Investors Value IPA Services across the Investment Life Cycle

Insight on which investment promotion activities matter most, and to whom, can be drawn from a review of investor responses from the 2019 GIC Survey.[14] The results reveal that MNEs generally find IPA services valuable. More than 60 percent of surveyed investors consider at least one IPA service to be "critically important" to their operations, and nearly 90 percent consider at least one service to be "important" or "critically important."

When looking more closely at the types of services valued, foreign investors

FIGURE 5.2 Better-Quality IPA Services Attract More FDI Inflows

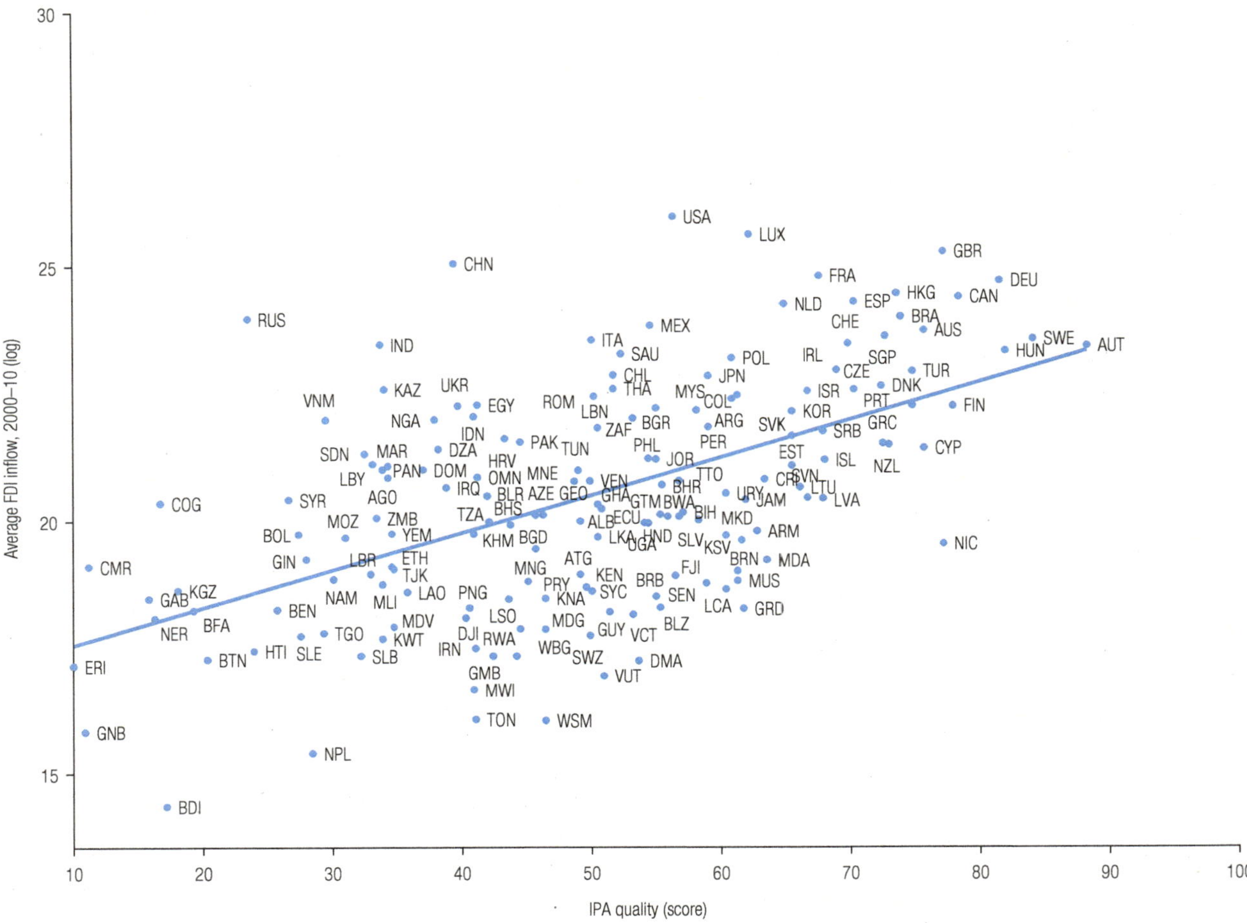

Source: Harding and Javorcik 2012.
Note: The dependent variable is the average FDI inflow received by each country during the 2000–10 period as reported in the IMF's *International Financial Statistics* and expressed in the log form. Investment promotion agency (IPA) service quality is measured based on ratings on a scale from 0 to 100 from "Global Investment Promotion Best Practices 2012" (World Bank 2012) which measured the quality of each IPA's inquiry handling and website. Country and economy labels are International Organization for Standardization (ISO) codes. FDI = foreign direct investment.

indicate that IPA services offered across the investment life cycle—not just during the investment attraction and establishment stages—are important to their business decisions (figure 5.3). About two-thirds or more of surveyed investors consider each IPA service (including postinvestment services such as assistance with operational issues) to be "important" or "critically important." The results also highlight the importance of IPAs' role in advocacy: 35 percent of the surveyed investors consider IPAs' efforts to improve countries' business environments to be "critically important," the highest percent of such responses among IPA services.

Certain groups of investors value IPA services more than others (figure 5.4). IPA services are considered more important to investors from developing countries. For example, about 33 percent of investors from developing countries report that preinvestment assistance (such as site visits and briefings) is "critically important," compared with 24 percent of investors from developed countries. Relative to investors from developed countries, investors from low- and middle-income countries may lack the financial

FIGURE 5.3 IPA Services across the Investment Life Cycle Are Important to Investors

Question: How important are the following services offered by investment promotion agencies to your company in this country?

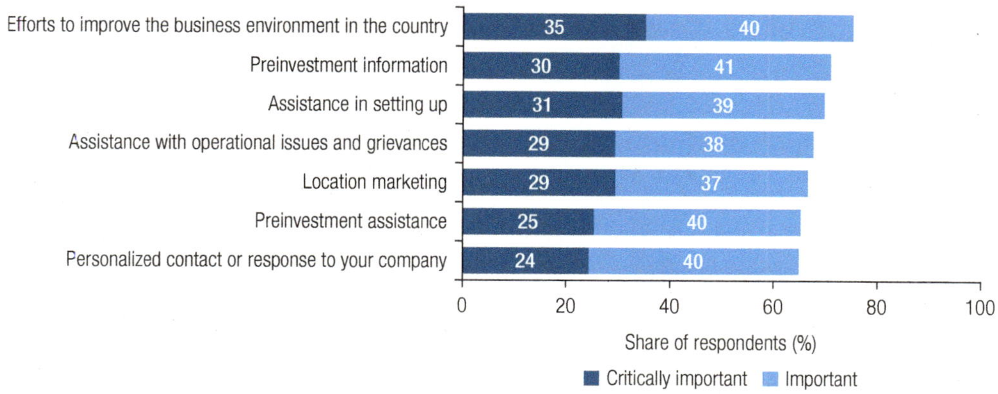

Source: Computation based on the 2019 GIC Survey.
Note: Affiliates of multinational enterprises were surveyed in 10 middle-income countries: Brazil, China, India, Indonesia, Malaysia, Mexico, Nigeria, Thailand, Turkey, and Vietnam. IPA = investment promotion agency.

FIGURE 5.4 Investors from Developing Countries Value IPA Services More than Those from High-Income Countries

Question: How important are the following services offered by investment promotion agencies (IPAs) to your company in this country?

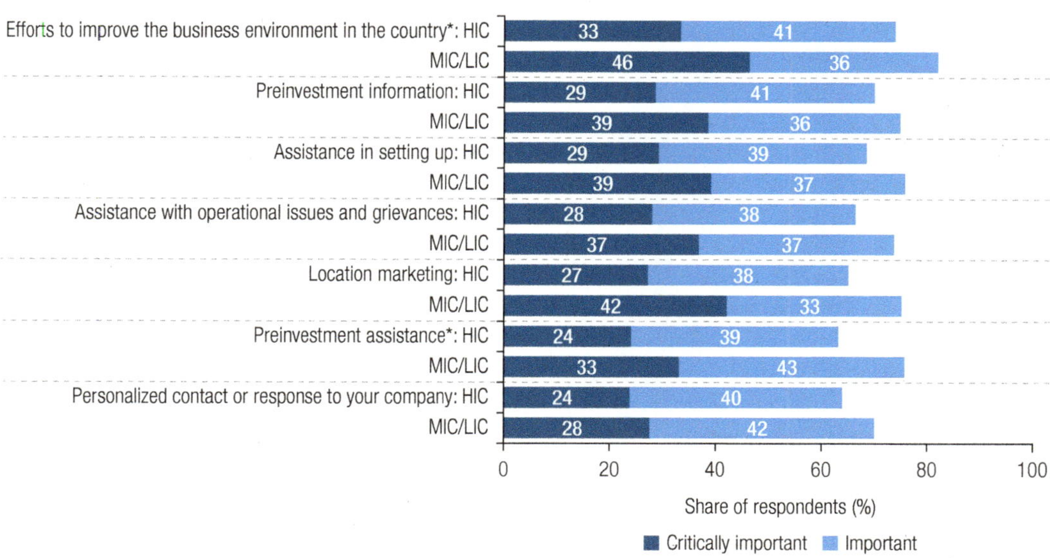

Source: Computation based on the 2019 GIC Survey.
Note: Affiliates of multinational enterprises were surveyed in 10 middle-income countries: Brazil, China, India, Indonesia, Malaysia, Mexico, Nigeria, Thailand, Turkey, and Vietnam. All country income categories use World Bank-defined classifications; "developing" countries refers collectively to all low- and middle-income countries. HIC = high-income country; LIC = low-income country; MIC = middle-income country.
Statistical significance denoted by asterisk: $^*p < .10$ in an ordered logistic regression incorporating controls for sector, a dummy variable for exports comprising over 50 percent of revenues, sector-export interactions, import share of inputs, sector-import interactions, source country income group, a dummy for employment over 250 employees, a dummy for investment stock over US$10 million, number of years in country, percentage foreign ownership, and country fixed effects.

capacity or connections to hire external consultants to help scope and select potential investment location sites. They are also less likely to have access to binational chambers of commerce in host countries. Thus, they are more likely to rely on IPAs for preinvestment assistance.

In addition, IPA services that focus on early stages of the investment life cycle are more important to new investors with less in-country experience. Of investors with 0–10 years of experience in surveyed middle-income countries, 27 percent consider preinvestment assistance such as site visits and briefings to be "critically important," versus 23 percent of investors with more than 30 years of experience in a market. Similarly, 35 percent of investors with less than 10 years of experience consider business setup assistance (such as help with entry permits) to be "critically important," compared with 30 percent of investors with more than 30 years of experience. In contrast, services like assistance with grievances and operational issues are valued by newer and older investors alike.

IPAs May Not Be Evolving as Dynamically as Needed

Despite important changes in the FDI landscape, IPAs have evolved surprisingly little over the past 12–13 years. Comparing IPA characteristics surveys from 2005 to 2017/18 (see annex 5B for summary of data sources and methodology), a few shifts are observed, but many IPA features remain the same (see annex 5B, table 5B.1). This suggests that IPAs may not be as dynamic or responsive as needed, especially in the context of a more challenging FDI climate and broader economic shifts such as a heavier reliance on automation, the growth in GVCs, and the rise of the services sector. Such limitations are particularly concerning in light of the serious and unprecedented challenges posed by the novel 2019 coronavirus disease (COVID-19) pandemic; IPAs need to be able to adapt and provide the necessary support to investors and other government agencies during crises.

IPAs are not advancing on several practices associated with better performance:

- Only 55 percent of IPAs in 2017/18 (compared with 53 percent in 2004) have an investor tracking system
- Only 64 percent of IPAs are targeting specific countries (compared with 61 percent in 2004)
- Few are reporting to higher levels of government (12 percent in 2005 versus 16 percent in 2017/18)
- Despite significant growth in the number of overall staff, the growth of staff engaged in investment promotion has not increased as notably (suggesting that staff are engaging in other mandates).

At the same time, IPAs are expanding, signaling their increasing prominence as public agencies. IPAs' FDI and investment promotion budgets have grown since 2005. In 2005, more than 50 percent of agencies had budgets up to US$500,000, whereas in 2018, most of them had budgets up to US$1 million.[15] Alongside the growth in budgets, the average number of agency staff increased from 208 in 2005 to 337 in 2017/18. The average number of offices abroad also increased from 11 to 18. Simultaneously, the role of subnational IPAs has also been growing, with larger budgets and expanded mandates.

Encouragingly, national IPAs are engaging in more proactive, research-based sector targeting (figure 5.5). When asked whether the agency engages in proactive investor targeting, all IPAs in 2017/18 responded affirmatively, compared with 77 percent in 2005. Similarly, all IPAs in 2017/18 reported undertaking sectoral or market research, compared with 74 percent in 2005. Nearly all IPAs (93 percent) reported targeting specific sectors in 2017/18, whereas only 77 percent did so in 2005.

However, IPAs are still targeting more-traditional economic sectors, mostly in the primary sector (raw materials) without reflecting the global FDI emergence in the tertiary sector (services). Comparing the global percentage growth in 2009–18 FDI projects to percentage point increases in sector

FIGURE 5.5 IPAs Are Becoming More Proactive and Focusing More on Sector Targeting

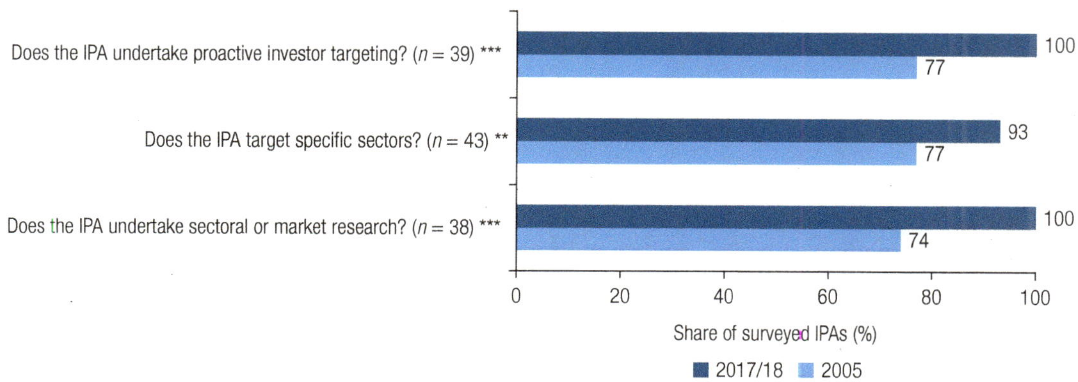

Sources: 2005 World Bank Group IPA Census and 2017 World Bank Group Global IPA Survey; 2017 and 2018 World Association of Investment Promotion Agencies (WAIPA) annual surveys; OECD 2018.
Note: For details about the data sources and methodology, see annex 5B. IPA = investment promotion agency; n = sample size (number of IPAs). Because the data are sourced from samples, the statistical significance of the increase over time is presented: *$p < .10$, **$p < .05$, ***$p < .01$

targeting by IPAs,[16] a misalignment appears between the sectors that IPAs are prioritizing and the global trends in the FDI landscape (figure 5.6).

This trend suggests that IPAs may not be engaging in an evidence-based approach to their proactive promotion efforts—focusing on historical priorities rather than targeting those segments with higher traction—or very likely, they could be under pressure from their governments and local interest groups to promote the primary sector regardless. The growth in IPA sector targeting in the primary sector from 2005 to 2017/18 also suggests a continued prioritization of natural-resource-seeking FDI, which means that IPAs may be missing opportunities to support their home countries in leveraging efficiency-seeking FDI for development impact, especially given its potential role in GVC integration and economic upgrading.

Nor have IPAs evolved much in their targeting of source countries for FDI despite the global shift toward increased investment flows from developing countries to other developing countries. Although IPAs should be consistent in their targeting efforts, they also need to adapt and revisit their strategies every year.

Looking at selected performance indicators over time—drawing on the World Bank Group's Global Investment Promotion Best Practice (GIPB) reports from 2006 to 2012—IPAs have responded poorly to inquiries, a basic information service to investors.[17] Service delivery ratings for inquiry handling were quite low in 2006, did not improve in 2009, and surprisingly declined in 2012, the year of the last GIPB report (figure 5.7). Another basic service IPAs need to provide is information available through their websites. Between 2009 and 2012, the average website score remained relatively low and stagnant, only reaching 61 percent in 2012.

In addition, as of 2012, only 3 percent of all national IPAs provided good-practice inquiry handling.[18] Of 181 IPAs included in the GIPB report, 165 had a website, but only 102 provided an email address, and only 53 replied to investor inquiries in a reasonable, business-like time frame. Only 24 provided an adequate response, and only 6 followed up afterward to help convert interest to investment.

Common Challenges Prevent IPAs from Performing Better

Uneven Investor Service Coverage

As part of their goal to harness more and better investment for their locations, IPAs

FIGURE 5.6 IPA Sector Targeting Maintains a Traditional Focus on the Primary Sector, Indicating a Misalignment with Evolving Global FDI Trends

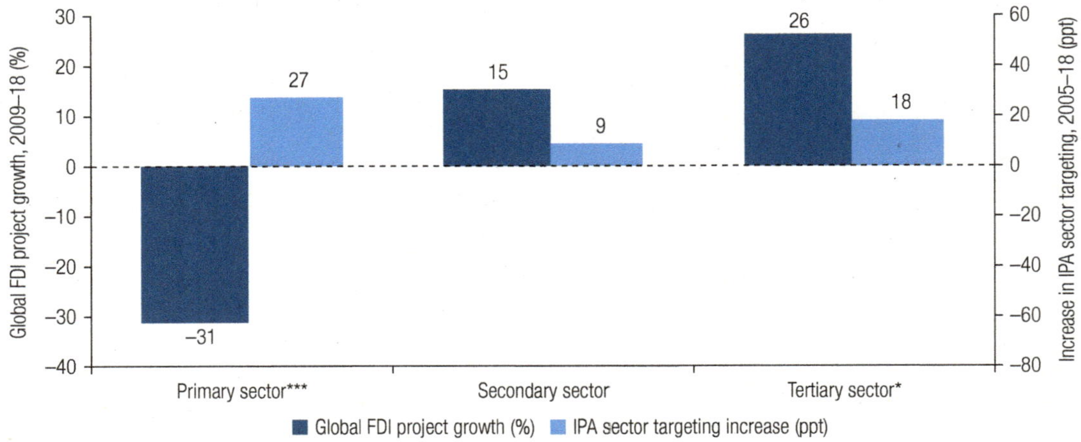

Sources: FDI project data from fDi Markets, a *Financial Times* dataset (https://www.fdimarkets.com/); sector targeting data from the 2005 World Bank Group IPA Census and a combination of 2017/18 IPA surveys from the World Bank Group, World Association of Investment Promotion Agencies (WAIPA), and Organisation for Economic Co-operation and Development (OECD). (For more informat on, see annex 5B).

Note: Because of open responses to sector targeting in later investment promotion agency (IPA) surveys, the sector groups have been defined by the authors to allow concordance between fDi Markets data (comparing total global projects by sector over time) and the IPA surveys. The comparison date range uses the longest reliable information available in each of the data sources, so foreign direct investment (FDI) projects start in 2009 and sector targeting in 2005. For IPA sector targeting, the sample size of national IPAs varies by sector depending on available comparison data over time (51 IPAs for the primary sector; 45 for the secondary sector; and 44 for the tertiary sector). The number of FDI projects is a global figure. "Primary sector" refers to raw materials, "secondary sector" to manufacturing, and "tertiary sector" to services. ppt = percentage point(s).

Significance levels: Given that the IPA surveys are samples, changes in targeting are presented with statistical significance (*$p < .10$, **$p < .05$, and ***$p < .01$) and represent percentage point changes in the fraction of IPAs targeting that specific sector. (The authors believe this is more informative than a percentage change, given that a 1–2 percent change would otherwise represent a 100 percent increase in targeting.)

FIGURE 5.7 IPA Inquiry Handling Deteriorated in 2012 from an Already Poor Level in 2006

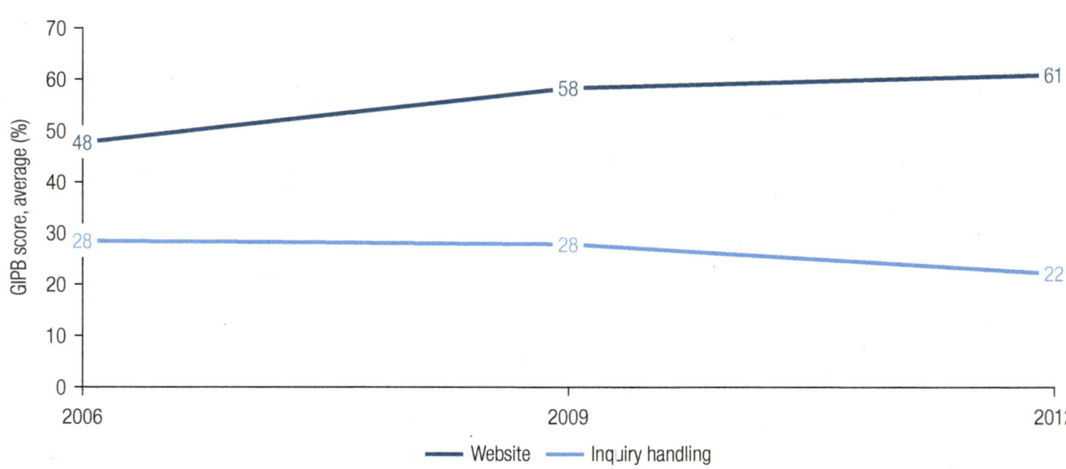

Sources: World Bank, using data from MIGA 2006b and the Global Investment Promotion Best Practices/Benchmark (GIPB) studies (World Bank 2009, 2012).
Note: Average scores for website and inquiry handling were compiled by using the three rounds of the World Bank Group's GIPB reports. Highest possible score = 100 percent. IPA = investment promotion agency.

are supposed to provide quality services to investors throughout the investment life cycle (box 5.1.). However, the 2017 World Bank Group Global IPA Survey finds that most IPAs are providing services predominantly at the attraction stage, with decreasing coverage starting at investment entry and establishment, followed by the retention and expansion stage. Services to foster linkages between MNEs and domestic firms are rarely covered by IPAs (table 5.1).

This distribution of effort reflects the focus of IPAs on the attraction stage but leaves important gaps in terms of investor needs. The World Bank Group is piloting detailed investor service satisfaction surveys in client countries. Preliminary findings show investors attach a high relevance to investment assistance, advocacy, and information services provided by IPAs, but at the same time, investors largely do not give good satisfaction ratings in those three service categories. Poorly serviced investors may decide to discontinue investing or divest. In contrast, well-serviced investors may decide to reinvest, either to expand the current activity or to diversify into new activities.

Inadequate Sector Prioritization and Focus

Based on the 2017 World Bank Group Global IPA Survey, the vast majority of IPAs (84 percent) list five or more "priority" sectors for investment promotion; 44 percent have more than eight (figure 5.8).[19] Moreover, IPAs show varying levels of specificity when designating their priority sectors—with some identifying broad economic categories (for example, manufacturing) and others, mostly in more advanced economies, selecting specific segments. (See box 5.2 on the need for more precise targeting.) World Bank Group experience in developing countries suggests that IPAs working with more than five priority sectors or segments may be diluting their scarce resources, making it more difficult to provide high-quality services demanded by investors, thus achieving weaker results.

Wide Range of Mandates

Many IPAs are taking on too many mandates that cover a wide range of functions, requiring very different skill sets (figure 5.9). The 2017 World Bank Group Global IPA Survey finds that the average number of mandates is 7.8 globally, with developing-country IPAs pursuing more (8.1, on average) than developed-country IPAs (7.0, on average). Developing countries are more likely to be mandated to support domestic direct investment (DDI), negotiate investment agreements, issue licenses, promote exports, negotiate public concessions, and administer public-private partnerships (PPPs), in addition to providing core investment promotion functions.

Pairing data from the 2017 World Bank Group Global IPA Survey with FDI figures reveals a strong negative association between

TABLE 5.1 IPAs Self-Report Providing Services Mostly at the Attraction Stage, with Service Delivery Rapidly Declining in Later Stages of the Investment Life Cycle

Share of respondents (percent)

Service type	*Attraction*	*Entry and establishment*	*Retention and expansion*	*Linkages and spillovers*
Marketing	92	52	39	20
Information	94	61	49	23
Assistance	78	78	63	29
Advocacy	93	53	36	22

Source: Adaptation of Heilbron and Aranda-Larrey 2020.

Note: The figures presented in this table are computations based on the 2017 World Bank Group Global IPA survey. The survey received responses from 83 national IPAs globally. (For more information, see annex 5B.) Stages are drawn from the World Bank Group's investment policy and promotion life cycle (attraction, entry and establishment, retention and expansion, and linkages and spillovers). IPAs were asked which specific services they provided to investors. Their responses were grouped across the four investment life cycle stages and four service categories. IPAs = investment promotion agencies.

FIGURE 5.8 Eighty-Four Percent of IPAs Have Five or More "Priority" Sectors

Share of IPAs claiming to have the indicated number of strategic sectors (percent)

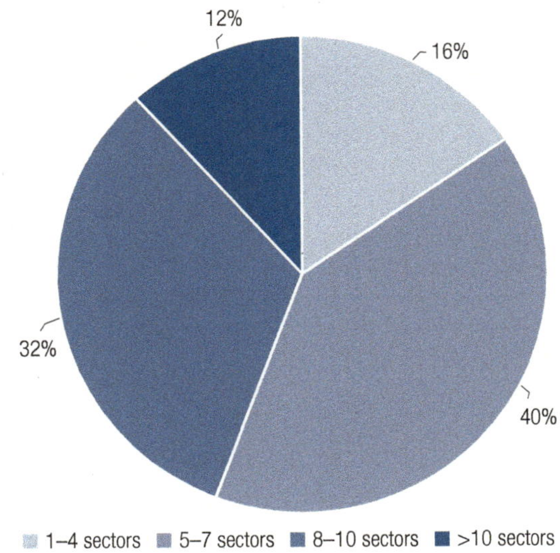

Source: World Bank Group 2017 Global IPA Survey.
Note: The survey received responses from 83 national IPAs globally. (For more information, see annex 5B.) IPAs = investment promotion agencies.

BOX 5.2

From Sectors to Segments: Making IPA Targeting More Precise

Most sophisticated investment promotion agencies (IPAs) have evolved from promotion during the 1980s of broad economic sectors—such as the primary sector (natural resources) or the secondary sector (manufacturing)—to more specific industries within sectors. This evolution mirrored the advent in the 1990s of better, more detailed data such as the Standard Industry Classifications and commercial databases.

In the 2000s, the focus has sharpened toward subindustries and specific business activities within industries or global value chains (GVCs), such as "assembly of electronic components," that could be clustered under an "advanced manufacturing" sector.

For example, the Costa Rican Investment Promotion Agency (CINDE) has been promoting segments such as the assembly and sterilization of therapeutic devices. IDA Ireland focuses its promotion efforts by using a matrix of sectors and activities—for example, research and development (R&D) within the life sciences sector.

Many policy makers and practitioners in the field often still refer generically to sectors, especially in the developing world. Refinements toward more precise identification of target segments follow good-practice techniques for marketing segmentation and can effectively improve IPA impact.

the number of IPA mandates and FDI inflows in developing countries (figure 5.10). This suggests that the more mandates IPAs in developing countries cover, the more challenges they may face in attracting FDI.

Findings from World Bank Group operational experience reflect this trend, especially at the early stages of an IPA's development. For instance, the Rwanda Development Board, which has multiple mandates, has achieved important results but has taken many years to ramp up FDI inflows.[20] The same association for developed-country IPAs does not seem to exhibit a significant statistical correlation, suggesting that the relationship between the

FIGURE 5.9 Most IPAs Cover a Wider Range of Mandates than Just FDI Promotion, Especially in Developing Countries

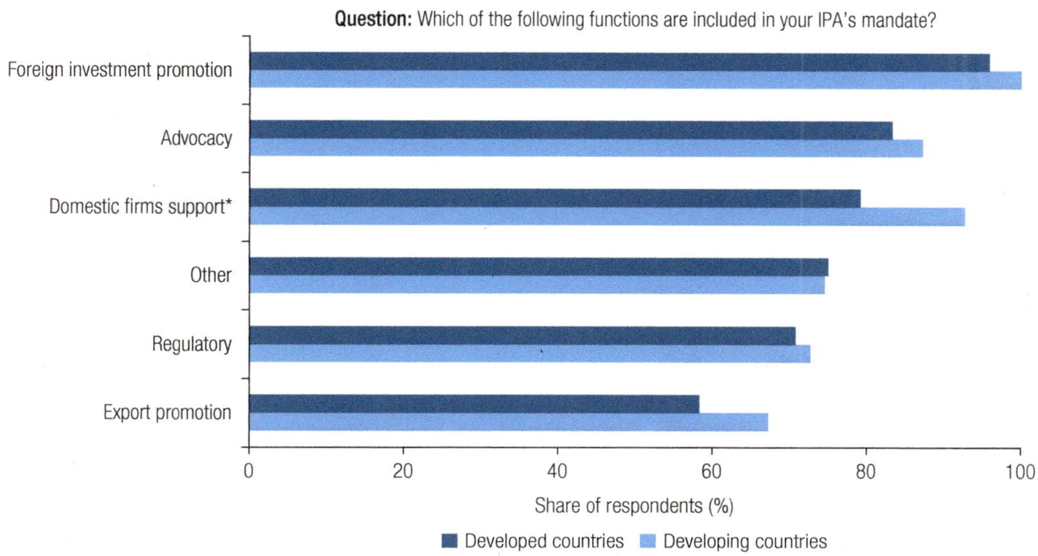

Source: Computation based on 2017 World Bank Group Global IPA Survey.
Note: The survey received responses from 83 national IPAs globally. (For more information, see annex 5B) "Advocacy" includes mandates related to policy advocacy as well as investment climate reform. "Domestic firms support" includes mandates related to domestic investment promotion and development of small and medium enterprises and local suppliers, as well as matchmaking between foreign investors and local suppliers. "Regulatory" includes mandates related to incentive administration and investment project screening or approval, as well as issuing other licenses or permits. "Other" mandates include outward investment support, administration of public-private partnerships, special economic zones, industrial parks, or other state assets, as well as negotiation or administration of investment agreements or public concessions. All country income categories use World Bank-defined classifications; "developing countries" refers collectively to all low- and middle-income countries and "developed countries" to high-income countries. FDI = foreign direct investment; IPAs = investment promotion agencies.
Significance levels: $*p < .10$, $**p < .05$, $***p < .01$.

number of mandates and FDI inflows is not clear. IPAs may be able to adopt more mandates without curtailing FDI as they mature.

Resource Constraints

Despite growing budgets and staffing over time, the 2017 World Bank Group Global IPA Survey reveals that the biggest challenges facing IPAs in developing countries are related to financial resources (52 percent of respondents citing it among their top three challenges), government support and public policies (49 percent), and human resources capacity (44 percent), as shown in figure 5.11.

Developed-country IPAs indicate that they are most concerned with the economic environment (57 percent), followed by processes and bureaucracy (43 percent), and then by financial resources (33 percent). The challenge pertaining to limited resources is more pronounced for IPAs in developing countries, which also carry wider mandates, in turn putting more pressure on scarcer resources.

Inadequate Institutional Coordination

Institutional coordination and partnerships are critical for IPAs to effectively service investors. Based on the 2017 World Bank Group Global IPA Survey, 77 percent of respondent national IPAs maintain close or regular contact with their subnational agencies (box 5.3).

Nearly all IPAs use coordination mechanisms with other entities such as memorandums of understanding (MoUs) or regular inter-agency meetings. Nevertheless, IPAs still face significant obstacles in their institutional coordination efforts: 65 percent cite having unresponsive partner entities, and 64 percent cite the absence of mandate or power to ensure effective cooperation.

FIGURE 5.10 IPAs in Developing Countries That Have More Mandates Also Have Lower FDI Inflows

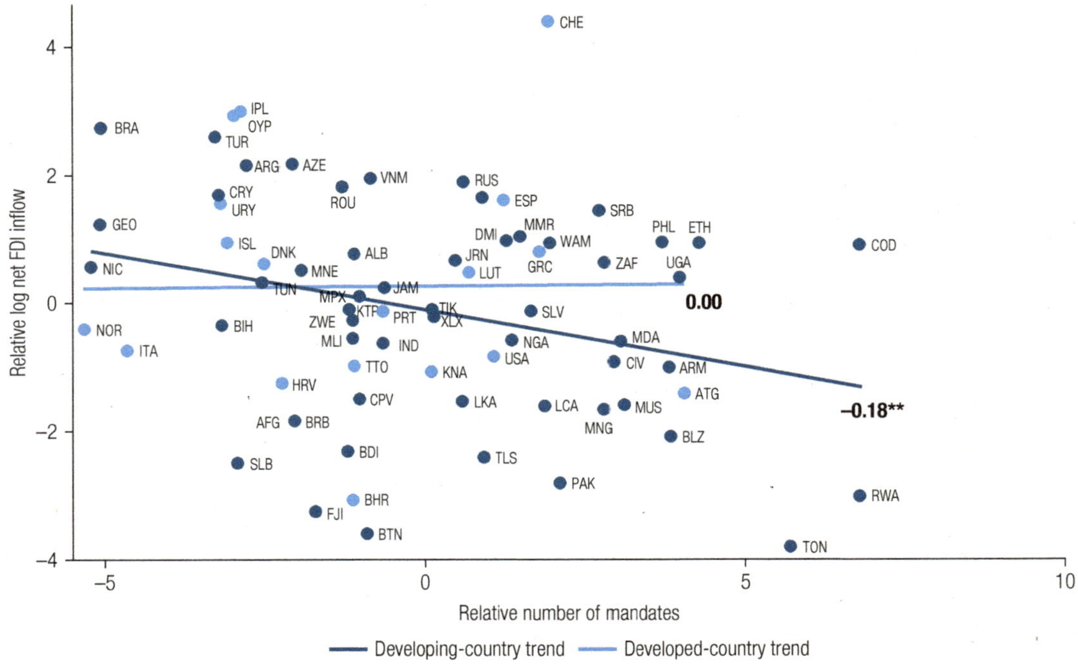

Sources: Computation based on 2017 World Bank Group Global IPA Survey; World Development Indicators database.
Note: The figure is a scatterplot of the regression of log net FDI inflow and number of mandates, controlling for total investment promotion staff, country gross domestic product (GDP), and country population. "Relative number of mandates" refers to the number of mandates after partialing out the effects of the predictor variables used. The survey received responses from 83 national IPAs globally. (For more information, see annex 5B.) All country income categories use World Bank-defined classifications; "developing countries" refers collectively to all low- and middle-income countries and "developed countries" to high-income countries. Country labels are International Organization for Standardization (ISO) codes. FDI = foreign direct investment; IPAs = investment promotion agencies.
Significance levels: $^{*}p < .10$, $^{**}p < .05$, $^{***}p < .01$

What Can Governments Do to Improve the Development Impact of Their IPAs?

The World Bank Group proposes a new framework to help countries establish or strengthen their IPAs' ability to achieve development objectives, especially through increased and higher-quality FDI inflows (Heilbron, and Aranda-Larrey 2020). This framework is based on the literature as well as on the World Bank Group's research and operational experience.[21] It consists of three thematic pillars that IPAs should consider to increase investor satisfaction and confidence as a means toward higher development impact (figure 5.12):

1. Strategic alignment and focus
2. Coherent institutional framework
3. Strong investor service delivery.

The three pillars should have a strong foundational base—that is, a national development plan or vision, coupled with corresponding investment policies or FDI strategy. The pillars are also interrelated: the strategies should inform the institutional framework, not the other way around, and both would determine service delivery strength. The framework is proposed to serve as an assessment tool to help determine how an IPA is performing on each of the specific indicators under each pillar. It is also intended to function as a road map for IPA improvement.

FIGURE 5.11 IPAs in Developing Countries Indicate That Financial and Human Resources, as Well as the Economic Environment, Are Their Top Challenges

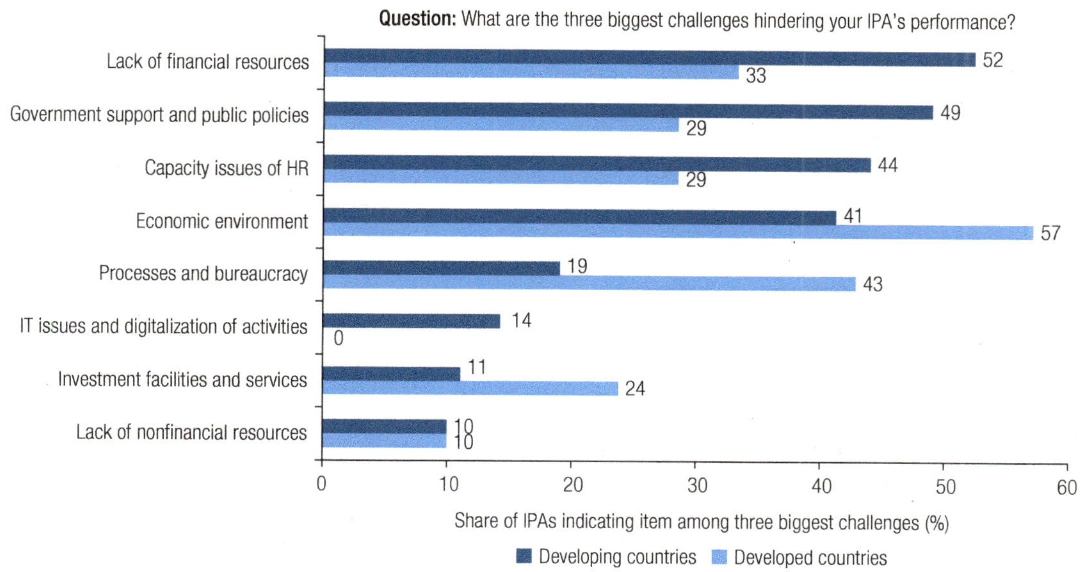

Source: Computation based on 2017 World Bank Group Global IPA Survey.
Note: The survey received responses from 83 national IPAs globally. (For more information, see annex 5B.) All country income categories use World Bank-defined classifications; "developing countries" refers collectively to all low- and middle-income countries and "developed countries" to high-income countries. HR = human resources; IPAs = investment promotion agencies; IT = information technology.

BOX 5.3

The Role of Subnational IPAs in Attracting FDI

The field of investment promotion is increasingly taking on a local focus, with subnational investment promotion agencies (IPAs) growing in prominence alongside their national counterparts. In parallel, investors are becoming increasingly sophisticated in evaluating the benefits of particular cities, provinces, or regions within a country, particularly in larger countries.

Subnational IPAs play unique roles and have distinct characteristics compared with national IPAs. Given their smaller jurisdictions, these agencies often have deeper knowledge of the local business environment and its value proposition to investors, as well as stronger ties to local agencies more heavily involved in the day-to-day operational needs and issues facing investors. Despite these benefits, subnational IPAs may raise particular concerns for policy makers about a "race to the bottom" within a country, whereby subnational locations compete on the basis of incentives for new investments coming into the country or even displace investment from one jurisdiction to another.

Despite the apparent importance of these local entities, the literature on subnational IPAs is almost entirely absent. A recent study by the MASSIVE (Multinationals, Institutions and Innovation in Europe) project, funded by the European Research Council at the London School of Economics, has taken a more thorough look (Crescenzi, Di Cataldo, and Giua 2019a). It leverages a survey on national and subnational IPAs in Europe to systematically evaluate the impact of investment promotion efforts to attract foreign direct investment (FDI) toward areas and sectors that would otherwise not be targeted.

Box continues next page

BOX 5.3

The Role of Subnational IPAs in Attracting FDI *(continued)*

The study finds that subnational IPAs help generate FDI inflows at the local level, in terms of both the probability of receiving FDI and the total amount of FDI received. This impact is more pronounced in less-developed jurisdictions, likely pointing to the role of subnational IPAs in helping investors address information gaps, inadequate transparency, and weaker institutional conditions in these areas. Moreover, subnational IPAs in the study have demonstrated a better capacity for attracting FDI in knowledge-intensive sectors than in other sectors.

Although further analysis and global coverage is needed to address this underresearched topic of subnational investment promotion, these findings suggest that policy makers ought to carefully consider and potentially highlight the unique role that subnational IPAs can play in fostering FDI.

Source: Crescenzi, Di Cataldo, and Giua 2019a.

FIGURE 5.12 Core Elements for Increasing the Development Impact of Investment Promotion Agencies

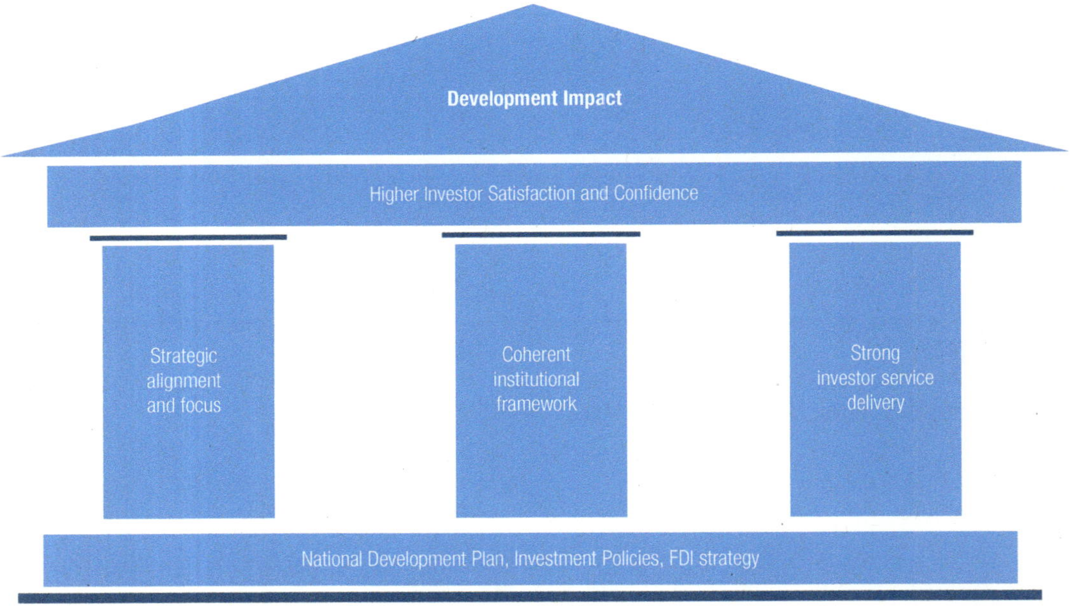

Source: World Bank. See Heilbron and Aranda-Larrey 2020 for more information.
Note: FDI = foreign direct investment.

Pillar 1: Sharpen Strategic Alignment and Focus

Sharpening a country's strategic alignment and focus is a key pillar to strengthen the development impact of IPAs. Doing so requires developing a shared vision while making difficult strategic decisions.

A strategic planning framework should foster stakeholder dialogue among the public and private sectors, organized labor, academia, and civil society on national priorities and the role of each of them in development. However, this process is difficult. Many countries lack key pieces of this strategic framework, leaving stakeholders to deal with investment in an uncoordinated fashion, sometimes duplicating functions or leaving important gaps in the investment ecosystem and investor services.

Adopt a Cascading Strategic Framework for Investment

Several levels of strategic planning should cascade down from an overarching national development plan that would likely aim at achieving the Sustainable Development Goals (SDGs) of the United Nations' 2030 Agenda for Sustainable Development. The planning process should help clarify expectations and roles for each stakeholder based on a broad consultation.[22]

This step provides the opportunity for countries to discuss sentiment concerning FDI, evaluate pros and cons, and decide how to best leverage FDI for development. The resulting national vision, strategy, or development plan should clearly indicate the roles of the private sector and FDI while providing direction for more coherent policies and institutional frameworks for investment. That has been the case in Ireland since the 1960s, in Malaysia since the 1990s, and more recently in Colombia, Myanmar, and Rwanda.[23]

The strategic process should continue cascading down to develop the country's investment and industrial policy as well as its FDI strategy. The latter should identify, through a data-intensive process, the country's most competitive segments to promote, the reforms or measures to help improve the country's competitiveness for desired segments, and the target markets and investors.

These high-level strategies should inform the more specific institutional strategies, such as the IPA corporate plan and investment promotion strategies for individual targeted segments. Scotland's IPA, Scottish Development International (SDI), illustrates this strategic development process well, with the added layer of alignment at the UK level. An IPA's corporate plan (also called an IPA business plan or strategy) is the road map for the IPA to achieve meaningful developmental goals, with clear milestones for each key performance indicator (KPI) along the way. It lays out actions to establish the IPA (if new) or reinforce it (if existing), giving it a stronger strategic focus, institutional capacity, and commensurate resources.

IPAs need to monitor global trends—including changing sources and modalities of FDI, dynamic segment and GVC trends, technological advances, geopolitical tensions, and other global opportunities or threats to inform the strategic development process. Notably, for example, in the context of the COVID-19 pandemic, strong strategy, coupled with business intelligence, can help IPAs identify changes in GVC activities and advocate for needed reforms to support struggling businesses, while proactively promoting new opportunities. This type of data-driven, proactive approach is needed for IPAs to foster their influence to reposition their locations, respond to investor needs, and capture higher levels of FDI.

IPAs should become active providers of feedback on policy making and identification of strategic segments, banking on the valuable insights the IPAs gain from their daily contact with investors and by connecting investors and policy makers. Highly desirable segments that remain unattractive to investors in the short-term require the IPA to advocate for related reforms or improvements in the investment ecosystem. When economic conditions turn unfavorable, including times of global crisis like the COVID-19 pandemic, IPAs should emphasize measures that support business continuity—by bolstering investor services around investor communications, retention, and advocacy.

Define Target Segments, Source Markets, and Investment Types

IPAs need a strong focus on a few segments, markets, and even investment types, which is achieved as part of the strategic planning process and based on strong analytic capacity. Fortunately, GVCs have broken down products and services into business activities. At the same time, data are increasingly available, allowing countries and their respective IPAs to identify more specific "segments" and develop investment promotion strategies for focused business or GVC activities (such as manufacturing, marketing and sales, customer support center, headquarters, and R&D), as discussed in box 5.2. These activities determine motivation and location selection factors (Crescenzi, Pietrobelli, and Rabellotti 2014).

Although countries may foster investment in many segments, IPAs should focus on just a few (three to five) competitive segments for proactive promotion efforts and high-level service offerings. Such a focus does not mean that IPAs would ignore or reject FDI in other segments but that a much higher level of resources would be dedicated to seeking and supporting projects in those identified strategic segments. Evidence suggests that the number of targeted segments an IPA can manage varies with its level of maturity and resources (see figure 5.10). Developing or fragile and conflict-affected contexts may require further focus (Whyte and Griffin 2014).

Identifying dynamic and competitive segments to proactively promote requires an evidence-based approach. The United Kingdom recently launched an approach to prioritize segments on the basis of the value that FDI will have on the economy, as estimated by an econometric model that includes several impact indicators (DIT 2018). Robust research and consultation with investors help IPAs understand trends, investor factors, challenges, and needs as well as how a country's location compares with competing locations for these segments so that the IPA can build compelling value propositions and effectively attract FDI into these segments. CINDE (box 5.4) and IDA Ireland (box 5.5) are examples of IPAs that have successfully operated this way for years.

World Bank Group experience indicates that a top-down imposition of target segments on an IPA by higher authorities often does not yield the expected results, likely because these segments have not been properly validated on competitiveness. As mentioned, IPAs can still provide services reactively to investors.

IPAs should also take into account the SDGs when designing their strategies and considering the type of investment they are seeking to attract. Good alignment with SDGs will result in higher-quality FDI, with investment projects that go beyond economic considerations to integrate social and environmental dimensions. To date, IPAs have mostly focused on the economic development and environmental dimensions (Filippov and Guimon 2012; VCC and WAIPA 2010).

To maximize their impact, IPAs should not only target MNEs (for example, PVH in Ethiopia or Volkswagen in Rwanda) but also consider their global suppliers to more fully develop the respective cluster. IPAs could offer a linkages service by mapping MNE demand and introducing domestic suppliers to MNEs. However, building suppliers' capacity should not be part of an IPA's mandate.

In certain countries, IPAs could consider brownfield forms of investment, beyond attracting and retaining greenfield FDI, their traditional domain (see chapter 2). Governments have various development motives and means to foster the potential of brownfield FDI ventures. IPAs could provide services, for example, of connecting foreign investors to potential mergers and acquisitions (M&A) or joint venture candidates.

Develop a Strong Investment Promotion Mandate

Developing-country IPAs and most disadvantaged regions in developed countries should strengthen their strategic focus on the investment promotion mandate (Crescenzi, Di Cataldo, and Giua 2019a). This clarity and focus of mandate are especially important for young IPAs or those that need to be strengthened. Policy makers need to carefully consider the pros and cons when adding either an investment promotion mandate to other entities or nonpromotion mandates to the IPA, especially in developing countries.

Examples of good-practice IPAs exclusively focused on investment promotion include the Austrian Business Agency (ABA-Invest in Austria); CINDE; Invest in Bogotá (Colombia's subnational IPA);

BOX 5.4

Costa Rica's IPA (CINDE) Follows Several Good Practices, Particularly around Strategic Focus

Although the Costa Rican Investment Promotion Agency (CINDE) is a private sector-led IPA with significant autonomy, it has benefited from high levels of government support and strong partnerships since the late 1990s. These factors helped the IPA land not only technology giant Intel in 1996—which subsequently shaped the country's economic landscape (MIGA 2006a; Nelson 2000, 2005, 2009; Spar 1998)—but also Abbott Laboratories (now Hospira), P&G, and other anchor investors in the country's most dynamic segments (health sciences and information technology [IT]-enabled services).

CINDE has continuously sharpened its strategic focus, evolving from an all-purpose development agency when founded in the mid-1980s to a fully focused IPA attracting and expanding foreign direct investment (FDI) projects by the turn of the century.

It has also refined its sectoral focus from broad light manufacturing in the early 1990s to strategic and specific global value chain (GVC) links by the late 1990s, including the assembly and testing of electronic circuits, assembly and sterilization of therapeutic devices, and legal and financial global shared services.

At the same time, CINDE improved its service offerings beyond the initial stage of attracting investment. It now proactively accompanies strategic investors throughout their investment journeys. Advocating on behalf of investors and proactively connecting investors and government, CINDE has helped catalyze key reforms, unlock strategic investments and increase the country's participation in GVCs tenfold in the past three decades (figure B5.4.1).

FIGURE B5.4.1 Costa Rica's FDI Inflows and GVC Participation Have Increased Tenfold since the 1990s

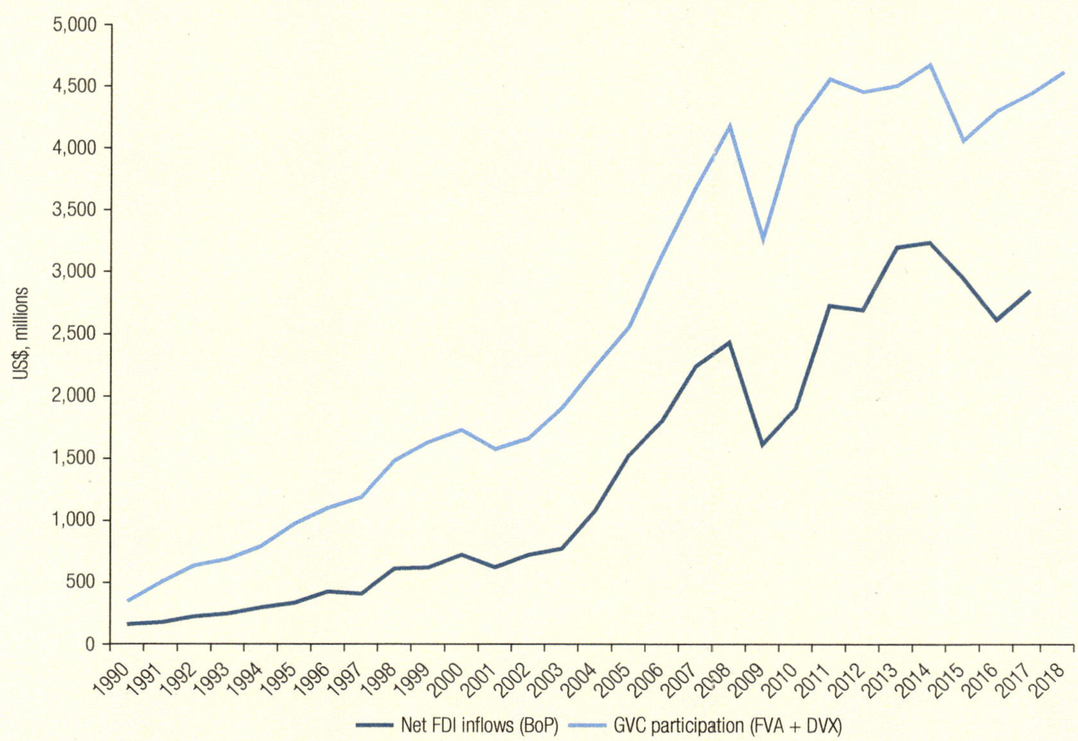

Sources: World Development Indicators Database; United Nations Conference on Trade and Development (UNCTAD)-Eora GVC database (https://worldmrio.com/unctadgvc/).

Note: Global value chain (GVC) participation is measured by adding foreign value added (FVA) and domestic indirect value added (DVX). BoP = balance of payments; FDI = foreign direct investment.

BOX 5.5

Learning from the Success of a 70-Year-Old IPA: IDA Ireland

Founded in 1949 and incorporated as an autonomous state-sponsored body in 1969, Ireland's investment promotion agency (IPA), known as IDA[a] Ireland, has a decades-long track record of consistent achievement. When IDA Ireland was restructured in 1969, Ireland was not regarded as an attractive investment destination (because of economic stagnation, limited natural resources, one of the lowest incomes per capita in Europe, and a total population of just 2.9 million). IDA Ireland managed to change global perceptions and helped transform Ireland into a foreign direct investment (FDI) powerhouse and a US$383 billion economy.[b]

Ireland's cumulative FDI stock of US$909 billion (UNCTAD 2019) is 237 percent of GDP and 2.6 times the European Union (EU) average. IDA Ireland reports that the 1,444 FDI companies it helped attract have generated 229,000 jobs (up to 2018), spent about US$20 billion in the Irish economy (in 2017), and represent 67 percent of the country's total exports.[c] Several key elements contributed to this success.

Clear mandate and sector strategy. With the focused mandate of attracting FDI, IDA Ireland has developed a deliberate strategy to promote industrial development by targeting three sectors and three business activities (resulting in strategic segments) in which Ireland could achieve a competitive advantage. In 2018, IDA Ireland reported having created 124,000 jobs in international and financial services; 64,000 in life sciences; and 22,000 in computers, electronics, and optical equipment. It has managed to build a critical mass of firms in each of these sectors, which has a self-reinforcing clustering effect (IDA Ireland 2018).

Commitment toward improving the investment climate and forging effective partnerships. IDA Ireland's success would not have been possible without a national commitment to free trade from the 1960s onward and a social partnership agreement whereby government, employers, labor, farmers, and nonprofit organizations collaborated closely to reach a consensus on development priorities, moderate wage increases and cut taxes, and share efforts to achieve national goals.

In addition, having identified low labor skills as a main constraint, the government invested significantly on education (amounting to 13.5 percent of public spending in 2016).[d] The Irish government focused education and training on the key technology sectors that the IPA was targeting. An expert group on future skill needs was formed in 1997 to guide these decisions. Today, one-third of college graduates specialize in sciences and engineering, and one-fourth are in business.

The government also created a combination of well-funded state agencies and advisory councils with specialized functions, such as (a) IDA Ireland, which focused on FDI attraction; (b) Forfás, which focused on strategic planning for enterprise, trade, science, technology, and innovation—absorbed by Enterprise Ireland in 2014; (c) Enterprise Ireland, which supports indigenous industry and export development; and (d) Science Foundation Ireland, which fosters innovation.

In addition to their own synergies, these agencies have good working relationships with key regulatory agencies at the national and local levels as well as with private sector organizations. All employ professional and permanent staff who do not change when the government changes.

Strong monitoring and evaluation (M&E) capabilities. Government support for FDI attraction was greatly helped by IDA Ireland's development of a simple cost-benefit model, which demonstrated to the government and taxpayers the economic benefits and the inherent self-funding nature of investment promotion.

The model uses a simple economic table to calculate the costs and benefits over a period of seven years (to allow sufficient time for investment projects to build up to full production capacity) for every individual project supported by the government. IDA Ireland has established a target cost-benefit ratio of four to one—that is, the value of the future benefits over seven years must be at least four times greater than the (shared) costs to the state of running IDA Ireland and the cost of all financial incentives to the specific investment over that period. IDA Ireland publishes the results of its aggregate cost-benefit analyses every year to show that economic benefits exceed costs over time. This model is now a standard tool used by IDA Ireland in its requests to the government for funding.

Adequate institutional and financial autonomy. IDA Ireland has a separate legal mandate that grants it a substantial degree of institutional and financial autonomy and a sufficient and sustained budget, year in and year out.

Box continues next page

BOX 5.5

Learning from the Success of a 70-Year-Old IPA: IDA Ireland *(continued)*

Its board of directors counts on private sector representation, but board members are clearly appointed to represent public interests instead of private ones. Staff are paid at market rates and have both public and private experience. The stability of senior management has avoided frequent changes at the top level—for example, IDA Ireland has had only six chief executive officers (CEOs) since its creation.

IDA Ireland has sector-based staff both in its headquarters and in 20 offices in 13 countries. Its overseas offices are staffed by about 40 professionals. Targets are set annually by sector, by country, by office, by Irish region, and by staff member. Staff are offered merit bonuses tied to their performance against these targets. The strong support received from the government has enabled long-term, strategic, and consistent policies to survive outside political or electoral time frames.

Sources: IDA Ireland 2018; IDA Ireland website: http://www.idaireland.com; interviews with former IDA Ireland staff; UNESCO Institute for Statistics data: http://uis.unesco.org; UNCTAD 2019; World Bank's World Development Indicators database.

a. The agency was founded in 1949 as the Industrial Development Authority.

b. Ireland economic data from the World Bank World Development Indicators Database.

c. FDI impact data from the IDA Ireland website: http://www.idaireland.com.

d. Education spending data from United Nations Educational, Scientific and Cultural Organization (UNESCO) Institute for Statistics 2016 data: http://uis.unesco.org.

InvestHK (Hong Kong SAR, China); Invest India; and Scottish Development International (SDI). Standard components of an investment promotion mandate include the following:

- *Attract FDI inflows* by influencing investor location decisions with marketing, information, and assistance services (such as an outreach program)
- *Support investments from announcement to start-up* with information and assistance services (such as an establishment program)
- *Retain and foster expansion of existing investors* with marketing, information, assistance, and advocacy services (such as full-service aftercare programs)
- *Encourage and facilitate business linkages* between foreign firms and domestic ones as well as other mechanisms for the spillover of skills, technology, know-how, and international market networks (such as a linkages program)
- *Advocate for improvements to the location's competitiveness, general investment climate, and sectoral ecosystems* before the government, private sector, and any relevant stakeholders (such as an advocacy program)
- *Inform the national vision for FDI, and develop and implement an investment promotion strategy,* in collaboration with relevant public and private sector partners in the country.
- *Monitor, research, and gather intelligence* about investment.

There could be a case for placing trade or export promotion and investment promotion under the same agency when there are strategic synergies, as in the case of a country looking to attract and expand investment geared toward exports. Such functions should not merge solely as a budget-cutting measure (Heilbron and Whyte 2019; UNCTAD 2013). Each division must have sufficient resources to deliver on its specific mandates. Cost savings may accrue from combining common back-office functions—administration, finance, IT, human resources, legal—and some international offices (when the market is a target for both functions). However, this is rarely successful when institutions are starting up or have low capacity. Policy makers need to recognize the differences between the two mandates (different goals, company targets, company decision levels, markets, sales cycles, promotion instruments, job requirements, and budgets).

Support for outward FDI (OFDI) is a natural extension of export promotion, as domestic firms move from exporting to establishing a presence in that foreign market. IPAs, especially in developing countries, should not include or add a mandate to promote OFDI because the needs of such domestic firms are quite different from those of foreign investors coming into the home country (Heilbron and Whyte 2019).

IPAs, particularly in the developing world, should also ideally not have mandates covering regulation, investment incentives, small and medium enterprise (SME) development, special economic zones (SEZs), or PPPs. Governments often struggle when delivering support to private sector investors. At times, mostly to cut costs, they combine several functions within the same institution. However, especially in developing countries, this may create issues—such as conflict of interest when the promoter is under the same roof as the regulator or incentives approver or when resources favor domestic investment to the detriment of FDI promotion (Heilbron and Whyte 2019). Table 5.2 summarizes this guidance for IPA mandates in the developing world.

The World Bank Group's operational experience has shown that separation of investment promotion function from other government units—including those dealing with regulatory and incentive approvals, SME development, SEZ supervision, SEZ development, and PPP administration or concessions—produces better results for both the investment and the specialized mandates in developing countries. At the same time, strong intergovernmental cooperation between the IPA and the specialized units is essential to improve effectiveness.

If the IPA is assigned mandates beyond promotion, sequencing the mandates over

TABLE 5.2 Dos and Don'ts of Mandates for IPAs in Developing Countries

Category	*Institutional function*
Investment promotion services	Marketing
	Information
	Assistance
	Advocacy
Other promotion types	Foreign investor and local supplier matchmaking
	Export promotion
	Support for outward investment
	SME development
Administration or regulation	Administration of incentives
	Screening or approval of investment projects
	Issuance of noninvestment licenses or permits
	Administration or negotiation of government concessions (such as in infrastructure or extractive industries)
	Administration of public-private partnerships
	Management of state land or assets

■ Must do ■ Okay to do, but with care[a] ■ Do not do

Source: World Bank.

Note: This table captures general guidelines based on more than 30 years of World Bank Group operational experience in developing countries. Country-specific characteristics may warrant different approaches and considerations. FDI = foreign direct investment; IPA = investment promotion agency; SME = small and medium enterprise.

a. These functions can be included with certain strict organizational prerequisites to avoid impeding investment promotion.

time may produce the best results. Many of the IPAs that have added mandates beyond investment promotion have struggled to adapt effectively to their expanded portfolios without losing promotional effectiveness. Among the few with decades-long success in managing additional mandates is IDA Ireland, which includes incentives and property management. More recently, the Rwanda Development Board has been forging a solid international reputation in this regard (See box 5.6 for more information on the mandates of IDA Ireland and the Rwanda Development Board). These cases appear to have at least the following characteristics in common:

- Their mandate expansions were deliberate and motivated by strategic objectives—as opposed, for example, to cost-saving or political motives.
- Different mandates (promotional and nonpromotional ones like regulatory functions) have been sequestered, allowing promotional staff to operate somewhat autonomously according to their own strategies and resources, and with a private sector mindset.
- Promotional staff have been held accountable for performance against their own impact indicators.
- There are no mandate overlaps with other agencies, especially for investment promotion.

Pillar 2: Build a Coherent Institutional Framework

Building a coherent institutional framework for investment is crucial to FDI effectiveness, even if it takes significant time and effort. This is especially important when setting up an IPA or restructuring the existing one. The right institutional setup varies, depending on the country's political economy, the government's existing institutional framework, available legal institutional formats, the civil service culture, and the institutional collaboration culture (Heilbron and Whyte 2019).

In determining the right institutional framework for investment promotion, policy makers should address the following key elements and consider the recommendations described in more detail below:

- A common vision and strategic alignment
- Corresponding institutional network KPIs
- Clearly identified institutional partners with focused mandates, division of roles, focal points, joint promotion activities, and some shared assets (such as an information library, online portals, and tracking tools)
- Institutional coordination/collaboration guidelines and protocols
- Capacity building in the area of investment promotion.

Provide High-Level Government Support to FDI and the IPA

If the government is serious about leveraging FDI for development, it must build an institutional framework with a strong IPA at its core. This IPA should integrate key institutional characteristics that are associated with stronger performance, starting with the highest level of government support (from the president or prime minister) directly or indirectly championing the needed legal, regulatory, and institutional reforms.

As part of its high-level support, the government should send clear signals that instill confidence in investors and back the IPA with the appropriate legal status and hierarchy within the government for the difficult task of mobilizing stakeholders typically required to bring about significant or transformational investment. Being a unit of a department or ministry may, in most developing countries, undermine the IPA's influence to mobilize stakeholders to reform and obtain investment. The right attachment—but more importantly, the right support from the highest levels of the government—gives the IPA a certain stature and visibility in the country. It also sends strong signals to investors and government alike about the priority the government places on investment and FDI.

BOX 5.6

How Different Institutional Setups Respond to Multiple Mandates: The Cases of Ireland and Rwanda

IDA Ireland

IDA Ireland[a] has undergone several major reforms to its mandate in the 70 years since its creation, as government priorities have shifted and as good practices in investment promotion have emerged. IDA Ireland was established in 1949 as a subministerial unit, during a period of protectionism, to stimulate the development of exporting enterprises. Nine years later, its focus was changed to foreign direct investment (FDI) and export promotion. Recognizing the need for a more private-sector-like approach and greater operational flexibility, the government changed IDA Ireland's legal form in 1969 from a subministerial unit to an autonomous state-sponsored body. Twenty-five years after that, in 1994, enterprise development and export promotion were moved out of IDA Ireland so that it could be dedicated to the promotion and development of high-quality FDI. Two of its prior mandates, seen as assets in landing FDI, were retained: the regulatory function of incentive administration and the management of industrial estates.

In short, IDA Ireland came to its current set of mandates not by addition but by subtraction. Although it does more than other leading IPAs today, its mandates have actually decreased over time—the result of many years of policy experimentation and lessons learned. In its current form, IDA Ireland organizes its promotional work through 11 units, mostly focused on sectors, reporting to the chief executive officer (CEO). Its nonpromotional work is conducted through nine units, mostly functional units, under a single executive director in charge of all noncore functions such as human resources, legal affairs, finance, and corporate strategy and planning as well as incentives and real estate management.

Rwanda Development Board

Rwanda went the other way, by expanding mandates. Since the Rwanda Development Board (RDB) was founded around 2008, it has accumulated functions, building on those of its predecessor body, the Rwanda Investment and Export Promotion Agency (RIEPA). Today, the RDB includes a one-stop shop for investment-related procedures; sector development of two of the government's highest-priority sectors, information and communication technology (ICT) and tourism; and the administration of special economic zones (SEZs), public-private partnerships (PPPs), and special projects with international donors and partners. It reports directly to the president of Rwanda.

Given the RDB's strong track record of economic reform and growth, the decision to add the one-stop shop was seen as a way to extend its influence and good performance to areas that were impeding investment (such as procedures for establishment). This is a common motive for the assignment of one-stop shops to IPAs. At the same time, a shift in organizational culture away from promotion in favor of regulation is also a major reason for IPAs not performing on their promotion mandate. The RDB tries to mitigate this risk by dividing its investment division into (a) a promotion department with 11 sector-focused units, which list proactive outreach to potential investors as their first activity; and (b) its "one-stop center," which has limited its focus to business registration, duty exemptions, work permits, and environmental impact assessments. SEZs, PPPs, and sector development have their own divisions. Close attention and high expectations from the president are also seen as having much to do with the RDB's continued success.

Sources: Interviews with RDB staff and former IDA Ireland staff; RDB website (https://rdb.rw/); IDA Ireland website (http://www.idaireland.com).
a. The agency was founded in 1949 as the Industrial Development Authority.

Ethiopia's recent tenfold growth in FDI stems from a high-level engagement by the former prime minister and his economic adviser in opening the economy to foreign investors and restructuring the institutional framework for investment. This restructuring, guided by the government's Growth and Transformation Plans I and II (covering the five-year periods of 2010/11–2014/15 and 2015/16–2019/20, respectively), included elevating the Ethiopian Investment Commission to report to a newly created Investment Board, chaired by the prime minister.[24]

Turkey offers another good example of a national IPA with a high position in government. The country's Investment Office is situated within the Presidency of the Republic of Turkey and reports directly to the president. In India, Prime Minister Narendra Modi's support of Invest India helped transform the country's IPA from a small, uninfluential 10-person unit to a vibrant operation with more than 100 staff that has contributed to higher levels of FDI and is in the process of upgrading the capacity of Indian subnational IPAs (box 5.7).

Some countries achieve high-level visibility by attaching the IPA to the president's or prime minister's office. However, policy makers need to be aware of the risk that the IPA may get little attention from an already busy president or prime minister and become unstable in a political transition. Accordingly, an empowered autonomous unit reporting to a formal board of directors, investment board, or advisory board chaired by the head of state or by a strong ministry may be a good combination of high stature with a more sustainable approach.

Grant the IPA a Sufficiently High Level of Autonomy

IPAs tend to perform better when they have a high degree of financial and operational autonomy or independence. IPAs should be allowed to operate following an approved strategic plan with minimal political interference; hire staff with private sector experience independently from the civil service (as do CINDE, Invest Bogotá, and Invest India); be accountable and report results to a board of directors; and maintain continuity throughout political cycles.

In addition to top government officials, the IPA board needs to have active and strong private sector representation (ECORYS 2013; Miškinis and Byrka 2014) from key chambers of commerce or business associations, foreign private sectors, and professional advisers. Their expertise helps the IPA better understand investors and deliver relevant services to them. Nonautonomous IPAs should at least have an advisory board with functions and composition similar to a board of directors, even if it does not have legal authority over the IPA's operations.

Ensure the IPA Is Staffed with the Right Expertise

IPAs need a good mix of IPA management and staff with private sector experience. Many IPAs are already incorporating more private sector expertise as both empirical research and operational experience highlight the need for IPAs to develop transnational learning capacity and adopt an investor-minded, service-oriented, and consultancy-like democratic organizational culture (ECORYS 2013; Nelson 2009; Ortega and Griffin 2009). The IPA's CEO, promotion director, and key promotion staff should have private sector experience, international exposure, and fluency in relevant languages, as well as strong interpersonal abilities. The CEO needs to enjoy a high level of credibility with both the private and public sectors. For this to happen, the IPA requires independence from the civil service restrictions for human resources.

Invest India, for example, rapidly ramped up from a weaker promotional unit with little impact to an award-winning IPA that has helped raise FDI inflows to new levels after hiring high-caliber management and staff (90 percent of whom come from the private sector) and adopting an operating model that mirrors consulting firms, with young talented staff providing data-driven support to investors (box 5.7).

Provide Sufficient and Sustained Financial Support to the IPA

To perform effectively, IPAs require reliable funding over a three- to five-year period, given the long-cycle nature of investment promotion. In the 2017 World Bank Group Global IPA Survey, IPAs indicated that their most important challenge concerns financial resources and that financing comes mostly from public funds. Charging fees to investors is not a good practice because investment promotion should be seen as a public good. Fees can send a wrong signal to investors that FDI is not prioritized or encouraged.

BOX 5.7

Invest India: Building a High-Performing IPA from the Ground Up in Record Time

Invest India illustrates how a new investment promotion agency (IPA) can be built up over just a few years by following a few key principles while avoiding many typical mistakes. Invest India was established in 2009 as a joint venture of the Department of Industrial Policy and Promotion (DIPP) of the Ministry of Commerce and Industry, the Federation of Indian Chambers of Commerce and Industry (FICCI), and state governments of India. The agency lay dormant for many years and, even as recently as 2015, had no more than a handful of staff reactively answering investor queries, with little or no traction with potential foreign investors.

Then, in September 2014, Prime Minister Narendra Modi launched "Make in India," a government initiative to persuade and encourage companies globally to manufacture their products in India (http://www.makeinindia.com). As part of this initiative, the government decided in 2015 to reinvigorate "Invest India," recognizing the need for a government agency to proactively tackle the attraction of foreign firms. Invest India was mandated to ramp up its investment promotion efforts and capitalize on the potential of India's economy.

Following international good practices, Invest India received the full support of senior-level government officials. A new chief executive officer (CEO) was appointed and given direct access to the line minister and the prime minister's office. The IPA's goals were linked to the country's broader development goals, and it was officially mandated to lead the country's national investment promotion as the single point of contact for foreign investors. Following global good practices, it was not assigned any regulatory functions. It was given sound financial support from the Department for Promotion of Industry and Internal Trade (DPIIT, formerly DIPP) and a functioning board with 51 percent private sector representation.

Invest India was permitted to adopt a much flatter organizational structure than typical Indian civil service entities and to recruit high-caliber management and staff outside the normal civil service recruitment procedures. It adopted a consultancy-like operating model designed to offer quality services to investors. The agency has now developed into a dynamic, service-oriented organization with highly qualified staff. As of mid-2019, 51 percent of the staff were women, 90 percent of its 138 dedicated professional staff had private sector experience, and 60 percent had graduate degrees.

Invest India also set about developing strong relationships with state-level IPAs across India. It took a proactive approach to better understand the strengths and the needs of each state in terms of competitiveness to attract new investment and capacity to support incoming investors. It provided direct support to subnational IPAs and invited all state IPAs to participate in a World Bank Group IPA assessment designed to further strengthen capacity. Confidential reports were delivered in March 2018 to 21 state IPAs offering tailored advice on areas for improvement.

Since the agency's rejuvenation in 2015, Invest India has been transformed into an award-winning IPA, receiving the United Nations Conference on Trade and Development's (UNCTAD) global award for best-practice IPA in 2016 and for sustainable development investments in 2019. It was also named best IPA in South Asia, East Asia, and Oceania at Dubai's Annual Investment Meeting (AIM) in 2016, 2017, 2018, and 2019, and was elected as co-vice president of WAIPA for 2019–20.

By mid-2019, Invest India had responded to more than 193,000 business requests from 126 countries and 41 sectors, 92 percent of which were answered within 72 hours. Working with some 760 companies, it had generated a project pipeline of US$138 billion, of which an estimated US$22.7 billion had been executed, with 135,000 direct jobs in the process of being created and contributing to making India the world's top-five greenfield destination in 2018.[a]

Sources: Invest India website: https://www.investindia.gov.in/; interviews with Invest India management.

a. Data on Invest India's outcomes from fDi Markets, a *Financial Times* dataset (https://www.fdimarkets.com/).

Develop Strong Partnerships

IPAs need to develop strong partnerships with both the public and private sectors at the national and subnational spheres to harness FDI. They are interacting on average with 25 different organizations (OECD 2018).

Strong partnerships develop through consultation and working together on common issues. For instance, jointly developing an investment vision or FDI strategy for the country helps strengthen these partnerships and improves effectiveness, stemming from aligning stakeholders behind a few priorities for economic (and social) development. Strong intergovernmental cooperation between the IPA and specialized units dealing with permits, incentives, and other noncore IPA mandates is essential in effectively delivering services to investors. Other national and subnational stakeholders playing a role in investment—such as sectoral ministries, environmental protection agencies, and utility providers—should also be integrated into the institutional framework.

Strong national IPAs in larger countries tend to have closer and more systematic working relationships with subnational IPAs—or at least more regular cooperation and contact with them. Institutional coordination mechanisms are essential to avoid investor confusion and frustration stemming from duplication or gaps in service delivery. Well-coordinated national and subnational IPAs complement each other and avoid such issues—taking on roles and delivering investor services based on their position within the typical investment cycle. For instance, it is most effective and efficient for the national IPA to devote resources to marketing, especially when dealing with investors abroad, as in the case of Apex-Brasil, Austrade (Australia), and Germany Trade & Invest (GTAI). In contrast, the day-to-day problem solving for an established investor is generally better dealt with at the subnational level (for example, by the SEZ or municipality).

Importantly, in creating a "national team" spirit for promotion, protocols should be in place to avoid "race to the bottom" behavior within the country, such as subnational IPAs competing for the same investors on the basis of incentives or concessions. Protocols of engagement and coordination mechanisms should help in this regard. India provides a good example (box 5.7).

Pillar 3: Strengthen Delivery of Investor Services

The 2019 GIC Survey reveals that investors value IPA services: 90 percent of responding investors value at least one IPA service, and two-thirds or more appreciate IPA services across different stages of the investment life cycle, not just at attraction or entry. World Bank Group experience and empirical research demonstrate that IPAs are mostly engaged in investment promotion events while underdelivering services beyond the attraction stage.

IPAs should aim at improving their service delivery across the investment cycle to increase investor satisfaction, especially for the services that strategic investors consider most relevant. The World Bank Group offers a new, comprehensive investor services framework linking four service categories (marketing, information, assistance, and advocacy) across four stages of the investment life cycle (attraction, entry and establishment, retention and expansion, and linkages and spillovers). The framework should be applied strategically to each of the targeted segments. (Heilbron and Aranda-Larrey 2020). The aim is to provide a well-balanced mix of services depending on the development level of the segments, with (a) proactive outreach and relevant information in carefully identified segments; (b) hands-on support to help investors establish and expand (aftercare programs); and (c) advocacy to continuously improve the investment ecosystem through fundamental reforms. For instance, quality IPA information would increase transparency, and the IPA's provision of effective assistance across all stages would build investor predictability. Both improve investor confidence, which can support FDI growth (see chapter 4).

Well-respected IPAs such as ABA–Invest in Austria, CINDE, IDA Ireland, InvestChile, InvestHK, and SDI all seem to apply the new framework's principles and most of the services listed under it.[25] The most notable differences of approach among these leading IPAs relate to the retention and expansion stage, as some of these national IPAs seem to be working in partnership with subnational IPAs taking care of such services.

As noted earlier, IPAs need to collaborate to provide services to investors seamlessly throughout their investment journeys. The national IPA is best placed to interact with investors during the attraction stage but could decrease its role once investors get established in a particular site if qualified subnational IPAs can take over. At that stage, the subnational IPAs can take ownership of the relationship and service provision, and consequently provide a higher level of attention. This suggested framework with a diminishing role for the national IPA and an increasing role for the subnational IPA in different stages of the investment life cycle is illustrated by the triangles of figure 5.13.

IPAs are (or could be) active connectors between investors and policy makers, channeling business-to-government (B2G) feedback and highlighting the role IPAs can play in delivering advocacy services. The 2019 GIC Survey revealed that investors consider advocacy to be the most critically important service IPAs provide.

Delivering top-quality, on-time services to investors across all stages of the investment life cycle requires systems, such as M&E on key KPIs; standard operating procedures; templates for repetitive tasks; a virtual library of the most frequently used documents; a website where investors can meet their initial information needs and download key documents and data; an investor relationship management system with CRM software at its core to track these interactions over long periods; and investor surveys. The United Kingdom has developed a monitoring, reporting, evaluation, and learning (MREL) framework to assess the effectiveness of all IPAs in the union, including its national Department for International Trade (DIT) and several subnational IPAs in achieving impact relative to their respective regions' characteristics (DIT 2018, 2019). Spain has a portal to share investment inquiries broadly with all qualifying subnational IPAs.

During the extremely uncertain times of the COVID-19 pandemic, selected IPAs from around the globe were showing resilience by operating remotely and delivering key services to investors. A WBG rapid survey, conducted in April 2020, showed that some IPAs were responding in the following ways:

- Strengthening communication via websites, newsletters, and social media to update investors daily on developments related to the virus and government responses

FIGURE 5.13 Proposed Division of National and Subnational IPA Roles in Service Delivery to Investors

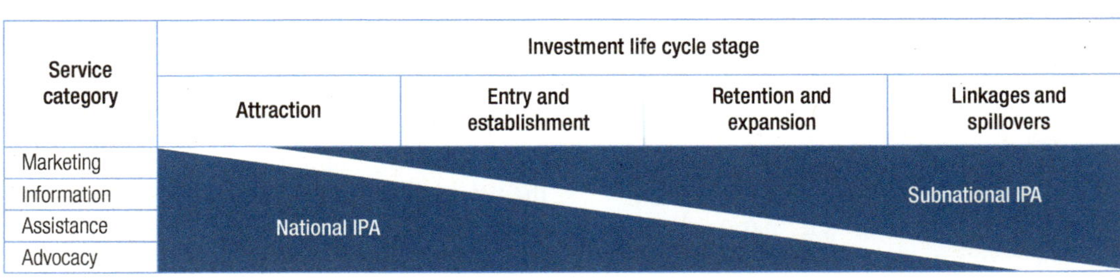

Source: World Bank.
Note: IPA = investment promotion agency.

- Bolstering direct assistance (aftercare) services to established investors to solve their individual issues
- Boosting advocacy services to systematically solve pressing issues facing investors.

IPAs have a pivotal role to play in helping governments respond to the COVID-19 pandemic. This role extends beyond the immediate term to include the post-outbreak recovery phase—providing relevant services to help investors return to operations as quickly as possible, while encouraging new investment and expansions into emerging strategic segments.

Conclusions and Future Research

The principal role of IPAs continues to be too often misunderstood, even by policy makers, as an exercise in simple marketing. At the same time, most IPAs are struggling to reach their full development impact because they lack strong support to evolve quickly with FDI market trends and more sophisticated investor needs, they lack strategic focus, and they do not adequately cover the services that investors value.

For IPAs to improve their contribution to development, several policy recommendations are key:

- *Provide the IPA with high-level government support* (from the president or prime minister), giving high priority to investment (or FDI) and directly or indirectly championing the needed legal, regulatory, and institutional reforms for investment.
- *Foster strong strategic alignment*, stemming from consultations with the public and private sectors and cascading from a national plan, vision, FDI strategy, or industrial strategy that clearly states the role of the private sector. These higher-level national strategies also need to consider IPA feedback and permeate the IPA corporate plans and sectoral strategies, which focus proactive investment promotion efforts on a few properly identified competitive segments.
- *Grant the IPA a clear, uncontested mandate focused on investment promotion*, especially when starting or restructuring the IPA to empower the IPA and avoid unnecessary duplication.
- *Grant the IPA a high degree of institutional and financial autonomy* (or semi-autonomy), emulating the private sector's flexibility to act according to strategic plans and hire staff according to specified and transparent job qualifications. This should avoid political interference and disruptions during political transitions. Having the IPA report to an independent and functioning board of directors or advisory board with strong and active private sector representation would help it better understand investors and provide direction in catering to their needs.
- *Foster a strong, investor-centric service orientation at the IPA and with partners.* This includes allowing the IPA to hire management and key promotion staff with strong private sector experience, international exposure, and language skills as well as building capacity for the IPA and its partners to design and provide relevant, high-quality services to those strategic investors throughout the investment life cycle.
- *Provide sufficient, sustained financial resources to the IPA* over three- to five-year periods to ensure continuity of strategic efforts over the long-cycle nature of investment promotion and to avoid struggling over funds every year or having to charge fees.

Regarding future research, emphasis should be placed on more rigorously assessing IPAs' performance, especially to identify which IPA characteristics (autonomy, staffing, budgets, and so on) are most effective at maximizing their development impact. More can be done to analyze the links between IPA services (type and quality) and investor satisfaction (and potentially investor confidence) and their effect on FDI.

To date, such research has been sparse, not only in the context of developing countries but also in picking up on nuances across different stages of economic development. In this vein, econometric analysis at the global level should be pursued and anchored in better collection of data across a wide international sample of IPAs, with time-series information on different IPA attributes and services, and critically, on performance indicators (ideally with firm-level data, or alternatively, with information on IPA segment targeting to link with data on FDI inflows).

Other areas that warrant deeper consideration include further analyses on the role of subnational IPAs as they become more prevalent in developing countries; the mechanisms for better national-subnational institutional collaboration and avoidance of "race to the bottom" behavior; the role of IT and digitalization on investment promotion; and the contribution of IPAs to countries' resilience in times of crisis (notably, for example, the COVID-19 pandemic), integration into emerging GVCs, and in achieving the SDGs.

Annex 5A. Key Measures of IPAs' Impact

Investment promotion agencies' (IPAs') top performance indicators, in terms of their direct contribution to development, are investment facilitated or generated (including foreign direct investment [FDI] inflows) and jobs created. Worldwide, 95 percent of IPAs responding to the 2017 World Bank Group Global IPA Survey reported collecting data on their contribution to FDI, and 81 percent collected data on job creation (figure 5A.1).

IPAs are especially concerned about economic development (the dimension most featured in IPA strategies), particularly employment creation (VCC and WAIPA 2010). However, most IPAs only collect information on *announced* investment and jobs, with few tracking FDI and employment levels that are *achieved* (based on established investments).

A few sophisticated IPAs such as IDA Ireland and the United Kingdom's Department for International Trade (DIT) have been measuring return on investment of public funds, using a basket of indicators that include FDI

FIGURE 5A.1 Nearly All National IPAs Collect Data on the Amount of Investment Facilitated and Jobs Created as Indicators of IPA Performance

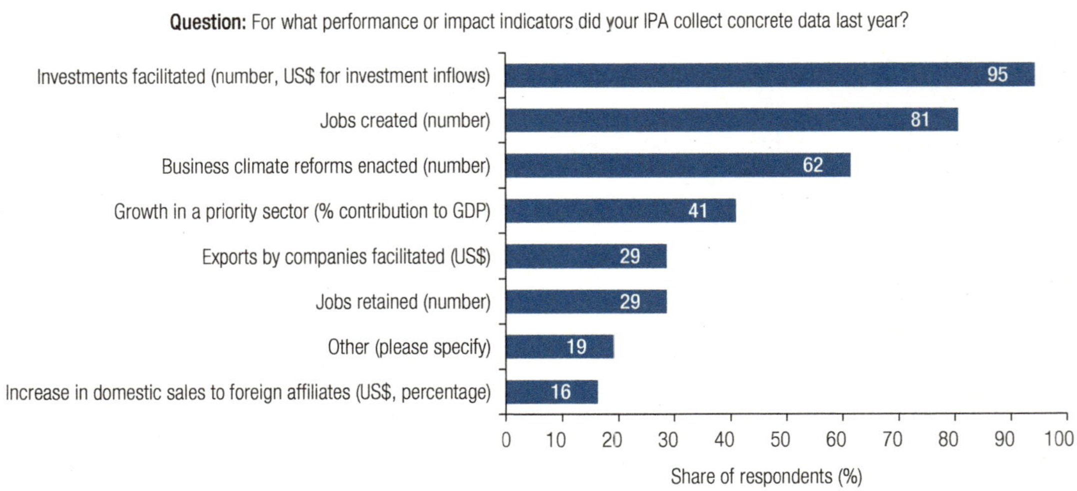

Source: 2017 World Bank Group Global IPA Survey.
Note: The survey received responses from 83 national IPAs globally. (For more information, see annex 5B.) GDP = gross domestic product; IPA = investment promotion agency.

inflows, gross value added, wages, and employment levels (DIT 2018; IDA Ireland 2018). Only a few developing countries measure the degree of embeddedness of the investments and their local impact in terms of additional growth and jobs generated directly and indirectly. The United Kingdom is moving to net value added and employment.

Most studies use the value of FDI inflows (Harding and Javorcik 2011, 2012; UNCTAD 2001; Wells and Wint 2000) or the number of FDI projects as the IPA's measure of performance, reflecting data availability. A more recent study proposes using four variables to measure the IPA's performance as perceived by survey respondents on the Likert scale, which measures intensity of feeling: (a) FDI inflows, (b) target investment amount, (c) investment promotion efficiency, and (d) survival rate of new invested ventures (Lim 2018).[26]

Soft and hard factors (perceptions, FDI amounts, job numbers, and wages) need to be considered when evaluating IPAs (UNCTAD 2008). That said, data in general, but especially for indirect impact and qualitative aspects, are not easily available. Such data issues are even more pronounced in the developing world.

Annex 5B. Analysis of IPA Surveys: Overview and Approach

2017 World Bank Group Global IPA Survey

From October 2016 to March 2017, the World Bank Group contacted 147 investment promotion agencies (IPAs) to gather information on their characteristics and activities through a web-based survey. Eighty-three national IPAs responded (a response rate of 56 percent). A regional breakdown of the respondents is presented in table 5B.1.

Comparison of Global IPA Surveys over Time

To compare IPA characteristics over time, data from five different surveys[27] are leveraged:

- 2005 World Bank Group IPA Census
- 2017 World Bank Group Global IPA Survey
- 2017 World Association of Investment Promotion Agencies (WAIPA) Annual Survey

TABLE 5B.1 Regional Coverage of the 2017 World Bank Group Global IPA Survey

Region	*Distribution of IPAs contacted (%)*	*Response distribution (%)*	*Number of respondents (number of IPAs)*
East Asia and Pacific	14	13	11
Europe and Central Asia	33	35	29
Latin America and Caribbean	18	18	15
Middle East and North Africa	10	7	6
North America	1	1	1
South Asia	4	6	5
Sub-Saharan Africa	21	19	16
Total	100	100	83

Source: 2017 World Bank Group Global IPA Survey.
Note: The survey received responses from 83 national IPAs globally. "North America" includes Canada and the United States.
IPA = investment promotion agency.

- 2018 WAIPA Annual Survey
- 2018 OECD report, "Mapping of Investment Promotion Agencies in OECD Countries" (OECD 2018).

Changes are evaluated across the following key areas: governance structure, activities and services, sector and country targeting, budget, staff, systems and tools, and foreign presence. Because country and question coverage of the different surveys vary dramatically, precise comparison across time posed challenges. The 2005 World Bank Group IPA Census covered the widest range of IPAs (106 in total) and provides a baseline for comparison over time. To maximize sample size, the analysis combines the remaining four surveys into single observations for the period 2017–18. The trend analysis is restricted to the subset of IPAs observed in both time periods, so conclusions are not swayed by changes in sample composition. Changes over time are calculated using IPA fixed effects to identify within-IPA changes.

A few caveats are in order. Sample size varies by question (based on presence and format of questions in the survey). More broadly, caution should be exercised when considering generalizability of results because the sample is nonrandom, and changes may be associated with other unobserved characteristics.

Annex 5C. Additional Data on Evolution of IPA Institutional Characteristics, 2005 to 2017/18

TABLE 5C.1 Selected IPA Characteristics with No Significant Changes between the 2005 and 2017/18 IPA Surveys

Topic	*Question*	*2005*	*2017/18*	*Sample size (number of IPAs)*
Governance structure	% of IPAs that are government run	93	89	52
	% of IPAs reporting to more senior levels of accountability (for example, prime minister's or president's office)	12	16	58
	% of IPAs with a board	71	75	56
	% of IPAs with private sector members on their boards	52	55	21
Activities	% of IPAs that advertise in the media	78	90	40
	% of IPAs engaging in analysis or policy advocacy to improve the investment climate	98	95	41
	% of IPA's budget devoted to image building	26	25	24
	% of IPA's budget devoted to investment generation	36	33	25
	% of IPA's budget devoted to investor servicing	25	32	18
Country targeting	% of IPAs that target specific countries	66	63	35
	Average number of countries targeted by IPAs	6	4	32
Staff	Average number of staff focusing on investment promotion	31	42	52
Systems and tools	% of IPAs with private sector database	96	100	25
	% of IPAs using an investor tracking system	53	55	38
Foreign presence	% of IPAs with overseas representation	74	78	27

Sources: 2005 World Bank Group IPA Census and 2017 World Bank Group Global IPA Survey; 2017 and 2018 World Association of Investment Promotion Agencies (WAIPA) annual surveys; OECD 2018.

Note: For details about the data sources and methodology, see annex 5B. Changes over t me are calculated using IPA fixed effects to identify within-IPA changes. Significance of changes across time is calculated using IPA samples for which the question is commonly available in both 2005 and 2017/2018 to avoid changes being driven by changes in the sample composition. This table summarizes selected features where no significant changes, up to the 10 percent level, are observed. Nonsignificant changes do not necessarily indicate that no meaningful changes have occurred but may indicate that the sample size is too small to draw generalizable conclusions. Discrepancies in the phrasing of questions across surveys means that the authors have matched questions across surveys based on their judgment of sufficient comparability.

Notes

1. Throughout the chapter, investment promotion agencies (IPAs) refer to institutions that include an investment promotion function or mandate (covering both dedicated agencies as well as units that do so within larger institutions, such as economic development boards).
2. As throughout this report, "developing countries" refers to low- and middle-income countries, and "developed countries" to high-income countries, based on World Bank Group classifications: https://datahelpdesk.worldbank.org/knowledgebase/articles/906519-world-bank-country-and-lending-groups.
3. FIAS—now called the Facility for Investment Climate Advisory Services (still abbreviated as FIAS)—is a joint service of the World Bank and the International Finance Corporation (World Bank Group) that focuses on helping countries attract foreign direct investment, supporting reforms in more than 100 countries over three decades. For more information, see the World Bank's FIAS web page: https://www.worldbank.org/en/topic/competitiveness/brief/facility-for-investment-climate-advisory-services-fias.
4. WAIPA, the World Association of Investment Promotion Agencies, is an international nongovernmental organization, established in 1995 by the United Nations Conference on Trade and Development (UNCTAD), that acts as a forum, provides networking, and promotes best practices for IPAs. For more information, see the WAIPA website: https://waipa.org/.
5. For this section, the authors reviewed a wide range of resources to provide a broad overview of the literature on investment promotion and then classified them by topic but not by empirical strength.
6. Crescenzi, Di Cataldo, and Giua (2019a) find a positive impact of subnational IPAs in attracting FDI and a mixed impact of national IPAs, based on empirical research in Europe.
7. "Cultural distance" is defined as differences between one country and the United States in terms of language and business conduct. The 2011 study by Harding and Javorcik uses US FDI outflows, for which cultural distance from the United States might be relevant. This may not be the case for FDI sourced from other countries, such as China.
8. CINDE identified the right competitive segment to target, engaged in one-on-one strategic outreach, and provided top-notch individualized services to investors.
9. "Efficiency-seeking" FDI leverages cost savings and competitive features of a location to serve as an export base.
10. For more information about the 2017 World Bank Group Global IPA Survey, see annex 5B.
11. At the same time, Bauerle Danzman and Gertz (forthcoming) also indicate that autonomous IPAs are less likely to align their activities with other government priorities.
12. Transnational learning capacity, in this context, refers to the IPA's capacity to understand multinational enterprises and learn from them, usually by leveraging the expertise of staff who have had experience working with, or for, such enterprises.
13. The 2017 GIC Survey data were collected through telephone interviews with 754 business executives involved with operations in developing countries (picked from among 8,000 eligible companies in the Dun & Bradstreet database). The survey captures perceptions of international business executives on the role that investment climate factors play in their FDI decisions.
14. The 2019 GIC Survey data were collected through telephone interviews with over 2,400 business executives of MNE affiliates in 10 developing countries: Brazil, China, India, Indonesia, Malaysia, Mexico, Nigeria, Thailand, Turkey, and Vietnam. The survey captures perceptions of international business executives on the role that investment climate factors play in their FDI decisions.
15. IPA data are from the 2005 World Bank Group IPA Census and the 2017 World Bank Group Global IPA Survey (see annex 5B). Regarding the comparison in IPA budget size, the 2005 World Bank Group IPA Census asks about the "FDI promotion" budget, while the 2017 World Bank Group Global IPA Survey asks about the "investment promotion" budget. Values are presented in 2018 US dollars, adjusted for currency convertibility and inflation.
16. FDI project growth from 2009 to 2018 was calculated from the *Financial Times*' fDi Markets

dataset (https://www.fdimarkets.com/), representing that survey's coverage of more reliable data (through systematic collection of information on FDI project announcements). Data to measure changes in IPA sector targeting were sourced from the 2005 World Bank IPA Census and a combination of 2017/18 IPA surveys from the World Bank Group, World Association of Investment Promotion Agencies (WAIPA), and Organisation for Economic Co-operation and Development (OECD). (For more information, see annex 5B.)

17. GIPB reports are based on the review of each IPA's website and its responses to investor requests for information. These inquiries are made using a "mystery shopper" approach, whereby a global site selection firm submits GIPB inquiries as the inquiries of a supposed anonymous investor. Each IPA receives a confidential report with results.
18. The GIPB was discontinued after 2012. There have been no similar evaluation data since then.
19. The question in the 2017 World Bank Group Global IPA Survey was phrased as an open-ended question to IPAs to write in which sectors they are prioritizing. Consequently, there were variations in how sectors were described and classified. But the numbers still indicate a comparable magnitude of the number of sectors considered to be a "priority" for investment promotion efforts.
20. Rwanda's FDI inflows have increased over time, from US$14 million in 2005 to US$398 million in 2018, according to UNCTAD *World Investment Report* data.
21. The World Bank Group has over 30 years of operational experience in the field of investment promotion, providing assistance to countries across the world.
22. Countries are increasingly linking their national plans with supranational visions and development plans. For instance, the Association of Southeast Asian Nations (ASEAN) community is working toward its common Vision 2025. Rwanda has supranational commitments through the African Union Agenda 2063 and East African Community Vision 2050.
23. Malaysia developed "Wawasan 2020" (Vision 2020), a 30-year national development plan spanning 1991–2020. Colombia's National Development Plan 2018–2022 and Myanmar's Sustainable Development Plan 2018–2030 take steps toward the SDG targets for 2030. Although Rwanda is still within its 20-year plan (2000–20), it is now preparing a 30-year plan (2020–50).
24. These reforms, which continue under the current government, have helped the country move toward needed labor-intensive industrialization (a significant achievement in Sub-Saharan Africa) and contributed to boosting FDI inflows from US$279 million in 2012 to US$3.6 billion in 2017 (UNCTAD 2018).
25. This finding is based on two-hour, one-on-one detailed interviews carried out with the mentioned IPAs in 2019.
26. A Likert scale is a psychometric scale widely used to gauge responses in survey research. Specifically, it measures how people feel about something by asking respondents to choose from five to seven balanced responses.
27. The analysis drew on the full datasets (only available internally) of the 2005 World Bank Group IPA Census; the 2017 World Bank Group Global IPA Survey; and the 2017 and 2018 World Association of Investment Promotion Agencies (WAIPA) Annual Surveys. More information on the 2005 WBG IPA Census, and the WAIPA 2018 Annual Survey can be found in Harding and Javorcik (2011), and WAIPA (2019), respectively. Any data leveraged from the 2018 OECD report, "Mapping of Investment Promotion Agencies in OECD Countries" were drawn from the figures and charts included in the publicly available publication (OECD 2018) as the authors did not have access to the full dataset.

References

Anderson, John, and Dylan Sutherland. 2015. "Developed Economy Investment Promotion Agencies and Emerging Market Foreign Direct Investment: The Case of Chinese FDI in Canada." *Journal of World Business* 50 (4): 815–25.

Bauerle Danzman, Sarah, and Geoffrey Gertz. Forthcoming. "Facilitating Sustainable Investment: The Role and Limits of Investment Promotion Agencies." In *World Trade Forum 2018: Trade, Development, and Sustainability*. Cambridge: Cambridge University Press.

Charlton, Andrew, and Nicholas Davis. 2007. "Does Investment Promotion Work?" *The B.E. Journal of Economic Analysis & Policy* 7 (1): 1–21.

Cho, Joong-Wan. 2003. "Foreign Direct Investment: Determinants, Trends in Flows and

Promotion Policies." *Investment Promotion and Enterprise Development Bulletin for Asia and the Pacific* 1: 99–112.

Crescenzi, Riccardo. 2018. "Why Foreign Investment Clicks in Some Cities and Regions, while Others Are Left Behind." *Global Investments and Local Development* (blog), London School of Economics, November 30. https://blogs.lse.ac.uk/gild/2018/11/30/why-foreign-investment-clicks-in-some-cities-and-regions-while-others-are-left-behind/.

Crescenzi, Riccardo, Marco Di Cataldo, and Mara Giua. 2019a. "FDI Inflows in Europe: Does Investment Promotion Work?" Working Paper 10/2019, Institute of Global Affairs, London School of Economics and Political Science.

Crescenzi, Riccardo, Marco Di Cataldo, and Mara Giua. 2019b. "Governments Strive to Attract Investment, but So Far There's No Evidence of What Works." *LSE Business Review* (blog), February 22. https://blogs.lse.ac.uk/businessreview/2019/02/22/governments-strive-to-attract-investment-but-so-far-theres-no-evidence-of-what-works/.

Crescenzi Riccardo, Carlo Pietrobelli, and Roberta Rabellotti. 2014. "Innovation Drivers, Value Chains and the Geography of Multinational Corporations in Europe." *Journal of Economic Geography* 14 (6): 1053–86. doi:10.1093/jeg/lbt018.

DCI (Development Counsellors International). 2017. "A View from Corporate America: Winning Strategies in Economic Development Marketing." Survey report, DCI, New York.

DIT (United Kingdom, Department for International Trade). 2018. "Estimating the Economic Impact of FDI to Support the Department for International Trade's Promotion Strategy: Analytical Report." DIT, London.

DIT. 2019. "Department for International Trade Inward Investment Results 2018–19." Statistical report, DIT, London. https://www.gov.uk/government/collections/dit-inward-investment-results.

ECORYS. 2013. "Exchange of Good Practice in Foreign Direct Investment Promotion: A Study Carried Out under the Framework Contract ENTR/2009/033." Final report, 2nd rev., ECORYS, Rotterdam, the Netherlands.

FIAS (Foreign Investment Advisory Service). 2011. "Investment Generation Toolkit." Online resource (unavailable after 2017), World Bank, Washington, DC.

Filippov, Sergey, and José Guimon. 2012. "From Quantity to Quality: Challenges for Investment Promotion Agencies." *Institutions and Economies* 4 (2): 25–44.

Freund, Caroline, and Theodore H. Moran. 2017. "Multinational Investors as Export Superstars: How Emerging-Market Governments Can Reshape Comparative Advantage." Working Paper 17-1, Peterson Institute for International Economics, Washington, DC.

Harding, Torfinn, and Beata S. Javorcik. 2011. "Roll Out the Red Carpet and They Will Come: Investment Promotion and FDI Inflows." *The Economic Journal* 121 (557): 1445–76.

Harding, Torfinn, and Beata S. Javorcik. 2012. "Investment Promotion and FDI Inflows: Quality Matters." *CESifo Economic Studies* 59 (2): 337–59.

Heilbron, Armando, and Yago Aranda-Larrey. 2020. "Strengthening Service Delivery of Investment Promotion Agencies: The Comprehensive Investor Services Framework." Investment Promotion for Impact Series. Investment Climate *In Focus* Note, World Bank, Washington, DC.

Heilbron, Armando, and Robert Whyte. 2019. "Institutions for Investment: Establishing a High-Performing Institutional Framework for Foreign Direct Investment (FDI)," Investment Climate *In Focus* Note, World Bank, Washington, DC.

IDA Ireland. n.d. http://www.idaireland.com.

IDA Ireland. 2018. "IDA Ireland Annual Report & Accounts 2018." IDA Ireland, Dublin.

Lim, Sung-Hoon. 2018. "Determinants of the Performance of Investment Promotion Agencies: Evidence form a Mix of Emerging Economies." *Emerging Markets Finance and Trade* 54 (8): 1907–23. doi: 10.1080/1540496X.2017.1334144.

Loewendahl, Henry. 2001. "A Framework for FDI Promotion" *Transnational Corporations* 10 (1): 1–42.

MIGA (Multilateral Investment Guarantee Agency). 2001. *Investment Promotion Toolkit: A Comprehensive Guide to FDI Promotion.* Washington, DC: World Bank.

MIGA. 2006a. "The Impact of Intel in Costa Rica: Nine Years after the Decision to Invest." Working Paper No. 37402, Investing in Development Series, World Bank Group, Washington, DC.

MIGA. 2006b. "Investment Promotion Agency Performance Review 2006: Providing

Information to Investors." Working Paper No. 37831, IPA Performance Review Series, World Bank Group, Washington, DC.

Miškinis, Algirdas, and Mariya Byrka. 2014. "The Role of Investment Promotion Agencies in Attracting Foreign Direct Investment." *Ekonomika* 4 (93): 41–57.

Monge-González, Ricardo, and Ezequiel Tacsir. 2014. "Policy Coordination: From FDI to a Broader Framework to Promote Innovation—The Case of Costa Rica." In *Science, Technology and Innovation Policies for Development: The Latin American Experience,* edited by Gustavo Crespi and Gabriela Dutrénit, 203–24. Basel, Switzerland: Springer.

Moran, Theodore H., Holder Görg, Adnan Serič, and Christiane Krieger-Boden. 2018. "Attracting FDI in Middle-Skilled Supply Chains." Economics Discussion Papers No. 2018-2. Kiel Institute for the World Economy, Kiel, Germany.

Morisset, Jacques, and Kelly Andrews-Johnson. 2004. "The Effectiveness of Promotion Agencies at Attracting Foreign Direct Investment." Occasional Paper No. 16, Foreign Investment Advisory Service, World Bank Group, Washington, DC.

Nelson, Roy. 1999. "Intel's Site Selection Decision in Latin America." Global Business Case No. A03-99-0016, Thunderbird School of Global Management, Arizona State University, Tempe.

Nelson, Roy. 2000. "Case Study: Intel's Site Selection Decision in Latin America." *Thunderbird International Business Review* 42 (2): 227–49.

Nelson, Roy. 2005. "Competing for Foreign Direct Investment: Efforts to Promote Nontraditional FDI in Costa Rica, Brazil, and Chile." *Studies in Comparative International Development* 40 (3): 3–28.

Nelson, Roy C. 2009. *Harnessing Globalization: The Promotion of Nontraditional Foreign Direct Investment in Latin America.* University Park, PA: The Pennsylvania State University Press.

OECD (Organisation for Economic Co-operation and Development). 2018. "Mapping of Investment Promotion Agencies in OECD Countries." Inventory and survey report, OECD, Paris.

Ortega, Celia, and Carlos Griffin. 2009. "Investment Promotion Essentials: What Sets the World's Best Investment Facilitators Apart from the Rest?" Investment Climate *In Practice* Note No. 6, World Bank, Washington, DC.

Pietersen, Pontévechio Hawarden, and Henri Bezuidenhout. 2015. "South African IPAs Attracting FDI: Investment Promotion Strategies." *Journal of Applied Business Research* 31 (3): 1057–72.

Spar, Debora. 1998. "Attracting High Technology Investment: Intel's Costa Rican Plant." Occasional Paper No. 11, Foreign Investment Advisory Service, World Bank Group, Washington, DC.

UNCTAD (United Nations Conference on Trade and Development). 1997. "Survey of Best Practices in Investment Promotion." Survey report, United Nations, New York and Geneva.

UNCTAD. 2001. "The World of Investment Promotion at a Glance: A Survey of Investment Promotion Practices." Study, Advisory Services on Investment and Training (ASIT), United Nations, New York and Geneva.

UNCTAD. 2007. "Aftercare: A Core Function in Investment Promotion." Investment Advisory Series, Series A, No. 1, United Nations, Geneva and New York.

UNCTAD. 2008. "Evaluating Investment Promotion Agencies." Investment Advisory Series. Series A, No. 3, United Nations, New York and Geneva.

UNCTAD. 2013. "Optimizing Government Services: A Case for Joint Investment and Trade Promotion?" *IPA Observer* No. 1, UNCTAD, Geneva.

UNCTAD. 2018. *World Investment Report 2018: Investment and New Industrial Policies.* New York and Geneva: United Nations.

UNCTAD. 2019. *World Investment Report 2019: Special Economic Zones.* New York and Geneva: United Nations.

UNESCO (United Nations Educational, Scientific and Cultural Organization). n.d. Institution for Statistics. https://uis.unesco.org.

VCC and WAIPA (Vale Columbia Center and World Association of Investment Promotion Centers). 2010. "Investment Promotion Agencies and Sustainable FDI: Moving toward the Fourth Generation of Investment Promotion." Report of the findings of the VCC-WAIPA Survey on Foreign Direct Investment and Sustainable Development, New York and Geneva.

Volpe Martincus, Christian, and Monika Sztajerowska. 2019. "How to Solve the Investment Promotion Puzzle: A Mapping of Investment Promotion Agencies in Latin American and the Caribbean and OECD Countries." Monograph, Organisation for

Economic Co-operation and Development and Inter-American Development Bank, Washington, DC. http://dx.doi.org/10.18235/0001767.

WAIPA (World Association of Investment Promotion Agencies). 2019. "Overview of Investment Promotion: Report of the Findings from the WAIPA Annual Survey of 2018." WAIPA, Geneva.

Wells, Louis T. Jr., and Alvin G. Wint. 2000. "Marketing a Country: Promotion as a Tool for Attracting Foreign Investment." Revised ed. Occasional Paper No. 13, Foreign Investment Advisory Service, World Bank Group, Washington, DC.

Whyte, Robert, and Carlos Griffin. 2014. "Promoting Foreign Investment in Fragile and Conflict-Affected Situations." Investment Climate *In Practice* Note No. 22, World Bank, Washington, DC.

Whyte, Robert, Celia Ortega, and Carlos Griffin. 2011. "Investment Regulation and Promotion: Can They Coexist in One Body?" *In Practice* Note No. 16, World Bank, Washington, DC.

World Bank. 2009. *Global Investment Promotion Benchmarking 2009 (Vol. 2): Summary Report.* Washington, DC: World Bank.

World Bank. 2012. *Global Investment Promotion Best Practices 2012.* Washington, DC: World Bank.

World Bank. 2018. *Global Investment Competitiveness Report 2017/2018: Foreign Investor Perspectives and Policy Implications.* Washington, DC: World Bank. doi:10.1596/978-1-4648-1175-3.

World Bank. 2020. *World Development Report 2020: Trading for Development in the Age of Global Value Chains.* Washington, DC.

World Bank World Development Indicators database. http://datatopics.worldbank.org/world-development-indicators/.

Glossary

Bilateral investment treaty (BIT). A bilateral investment treaty is an agreement between two countries establishing the terms and conditions for private investment by an entity of one country in another country.

Brownfield FDI. Brownfield FDI refers to any purchase of more than 10 percent of a target company's assets by a foreign entity. Ten percent is the threshold for a foreign investment to be considered direct (FDI), according to the International Monetary Fund (IMF) and the Organisation for Economic Co-operation and Development (OECD). The purchase can be friendly or unfriendly and result in various combinations of outcomes in terms of creating a new legal entity, including a simple acquisition or a merger. Joint ventures do not fall under the category of brownfield foreign investment because they refer to the establishment of new facilities—greenfield investment—involving a local and a foreign entity.

Developed countries. Developed countries include high-income countries as classified within the World Bank's country and lending groups.

Developing countries. Developing countries include low- and middle-income countries as classified within the World Bank's country and lending groups.

Doing Business. This World Bank project provides objective measures of business regulations and their enforcement across 190 economies and selected cities at the subnational and regional levels. Launched in 2002, the project looks at domestic small and medium-size companies and measures the regulations applicable to them throughout their life cycles.

Efficiency-seeking FDI. Efficiency-seeking FDI occurs when investors seek to increase the cost efficiency of production by taking advantage of location-specific factors. These investors are also known as "cost-competitive investors," and their main investment motivations include lowering production costs and establishing a new base for exports.

FDI inflows. FDI inflows comprise all liabilities and assets transferred between resident direct investment enterprises and their direct investors into the reporting economy for the reporting period, usually for one year.

FDI outflows. FDI outflows comprise all liabilities and assets transferred outward between resident direct investors and their direct investment enterprises away from the reporting economy for the reporting period, usually for one year.

FDI stock. According to the OECD, FDI stock measures total direct investment at a given point, usually at the end of a quarter or year. It represents the value of the resident investors' equity in and net loans to enterprises resident in the reporting economy.

Foreign affiliates. "Foreign affiliates" refers generically to various types of entities that a foreign investment might take. These affiliates may be subsidiaries, branches, or any other enterprise resident in a host country that is controlled by a nonresident institutional unit.

Foreign direct investment (FDI). According to the IMF, FDI is a category of international investment made by a resident entity in one economy to establish a lasting interest in an enterprise resident in an economy other than the investor's. A "lasting interest" refers to a long-term relationship between the direct investor and the enterprise as well as a significant degree of influence by the direct investor on the management of the direct investment enterprise. Components of FDI include equity, intracompany debt, and reinvested earnings.

Global Investment Competitiveness (GIC) Survey. The GIC Survey is a World Bank survey of executives of the affiliates of multinational enterprises (MNEs) in developing countries. For the purposes of this report, the 2019 GIC Survey data cover more than 2,400 foreign investors with operations in 10 middle-income countries: Brazil, China, India, Indonesia, Malaysia, Mexico, Nigeria, Thailand, Turkey, and Vietnam.

Global value chain (GVC). A GVC refers to the series of stages required to produce a good or service that is sold to consumers, with each stage adding value and with at least two stages conducted in different countries.

Government effectiveness. Part of the World Bank's Worldwide Governance Indicators, "government effectiveness" is an aggregate indicator that reflects perceptions of the quality of public services; the quality of the civil service and the degree of its independence from political pressures; the quality of policy formulation and implementation; and the credibility of the government's commitment to such policies.

Greenfield FDI. In greenfield FDI, the investor builds its business operations from the ground up. In this report, greenfield refers to a mode of FDI entry whereby a foreign investor builds its operations in a host economy.

GVC activities (or stages). GVC activities, or stages, are those required to produce a good or service in the context of a global value chain. Spread across several locations, these activities span the conception of the good or service to its end use and include research, design, production, marketing, and distribution.

GVC participation (or integration). GVC participation, or integration, refers to the engagement of a country, sector, or firm in at least one stage of a global value chain. Overall participation may take the form of two broad types: backward or forward participation.

High-income countries. For the World Bank fiscal year 2020, high-income economies are defined as those with a gross national income (GNI) per capita (calculated using the World Bank Atlas method) of US$12,376 or more in 2018.

Home economy. The home economy is the country of origin of the foreign investment.

Host economy. The host economy is the country that receives the foreign investment.

International investment agreement (IIA). An IIA is a type of treaty between states that addresses issues on cross-border investments. IIAs exist on three levels: *bilateral* (such as BITs); *regional or preferential* (such as regional customs unions and free trade areas or preferential trade agreements); and *multilateral* (such as applicable rules in World Trade Organization agreements and other international investment conventions).

Investment incentives. Investment incentives are measurable economic advantages that governments offer to specific enterprises or groups of enterprises to steer investments into preferred sectors or locations. These benefits can be either fiscal (for example, tax concessions) or nonfiscal (for example, loans or rebates).

Investment linkages. Investment linkages are transmissions of foreign knowledge and practices that may improve the production capabilities of domestic suppliers, as a result of contractual arrangements between local suppliers and multinational corporations.

Investment promotion agency (IPA). An IPA is a government agency or nonprofit organization whose mandate is to attract investment to the host economy.

Investment protection guarantees. An investment protection guarantee is a guarantee or insurance provided by law, government, multilateral agency, or any party for an investment made.

Lead firm. A lead firm is the hierarchically dominant actor within a GVC.

Lower-middle-income countries. For the World Bank fiscal year 2020, lower-middle-income economies are defined as those with a GNI per capita (calculated using the World Bank Atlas method) between US$1,026 and US$3,995 in 2018.

Low-income countries. For the World Bank fiscal year 2020, low-income economies are defined as those with a GNI per capita (calculated using the World Bank Atlas method) of US$1,025 or less in 2018.

Mergers and acquisitions (M&A). M&A refers to transactions that result in the consolidation of companies or assets.

Multinational enterprise (MNE). An MNE is an enterprise that has operations in more than one country and usually has a centralized head office that coordinates global management.

Parent company. The parent company is the institutional unit that owns enough interest in another firm to manage or operate the firm.

Regulatory risk. As defined for the purposes of this report, regulatory risk is a subset of political risk related to select features of countries' regulatory frameworks that can reduce risks for investors and limit the potential for unexpected losses due to arbitrary government conduct. Specifically, the new regulatory risk measure introduced in this report examines (a) the level of *transparency* in both the content and process of making laws and regulations that apply to investors; (b) the extent of legal *protection* provided to investors against arbitrary, unpredictable, and nontransparent government interference; and (c) the existence of effective *recourse* mechanisms for investors.

Reinvested earnings. Reinvested earnings are net earnings not paid out as dividends but retained by the firm for reinvestment in its business operations in the host country.

Trade diversion. Trade diversion is the process of diverting trade from a more efficient exporter to a less efficient one by means of a free trade agreement or a customs union. For example, when two countries sign a trade agreement, they could reduce their imports from the rest of the world and source their imports from each other. To the extent that this strategy of import reallocation has been triggered by the trade agreement, it can be considered a trade diversion.

Upper-middle-income countries. For the World Bank fiscal year 2020, upper-middle-income economies are defined as those with a GNI per capita (calculated using the World Bank Atlas method) between US$3,996 and US$12,375 in 2018.

ECO-AUDIT

Environmental Benefits Statement

The World Bank Group is committed to reducing its environmental footprint. In support of this commitment, we leverage electronic publishing options and print-on-demand technology, which is located in regional hubs worldwide. Together, these initiatives enable print runs to be lowered and shipping distances decreased, resulting in reduced paper consumption, chemical use, greenhouse gas emissions, and waste.

We follow the recommended standards for paper use set by the Green Press Initiative. The majority of our books are printed on Forest Stewardship Council (FSC)–certified paper, with nearly all containing 50–100 percent recycled content. The recycled fiber in our book paper is either unbleached or bleached using totally chlorine-free (TCF), processed chlorine–free (PCF), or enhanced elemental chlorine–free (EECF) processes.

More information about the Bank's environmental philosophy can be found at http://www.worldbank.org/corporateresponsibility.

green press INITIATIVE